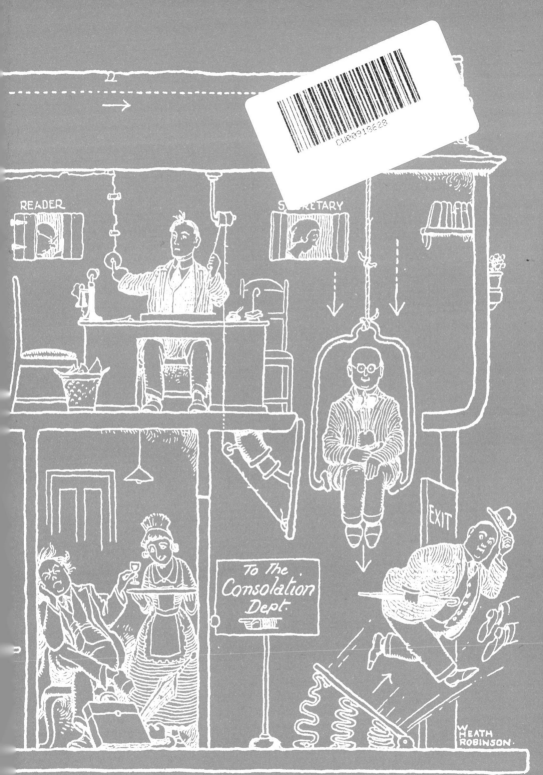

AFTERNOON IN A PUBLISHER'S OFFICE

'Spine tingling.'
Warwick McFadyen, *The Age*

'Spellbinding.'
John Hamilton, *The Herald Sun*

'What makes *Rare* such a treat is the unlikely triumph
of its subject [and] the everyday anecdotes and larger-
than-life characters that accumulate with the years.'
Geordie Williamson, *The Weekend Australian*

'A collection to treasure . . . Tasty . . . Revelatory . . .
Wry . . . *Rare* is a biography with many detours,
all of them interesting to anyone who loves books
and book people.'
The Saturday Magazine

'The biography of a remarkable woman making her
way and leaving a big mark in a largely man's world.
Kay Craddock's is a memorable life, ably told.'
William Butts, *Manuscripts*

'The author Stuart Kells is observant and quietly witty.
His book is captivating, partly because it discusses
other booksellers and their prizes and eccentricities.'
Geoffrey Blainey

'I have just spent some of the most wonderful hours
of reading I have ever experienced, reading *Rare* . . .
It flows seamlessly and presents such a finely balanced
work of the personal and professional.'
Mary Dalmau, Readers' Feast

PENGUIN

and

THE LANE BROTHERS

THE UNTOLD STORY OF A PUBLISHING REVOLUTION

STUART KELLS

Published by Black Inc.,
an imprint of Schwartz Publishing Pty Ltd
37–39 Langridge Street
Collingwood VIC 3066 Australia
enquiries@blackincbooks.com
www.blackincbooks.com

National Library of Australia Cataloguing-in-Publication entry:

    Kells, Stuart S., author.
    Penguin & the Lane brothers: the untold story of a publishing revolution / Stuart Kells.
    9781863957571 (hardback)
    9781925203417 (ebook)
    Lane, Allen, Sir, 1902–1970. Lane, Richard, 1905–1982. Lane, John, 1908–1942. Penguin (Firm)—History. Penguin Books Australia Ltd—History. Publishers and publishing—England—History. Publishers and publishing—Australia—History.
    070.50922

Cover design by Peter Long
Cover images: Brian Maudsley/Dreamstime.com (book);
Tolpeeva Nadezda/Shutterstock (bowler hat)
Text design and typesetting by Tristan Main

Printed in Australia by McPherson's Printing Group.

To Steve Hare
(1950–2015)
Penguineer extraordinaire

CONTENTS

Preface   ix

PROLOGUE   1
1   WILLIAMSES BEFORE LANES   2
2   THE JUMP START   13
3   THE BARWELL BOYS   25
4   COLD DIP   39
5   WHICH IS THE ENGLISHMAN?   51
6   PRACTICALLY EVERYTHING   66
7   THE LORD OF ALEXANDRIA   78
8   SWARMING BEES   90
9   BOOKMEN   100
10   'AT LENGTH DID CROSS AN ALBATROSS'   112
11   GETTING HOME   123
12   AN AIR OF FRIENDLINESS   135
13   SWATCHWAY AND KINGFISHER   142
14   PENGUINS GO TO SEA   152
15   A QUESTION OF TIMING   159
16   PECKING ORDER   167
17   IN ARMOUR   179
18   POWER AND GLORY   187
19   THE NELSON TOUCH   197
20   THE BEST MAN   209

21 SMALL FRY 223
22 A PERSONAL LETTER 236
23 GAMESMANSHIP 248
24 SHOCK TROOPS 258
25 CHATTERLEYS 270
26 THE GREAT ADVENTURE 280
27 THE MASTER BUILDER 294
    EPILOGUE 301

    Acknowledgments 303
    Notes 305
    Index 329

PREFACE

T he Penguin publishing history bookshelf is crowded. Arcane
studies of typography, glue, watermarks and the mysterious
odour of the first Penguin paperbacks – rubbery, musty and
even mousy – stand alongside the major works on the subject: Jack
Morpurgo's *King Penguin* (1979), Steve Hare's *Penguin Portrait* (1995)
and Jeremy Lewis's *Penguin Special* (2005). Why, then, another book
about the famous Antarctic bird?

Subtitled *Allen Lane and the Penguin Editors 1935–1970*, Hare's book
is a priceless trove of primary sources: smartly annotated letters and
documentary extracts selected with the specific purpose of showing the
development of Penguin's house style and the formation of a literary
legacy. The books by Morpurgo and Lewis are laudable, too, for the
breadth and depth of their research and insight. They are, however,
above all biographies of Allen Lane, the eldest, craftiest and most thrust-
ing of the three brothers who founded and ran Penguin. Morpurgo and
Lewis were, as Lane's biographers, naturally inclined to elevate his role
over that of his siblings, Richard and John. At times, they went so far as
to attribute to Allen ideas and decisions that were had and made by one
or both of his brothers, or by the three brothers jointly.

Yet the younger Lane brothers were publishers of importance, ahead
of Allen as often as behind, and they deserve more than a shunt into the
shade. Richard, for example, worked in the fine-press avant-garde
before applying what he learnt there to the publication of a Modernist

masterpiece, James Joyce's *Ulysses*. At Penguin, he was the firm's first editor, and the chief custodian of its cheerful ethic of well-designed books that offered high-quality literature at a low price. But a bigger issue than fraternal fairness is at stake in the writing of Penguin's history. When the biographies mis-describe the younger Lanes' contributions, they present a flawed picture of Allen Lane's achievement. Worse still, a chauvinistic focus on Allen blurs a unique dynamic in the history of publishing and media: the creative opposition among the brothers that constituted Penguin's secret weapon, a spry and idiosyncratic engine that drove a powerhouse.

The first Penguin books appeared in 1935, and for seven years thereafter the three brothers led Penguin as a triumvirate. The Lane boys did their best thinking together in bathroom board meetings where at least one director would always be 'mother naked'. In the Second World War, two of the brothers served in the Navy and, with the blessing of the war authorities, continued to nurture Penguin through initiatives such as the Forces Book Club. Integration into wartime officialdom made Penguin a national institution, but the war brought tragedy for the Lane family. John Lane's death in action during the North African landings of 1942 shattered the brothers' intimate partnership.

Though Richard served alongside John for much of the war, he survived and went on to share with Allen for almost two more decades the leadership of a company that became one of the first truly global media businesses. The Lanes built a firm and a brand that became synonymous not only with paperbacks but with a certain kind of publishing. Switched-on, progressive, accessible. Reader-focused, reader-engaged, reader-respecting. With its low-price, mass-distribution model, and a flourishing list encompassing literature, science, politics, journalism, education, children's books, classics, cooking, maps, music, games, art, architecture, history, sociology, humour and sex, Penguin became a vast 'poor man's university', and a prototype internet made from paper and ink.

Perhaps the best argument for looking again at Penguin is that the existing biographies of Allen Lane do not do justice to what is a rich and fascinating story. That story is at least as interesting as the plot of *The Social Network* (2010), David Fincher and Aaron Sorkin's account of the turbulent genesis of Facebook. Instead of Mark Zuckerberg's character-forming break-up with Erica Albright, we have Allen Lane, a dashing young man dressed in tails, taking a girl home after a late-night theatre party, riding in a hansom cab through Hyde Park under a full moon. Allen chose this perfect moment to propose marriage to his beautiful companion – and was summarily rejected. Instead of the notorious law-suits brought by Eduardo Saverin and Cameron and Tyler Winklevoss, we have the 1961 share float in which, after spectacular sales of *Lady Chatterley's Lover*, demand for Penguin shares exceeded supply by 15,000 per cent. The stockbrokers labelled the shares 'Chatterleys' and enjoyed a lavish dinner, celebrating a stag profit with few precedents. Allen made a fortune but his surviving brother was left feeling cheated and betrayed. In 2013, Penguin merged with Random House to form a £2.4 billion business, at a time when traditional publishing was under threat from ebooks, print-on-demand and other challengers. Allen Lane and Zuckerberg were cut from very different cloth, to be sure, but they both displayed the ferocious determination that feeds success. Both businesses were founded with audacity and as a bit of a lark. Both have had irreversible influences on world culture.

With unprecedented access to Richard's diaries and other family papers (many of them never before studied), the present volume is the first serious biographical treatment of the lives of Richard and John Lane, but it also seeks to shed new light on Allen's life and impact, and to describe and understand the multifaceted and changing relationship between the brothers, so crucial as a driver and influencer of Penguin's spirit and success. For most of Allen's life, Richard and John were his only true peers, and Richard was his conscience, his chief collaborator and his best friend. Though John's part in the Penguin story was cut short, he would continue to be a potent presence at the firm long after his passing.

Before starting Penguin with his brothers, Richard Lane spent a formative part of his youth in rural South Australia and New South Wales. His experiences there, and how they influenced the character and price of the first Penguins, are explored here for the first time. Those experiences and influences provide a wholly new perspective on the company's origins. Richard's priceless diaries and reflections also bring to light new information about the brothers' childhood, their family origins, their entry into the book world via The Bodley Head (publisher of Oscar Wilde and *The Yellow Book*) and the other moments that shaped their lives. The present book has also been informed by research in the invaluable Penguin corporate archive at Bristol University, and by interviews with the Lane family and others who knew their story. In examining the brothers and their relationship, *Penguin and the Lane Brothers* seeks to offer insights into the history of Penguin as an enterprise, a publishing innovation and a pioneering media company. The overarching intention is to tell truly and completely the remarkable story behind the twentieth century's greatest publishing house.

Stuart Kells
July 2015

PROLOGUE

Two boys ramble in an ancient wood. They are brothers, three years apart in age but roughly the same size. High up in an oak they spy a rookery. The elder of the two, Allen, climbs up to a nest, steals the blue speckled egg and wombs it in his mouth. The younger, Richard, steering his brother down with great care, tells Allen not to fall or he will addle the egg.

This Arcadian fragment of a true childhood story supplies a metaphor for two brothers who, with a third, John, founded Penguin Books, one of the most famous enterprises of the modern era. The metaphor is ornithologically apt. It fits because Allen was often seen striking out first, and Richard often found himself cautioning his more reckless brother. It fits, too, because the metaphorical egg was nearly stolen, and addled, a number of times.

Sublime moments like this one, in Leigh Woods, would become a touchstone in memory for the brothers, as would much of the early family life they shared. For the next half-century, a part of Richard would always believe that the increasingly wealthy and powerful Allen was still the boy with whom he had romped in the woods and shared other innocent adventures in Bristol and the West Country.

But to understand that touchstone and that metaphor, we have to go back to the beginning.

WILLIAMSES BEFORE LANES

I t started with a broken promise.

Camilla Matilda Lane came from a vigorous family of yeoman farmers in the North Devon village of Buckland Filleigh. In 1901, she was twenty-eight years old and eight years into her engagement with Bob Harris from the farm next door. Her parents relished the prospect of a match that would combine the neighbouring properties. Then, while staying with relatives in Bristol, she noticed a handsome man singing in the choir at St Mary Redcliffe. She went back the following Sunday and made sure she sat next to him in the congregation. They shared a hymn book, they spoke, and they sought out a mutual friend who might introduce them properly.

Camilla was smitten, Bob Harris was out, Samuel Allen Gardner Williams was in, and Jabez, Camilla's father, was furious. He refused to allow his daughter to marry Samuel in the Lane home, so they married in the beautiful church where they had met. Looking back on the courtship, Camilla would always say that she 'did all the chasing'.

Allen, Richard, John, Nora. 1902, 1905, 1908, 1911. Camilla and Samuel's children arrived with a regularity that suggests, on the face of it, an underlying design. Plans for the Williams children were, however, remarkably undeveloped, if indeed any existed, apart from the general ambition to create a loving home in which the children could thrive. Two kind-hearted souls, Camilla and Samuel were better at arranging births than lives.

Abstemious, diligent, precise: Samuel, like Camilla, had an external seriousness that hid an inner romantic. In choosing a career, he had decided neither to follow his father into seafaring nor his grandfather into the funeral industry. Samuel landed somewhere in the middle, becoming a civil architect and surveyor for Bristol council, where he helped manage the city's planning schemes and urban development. Outside work, he dabbled eccentrically. Apart from singing in the church choir, he experimented with photography and was a recognised authority on cheddar cheese. He brewed cider (allowing himself one pint a day at dinnertime in his Royal Doulton cider mug) and made vegetable wines (allowing himself none at all) by fermenting parsnip, cowslip and dandelion. An accomplished carpenter, he made chairs, a chest of drawers and other furniture by applying the principles of Scandinavian *sloyd* woodworking. As President of the Cornish Association, he wore a chain of office on civic occasions.

Later writers cast Samuel Williams unflatteringly as a short, round-headed, ruddy-faced, walrus-moustachioed weakling, dominated by his wife and bumbling inconsequentially through life with his ragbag of interests. But that image is unfair, and very far from how his children saw him. To Allen, Richard, John and Nora, their father was a Welsh colossus. Richard described him in his diary as 'the best man I have ever known and ever will know'.

In a northern suburb of Bristol, Samuel's modest public-sector income funded a medium-sized household in a largish house: Broomcroft, a labyrinthine four-storey edifice built of pinkish stone at the end of a terrace on a steeply sloping block. When Samuel asked his sons to paint all the ground-floor doors, they counted seventeen of them. Broomcroft's orientation turned the hillside-facing kitchen into a gloomy basement. Samuel cosied it up somewhat by paving the floor with repurposed wooden roadway blocks. The kitchen had no water laid on so this had to be brought in from the scullery. Nor was there water on the top two floors, and nowhere in the coal-fired house had constant hot water. Saturday night was bath night, and in summer the baths were cold. Under the front path lurked a huge coal cellar and, directly in front of the kitchen, a garbage dump that was not fly-proof. Allen and Richard worried that this juxtaposition was unhygienic.

Broomcroft stood on Cotham Vale, a street of pretty stone-built

Italianate and Victorian homes. Everyone in the neighbourhood knew the old man who paraded with a bundle of newspapers and an umbrella. Nora loved to imitate his squeaky cry of 'pay-per!' Another local character was the harpist who, on winter evenings, wheeled his instrument round on a dolly and played outside the house. The Williamses and their neighbours applauded with a shower of pennies. Cotham Vale was a charming place in which to grow up.

From a young age, the Williams children were proud Bristolians. They witnessed a procession of eminent men in ermine-lined gowns, led by the lord mayor, who carried a silver mace and a gold chain. Like every good Bristol boy, Richard could identify the major institutions: the central fire station, the central police offices, the waterworks, the cigarette makers W.D. & H.O. Wills, and the acclaimed contralto Dame Clara Butt in her regular concert appearances. He knew all the local churches: St Mary Tyndalls Park, St Mary Redcliffe, All Saints, St John's, the Cathedral, St Anselm's and St Mark's. At St Mark's, in the Lord Mayor's Chapel, Richard first heard the stirring hymn 'Hark, Hark My Soul'. St Mary Redcliffe, though, was his favourite church – in Bristol, in England, and in the whole world.

Every Sunday evening, the Williams family sang hymns and songs in the drawing room at Broomcroft. Camilla played the piano fitted with candlesticks, and the rest of the family gathered round. Samuel sang in the deep bass voice that had first beguiled Camilla. Richard loved to sing and could play the first few bars of 'God Save the King' on the violin, but only by holding the delicate instrument on his lap and sawing the music out of a single string. In this way, Richard accompanied his brothers in a rendition of 'The Dutchman's Dog'. Allen banged out the tune on the piano with the sustain pedal on. Chubby-cheeked John grabbed a concertina and, with all the stops held down, stretched it to breaking point and closed it just as violently until every ounce of air had been expelled. 'Oh where, oh where can he be?' sang the brothers at full volume to this discordant accompaniment. Had the old Dutchman displayed but half their exuberance, Richard later remarked, the dog would have heard its owner at once and the song need never have been written.

Of all the Williams children, Richard found the greatest pleasure in poetry and literature. His childhood reading furnished him with a good knowledge of Ovid, Shakespeare, Spenser, Milton, even Euclid, and an up-to-date, upper-middlebrow taste. He admired Walter Scott and Mark Twain, and Oliver Wendell Holmes' *Autocrat at the Breakfast Table*, but Francis Palgrave's compilation of meritorious songs and verse, the *Golden Treasury*, reigned supreme. For Richard, that book became a family of old friends, and the head of the family was Thomas Gray's 'Elegy Written in a Country Churchyard' (1750), especially the passage:

The curfew tolls the knell of parting day,
The lowing herd wind slowly o'er the lea,
The ploughman homeward plods his weary way,
And leaves the world to darkness and to me.

At home there was also a sixteenth-century edition of the so-called Breeches Bible ('and they sowed figge-tree leaves together, and made themselves breeches'); and back issues of the *Strand* magazine, and Wilfred Whitten's *John O'Londons*, which Richard cherished for the quality of their writing and the smart tales of modern life. But in spite of these attractions and his sincere love of books, Richard's childhood was not overly bookish. It was, rather, a childhood filled with adventure and earthly delights.

From Cotham Vale, Nature could be reached on foot. In the *Golden Treasury*, Richard read about rivulets, meadows and the wood 'that is dearer than all', but around Bristol he and Allen could see and touch and climb the real thing. Redland Green was a stone's throw away from Broomcroft, and Durdham Down led to the River Avon. Farther west lay the inviting expanses of Leigh Woods. Allen and Richard climbed in Avon Gorge, navigated the steps to Laura Falls, explored Nightingale Valley, and came to know these places intimately. Their favourite walk took them across Isambard Kingdom Brunel's precipitous suspension bridge, where they drank in the view from the half-way point – the left side of the deep gorge covered with trees every shade of green, the tallest swaying in the wind; the right side all unhewn rock with islands of stranded flora. The kind of beauty that can be pictured in soft light. Passing under the tall arch and pillar at the Somerset end of the bridge, the ramblers read the Latin inscription, SUSPENSA VIX VIA FIT, 'A suspended way made with difficulty'. In springtime, primroses and bluebells carpeted Leigh Woods.

The sweet scent filled the brothers' lungs. Apart from wild rooks' eggs, Allen and Richard gathered newts, collected butterflies, picked bluebells and caught sticklebacks in the River Trym at Coombe Dingle with home-made rods and bent pins for fishhooks.

When the brothers could afford basic single-gear bicycles, they cycled far and wide. Traversing hilly Bristol on fixed-gear bikes was gruelling work, especially over Blackboy Hill and Cotham Hill. Any mishandling of the descent would be punished by skinned knees and, where the surface was gravelly and the camber wrong, a skid into the railings. The boys also had an old trolley, which they pushed and rode around like a billycart. Richard later wrote to his family about the trolley, recalling 'the thrills we experienced when descending hills at fifteen miles an hour, and the thrills we didn't have in pushing it up hills at two miles an hour'. On holiday, the family visited the brickworks at Axbridge, where another trolley ran on tracks the full length of the works. All three brothers pushed and pulled it up to a spot where they could climb on board and accelerate to breakneck speed.

Regarded as the oddballs of the Lane and Williams clans, Samuel and Camilla were less well-off but better educated than most of their relatives. They had progressive views about how best to bring up their children. Broomcroft's system of government was somewhere between a sovereign democracy and an anarcho-syndicalist collective. Seeing no place for beatings in the home, Samuel and Camilla instead promoted individualism and freedom, long before that style of parenting was pop-ular. Allen, Richard, John and Nora were loved but not spoilt. Their par-ents taught them to hold happiness above prosperity, and mindful work above possessions. Samuel and Camilla said they appreciated anything their children had done with their hands and brains. Naturally, in this environment all the Williams children took pleasure in making things. Nora made calendars and painted in watercolour. At the Royal show, Richard and Allen gathered up corks and sewed them together to make a sort of jacket. The boys enjoyed practical pursuits and studied the farming methods of Camilla's relatives. Richard had a talent for puzzles and riddles, and a liking for fine and precise instruments and mecha-nisms like locks and guns and engines, quickly learning how to dis-mantle and then reassemble them. As a boy, he began collecting keys; as a youth, he would collect firearms; and as an adult, he would own and tinker with a long succession of cars; but one constant throughout his life would be his collection of books.

Samuel was the model for Richard's interest in precision, and he too possessed an inquisitive mind. He converted a bedroom at Broomcroft into a studio where he developed and printed images from his quarter-plate camera. Another room housed the maid, so the remaining bedrooms had to be shared. For several years, Allen and Richard occupied the best room in the house. Their bedroom over Broomcroft's front door had bright red wallpaper and was well lit, even at night thanks to a nearby lamppost: two princes in their perpetually illumined chamber.

The brothers' outward appearances belied their difference in years. From an early age Richard challenged his elder brother for height and indeed they looked similar, almost like twins, though Allen had a tendency to put on weight. They shared the same strong jaw, roundish face, fair skin and fair hair, though Richard's was a few shades fairer. In early black-and-white photographs, it is hard to say which brother is which; one tell is that Richard is almost always smiling, as if Allen has just made a joke off camera. In life they were inseparable. After their musical Sunday evenings, Allen and Richard would walk to Clifton Down and stargaze in the grounds of Mortimer House. They joined the same Boy Scout troop, and the choir at St Anselm's – 'Allen for his voice and Dick for his appearance because he looked angelic with his blue eyes and pink cheeks'. (In 1907 the Clifton-based Prussian artist Fritz Von Kamptz painted a cherubic portrait of Richard; Fry's Chocolates asked if it could use the image on its tins, but Samuel refused.) Sharing a room deepened the brothers' attachment. In quiet moments at Broomcroft, they were for ever planning new escapades.

Yet the brothers did differ in character and personality. They both counted their blessings, but Richard as if they were really blessings, and Allen as if they were his due. Compared to Richard, Allen was less sanguine, more self-serious and reserved, perhaps more cynical, slower to make friends. And he could not care less about Thomas Gray, with his tolls and knells and herds and plods. But Richard loved his brother and saw the best in him. The middle brother cultivated an ear for the absurd, and Allen had the quality Richard found irresistible: a zestful preparedness to muck in with a project, no matter how offbeat or ill-conceived. The middle and eldest Williams brothers had in common a degree of confidence that bordered on invincibility. Richard was never happier than in Allen's company.

In their various schemes, the Williams boys were notably entrepreneurial, and that entrepreneurship was creative, lean and scattershot. When given the chance to rent a small garden allotment on land that used to be tennis courts, Allen and Richard pounced. The allotment needed to be dug up. 'This was quite heavy going as every sod of turf had to be buried a foot down,' Richard later recalled. 'Allen had the bright idea of telling all the boys at our next choir practice that in exchange for some pleasant light exercise, free sweets, cakes and lemonade would be available.' The Williams' allotment was the first to be planted. Allen and Richard fortified their soil with potato waste, and at the first exhibition of produce from the allotment they won the prize for the heaviest potato.

Mr Bingham helped manage Bristol's waterworks and was, like Samuel Williams, a medium-sized cog in the local administrative machine. The Williams and Bingham families became friends and went to the Bristol Downs for picnics and cricket. On fine summer days, dozens of informal matches paved the Downs. Despite the dubious musical talents of the Williams boys, the two families formed the Bingham–Williams Concert Party. At Broomcroft, they put on shows for small audiences to raise money for war horses and other causes championed by the Blue Cross. At the climax of the performance, Samuel appeared dressed as Kaiser Wilhelm, complete with military helmet and sword; the whole cast tackled him and fell into a scrummage. A hit with the audience – Samuel outwardly made a convincing Kaiser – the climax had to be repeated many times.

The Williams children's schooling was chaotic from beginning to end. All four had different pre-school educations. After Richard's time at kindergarten, he joined Allen at Tellisford House, where the sadistic headmaster Mr Crawford caned the boys daily on flimsy and not-so-flimsy pretexts. Allen on his own at Tellisford seemed a benign student, but Richard brought with him a brotherly competitiveness that got the two of them into trouble. Their schoolmasters likened them to two facets of Seidlitz powder: harmless when kept apart, but explosive when mixed. Reflecting years later on his time at Tellisford House, Richard only recollected punishment.

Richard left Tellisford for a stint at Clifton College, before joining Allen again, this time at Bristol Grammar School. The boys called it 'the Gram' and themselves 'Britain's Greatest Scholars'. In and around the playing fields, the Great Hall and the other elegant school buildings, life centred on the masters, the corps, sports, games, fights, jokes, pranks and 'going on det'.

Richard was interested in cricket and followed closely the school's first eleven in their matches against Downside, Cheltenham Grammar and other peer schools. Allen, whose smirk tended to aggravate his masters, cared even less about cricket than he did about Gray's 'Elegy'. He had little interest in team sports of any kind – weakness in one of his feet was blamed – though he did climb, via the bike sheds, up to the gym roof, where he had an illicit picnic with his schoolfellow Ernest Wilmott. During the feast, Wilmott pointed out his sister, 'who with other girls was cultivating a void piece of ground on the other side of the road'. Enjoying this intriguing vista cost Allen a two-hour detention. Allen and Richard were in trouble at the Gram almost as often as at Tellisford.

Nora Williams learnt a lot from her brothers, and even surpassed them as a virtuoso of mischief. She boarded at the Friends' School, a Quaker establishment at Saffron Walden in Essex, and was a senior there when measles broke out. Clocking a couple of juniors walking down a corridor, Nora instructed them to follow her into an empty classroom where she 'produced her paint box and covered their faces with red spots'.

> She then set them free. They were barely out of her sight when they were seen by a mistress who, without a close examination, marched them smartly into the san where all the real measles cases were in isolation. Soon it was noticed that the spots were artificial but the damage had been done, they had been in contact with genuine measles cases and were therefore unable to rejoin their own classes and had to be kept in isolation.

The strict headmistress, Miss Priestman, took a dim view and reprimanded Nora severely. This would not be their last encounter. Every pupil at the school had an 'undermug', a metal pan kept under the bed.

Nora challenged anyone in her dormitory to roll a mug along the corridor. No one accepted the dare, so she proceeded to do it herself. At the end of the corridor was a long flight of stone steps and the mug, getting up speed, rolled down these steps making a considerable noise. Nora tried in vain to arrest its progress and when eventually it reached the bottom there was Miss P, not at all amused. She said to Nora, 'Tomorrow morning after prayers you will come to my office bringing that object.' In due course, she turned up to find Miss P had rearranged the furniture in her office, leaving a circle or course which could be used for rolling a mug. Miss P said, 'As you appear to like this form of exercise, for the next hour you will proceed to roll your mug around my office,' and in spite of all pleas of an aching back, this she had to do.

The 'Undermug Episode' became famous at the Friends' School and beyond. Nora's aunts warned their daughters – and Frances Collihole in particular warned Joan and Evelyn Collihole – to steer clear of their cousin as she was 'always leading them into trouble', what with her three brothers and their 'awful pranks'.

At the Gram, Richard befriended another heat-seeker. On the hard courts at Clifton Zoo, Richard played tennis with Doug Gael, who had the same incendiary quality that Richard appreciated in Allen. Richard and Doug shared an interest in guns and explosions. When they made their own gunpowder, they tested it on the tramline in front of Doug's home on Whiteladies Road. A passing tram ignited the blast, which 'could be heard for miles'.

Richard was a pupil under three memorable masters: Mr Beames, Mr Hutchings and Mr Fortey. 'Dear old Billy, dear old Eggy, dear old Fifty.' Like many Bristol Grammar students and old boys, Richard had a soft spot for Mr Hutchings. Richard felt affection, esteem and even veneration for the master whom everyone called Eggy, and whose secret name, in the hugger-mugger language of Britain's Greatest Scholars, seems to have been Chumblepump. Beneath Mr Hutchings' well-cut clothes and mild, gentle voice lay a mild, gentle nature. Richard's first impression was that Eggy took little interest in the affairs of life that meant so much to the schoolboys, like world-champion boxing bouts. But after an English lesson in which the master handed out corrected essays, the conversation turned to the question of the hour: who would win the Carpentier–Dempsey fight? Joe Dempsey would certainly win, Mr Hutchings declared, backing up his statement with a technical knowledge – of the fighters' records, weight and technique – that the boys had never dreamt he possessed. When Dempsey ultimately thumped Georges Carpentier, Eggy's stock rose still further in the eyes of his pupils.

During Allen's first term at the Gram, a master asked him to take a note to Mr Hutchings. Allen hesitated. Who was Mr Hutchings? Seeing his puzzlement, a boy in the class whispered, 'Eggy,' and off Allen went.

Mr Fortey, aka 'Fifty', was a welcome addition to the Gram. For three terms he was Richard's form master; three 'very pleasant' terms, in Richard's recollection. Richard attended Mr Fortey's Monday afternoon scripture classes, which followed a predictable pattern: 'We would start on scripture and one subject would lead to another and we nearly always finished up by listening to him telling us how he nearly ran down the *Aquitania* with a half-ton yacht.'

Summer holidays were mostly spent at Camilla's relations' farms in rural Devon. The farmhouses 'were centuries old',

> a bit of lawn, trees, flowers, kitchen garden, small orchard, large kitchen, cool pantries with slate shelves for pans of cream in the making, a well with hand pump that delivered icy cold water on the hottest day, lots of outbuildings, stables, calf sheds, implement sheds, Dutch barns and the whole surrounded by green fields and hedges with primroses, hollyhocks and wild strawberries.

For the Williams boys, the farm meals were the stuff of legend – the farmer and his family, the visitors and all the farm staff, eating together at a single long table. Home-cured bacon, fried and boiled potatoes, 'as many eggs as you liked'. On other visits, the Williamses enjoyed a souped-up high tea around a 'highly polished table really groaning with ham and turkey, goose and duck, and for "after" always fruit and junket served in a large glass bowl smothered in Devonshire cream – and to fill in any empty spaces freshly made scones with strawberry jam and cream'.

When Samuel took his sons to a dairy to buy more Devonshire cream, they were each given a delicious glass of scalded skimmed milk that cost a ha'penny. Their uncle, William Collihole, owned a general store opposite a pub, the Ring of Bells, at Winkleigh. In the store, the Williams boys were allowed to help themselves to sugar from great wooden bins. (Winkleigh had been the scene of an infamous family episode. In 1910, when the boys were eight, five and two years old, the Williamses went to Uncle Collihole's wedding. The well-wishers erected a celebratory floral arch outside the church and planned a fine display of bellringing to follow the service and the wedding breakfast. However, before the bellringers' performance, Samuel took them to the Ring of Bells. In due course the performance flopped, and Nora's would not be the only Williams name to be written into the Colliholes' bad books.)

In the final years of the First World War, and in the immediate post-war period, social and economic upheaval threatened to sweep away much that was cherished of rural England. Against that backdrop, all four Williams children faced the same mundane question of what to do after leaving school. For each of the children, this question would be answered in a remarkable way.

The Jump Start

At Bristol Grammar School, Allen left behind a miserable record in English and arithmetic. Richard did somewhat better, but both boys left school early and neither obtained the qualifications necessary to go on to university. For Richard, though, university was not so far away. He and his brothers loved drinking cider; their father enjoyed brewing it at Broomcroft. Richard would learn how to make it on a commercial scale, and in doing so he would learn a trade. On leaving school, Richard joined the Agricultural and Horticultural Research Station of Bristol University as a working student.

The locals knew the research station at Long Ashton, a few miles to the south-west of the city, as the 'cider institute'. Richard bicycled to and from the institute, until Samuel bought him a second-hand motorbike. Sixteen-year-old Richard revered his two-and-three-quarter-horsepower Douglas, which he took for exhilarating rides over rolling green hills and along ancient twisting roads. The machine that he christened the 'old bus' was fast: on Christmas Eve, Allen and Richard watched the sun set from New Passage and were back home before lighting-up time. Allen and Richard rode the Douglas around the district, through a landscape of thatched cottages, hedgerows, climbing roses, stone walls and fine English trees. To Westbury, Flax Bourton and Chard; to Bedminster Down, where at night the brothers could see the lights of the city. The elder Williams brothers were never closer than during their peregrinations on the Douglas.

In his diary, Richard left enough details for us to reconstruct a typical journey to the cider institute – a vivid slice of daily life that reveals much about him at that time. On a fine, bright morning a healthy nip spikes the air as a young man emerges from Broomcroft pushing the Douglas and wearing a neat collar and tie, highly polished field boots, breeches, a trench coat and a cap pulled down on one side. He turns a tap on the Douglas, tickles the carburettor, adjusts several levers, then with a farewell glance at home he pushes the bike forward. (The Douglas has no clutch and always starts with a jolt.) A couple of bangs, the engine comes to life and the boy gets on the bike ... Turn into Aberdeen Road, pull coat straight, grip petrol tank with knees, give cap a final pull and gauntlet gloves a tug. Slow for the dangerous crossing at Cotham Hill and the nasty corner at Whiteladies Road. Then all clear down the shady avenue from Oakfield Road to the Victoria Rooms. Slow past the policeman. Extend right hand and cross the tramlines, then cut down the Triangle and turn right. The road is very narrow; bear to the left and it is wide once again. Always lots of children here so 'safety first'. Swing to the right and on to busy Hotwells Road, stop at the newsagent and buy the *Daily Mail*, stuff this into coat and on again. Policeman on point duty at the next corner, sharp left, then on to the first swing bridge, just wide enough for two cyclists to pass. Up a short incline to the second swing bridge; if this has swung away, wait till it has swung back. Real good spin for a couple of hundred yards then over a narrow bridge and out into the country. Up, bear right then down towards the Smyth Arms. Slight rise again then sharp left just by one of the Lodge Gates of Ashton Park. Pass a girl walking to the bus stop, rather good looking. Up and down, left and right, race past the Bird in Hand and the almshouses with the lines from Spenser over the main porch: 'Sleep after toyle, Port after stormie seas, Ease after warre, Death after life doth greatly please.' On the left the ground slopes away to the railway and on the right the green fields stretch up to Paradise. Now the engine is purring. Pass the men on their way to the Institute; just enough time for a 'Morning'. Slow right down, drop into low gear, squeeze between the green gates in front of the office, push the old bus into the shed, kick down the stand, and on with the daily tasks.

Going home, Richard passed the same people every day, and he measured them according to how well they reciprocated his good cheer.

A silent man on a Rudge; a man driving a Ford lorry, always jolly; a man on a pushbike who would bid Richard 'Goodnight'; an eight-horsepower Rover whose driver never waved; a friendly acquaintance on another Douglas; and 'the Athlete', a man about six feet three inches in height and 'of splendid build' who dressed in a light tweed suit, carried a stick and unfailingly greeted him. On to a lovely hairpin bend that Richard always hoped to round without any footwork. The engine was warm now. From the top of the hill it was a good run home, where Richard parked his bike in the garage or in the hall, and was soon 'sitting down to tea in the best company in all the world'.

At Long Ashton, 'under the superintendence of the Pomologist and Fruit Foreman', Richard studied cider-apple yields and growing methods, and generally helped run things. Erb Watts, the foreman, would impress his colleagues by lifting and pushing massive crates and vats and presses, and performing other feats of strength. On a good day, the men produced a thousand gallons of cider.

Richard passed the beautiful girl at the bus stop many times, but was always too shy to speak to her, or even to smile as he sped past. Allen, in contrast, never shied away from the opposite sex. He appreciated girls in general, and took any opportunity to get close to them, including church services. A different disposition towards girls was one significant consequence of the three-year age gap between Allen and Richard. Allen's more mature interests were, for the other brothers, a source of fascination and, to begin with, amusement. In the sphere of grown-up gender relations, Allen would always be several steps ahead.

Richard's friend Doug Gael had two attractive sisters, Roma and Rosemary, and a hutch for breeding rabbits. When Allen was fifteen, and beginning to take a serious interest in girls, he found the easiest way to arrange meetings with the Gael daughters was to rendezvous at the rabbit hutch. In 1918, a distant uncle on Camilla's side called at Broomcroft. John Lane senior was a celebrated figure in the book world. He owned the august firm The Bodley Head, which two decades earlier had published Oscar Wilde and Aubrey Beardsley. Lane and his wife Annie had moved to Bath, barely fourteen miles from Bristol, after a German bomb partly destroyed their London home and prospective servants refused to live in a bombed-out house. At Broomcroft, Lane put forward a proposal with massive implications for the

Williams family. After the war, Lane said, Allen could, if he so chose, join his uncle at The Bodley Head and learn about making and selling books. The great man was offering not just a publishing job but, potentially, a publishing inheritance. Presented with a life-changing opportunity, Allen wavered. His mind was elsewhere.

Richard recorded Allen's unpromising first contact with the possibility of a career in books: 'Uncle John was ... attempting to interest Allen in the Bodley Head, when suddenly Allen said he had to go off to feed his rabbits. Uncle John remarked that if he was more interested in animals than books, he might as well take up farming instead of publishing.' Later in life, Allen would have many more opportunities to 'feed his rabbits'. (When, for example, as a popular bachelor in London, he had four liaisons on the go at once, all with girls called Phyllis from different parts of the metropolis, he enlisted Nora to screen phone calls so that he would know whether it was Phyllis north, Phyllis south, Phyllis east or Phyllis west on the line.) Even though Allen found Roma and Rosemary Gael much more interesting than talking to John Lane about a publishing job, the conversation did ultimately take place and Allen signed on as Lane's apprentice, office boy and dogsbody.

Lane, who had no children of his own, would open this door on one condition: Allen would have to change his surname from 'Williams' to 'Lane'. Camilla and Samuel obliged, thereby encumbering Allen with the slightly absurd name of Allen Lane Williams Lane. In April 1919, all six members of the Williams family adopted the Lane surname. Camilla wisely thought it would be odd for Allen alone to have her family name; society might find it confusing, even improper. Within the family circle, Camilla did not want any of her children to feel alienated or left out. Samuel's paternal ego does not seem to have been bruised. A week after the name change, Allen Lane, aged sixteen, started work at The Bodley Head.

Shortish, roundish Uncle John had also started work in his middle teens. He cultivated an impeccable eye for literary and artistic talent, which saw him succeed in two countries as a publisher and bookman. For more than three decades, Lane was a pillar of the literary scene and enjoyed a fame rare in the book world. Could there be a better mentor and role model for Allen than this son of Devon farmers who was born in the village of West Putford, grew up in the countryside and would later cherish romantic childhood memories of tickling trout, farming sheep, growing corn and roaming the woods and moors?

Meeting John Lane was a boon for the Williams family, but Uncle John had his faults. After moving to London as a boy, Lane had started work at the railway clearing house where he administered, badly, a complex regime of payments between railway businesses. Outside work, he dealt in books and antiques. In time, his extracurricular entrepreneurship succeeded to such an extent that he could bring his entrepreneurship back into the office and pay colleagues at the clearing house to do his work. With Elkin Mathews, an apparently like-minded and definitely like-sized bibliophile and antiquarian, Lane set up business more formally. He chose for their premises a shop in Vigo Street, an edgy locale known as the scene of a destructive fire and as 'a gathering-place for the better class of whore'. Lane grew an Elizabethan beard and began dealing in 'First Editions and Scarce Books', some of them mildly disreputable in subject or presentation. Lane and Mathews called their bookshop The Bodley Head, after the great Devonian Sir Thomas Bodley, and they kept the name when they began making books and not just dealing in them.

At that time, a hefty slice of London society craved finely made books, bibliographical rarities, and the subtle distinctions – like inscriptions and priority of issue – that lifted certain books from the run of the mill. In this atmosphere, the underbelly of the antiquarian book scene thrived. Lane moved in the same circles as the bibliographers Thomas Wise and Harry Buxton Forman. The Bodley Head issued a Buxton Forman volume on Keats. With this kind of help, Wise and Buxton Forman climbed to the top of the rare-books ladder, only to be exposed as thieves, pirates, forgers and scammers on a spectacular scale. But The Bodley Head thrived too, issuing a series of books in beautiful Art Nouveau covers that were widely acclaimed and sought after.

In the firm's illustrious formative years, when it supported the decadent aesthetic movement in art and literature, poetry underpinned the firm's list. With Richard Le Galliene as his literary advisor, Lane corralled a stable of virile, whoring poets so fervently invested in the movement that a carelessly high proportion of them chose to depart this Earth ahead of time. Apart from the writings of Oscar Wilde and the art of Aubrey Beardsley, The Bodley Head published scores of other authors and illustrators, and the ground-breaking periodicals *The Yellow Book* and *B L A S T*. Though initially helpful to the firm, the connection to Wilde quickly lost its appeal. Caught up in the storm of publicity surrounding Wilde's indecency trial in 1895, Lane was a willing part of the ensuing retreat from the moral experimentations he had formerly embraced.

The ink on The Bodley Head partnership agreement was barely dry before Lane enlisted spies and started plotting against Elkin Mathews. When the inevitable separation occurred, the partners split their stock and their herd of authors. Astutely, Lane took the firm's name and sign, while Mathews kept the lease at Vigo Street. As if to taunt his former partner, Lane set up nearby at The Albany apartments in Piccadilly. By the time Lane met the Williams family, he was getting on in life (he was sixty-three) and getting on in a career in which he had published scores of authors and hundreds of titles, and had demonstrated a flair for publishing that bordered on genius. He was an influential pioneer in the formal and informal marketing of books through window displays and advertising. Though his list had initially concentrated on poetry, it broadened to encompass cooking, music, drama, ballet, art, architecture, transport, engineering, gardening, theology, *belles-lettres*, economics, novels, travel, history, classics, fashion, militaria and gynaecology.

John Lane senior was perturbed by young Allen's excuse about visiting rabbits, but he would have empathised had he known the real reason. There was a chafing contrast between the outwardly fuddy-duddyish Lane and the rampant young visionaries he published. In the company of long-haired, absinthe-drinking poets, John Lane was never more than an inside–outsider, occupying a curious bohemian nether world. He was nonetheless a man of the world; he exchanged raw and adult correspondence with the prolific poet William Watson, and bonded with Le Galliene, the owner of 'a consuming passion for anything in print, or in skirts, or in a glass'. Lane himself was popular with the ladies. When he met his future wife in 1896, he had more than one other affair on the go.

*

Annie Philippine Eichberg, born in 1856, was the daughter of Julius Eichberg, founder of the Boston Conservatory of Music. In 1884 she married the celebrated war correspondent Tyler Batcheller King. His extraordinary diaries reveal an intense regard and tender feelings for his wife. After King's death, his intimate messages to Annie were paid forward in her effusive love letters to John Lane. Annie and John had met in the drawing room of the London salon of Boston-based writer and socialite Louise Chandler Moulton. They married in 1898, when John was forty-four and Annie forty-two. The couple bought No. 8 Lancaster Gate Terrace, in what became a fashionable part of London. Annie wrote essays and short stories, the successful series of Maria novels, and a pamphlet on grapefruit. Mr and Mrs Lane filled their house with beautiful objects, and Lancaster Gate Terrace became a temple of good taste where the engaging host and hostess entertained literary London.

Their effusive letters aside, John and Annie Lane were a curious match. Awkward with foreigners, John was, according to Richard Lane, a member of the 'old school' who thought that, as long as he spoke English slowly and loudly enough, anyone anywhere should be able to understand him. Annie, by contrast, was the multilingual translator of Anatole France. John only went to North America and the Continent because he had to, for his work; otherwise, he would happily have stayed in England. Annie Lane, on the other hand, was innately international and cosmopolitan. Her father was German, she was born in Switzerland and in her childhood she moved to America, where she became a stylish member of Boston society. Though Lane could dance up to a point, his dislike for music was well known. When William Rothenstein took Lane to a Brahms concert in Paris, the publisher fell asleep. Annie, though, was deeply musical. At the age of sixteen she wrote the words for a patriotic hymn, 'To Thee O Country', which her father set to music. In 1906, to buy herself a Bechstein piano ('a Boudoir Grand Pianoforte'), she went with Edvard Grieg to choose the ideal instrument directly from Bechstein's Wigmore Street shop. Annie hosted regular 'musical evenings' at Lancaster Gate; on these occasions, Lane always made sure he was somewhere else.

According to a popular book-trade aphorism, the publisher's role is to publish as few books as possible. John Lane refined the aphorism to one of paying royalties as seldom as possible. In business, Lane was both fire starter and fire blanket. The authors, collaborators and competitors who knew him best used words like 'wily', 'devious', 'treacherous', 'swindler', 'villain' and 'fraud' to describe what they thought of him and his methods. But nearly every time he found himself in trouble, he managed to pull through, in part because his sharp approach was softened by an affable and sympathetic personality, a gentle voice and kindly weepy eyes – a symptom of gout. It was Lane's good side that Annie King noticed, and the odd coupling worked for the same unaccountable reasons that stopped Lane's authors from strangling him.

Apart from seeing a Zeppelin raid destroy much of his house, Lane had no direct involvement in the Great War. After moving to Bath and reconnecting with his Bristol and Devon relations, he and Aunt Annie became frequent visitors to Broomcroft, and in return hosted the Williamses in Bath, London, Clifton and Brighton. Over dinner, and in the drawing room at Broomcroft, he spoke about the goings-on in London and the publishing world. Thanks to these audiences, by the age of twelve or thirteen Richard Williams-Lane understood publisher's copyright and the basics of making and marketing books. When Uncle John brought books for Allen to read – to expose him to good writing and good thinking – the anointed protégé nibbled, while Richard feasted. He saw his uncle as a remarkable man who possessed marvellous energy and vitality. Though Richard shared with Annie and John a love of scenery, poetry and music, the Lanes were to him 'almost people from another world'. He had little sense of the great publisher's fame or influence, but he knew his uncle must be important because, among other hints dropped, Lane was on very friendly terms with J.E. Barton, headmaster at the Gram.

Though John Lane 'always had an eye for a likely-seeming, good-looking young man', Annie as much as her husband was behind the dynastic train of thought that carried him to Broomcroft and Allen to London. The inhabitants of Broomcroft were as impressed by Annie as they were by Uncle John. With the Williams-Lane children, Annie was self-effacing and always ready to tell an anecdote at her own expense, like the story of her umbrellas. She owned a large variety in different colours and styles, and nearly always carried one with her wherever she went. Every year, she sent off half a dozen to be repaired or re-covered. One day, she took the bus to collect a batch of brollies. She was not carrying one herself on this occasion but sat next to a lady who was. On getting up to leave, Annie reached for the item instinctively. Its owner protested and Annie apologised profusely. After she had done her shopping, Annie collected her repaired umbrellas and, returning by bus, happened to sit next to the same lady, who took one look at the brollies and said, 'You've had a good day, lady!' Richard felt a great affection for his new aunt and they began a long and warm correspondence.

After the Great War, Mr and Mrs Lane returned to London, reopened their house in Lancaster Gate and continued to entertain England's literary elite. When Allen joined them, his future was somewhat assured but, for Richard, things were far less certain. At the cider institute, he found the daily lessons and tasks with Erb, Jack, Bill, Cecil, Mac, Purren and Sweet William to be easy and pleasant but undemanding. The trips to and fro on the Douglas were the most enlivening events of the day. With his friend Mac, he began to talk of adventure beyond the compass of Long Ashton, Cotham Vale and Leigh Woods.

*

Mac – surname McMinn – lived in digs opposite the institute. His father had travelled to the Subcontinent and worked for some years in Ceylon. On little more than a whim, Richard and Mac decided to go abroad. After spinning a school-room globe made from tin, they thought at first that they might go to South Africa or America. The immigration rules in those countries turned out to be too circumloquent, however, so the boys decided on Australia. Samuel Lane encouraged his son's restlessness: he and Camilla had recently considered relocating the whole family to Australia; and, as a young man, Samuel had himself left home in search of adventure, which he found as a gold-seeker in South Africa and then as a volunteer in the Boer War. Samuel had been to Cape Town, had seen Lion's Head and Cecil Rhodes' estate. Speaking to Richard of his travels, he laid out the highlights enticingly. Samuel said that if Richard did not go abroad while he was young, he would regret it all his life.

Samuel and Camilla made one stipulation: that Richard would travel to a job. Richard and Mac looked for opportunities that offered work in Australia without requiring them to front the full cost of the passage out – then about twenty-four pounds. They came across an advertisement for an Empire scheme championed by Henry Barwell, the conservative premier of South Australia. The scheme aimed to attract British boys to South Australia, in part to make up for the loss of young Australian men in the Great War. Participating boys – who came to be known as Barwell Boys – had to sign on for a period of up to three years, during which time they would work on the land as apprentice farmers. The scheme offered the boys a deal: if they contributed ten pounds up front towards their fare, the balance would be paid by the government and recovered over time from their employers. For their labour, the apprentices would receive four shillings a week.

Richard completed the Department of Migration and Settlement's application form, which got to the heart of the matter:

Can you milk? *Yes*
Can you plough? *No*
Can you handle heavy horses? *Yes*
Have you any relatives or friends in Australia? *No*
Are you the son of an ex-Service man? *No*

The form also asked the applicant to identify his religion – Church of England – and, flirtatiously, asked whether he wished to travel on any particular line. Richard answered: Orient or CGL.

Applicants had to supply references. B.T.P. Barker, the director of the cider institute, had barely met Richard but happily attested that the applicant was 'thoroughly reliable, honest, intelligent and willing to learn ... Since being here he has taken part in the various seasonal operations on the farm which consists of ninety acres principally under mixed fruit, and has shown promise of turning out an extremely useful man.' In another reference, Headmaster J.E. Barton complimented Richard's character and designated him 'a thoroughly suitable candidate for emigration to Australia'.

Under the rules of the scheme, host farmers also had to apply to participate. Lenden Athelburt King, lately of Moorook, disclosed that he was married and lived about twenty-five miles from a railway station and three miles from Australia's longest river, the Murray. He sought a Protestant boy, aged fifteen to sixteen, who would 'assist in pruning cultivating spraying picking and drying fruit' and who in general would help work the irrigated soldier-settlement block. 'The lad will eat from our own table, sleep in the house and be one of the family.'

A migration official, possibly unaware that Bristol Grammar's motto was 'Grapes from Thorns', diligently mated the two applications. When Allen Lane (aged nineteen) learned that Richard Lane (aged sixteen) was leaving home for Australia, he wrote his brother a tender letter about their shared experiences and hopes, the affection he felt for him, and his pride at Richard's entry into the Barwell scheme. Richard took a prized photo of Allen with him to Australia; Samuel may have been his colossus, but Allen was his idol.

Uncle John understood and endorsed Richard's Australian fruit-drying apprenticeship. Lane had read Fraser Hill's *The Land and Wealth of New South Wales* (1894) and was optimistic about Australia's growth and development. In fact, for Lane, his nephew's plans were peculiarly resonant. In 1912, The Bodley Head's charismatic apprentice Arundel Dene had emigrated to Australia, from whence he joined the Australian Army and served in the war, before settling in Melbourne and working for the state electricity utility. Dene's replacement at The Bodley Head, Ben Travers, came from a family of dried-fruit merchants. Lane armed Richard with letters of introduction to people who might help him in his travels and his work.

The Sunday evening before Camilla and Samuel's second son departed, the family put on their best clothes and went to the evening service at St Mary Redcliffe. Camilla gave her son a small prayer book. He was still a boy when he left England, but the decision to go to Australia closed a critical chapter of his childhood, in which innocent pleasures and a tight family circle had helped foster the optimism, humility and industry that would define him as a person. Every man's childhood establishes a set of benchmarks and expectations, both conscious and unconscious. For Richard Lane, his childhood in Bristol scored marks more deeply than most. Some of his expectations were low but many were high. The poor plumbing and unhealthy layout of the family home set a low bar against which the Lane brothers would for ever measure their living arrangements. Broomcroft in particular implanted an obsession with bathrooms that the brothers shared – that is, they shared the obsession and would share bathrooms, too, to an extent that would play a surprisingly important part in their lives. On the other hand, generous meals across Devon, in farmhouses more affluent than Broomcroft, set the bar very high for every other meal the brothers would consume, and engendered a culinary obsession almost as intense as the ablutory fixation. Richard's friendships with Doug Gael, Mac McMinn, the Binghams and above all with Allen were the model for his future friendships. The Williams-Lanes' home life was the yardstick against which Allen, Richard, John and Nora would measure every other family.

Allen and Richard took different lessons from the same experiences. In their long conversations with John Lane senior, Richard appreciated what Lane had done for the literary world, especially his help for budding authors and artists, while Allen was intrigued by industry gossip, and by Uncle John's convoluted moves against Elkin Mathews and the benighted holders of Bodley Head preference shares. Allen and Richard had been partners in the garden allotment project: Richard thrilled at the joint activity and the idea of entrepreneurship leading to money; Allen noticed what he could make people do. Sometimes, in their boyhood games and pursuits, what Richard saw as collaboration, Allen interpreted as competition.

Bristol nevertheless provided the reservoir of shared experiences that Richard hoped would for ever bind him to Allen and John. He hoped the Lane brothers would always be the Williams boys, fishing and climbing and exploring, and riding their trolley at breakneck speed.

Though sad to be leaving family and Cotham Vale, Richard had an openness to new experience that was characteristic of the Williams-Lanes and that drove him out into the wider world. From his childhood, Richard took many formative lessons about the value of family, friendship, respect, money, love. All these values would be challenged during his Australian escapade.

THE BARWELL BOYS

I n September 1922, from Tilbury Docks in the Thames estuary, Richard and Mac and seventy-nine other Barwell Boys set sail for Adelaide on the maiden voyage of the SS *Bendigo*. The P&O Steam Navigation Company named its ship after the great Australian gold-rush town and, indirectly, a famous bare-knuckle boxer. Thirteen-thousand tons, two quadruple-expansion steam engines, 1016 passengers, 225 crew, 'and quite a number of cats'. Many lies were told to the Barwell Boys, and some of the first were in the P&O prospectus, which displayed agreeable two- and four-berth cabins with portholes and washbasins. The prospectus also showed a sample lunch menu: 'soup, cut off the joint and two vegs., pudding and fruit'. The reality of the boys' living conditions was very different: cramped temporary cabins 'knocked up in one of the holds'.

> Mac and I were in an inside eight-berth cabin and not only was there no washbasin but in fact there was no water on our deck. In our cabin was a save-all, a contraption that held a small bowl that could be filled from a small tank that was supposed to be filled by the steward. When the door on which the basin rested was shut the contents fell into the bottom tank, that was in turn supposed to be emptied by the steward. But, apart from the first couple of days, neither operation took place [and] as there were no toilet facilities one can imagine to what use the contraption was put.

No ventilation, no natural light. The 'cabins' were inferior to third class. In hours they could be re-converted into storage for cargo. Eight boys occupied an improvised cabin much smaller than the red room at Broomcroft. In the fit-out and furnishings, every expense had been spared. The hard pillows made the boys' ears ache.

The prospectus lunch menu also turned out to be atypical. Yes, there was fruit: one apple every other Sunday. Meagre and unwholesome meals meant the boys were always hungry. Richard's belt had two extra holes added but soon divorced his waist; 'at the rate I am going I shall be able to wind it around myself twice'. Calavances were a staple offering on the *Bendigo* – 'very hard small nasty musty rotten little beans, and the chief use made of them by a lot of the pupils is to throw them at each other'. For protein, the boys were served foul-smelling meat, and sausages made from bacon rind and potato peelings. There was also soup, which Billie Askwith renamed 'galvanized seawater'. Richard thought some of the food was unfit even for the albatrosses that shadowed the ship. Meals were served on unclean crockery and cutlery, and under no circumstances were there second helpings.

The Barwell Boys came from most classes and counties but were collectively a rough and hard lot. They fought and played cards and argued and swore like the stokers who fed the engines far below. They smashed the naked lightbulbs in their cabins and stole replacements from the dining saloon and elsewhere on the ship. All short of money, the boys instituted a complex system of barter and piecework. They would 'do almost anything for cash or cigarettes … shirts washed for tuppence, collars one fag each, boots cleaned one fag a pair or one person cleans them if you will let him use the polish and brush for his own boots. One boy in our cabin will draft out a letter to anybody for tuppence.' Some boys sold their clothes.

In the wider population of passengers, there were violent drunks, men held in irons, stowaways, illicit affairs, and rumours of a girl having fallen overboard. At the first foreign port, one passenger slept the night in a police cell and another, a drunken Scotsman referred to as 'the old man', fought his way back on board. After fighting six men at once, he fell and refused to get up. 'He was so violent with his arms and with his legs when he was on the ground that somebody had to punch him in the stomach to keep him quiet … a rope was slipped under his shoulders and he was hauled up amid tremendous laughter. His hat fell off and he banged his face a good deal.' Richard was soon a long way from the cosy hearth of Broomcroft. For a child from Cotham Vale, the *Bendigo* presented a grotesque tableau of moral horrors. Boys younger than sixteen drunk to oblivion on spirits. Young children gambling and playing cards for money – 'one of the worst evils of this world', said Richard in his diary. Pools of blood at a crime scene witnessed at a port of call. Richard had thirsted for experience; on the journey to Australia he got it. Twelve days into the voyage, in tropical humidity 'like a Turkish bath', a Barwell Boy from a neighbouring cabin went mad.

> He will not sleep in the top bunk as he is afraid somebody will stab him with a knife and a couple of nights ago he woke everybody in his cabin up and told them the ship was sinking, he then rushed up on deck with a lifesaving jacket on. Last night he prayed aloud for his cabin mates and blessed them. He has seen 'sawbones' the doctor several times, but he does not seem any better.

The next night, the boy drank brilliantine 'to oil his throat'. His name was Bourne but the Bendigonians only ever referred to him as Loony or Loopy. In the course of his descent he forgot when to hold his tongue. He interrupted the ship-board lectures, proselytised maniacally, and generally made a nuisance of himself. The last straw came when he tried to convert the purser. The managers of the migration scheme decided he would be sent back to England without being allowed to disembark at Adelaide or Sydney. Richard and other boys had tried to reason with him, and to curb his wildest flights. When the final adjudication came, Richard wrote home, 'I am very sorry for him.'

In South Africa, a friend of Samuel Lane – Mr Moore, the assistant chief of prisons and recent superintendent of a leper colony – took Richard out to lunch. With overflowing gratitude Richard consumed the first decent meal he'd had since leaving home: 'soup, curried eggs and rice, roast beef, potatoes, jelly and cabbage, fruit salad and junket, toast and butter, dry ginger ale, coffee, Egyptian dates', followed by a high tea of meat and potato pie, pineapple, oranges, bananas, gooseberry jam and *mostbolletjies* – 'a kind of bun made from moss and a certain part of grapes'. Mrs Moore gave Richard more *mostbolletjies* to take on board.

To the Williams-Lane family, Richard's transit through Cape Town mattered. Samuel's time there had influenced Richard's decision to leave England, and Richard was determined to connect with his father's memories of the place. In and around the city, Richard reverently traced his father's footsteps: Lion's Head, Table Mountain, Devil's Peak, Kloof Nek, the Twelve Apostles – and Hout Bay, where small children sold strings of brittle shells at exorbitant prices; Cecil Rhodes' estate, with its verdant oaks, vines, peach trees, fields of wild lilies and long avenues of Port Jackson willows. Lions, baboons, monkeys, peacocks and wilde-beest, all caged. The Rhodes memorial among the trees.

Apart from the sights and surrounds of Cape Town, Richard made a close study of his fellow passenger, 'the old man' from Scotland.

> Every time he goes on shore he gets drunk ... He is very canny and keeps all his money in a metal box double padlocked and he only takes out enough to get properly drunk on, usually ten shillings a time. He was tight Monday and Tuesday night and last night after he had been brought on board I went and had a look at him. He was lying on his bunk, his clothes covered in dirt, dust and mud. He had been sick all over his chin ... Mr Tyler and Mr Tomlin refused to sleep in the same cabin ... but Mr Garvie said he would stick there for the night and give him a good telling off as soon as he was in a fit state to understand anything.

On the first leg of the voyage, Mac, Richard, Billie Askwith, Mr Garvie, Mr Tyler and four other 'broad minded men' had formed a group they called the Intellectuals. To dilute the general anarchy, they convened debates on literature, philosophy, theology and current affairs, and organised 'grand supper parties' that were convivial but far from grand. The Intellectuals attended classes in first aid with Mr Ker, took dancing lessons with Mr Garvie, exercised daily with 'physical jerks' under the instruction of Mr Tyler, and vowed to restrain their smoking, at least for a few days.

In the span of a peripatetic career, Keith Garvie had been, among other things, 'a private secretary, an actor, a dancing instructor, a book traveller, a clerk of works'. After Cape Town, the ship listing heavily to starboard due to a supernumerary load of coal, he gave an informal lecture about his 40,000 mile trip, 'Around the world, from Melbourne to Melbourne'. Garvie and Richard became friends. They discussed the *farceur* and novelist Ben Travers and other favourite authors, and shared their thoughts on life, love and the future. Garvie read the departure letter Richard had received from Allen. Richard recorded the man's reaction:

> He was very interested and said that although he had got a brother, he never knew what brotherly love was and had never received a letter like that from him all his life, nor from anybody else until he was a good bit older than I was. He thought it was a beautiful letter and that the love that existed, and always will exist, between Allen and my unworthy self was what he had longed for in the main when he was young.

The events put on by the Intellectuals were not the only way to socialise on the *Bendigo*. On behalf of the captain, the purser sponsored festivities that drew passengers from all decks. One Saturday night, a fancy-dress parade ended in a dance. 'Allen would have enjoyed it very much,' Richard wrote to his family, 'as the rolling of the ship compelled the partners to hold on to each other very tightly.'

> It was at first decided to postpone it because of the weather, but when the Captain heard of it he said have it by all means as the partners would have a good excuse to cuddle each other. And they did! When Allen reads this he will make a mental note that the Captain is a sport and he will be right.

Throughout the voyage, Richard's family was in his thoughts. Continually, almost religiously, he recalculated the time and wondered what his parents and sister and brothers would be doing.

When the ship docked at Fremantle, the Intellectuals were determined to get away. Mac, Richard, Garvie and Billy Askwith walked the twenty-five miles to Perth and back. Richard noted the price of everything. Fruit, film, meals, tobacco, shirt collars, cars, cream, cameras, postage, railway fares, books. For the Intellectuals, the highlight of the Perth jaunt was a bag of bananas, paid for and presented to them there by Mr Morgan of the YMCA. Despite bathing their feet in the Swan River, the four passengers rejoined the ship with spectacular blisters and feet generally 'in a very poor state'.

*

On 24 October 1922 the *Bendigo* arrived in Adelaide and the Barwell Boys – all except poor Loopy Bourne – began to disperse to their placements. Mac went to Berri with a Mr Spendiff. Billie Askwith went to Hindmarsh Island. Richard made the most of a two-day layover in Adelaide. He explored the city and visited the fine botanical gardens. And he called on Collier Robert Cudmore – a local solicitor with an international reputation. At the 1908 Olympic Games, Cudmore won rowing gold as a member of the British four; he was called to the Bar in 1910; and during the First World War he commanded a battery on the Western Front and was severely wounded, twice. The year 1922 saw him in the early stages of what would become a stellar legal and political career, in which he spearheaded reforms of parliament, universities, traffic rules, public health and prostitution. Cudmore knew at one remove both Samuel and Camilla, and he offered to do anything he could for their son.

Richard travelled by train and service car to Moorook. The car was an extended makeshift private taxi service, standing in for phantom train and bus connections, and travelling sometimes on winding bullock tracks that stood in for phantom roads. A soldier settlement in South Australia's irrigated and semi-arid Riverland, the township of Moorook had a church, a general store and a bakery. The settlement held on to the land by its fingertips. Three miles from town, Len King and his wife farmed twenty-two scraping acres planted with grape vines and, 'for personal use', straggling trees of apples, peaches, figs, nectarines, quinces and apricots. They owned two horses, two pigs and three cows but no stable or cowshed, so all milking was conducted in the open air. A network of snake-infested irrigation channels prevented the farm from rejoining the encircling semidesert of Mallee scrub and saltbush.

Richard received by mail a group photograph of his cohort of Barwell Boys, and a letter from Victor Ryan, state immigration officer and supervisor of the Barwell scheme, which offered encouragement:

Attend to all the little details that may appear at first sight too trivial to bother about, and don't be disheartened if at times you make mistakes. Your employer knows that Australian conditions are quite strange to you, and will make all allowances, so long as you will bear in mind and act upon the advice, 'if at first you don't succeed try, try, try again'.

The Barwell Boys called the migration officer 'Daddy' Ryan, the father of all the boy migrants. To King and the other host farmers, Ryan wrote:

The boys, being apprentices, should not be regarded as casual farm hands … might I mention that it will tend a great deal towards the boy's happiness and good behaviour, if your wife or other womenfolk will take a kindly interest in his welfare, and the boy will, doubtless, respond to any kindness received by giving better service and by little acts of usefulness about the house.

Tough, serious, tight-lipped, King had served in France in the Great War, and he retained many of his military traits. The Kings' home, like all the others in the district, was built from cement and had an iron roof. Richard's room stood outside the house proper, 'a sort of lean-to addition … about eight by five feet with a concrete floor'. The outer walls were made from hessian that let the dust in. For furniture: a camp bed, a chair, a mirror framed with canvas, a fragment of an old straw mat, a candlestick, kerosene (paraffin) cases, and old boxes with a piece of cloth thrown over them to act as a dressing table. For washing: a tin bowl on a bench outside the living room. Everyone in the household used the same roller towel in the kitchen. 'This was nearly always filthy and the result was that I got a bad case of impetigo and this together with the hot weather and the fact that I had just started to shave, really made life miserable.' For sanitation, a dunny can – 'a small wooden contraption with a seat with a hole in it and a bucket'. The contraption sat just outside Richard's bedroom window, and he was responsible for emptying it. At night, he could hear the rustling of maggots in the bucket.

Soon after Richard's arrival, a snake killed a fruit grower; Richard wanted to avoid the same fate. The Kings had two boys aged under three. They shared a birthday, which happened to be the day before

Richard arrived, so naturally they saw his possessions as presents for them to do with as they chose. At every opportunity they ransacked his room. When they ate his biscuits, Richard bought more and hid them in the pocket of his coat, which hung on a nail beside his bed. One night, a noise woke him and he felt sure it was a snake. He lit the candle, armed himself with a boot, traced the noise to his coat and gave it 'a hefty swipe', thereby evicting the tiny mouse that had been gorging on the biscuits.

From his first day at Moorook, Richard entered a consuming cycle of work that started before dawn, finished after dusk, purged all thoughts of reading and culture, and left little time for writing letters or his diary. The work was as strenuous as it was varied: pulling shoots off vines, feeding the pigs, milking the cows, letting the cows out into the bush ('they know when to come back'), helping separate the milk, hoeing, harrowing, and, most backbreaking of all, excavating a cellar from solid rock. Flies got in his 'eyes and ears and nose and everywhere'.

One night, he watched a frog swimming in the water tank. The creature crossed the moon's reflection, leaving a dozen moons behind it. Richard could not drink the briny froggy water as it was, so he masked the taste with lime juice. Sunburnt and aching all over, Richard suffered for the first time from what he called his 'fits of the blues', and wished he had never come out to Australia. He felt sharply the isolation from family. Before embarking on the *Bendigo*, he had always had Allen or John with whom to confer, conspire and laugh. He had never been away from them, or from Samuel and Camilla and Nora, for an extended period of time. Now, he was a very long way away, and the contrast between Moorook and Bristol jarred.

Moorook's weather varied wildly, from cold to extremely hot. On 12 November the temperature reached 102 degrees Fahrenheit at 8 a.m. and 108 at noon. In this heat, Richard rode the horse rake and hauled and stacked lucerne. 'Lucerne is about equivalent to the English clover,' he informed his family. Richard had to spray the vines with Bordeaux mixture: 'sulphate of copper, soda and water, also a little flour to help make it stick'. The caustic formula stung his sunburnt and peeling arms.

When Mr King decided to remove a barbed-wire fence from a lucerne patch, he coiled up a few yards of the wire, put them in a cart and told Richard to mount the cart and anchor the wire with his foot.

King then drove the horses, over uneven ground, to pull down the remaining wire. On the cart, the wire slipped and caught in Richard's feet, sending him sprawling. It cut through his trousers and socks and slashed his ankle. Richard asked for permission to return to the house for a bandage. King refused and said they would carry on and finish the fence first. Richard relayed the incident to his family but put on a brave face, playing down the injury and omitting King's refusal to allow the wound to be dressed.

Richard Lane strove to be the ideal boy migrant: obedient, diligent, punctual, respectful, resourceful. But Mrs King was unmoved by the immigration department's advice that she play a maternal role. She kept her distance while making up her mind about the new addition to the household. Clarity was not long in coming. Mrs King concluded that she hated the farm's new apprentice. She resented his presence at the dinner table and refused to speak to him. Instead she asked her husband, 'Does that Pommy bugger want any more food?'

By order of Mr King, Richard went to work on a neighbouring block owned by a man called Duncan. There, for several weeks, from 7 a.m. to 7 p.m. each day, Richard cut apricots. For this labour, Duncan offered a sweetener that, as Richard explained, wasn't very sweet at all: 'Whatever I earn over five shillings a day I can keep, but as I am inexperienced at the job I assure you I don't earn much.' Over and above his work on the Duncan block, he retained many of his duties for the Kings, including milking before dawn and after dusk, and emptying the dunny can. His work duties on Sundays were the same as on every other day.

The living conditions and strenuous work on the King block, Mr King's reckless methods, Mrs King's irrational contempt, the King boys' destructive sorties, and the impromptu secondment to Mr Duncan's apricots – here was ample evidence that Richard had made a grave mistake in joining the Barwell scheme. He stuck it out at Moorook for three months, but he had already decided that his circumstances there were diabolical. Richard was unafraid of hard work in the home and on the farm, but this regime devoured almost every waking moment and every skerrick of energy. Used to romping in woodlands, and riding his bike far and wide in rural England, Richard now had no say in how he spent his days. His first experience of the Barwell scheme felt like slavery. The blues intensified and he suffered a bleak, intense homesickness.

The mistreatment of Barwell Boys would be the subject of a damning official inquiry, but that was two years away and of no help to Richard.

Soldier settlement was a government program that subsidised the cost of establishing returned servicemen on farms. A good idea in theory, but in practice an ill-conceived failure. Many of the farmers were inexperienced and under-trained; many of the farms were undersized and under-capitalised; and many of the settlers would later forfeit their properties. Much of the land selected for the scheme was unproductive – land so unpromising that it had never before been farmed, or could be bought cheaply by the officials who administered the program. There was a high uptake of boy migrants among the South Australian soldier settlers trying to make their blocks pay. Farmers in struggling districts hoped the Barwell scheme would send cheap labour, and even some capital. For boys like Richard Lane, the Barwell scheme and soldier settlement blended into a double disaster. The boys found themselves indentured to properties that were poorly run and which, even with exemplary management, could never prosper.

Mired in the King fiasco, Richard needed an immediate lifeline. Mr and Mrs Matthews ran 'Meyrah', a nearby fruit block at Moorook. Mr Matthews was English but in the First World War had been an officer in the Australian Air Force. He and his Australian wife had travelled to England together and knew Mr and Mrs Stanley De Courcy Ireland, who in turn knew John and Annie Lane. At Richard's lowest ebb, the Matthews reached out to him at the Kings' block and did what they could to make his life bearable, and to pave the way to freedom. Mrs Matthews invited him over for Christmas dinner, took him on a picnic, gave him books, and delivered other favours and courtesies at a time when Richard desperately needed such kindness. Mr Matthews had already hosted a Barwell Boy; he decided to apply for another, and Richard pursued with all his residual energy the prospect of a transfer. To Mr Cudmore in Adelaide, he wrote that, if he could be transferred to Meyrah, 'I am sure I should be perfectly happy'.

> I quite understand that if I am moved to Mr Matthews there are bound to be some unpleasant questions asked, but I don't think they will worry me very much and, after all it will only last for a short time as the gossipers will soon find a fresh channel to turn their talk into.

Also there is the fact that there will be no expenses incurred if I am transferred locally. Mr and Mrs Matthews are 'two of the best' and as regards cleanliness, home life and comforts it will be second only to home, which although it is 12,000 miles away it is still home. There can be no comparison between Mr King's and Mr Matthews' houses ... To put it shortly where one is spotlessly clean the other is filthy ... Mr Matthews is a conscientious worker and, I am sure, as good a boss as you would find in the whole of Australia, exactly the same can be said of Mrs Matthews.

Richard told Mr Cudmore he had been working the Duncan block. On its face, this was a breach, by King, of the apprenticeship agreement, and Cudmore informed the immigration officer Victor Ryan. Richard also confided in Reverend Davis, the parson at Moorook. The clergyman listened to Richard for two hours before writing to Ryan:

As far as I can gather the boy is from a very refined home and is highly educated. I know the conditions under which he lives for I have been to his employer's place many times and so far as Lane's complaint of filth and dirt is concerned I know he is telling the truth. The house is not fit for people with the ordinary amount of respect for cleanliness to inhabit let alone one of a highly sensitive nature ... I do strongly recommend his transfer and that speedily for the boy is eating his heart out.

Reverend Davis supported Richard's preferred destination, writing that Mr Matthews 'seems to be in temperament similar to Lane ... I am well acquainted with Mr Matthews and know the living conditions well. I can say truthfully that there is not a better place in Moorook.' Ryan had no choice; official enquiries had to be made. In response to departmental questions, King wrote to Ryan defending Richard's presence on the neighbouring property. Duncan 'was unfortunately late in occupying his block and there being no casual labour available I decided to help him out ... it's the custom of country people to all help, when one man is in a hole. The lad is not hired to him or fixed any set of wages.' Then came King's lance for Mr Matthews: 'Your informant or a party to it is trying to make things bad for me, he has had a boy of his own (a farm apprentice) and if he requires another one just send a petition form along and it will be signed by nearly 100 people that no more lads be put under his care.' Ryan asked the local council at nearby Loxton to make enquiries on the ground. The council clerk was partial to King's views and wrote in words that might have come from King himself:

> Mr King is known to all the settlers around Moorook as a very fair man ... Mr Matthews is a man of no principle and is only trying to get the boy away from King because he is an extra good boy, and once he got him might treat him well for a month or so and then the boy would be very sorry he changed, neither is he a suitable man to train a boy.

Richard's migration file swelled with the flurry of letters. The conclusion for Ryan was unmistakable: there was a mess in Moorook, and Lane must be removed. Mr and Mrs Withers, childless and originally from England, sought a boy under the scheme. They lived in Renmark, about thirty miles from Moorook. In a letter appended to his application, Mr Withers wrote, 'As the boy will be entirely in the house and as there is only my wife and self, I am anxious to get hold of as nice a lad as possible.' An interview was arranged, the official transfer was effected, and a relieved Richard left Moorook, grateful to all who had helped. But he was rightly worried about the next phase of his Australian adventure, and how long it would be before he could re-enter the stream of life. The distress of unamenable work, physical exhaustion and isolation from family was compounded by a clash of expectations. A fundamental disconnect separated the parties to the migration arrangement. Richard had hoped the scheme would underwrite a rewarding interlude. South Australia saw his apprenticeship as an adoption and a marriage.

*

Though farther inland and a much larger town, Renmark resembled Moorook in many ways. It too had soldier-settlement blocks. It was at least as arid as Moorook, and the weather was at least as hot. In spring, the temperature in the shade was 110 degrees. Richard arrived at Mr and Mrs Withers' property – 'The Warren' – at the height of a punishing summer. He was greeted by a revised agreement from the immigration department, which stipulated a term of apprenticeship of two years and nine months. Richard refused to sign, replying to Daddy Ryan: 'When I signed an agreement in England, the term of apprenticeship was stated as not less than 12 months and not more than three years. I do not intend to sign an agreement for two years and nine months. Make it nine months and I will be perfectly satisfied.'

In England, Richard had received a pamphlet promoting the Barwell scheme. Like many other Barwell Boys, he understood 'the term of Apprenticeship would be for not less than twelve months or more than three years' to mean that the power to set the term, within these bounds, rested with the apprentice. The agreement he and Samuel Lane had signed was, however, 'for a period not exceeding three years as may be determined by the said Government', and the said government took a hard and narrow view: the commitment would be for the maximum time, three years. Ryan pressed Richard to sign the new agreement, playing dumb about the pamphlet.

> The original agreement with Mr King was for three years, but on transfer to Mr Withers, a new one was prepared for two years and nine months, as you had already served three months at Moorook. I do not understand your reference to 'not less than 12 months', as this does not appear in the document at all. I must accordingly ask you to comply with the Regulations and sign the agreement forthwith, so that you may be legally apprenticed.

Richard was in a bind. Homesick, exhausted, and now pressured by the department that had him in its control, he sat on the letter. Ryan wrote again with still greater pressure and half a threat. 'I am surprised that I have received no reply from you to my letter of 12th instant, and that the Agreements have not been returned duly signed. Will you please comply with my request for the documents to be signed without further delay, as I desire to save any unpleasantness if it is possible.' Richard, a youth of seventeen, 12,000 miles from home, found himself in an uneven dispute with a state bureaucracy. He knew that Daddy Ryan could deploy all kinds of 'unpleasantness'. Resigned to the fact that he would be trapped in South Australia, at least until a more lasting escape could be effected, he gave in and signed the new agreement. Richard's blues intensified. Not only was he away from home and facing all manner of troubles, but the duration of his absence was uncertain, and lengthening.

Richard's new home, The Warren, was on Chowilla Street in Renmark's rural outskirts. Two streets away, in Kulkyne Street, was Robert J. Beer's property. Beer was Withers' friend. After Richard arrived, Beer applied for his own Barwell Boy. Tom Nunn, aged seventeen, arrived in February 1924. He experienced the same culture shock that Richard had encountered at Moorook, and soon felt homesick and adrift. Richard naturally empathised and offered Tom advice and support, but the boy continued to struggle. Two months into Tom's apprenticeship, there was a party at Mr and Mrs Beer's home. Tom played the piano and sang. He played billiards. At seven o'clock the next morning, Bob Beer found Tom hanging from the crossbeam of an elevated water tank. Tom's passing would be one in a spate of Barwell suicides. The inquest that followed failed to shed any useful light. Saddened and uncomprehending, Richard could barely bring himself to write about the death. For Richard, Tom's suicide purged once and for all any remaining sense of 'Boy's Own Adventure' from his Australian experiment.

4

COLD DIP

The whole time Richard was away from England he kept a diary. He bought a series of notebooks, and when he'd filled one he sent it home. The resulting text, of more than 150,000 words accompanied by dozens of photographs and drawings, was in essence a long, loving letter to Camilla, Samuel, Allen, John and Nora, who were continually amazed, baffled and dismayed by Richard's reports from Australia. Yabbying. Battling a cyclone. Fighting fires. Chasing thieves with a truck and spotlight. What were the Williams-Lane family to make of it all? Apart from the notebooks, Richard wrote letters to the other inhabitants of Broomcroft and to John and Annie Lane and his other relatives and friends. The letters and diaries meticulously charted his travails and ambitions, his emotional highs and lows, his changing views of Australia and Australians, and his development as a boy and a man.

For Richard, writing was a precious activity because it shortened the distance between Australia and England. But writing in Renmark was difficult: 'while I write this the flies are walking all over me, they even walk down my forefinger and try to settle on the nib of my pen. Blow flies are buzzing everywhere, I am damp with perspiration, the atmosphere is almost stifling.' Richard devoted a large part of his diary to his fascination with Australia's wide skies and arresting landscapes. 'The golden streaky clouds appearing just above the bush, then some very light blue sky with dark almost purple clouds with a touch of red in them floating about. In the east the sky is light blue and very light pink and then there is the moon, the glorious moon.' 'Now the day is over, stars begin to peep. The sky is still bright in the west and it is all of a distinct lemon colour.' At other moments the sky was blood-red or made bright blue by vivid flashes of lightning. The cloudscape was striking, foreign, in Technicolor: 'a solemn Sunday stillness ... down on the horizon is a slate grey cloud, above it a cloud whose colour might almost be described as fawn, further westward, I am looking south west, the slate grey turns, oh so imperceptibly, to dark grey, the fawn disappears but in the centre of the grey cloud is one sharp streak of pink. As the sun sinks lower and lower, the light-coloured clouds take on a pinkish hue, from pink to a rich dark gold, from dark gold to light shining gold.' The bush was painted in matt with an imperfect palette, but it too held fascinations, so different from Nightingale Valley, but no less remarkable. Though unfamiliar to him, Australia's birds were, Richard thought, as beautiful and noble as their English cousins. He fell in love with Australia's natural beauty before he warmed to her citizens.

He observed the people he met with the acuity and detachment that Lemuel Gulliver brought to his encounters with the Brobdingnagians, the Balnibarbians, and the Japanese. Richard's new master, Mr A.B. Withers, was an odd blend of Wilkins Micawber and Forrest Gump, with a hint of Samuel Lane thrown in. As a young man, he had been articled to a solicitor in London but 'soon grew tired of it', or so he claimed.

He became a medical student and walked the hospitals, then to the Gold Coast for twelve months, back to London this time speculating, he had an office in King William Street, he gambled on horses and swore that he made money at it, he speculated in stocks and shares and lived at the end of a telephone. When King Edward was to be crowned, he bought up windows and sold seats. He was connected with the Bowden Wire people when they first started to make brakes, he was a buyer at Barkers for some time, a racing cyclist for some considerable period, he won a few championships and many medals, he drove one of the first cars in England, was a guide to an Expeditionary Force in West Africa, here he bayoneted many blacks and was in return shot in the knee, he still limps from this.

Withers then managed a theatre, before absconding with the actors to form a travelling company. He was 'private secretary to one of the great actor managers, and dozens of other things and of all of them he has hundreds of anecdotes'. Then Withers and his wife came to Renmark. He cleared his block of Mallee scrub, Murray Pine and eucalypts, and built a stone house.

When Richard arrived, the farm had one cow, two horses and thirty chickens, plus Joey the cockatoo and Tiddles the cat. Richard's living arrangements with the Witherses were far superior to those at Moorook. The comfortable homestead had a dining room, a large sitting room and 'a pleasant fireplace'. Richard's room 'was smallish but very nicely fitted out with a wardrobe and dressing-table.' His new lodgings were only temporary, however. When Mr Withers' family came to stay, Richard moved to the old nursery: 'no ceiling, only an iron (corrugated) roof, also it has no proper window, only mosquito wire and shutter. Also it has no furniture, but it is well filled without that, as it contains seven empty petrol cases, two leather trunks (one mine), several cardboard boxes, a wire stretcher with bedding, several small wooden boxes, the side boards of the trolley, two sweet boxes of peaches, one of apricots and one of prunes.'

Richard decorated his room with pictures, all sentimental, all reminders of home. One of Nora's smart calendars. A watercolour by Miss Watson. A picture of two kittens in front of a beehive, bees buzzing, 'Where innocence is bliss'. A colour print, *A June Garden* – 'old thatched cottage, climbing roses, old cobblestone pathway, beautiful flowers in the foreground and majestic trees in the distance'. A photo of Samuel Lane wearing his chain of office. A photo of the whole Williams-Lane family, taken at Marsh's when Richard was young. Another print, *The Avon at Clifton*, by Sutton Palmer, showing the suspension bridge, the Observatory and Leigh Woods. And in the most prominent position, Richard's prized photo of Allen.

Mr Withers welcomed Richard to The Warren. Here was someone to listen to his anecdotes and share the farm work. The Barwell Boy and his hosts settled into a domestic routine. When Mr Withers made custard, Richard tasted it, 'for the first and last time'.

I asked him how much sugar he had used. 'Sugar,' he replied. 'Sugar, what do you want sugar for in custard?' 'You didn't put any at all in

then.' 'No of course not, why? Don't you like the custard?' 'I'm not saying anything against it, but how much powder did you use?' 'I don't
know, just a few tablespoonfuls.' 'Don't you think it's a bit "powdery"?'
I asked him. 'Well, now you come to mention it, it certainly tastes as if
I had used too much powder. Just a little too much,' he added.

Richard kept the custard 'as a curiosity' for a few days. Joey and Tiddles
refused to go near it. When it began to change colour, he fed it to the
chickens. 'Strange to say the fowls haven't been laying half so well since
I gave them that custard.'

Mr Withers' unsystematic approach to washing dishes exasper-
ated his apprentice, who believed 'there is a right way and a wrong way
of doing everything. Certainly there is a right way and wrong way of
washing up.'

The boss washes, I wipe up. He has not much system and washes
whatever comes into his hand first. A cup, a saucepan lid, a basin, a
plate, two knives, a milk bowl, a few forks and spoons, several plates,
one egg cup, the rest of the knives, two milk basins, a saucepan,
another cup and so on. Occasionally, I refuse to wipe something as I
consider it is not properly washed. More hot water is required and as
there is none hot enough the boss lights his pipe again. 'What,' he
says looking at the clock, 'half past eight all ready. I promised to ring
up Smith soon after eight, I had better do it now.' I busy myself in trying to make the fire 'buck up', when in walks Mr Waters for his skim
milk, we give him all we have left over. He and the boss then have a
short talk usually about dried fruit matters. After he has gone we
start washing up again. The boss is now beginning to get desperate.
'A greasy saucepan, that must go in soak, a jam jar, also to be soaked,
two more jars, the water's not hot enough for them, they also must go
in soak, so must this saucepan and what are those three saucepans
and those two jars doing in the corner Dick?' 'Those are the ones you
put in soak yesterday.' 'Oh, are they, well the water's too cold, I must
do one though or we shan't be able to have any breakfast tomorrow.'

Bread was also unpredictable. The baker left his deliveries on a slate on
the back verandah.

We came up the block one day last week and were surprised to find that all the inside of the loaf had been eaten away, the crust only remaining. It was not hard to discover who were the culprits, for now whenever the baker arrives, the fowls rush to meet him. Needless to say, we immediately cancelled that arrangement, and the bread is now left in a tin.

Richard was impressed by how Mr Withers carried himself on visits to Adelaide: 'he is a real 100% hayseed, he strolls up and down the streets like a dog without his master, he aimlessly gazes into the shop windows, he positively gapes at high buildings.' Withers claimed that, as a young man in his prime and living in London, he had dressed in the height of fashion. The picture in Adelaide was somewhat different: 'now he is in a coat with bulging pockets, baggy trousers, dirty boots, socks hanging down over the top of his boots, collar and tie in a hopeless tangle and puffing away at a dirty old pipe in which he smokes aromatic Havelock by the plug, portions of which he cuts off with a small knife which he mislays an average of three times a day. This is the boss in town.'

Born on April Fools' Day, and wary of opening birthday parcels, Mr Withers was especially nervous on the eve of his initiation into Renmark's Masonic Lodge. He had 'got the wind up' over it.

Of course none of the masons have told him anything about it save the ridiculous. All they have done is to try and pull his leg and although they have not fully succeeded they have at least created a lot of mystery about it in the boss's mind. I think he will be glad when tomorrow night is over. Its very mystery is baffling.

In 1923, Renmark touched the trough of a long deep slump. Most local farms were set up to produce fruit for drying, but dried fruit prices had plummeted. The packing shed price for a ton of sultanas was ten pounds below the cost of production. Growers had lost money for the past three years. 'They have run up an overdraft at the bank and they now find that if they were to sell their block, they would not get enough to wipe off the overdraft ... 90 per cent of the growers are in this position. They would like to get out of it but they cannot.' The recession was just as bad among farmers growing fruit for wine or spirits. A government bounty on fruit was supposed to help, but only 'prolonged the agony'. To stay afloat, almost every grower had a sideline: selling vegetables, chaff, wheat or cool drinks; acting as agent for distant manufacturers of wirelesses, cars or motorbikes; professional or trade work; raising poultry or pigs; cutting or carting wood. 'Renmark at present is in a very bad way,' Richard observed. 'Very soon we shall be taking in each other's washing.'

On election day, all of Renmark turned out, in every type of vehicle, 'from wagons with eight-horse teams to dilapidated buggies drawn by cross-eyed knock-kneed pot-bellied old block horses'.

> From motor bikes and side cars to push bikes. There were buggies, sulkies, spring-drays, masher drays, traps, wagons, trolleys, Hilliards, Bettendorfs, in fact anything that could be drawn by a horse or horses. The cars comprised chiefly of Buicks, Dodges, Studebakers, Chevrolets, Fords, and a couple of Packards ... Men in light suits, dark suits, white suits, black suits, working suits of khaki, khaki pants with white, black, blue or khaki shirts ... and the 'Sweet young things'? White, black, blue, yellow, pink? Yes, sky blue, pink and every imaginable colour under the sun. The sun blazing down on this gay crowd made it quite a pretty picture.

Richard studied the Australians he met. He mastered their slang and judged their wit. His first impressions had been unfavourable, but he revised his view when he met the Potter family from Glenelg in Adelaide.

> I think that the greatest event that has occurred since I last wrote, half way through November, has been my meeting a class of people I had never met before. And for want of a better name I will call this class 'Educated Australians'. Before I only knew the workers and 'Uneducated Australians', and of course besides these I had met the educated and uneducated English people residing in Australia. As a class I like and greatly admire the educated Australian and as individuals I like them equally well.

Before that turning point, Richard applied his eye for the absurd to a series of disarming observations on the intellect of the 'average Australian'.

In one example, Richard mentions to an Australian the Bristol premises of the cigarette manufacturer W.D. & H.O. Wills. The Australian looks surprised for a moment, then says, 'Oh they have a branch in England have they?' And in another, he writes: 'You know the stories about an Englishman, a Scotsman and an Irishman ... Well, the same kind of stories appear in some of the papers out here. An Englishman does "x", a Scotsman "2x", and an Australian "4x". I was talking to an Australian one day and he, quite seriously, pointed out to me that the Australian nearly always "came out on top".'

Richard met another Australian who, when served a cocktail, 'complete with cherry and toothpick', asked why the hotel had 'such small straws'. The man's wife argued with Richard about whether grapevines had flowers or not. 'In the end, for the sake of peace, I assured her that vines never had and never will have anything which has the slightest resemblance to a flower, and that the grapes "just come".' Richard gathered a fund of stories about that good lady; one was about her first ride in a Renmark jalopy. Most cars with side curtains had on the driver's side 'a small aperture with a loose flap, this being for the driver if he wishes to place his hand outside the car, signalling when turning, stopping etc'. The lady noticed such a flap herself, while sitting in the front passenger seat, and asked what it was for. 'For the driver to spit out of,' came the reply. 'Oh,' she said. 'They don't allow you much room,' and then, after a pause, 'Why isn't there one on my side?'

Richard was egalitarian in his friendships. One of his best Australian friends, Don Mount, exemplified a particular type of cheerful hopelessness. Don lived in a grand 'humpy' (an improvised tent-cum-cabin) near The Warren.

> In the beginning there was a tent then Don covered this with a palm leaf shelter then he built on a dining room, lobby, sleeping out room, sitting room, a kitchen, all combined out of palm leaves and bamboo with a few mallee posts to keep the place together. The Westes have recently bought a new carpet and they gave Don the old one so now every room is carpeted. Over the entrance to this spacious mansion he has hung a section of a palm leaf bearing the name Burraboorlagar ... If it has nothing else the shack has at least a very artistic name.

Don was accident-prone and not very bright. He had two kerosene tins, one for water and one for flour and bread; when he placed a loaf of bread in the water tin he 'did not discover his mistake for two hours'. But he had a generous store of practical wisdom – about bush tucker, bush architecture, bush girls, and the bushman's handkerchief. Cars were a mystery to him. When Richard, examining an engine, removed the crank-case inspection plate, Don 'crawled underneath to see the connecting rods, crank shaft, cam shaft etc. He had never seen these portions of a car before.' For his trouble, he was doused in engine oil.

*

Richard's workload at Renmark was heavy but varied, and a merciful improvement on Moorook. The Withers grew sultana grapes and Doradillos, a variety of spirit grape that could also be used to make wine. The sultana grapes were dried on trays, and Richard busied himself cleaning trays, spreading fruit, rolling hessians, boxing fruit and carting it to the packing shed. He felt new strength come into his muscles, and became proficient at trellising, strutting, straining, irrigating and pruning vines, and rolling sultana canes. Before drying, the sultanas were dipped in boiling caustic soda to crack the skin so the grapes would dry more rapidly. That was how things were done before 'cold dip' conquered Renmark.

Cold dip made its first Australian appearance at Mildura, in north-western Victoria, when Greek migrant workers showed how grapes could be prepared in a cold solution of carbonate of potash, water and olive oil. 'Some very fine results have been obtained . . . the colour being far lighter, the skin not cracked, which prevents sugaring.' For fruit growers working in Renmark's heat, the new technique was far more pleasant than the boiling alternative. Renmark was alive with talk of cold dip. None of the locals could think or talk about anything else. Don Mount's brother Wally composed a poem on the subject and submitted it to the *Pioneer*.

Fruit growers who were not cold dipping were picking and packing Doradillos – everyone called them Doras – for the distillery. Wowserism was a potent political force in South Australia. Renmark had been founded as a dry town and for a long time had no hotels. Yet many of its

46

farms grew grapes, and during the economic slump there was a glut of wine, which everyone could buy directly from the distillery. The minimum order was five gallons, at a price of two pounds. 'So almost anyone can afford to buy five gallons of wine.' The wine had a high spirit content, but this was not advertised: 'a great number of growers (and others) are getting drunk on it. They have never been able to get drunk so easily and so cheaply before and do not know what to put it down to.' Richard's experience at Renmark was as much comedy as tragedy.

In the face of the slump, the Withers household needed its own sideline. The nearest railway stopped at Paringa, on the other side of the Murray River, so passengers going to Adelaide by train had first to cross the river by ferry – wasting time and energy in the process. After Richard had been in Renmark for a year, he and Mr Withers and Bob Beer launched a car service that would run directly the 187 miles between Renmark and Adelaide. Eager to embrace a project that involved neither hot nor cold dip, Richard sought official permission to leave the Barwell scheme and become a track driver and entrepreneur. In October 1924, he wrote to Daddy Ryan: 'I am now desirous of leaving the Boy Immigration Scheme as I have come to the conclusion that there is nothing in fruit growing at present.' Richard emphasised that he would not be leaving Withers' employment, so the scheme could not count his exit as another failure.

Mr Withers traded his clunker in as a down payment on a new American model called Moon. Richard had to contribute cash, and to do so he sought the money held on his behalf by the Barwell administrators. Mr Cudmore drafted a legal agreement to the effect that the car would be owned jointly and profits would be shared between Mr Withers and Richard. Bob Beer joined the arrangement as well; he had no ownership of the car, but 'a right on occasion to take alternate trips'. The prospect of Richard leaving the scheme was possibly a relief for Ryan, who was for ever chasing Withers' late remittances. But Ryan could never be a soft touch. He and Richard argued back and forth about the amount the state would release from the scheme for Richard. Ryan at first offered nothing, then six pounds, then twenty-five, and ultimately fifty pounds, which Richard used to pay the first instalment on the Moon.

Now Richard was no longer a Barwell Boy, and no longer just an apprentice fruit grower. He was a track driver, with an interest in a business from which he hoped to profit. Richard and Bob did two return trips each week, charging twenty-five shillings per passenger. Apart from those in Renmark itself, 'there were no made roads for the first hundred and fifty miles'. Depending on the state of the roads and tracks, the drivers chose routes through Eudunda, Kapunda or Gawler. Following unmarked and unsignposted tracks in the wild sand and scrub was in part an empirical exercise, and often a speculative one.

Richard and Bob transported some illustrious passengers. One of them was a parrot, another was cute Miss Curtis. When she and Sister Blair paid Richard to take them from Adelaide to Renmark, Don Mount came along for the ride. Sister Blair sat in the front of the Moon and Miss Curtis sat in the back with Don. It was a bumpy trip and Richard tried to avoid the worst of the pitted and corrugated track. 'Don had to hold on to Miss Curtis when going over a bump.' At Blanchetown, Don drew Richard aside and told him not to worry too much about the bumps. In Miss Curtis's company, he did not mind them at all.

At Bower, on the Morgan–Eudunda track, there was a church with a tower clock. The hour and minute hands were painted on. 'I suppose this is cheaper than a real clock with hands that move,' Richard wrote. Another track passed through Birdwood, which before the war had been called Blumberg. Between Birdwood and Gumeracha there was a low white building: 'a little cripple girl used to lie on a bed here, so placed that she could see all the cars and other traffic pass. First of all I used to wave to her, then one day when passing through Keyneton I saw some wild flowers growing on the side of the track so I picked a few and gave them to her.' After this, Richard always had something for the little girl: chocolates, sweets, flowers, a bunch of red prince grapes, or a bundle of *Punch* magazines that Auntie Annie had sent. 'She was a very cheerful girl and was always smiling. I am very pleased to state that she is fast improving, and the last time I saw her she had been taken out by her father in a wheelchair. She can also just hobble about, and in a few months the doctor thinks she may be able to walk quite well.'

Richard did 10,000 miles of track driving, without a single accident or broken spring. Driving had its delights, like racing down Adelaide's Esplanade late at night, or powering through the steep pinch at Gumeracha, or over Sedan Hill, or through the deep and picturesque Cudlee Creek gorge. Richard got to know a lot about cars – he did all his own on-the-run repairs – and a lot about people, in a way that only taxi drivers and perhaps bartenders can. Richard called Renmark the 'School of Experience'. He delighted in the entrepreneurship that reminded him of his childhood exploits with Allen. But 10,000 miles of track driving was not enough to make the car service pay, and not enough to get Richard back to England. The partners persisted for a year before the end came.

The service had attracted too few customers, and too many of them had refused to pay. The running costs, inclusive of speeding fines, were too high. Most disappointing of all, Richard thought Bob Beer had cheated his partners. Beer 'did us out of some money, quite a tidy amount', Richard wrote, believing Beer had pocketed fare revenue that was due to Richard and Mr Withers, who would otherwise have put it towards overdue payments on the car. At the time of Tom Nunn's suicide, Richard had defended Beer as 'one of the best'. After the car service folded, amid accusations and broken friendships, Richard formed a different view.

In February 1925, two payments were overdue and Richard wondered how long it would be before the Moon agents came for the car. Nor was Mr Withers keeping his part of the bargain; Richard said Withers had 'rather slipped me up': 'in hard cash all that he has paid toward the car and extras is one pound and I have paid well over sixty. I have also worked on the block for the ridiculous low rate of twenty-three shillings and keep per week, the basic wage for permanent hands being three pounds and sixteen shillings. I have also not worried him about paying me, at the present time I am paid up to the end of November. Why? Just because I am sorry for him.'

The same month saw a Biblical run of calamities. John Lane senior died. Richard Lane injured his wrist. The Moon was repossessed. And a plague of locusts came to Renmark. Richard reflected in his diary about his celebrated uncle.

I did not fully realise how much Uncle had done for me until I heard the sad news. Then I spent days during which I continually thought of all the pleasant times I had spent in his company at Clifton, Bristol, Bath, London and Brighton and the more I thought of him the more I realized what a remarkable man he was ... I was very sad for many days.

For the first time in twelve months, Richard got in touch with Mac McMinn, his fellow boy migrant and old friend from Long Ashton. Mac was full of news. Having met a girl of whom he was 'very fond', he was now anxious to make a home where he and the girl could settle down together. To be precise, he planned to buy a fruit block in the Riverland. Twenty-seven acres for £2850, with a deposit of £850. Richard had other ideas. 'If I had £850, I am jolly sure I would not buy a fruit block on the Murray.' Mac's love match spurred Richard's own thinking about girls and relationships.

> I wish my 'own true love' would come to see me, but she lives in the land of dreams . . . I have never seriously considered whether my ideal has dark or fair hair, whether she is a 'blonde' or a 'brunette'. Really I have not had time to think about ideal, I have thought about such things as the cold dip, compulsory pool, self-starters, carburettors, water pumps, fan belts, tyres, punctures, oil, petrol, grease and many other such things, and out of thinking about such things no ideal has arisen, but were I to dwell among peaceful lakes, sweet smelling flowers, gorgeous sunsets and beautiful scenery I think an ideal would arise. All this points at least to one thing, my ideal is not a female track driver.

Even more forcefully, the match made Richard think about the future. Uncle John's death and Mac's intentions to settle down sparked in Richard a *carpe diem* moment. He had wasted three years, he decided, and at the age of nineteen thought life was passing him by. But what to try next? Richard contemplated office work in Adelaide. He and Don Mount made plans to fix up a decrepit Ford truck and drive it to the east coast. Richard thought about sheep farming. He considered working as an auctioneer's clerk. None of these or the other options he entertained were viable. Having lost his investment in the Moon, Richard was nearly broke, and in danger of becoming stranded permanently in rural South Australia. He needed another lifeline.

WHICH IS THE ENGLISHMAN?

In the months before John Lane's death, he and Annie had sailed to America on the *Empress of France*. They met another passenger, Thomas Henry Rowlands, a sheep farmer from New South Wales who was travelling with his wife and daughter. The Lanes mentioned that they had a nephew living in South Australia, and Tom promised to invite Richard to Millamolong station, near Mandurama, 150 miles west of Sydney. Richard would holiday at Millamolong, and if he liked the sheep-farming life, then Tom would arrange for him to work as a jackaroo.

In June 1925, Richard left Renmark, avowing a hope 'never to return again'. Mac travelled to Adelaide to say goodbye to his friend, who boarded the steamship *Dimboola* and sailed via Melbourne to Sydney. After exploring Sydney's harbour and zoo, Richard travelled by train to Mandurama and by Fiat to Millamolong.

Moorook and Renmark were pale imitations of the Australian rural ideal, but Millamolong was the real thing. Ten thousand acres, a flock of exceptional Merinos, a grand homestead, even a well-stocked library. Mr Rowlands also half-owned another property, Canowindra, of 100,000 acres. Well-educated, successful in business and a generous philanthropist, Tom Rowlands was exactly the type of man that Richard Lane admired: 'he is always seeking for information. Always doing something, and always on the go. In this respect he is like that character of characters, like that person of whom volumes could be written, Mr

John Lane.' Millamolong was the kind of property, and Mr Rowlands the kind of man, on which Australia's pastoral legends were built.

The comparison between John Lane and Tom Rowlands was not far-fetched. Both men were clubbable, gregarious, industrious and generous – both donated money to their local hospitals, and gave many young men a kick-start in life (though there were disastrous consequences for the Bodley Head office boy whom Lane introduced to Oscar Wilde). Richard's description of Tom Rowlands mirrored the biographer James Lewis May's description of John Lane: 'always somewhere to go, something to see'. Little wonder that the two hit it off so well on the *Empress of France*, even though the publisher's health was fading. Between them, though, there was one important difference: everyone who knew Tom Rowlands trusted him and saw him as a man of integrity.

Richard spent three very happy months at Millamolong, doing light work, socialising with the Rowlands family and their employees and friends, and thinking about his life and ambitions. He adopted the idiom and appearance of Millamolong's inner circle. On a grand promenade around the central west of New South Wales, a party consisting of Tom Rowlands, his son Doug, Doug's friend Jack Hill, and Richard Lane met farm managers and associates, and classed sheep. To Dubbo and Cobborah, then Dunedoo for dinner. To Mundooran, Rocky Glen and 'Hillgrove'. To 'Bective' at Coonabarabran, back to Mundooran and via Dubbo to Wellington; on to Molong and Gamboola station with its fine homestead, then through Carcoar back to Mandurama and Millamolong.

A friend of Mr Rowlands owned Gamboola. 'Lady Ramsay was staying with him so we literally had a cup of tea with Lady Ramsay and then proceeded to Orange where we had a bonzer dinner at the Royal.' Hillgrove station was Bob Clifton's property. On meeting Bob's mother, Jack and Richard were introduced together. Mrs Clifton asked, 'Which is the Englishman?' 'This, let me assure you, is very amusing,' Richard wrote. 'Needless to say, Jack is an Australian.' In all, the party covered 800 miles and 'had a glorious time'.

At Millamolong, Richard Lane fell in love. Esme Rowlands was Tom's niece. Tom's brother Fred owned Werribee station – 'a fine house, tennis court, two cars' – near Woodstock.

We had dinner there and then back to Millamolong. With us came Miss Esme Rowlands, Mr Fred's only daughter. If this were in every sense of the word 'my private diary' I would state what I thought of Esme. As however this may be read by others besides myself, I had better not say too much. It might come back to 'Werribee' and then I should be done. However there is no harm done by stating that she is very good looking, likes the 'Great out of Doors', is a champion tennis player and is extremely fascinating. I had better not say any more or I might easily say too much ... We kept rather late hours while Esme was staying here. It was usually between one and two before we went to bed.

Richard sketched in his diary a full-blooded fantasy in which his heroic alter-ego, 'Allen Williams', a fruit grower from Renmark, falls in love at first sight with 'Esme Kirk', a station owner's daughter. Initially the love is not reciprocated but, in dramatic fashion, Allen woos and wins the heroine. There follows a motorbike race, a cricket match, a packing shed accident and a visit to Sydney Harbour and Taronga Zoo. The story reaches its climax 'one stormy night' while Allen is irrigating his orchards and vines. In mud and rain, Allen fights and bests a villainous foreign rival. Richard decided that Allen should not kill the villain, 'just make a mess of him'.

Richard also fell in love with station life. Unexpectedly, Millamolong proved a new rival to Broomcroft. Richard wondered: how could he get a position at Millamolong or a similar station?

If I could be appointed master of a small outback school at any decent salary and live on a station I should have plenty of spare time for learning something about sheep and I might also try to save a few pounds. You see sheep is what I am after, but to secure a position as jackaroo at a decent station is very hard ... Talking about trying to be a school master the place or rather school I am trying to get is at Torrington, not much like the place in Devon I'm afraid, but if I go to Torrington I shall be able to live with some friends of Mr Rowlands who have a station there, but if I can't live on a station I don't want to be a school master.

In the end, Richard had little say in his next move. Arnold Brown knew Tom Rowlands and owned the property Richard had visited near Coonabarabran. Bective was one-tenth the size of Millamolong, one-hundredth that of Canowindra. After speaking to Rowlands, Brown offered Richard a job as a jackaroo at a wage of one pound per week plus keep.

> I do not really want to go to Coonabarabran, I would much prefer to stay in this district but I do not like to say nay. Up in that district there are all small stations, nearly all owned by ex A.I.F. men whereas here the stations are much larger and owned by men who have been in the sheep business all their lives. So in some ways I think I should learn more here. It will be with much sorrow that I accept. If only I had enough to pay my fare home I would start tomorrow. As a jackaroo I cannot see much hope of getting home for a considerable time. Had I but forty pounds; it would not take me long to decide what to do with it. P&O branch service, Commonwealth third class or steerage on any boat at all. In fact at the present moment if someone offered me a job as a steward on a home going boat I would jump at it.

Richard's straitened finances became the standing joke at Millamolong. After three and a half years in Australia, he had about five pounds to his name. That was before he bought three pounds' worth of working clothes and boots. Then he had to pay for the train to Coonabarabran.

> On enquiring at the station what the fare was, I found out it came to £1.19.9. All Millamolong wondered what I should do with the odd three pence. It was at length decided that nuts were the most nourishing food, so I was to buy three pennyworths of peanuts, sometimes known as 'monkey nuts'. But a friend of Doug's . . . considered that it was 'more blessed to give than receive' and presented me with a large, very large, bag of Minties and peanuts.

Richard tried to thank the Rowlandses for the 'splendid time' he'd had at Millamolong, 'but Mr Rowlands said, "If you want to show your appreciation, come again." I should have liked to have made a little speech, but it was impossible. As it was, I said "But really" or "But seriously" a good many times.' Loaded with gifts of books, cigarettes, peanuts, mints and advice, with his heart 'almost breaking', Richard and his last thruppence left Millamolong.

*

Bective, Coonabarabran: a primitive house with walls of thin board. Richard could reach the ceiling, in the rooms that had a ceiling. Doors with broken hinges and no latches, handles or locks. Fences rotten and broken, and 'not a decent gate on the place'. Tumbledown farm buildings. When Mr Rowlands visited Bective, he leant against a sheep-yard fence and it collapsed. Brown's sheep were crawling with ticks and lice; Mr Rowlands confided that he would not have a single one of them at Millamolong. Except for his bed, Richard improvised all the furniture in his room from kerosene cases. He termed the style the 'late Kerosene period'.

The work was hard and the hours long. Richard soon reached the terrible conclusion that his labours on the King farm, the escape aided by Mr and Mrs Matthews, his work with Withers, quitting the Barwell scheme, 10,000 miles of track driving – all these things counted for nothing. For all intents and purposes, he was back at Moorook.

The Browns had three children: 'always making a row and they are the untidiest brats I have ever seen.' At shearing time, Richard's room became the shearers' dining room so he slept on the verandah. The children were inventive in their torments. When Richard lay in bed, one child crept up and tried to rub his face with a banana skin while another hit him with a stick; 'one pulled the clothes off the bed, while the other was trying to hit my face ... nothing in my room is safe, they look at everything, pull anything they can to pieces, ransack all my belongings.' Richard had to keep his books locked in his trunk, 'or else the brats would tear them all up. It's no good telling them not to do anything for their answer is always "but I want to".'

A hero of the Great War, Arnold Brown had started out as a private. 'When the Armistice was signed he was a Major and had it lasted another month he would have been a Colonel.' At the height of his involvement Brown commanded a battalion on the Western Front. Two days into an intense period of continuous fighting, he and his men were starved of sleep and supplies; 'the General sent along another battalion not to relieve them, but to support them.'

There was absolutely no place to put these men, to cram them in the one and only trench was equivalent to murdering them. [Brown] rang up the General and told him so. The General said, 'I have sent the men out to support you, use them.' [Brown] told the General to go to hell, he caught hold of the receiver of the telephone and tore it off, then after ordering the supporting battalion back to headquarters he went back to the fighting. Soon after he was wounded and after he had sufficiently recovered he was court-martialled. He was not cashiered and ultimately was presented with a DSO for this incident. General Birdwood also sent him a private letter telling him he was wrong to disobey orders, but he thanked him for doing what he did, in his own words 'practically saving the lives of a thousand men'.

After another display of intelligent courage, Brown won the Military Cross. Richard appreciated and respected Brown's military experiences, but realised that Brown had the same difficulties as Len King in adjusting to rural civilian life. When Brown collected his fine new car – a biscuit-brown Willys Knight with blue upholstery – he drove 400 miles with the back brake on. Bective was run along similar lines to King's block at Moorook. Near-fatal near misses were commonplace.

Bective's letterbox was half a mile from the front door. On Richard's first morning at the property he had to collect the mail. He mounted a horse that had won steeplechasing trophies and was a renowned 'goer'. On the return journey, 'the horse did not wait for me to get on'. Richard had one foot in a stirrup and one hand on the saddle when the horse 'tried to break the record for the half mile ... He jumped over the railway line which crosses the property and tore down the flat, approaching the house at a good sixty. I was holding on to the saddle for dear life.' Richard likened himself to the slave in 'The Slave's Dream': 'At each leap he could feel his scabbard of steel / Smiting his stallion's flank.' 'Only in my case it was a "stirrup of steel" which was smiting ... and which I was trying my hardest to prevent.'

On 16 November 1925, Richard Lane and Arnold Brown both had brushes with death. Brown was installing a pump in the well, which was 110 feet deep and held thirty feet of water. Richard helped lower eighty feet of piping down the well. The chain holding the pipe slipped twenty feet before jamming on a clamp, breaking the half-inch wire rope and saving the pipe from crashing into the abyss. 'I was holding on to the windlass handle at the time and had the rope not broken I should have been hurled half way to Coonabarabran,' Richard wrote.

Brown was then lowered into the well: 'just as he started the windlass slipped while the handle remained firm.'

> Mr Brown did not take any notice of this but I suggested fitting up a rope brake in case it should slip again, this was agreed to and when he had been lowered forty feet and was still forty feet from the water it slipped again and he would have dropped right down had it not been but for the brake. When we got back that night he told Mrs Brown that had I not suggested the brake he might easily have been killed, so we had quite an exciting day.

Richard rose soon after five o'clock to do all his morning tasks: 'lighting the kitchen fire, milking three cows, separating, chopping a large barrel load of wood, emptying the pig bucket, filling up two kerosene tins of water from a fresh-water tank, emptying three tubs which are used for washing, filling up the cool safe with water, and three times a week getting the mail from the front gate.' After breakfast, he rode the cultivator in extreme heat, and ploughed in dust so dense he could not see the horses, despite wearing motoring goggles and a pith helmet. Richard joined in with the shearing, 'a very dirty job', and did whatever else Brown directed: de-burring sheep, carting ringbarked timber, grubbing out thistles and Mexican Poppies, 'unstooking'.

> The boss is not too bad a sort of a chap but he has a very quick temper and goes off the deep end over nothing. The part I hate most is that there is nothing to look forward to during the day. There is nothing to do in the evenings, the Browns don't play cards, the gramophone has been smashed up by the kids, and there are no 'home comforts' at all.

When the Browns went on holiday to Manly Beach, they left Richard 'baching' on his own. He rode into town and bought steak; when he came to cook it the next morning it was green. He soaked and cooked apricots, then left them on the stove while he ploughed for a few more hours. When he returned he could not see the apricots or the saucepan for ants. He baked apples and left them on a kitchenette while he worked. A fowl got into the kitchen; 'besides losing all the apples, it took me a quarter of an hour to clean up the mess.' Richard ran out of bread so he decided to make a cake. The recipe called for butter but in the intense heat the butter had become 'butter oil'.

A native flower that was toxic and addictive for sheep, *Swainsona greyana* or the Darling Pea, had infested the district. 'Some sheep will feed on land covered with pea and not look at it,' Richard wrote, but others 'go mad on it' and, having acquired a taste, would eat nothing else. Sheep thus afflicted were said to be 'pea-struck'. 'In time it makes them poor and also very silly.' Presented with even the best-quality feed, pea-struck sheep would eat only enough to survive, and that barely: 'they walk about just a bundle of skin and bones.' Renmark had been devastated by the collapse in fruit prices; Coonabarabran was plagued by the Darling Pea.

One evening, Richard noticed a ewe looking especially unwell. He lifted her out of the enclosure and carried her and her lamb to the lucerne paddock. The following evening the ewe was still alive, 'but I expect to find her dead tomorrow morning'. The lamb, however, 'chummed up with another ewe that had lambed during the night and this ewe now kids herself that she has twins'. The next day, Richard saw a murder of crows cawing in the lucerne. He fired his rifle to disperse them and found the dead ewe that the crows had been 'making a mess of': 'it cannot have been dead long, but besides pecking the sheep's eyes out they had already made a start on its flesh.' Vowing vengeance on all crows, Richard set rabbit traps around the carcass. 'I soon had the satisfaction of seeing one caught, the rotten cruel brutes. I didn't call them this but something far more Australian.' The trapped crow got away, but at a cost; one of its legs remained in the metal jaws. Richard tied the leg to a post and wrote underneath, 'All Crows Beware.'

*

Richard was used to being around books. The Williams-Lanes always had books at home, and at grammar school and Millamolong he had enjoyed the use of well-equipped libraries. At Bective, however, the Browns' only bookcase contained nothing but agricultural gazettes and

books on military training. Most of the farmers in and around Coonabarabran were as interested as the crows in reading. Sheep were the
principal victims of pea strike, but some people in the district shared
the mental symptoms.

> Here if by some mistake a person reads a book they immediately for-
> get all about it. The love of poetry is unknown. Poetry is not consid-
> ered fit for men to read. If you want to read, there are plenty of good
> books such as 'The Agricultural Gazette of N.S.W.', 'The Blowfly
> Pest', 'Sheep Dipping', 'Lice in Sheep' ... but poetry and all that sort
> of stuff is 'slush'. Dickens, 'Oh I think I started a book by him once
> but it was too long winded,' or else, 'Never heard of the cove, what did
> he do anyway?' Scott, 'He's the bloke wot discovered the North Pole
> ain't he?' and so on. It is not funny but sad, it's this that makes me
> want to come home. The Rowlands are well educated, but they are not
> a family in a thousand, but a family in ten thousand.

Richard had hardly any spare time, and the Browns could not fathom
why he spent such a proportion of it writing in his diary. 'I am beginning to think that I should be thought better of if I did not write quite
so much. It "isn't done" in this district.' Mrs Brown told Richard out-
right that he would be better off reading the *Farmer's Handbook* than
writing in his notebook, but Richard resisted. 'The *Farmer's Handbook*
is no friend of mine whereas this book is and I am sure that after a hard
day's work I need friendship more than I do ... a reference book.'

> When I opened up my trunk and looked at my books I nearly wept
> with joy, they seem the only real friends I have up here. Good books,
> fine pictures, faithful friends; can one have too many of them? Old
> wood, old friends, old wine and old authors are best ... I must be
> something like the man of whom Crabbe wrote, 'His delight was all
> in books; to read them or to write. Women and men he strove alike to
> shun, and hurried homeward when his tasks were done.'

'Hurry homeward' was precisely what Richard wanted to do, but he was
still short of money. In debt to his tailor and being chased for car regis-
tration payments by the South Australian authorities, he hit financial

rock bottom. 'Not counting a pair of boots I bought and the freight on my luggage, I haven't spent one pound during the last two months. My financial condition can certainly be termed a crisis.'

Richard wrote to Daddy Ryan, Bob Beer and Mr A.B. Withers to call in debts. Ryan sent the remaining two pounds, nine shillings and eight pence in Richard's Barwell account. 'I regret that you should have found it necessary to make this application but trust that the small amount will help to tide you over your difficulty.' Beer owed materially more but refused to pay, writing that 'things are in a terrible bad way still and one cannot raise a cent more than necessary for the carrying on of the blocks'. Withers sent a five-page letter but no cheque. 'If I could possibly send you anything I would – the bulk of our income now comes from the cow and chickens, if things don't improve I fear it is impossible to last out much longer as we are gradually being reduced to less than nothing.' Withers could not even sell his gramophone as no one wanted it: 'everybody is getting a wireless set.'

For Richard, things were becoming desperate. He signed on as a drover to transport sheep from Lyndhurst to Coonabarabran for Mr Clifton. The 318 ewes and two rams were crammed into two double-decker train wagons. Each deck was two and a half feet high. Working solo, Richard had to travel with the sheep, to tend to them, and above all to stop them from lying down, 'for if they do they very soon die'.

> Some of the sheep were looking very crook and I had a fair amount of trouble making those that had fallen stand up. They would lie down in the middle of the [wagon] and let the other sheep stand and walk over them without trying to get up. If only they had laid down or had the sense to fall down near the sides they would have got more air and less trampling on.

It was dirty, difficult and dangerous work. In the cramped wagons, the sheep fell down a dozen at a time. Richard stooped and crouched and wrestled and lifted them up. Because the trains were slow and often stuck in sidings, the journey lasted two days. Because of the constant effort, there was very little time to eat. Richard was thirsty, hungry and exhausted, his head throbbing, 'like a blooming Ford car going slowly in top gear'. But all the sheep survived and Mr Clifton gave him a pound for the work. The trip cost Richard fourteen shillings, so in cash terms he netted six shillings. And he did one pound's worth of damage to his coat, and ruined his best hat, so overall the droving expedition was a shattering loss, and the financial crisis intensified.

A literate young man in a book desert, dead broke, with no way out. One evening at Bective, Richard had his worst bout of homesickness – worse than any time at Renmark or even Moorook. At his lowest ebb, Richard's mind churned with thoughts of the places he had seen and the people he had met; the doors that had opened and closed; the mess his life was turning out to be. And then, a vision. The rays of the setting sun had a beautiful effect on the clouds.

> It looked as if a gigantic explosion had occurred in that direction, the clouds were in a semicircular formation and the fringe was all of billowy white clouds. Towards the centre it grew darker and darker till low down on the horizon it appeared quite black. Out of this formation a solitary cloud drew apart from the rest and it assumed in almost perfect proportions the shape of England and it gradually floated on until the sun having departed, everything became dull and grey.

Allen rather than Richard had the stronger interest in mysticism and the occult. But this omen was unmistakable. When Richard finally resolved to return to England, Australia too delivered its verdict on its adopted fruit grower, track driver, jackaroo and drover. A kitchen conference convened at Bective.

> First one name was mentioned and then another, eventually practically everybody that I know or knows me was spoken of and his or her views given. Some were quite flattering and others were certainly not. Mr A. Brown thinks that I have plenty of common sense and my head screwed on the right way; but my chief interest does not lie in my work but in books. Mr R. Brown – 'Never do any good on the land.' Mr Thompson – 'That chap Lane is quite a clever fellow and will make a name for himself if he gets off the land' ... Mr T. Rowlands, Doug Rowlands, Bob Rowlands, Miss Rowlands and Mr Zell all told Mr Brown that in their opinion I should never be any good on

the land, not that I was a 'mug' but just that my heart was not in the game. These views were also expressed by Mr Clifton. And I think that they all know what they are talking about.

Charlie Thompson's father thought Richard would make an excellent newspaper reporter. Richard worked hard and was known as a young man of integrity, but everyone from Arnold to Zell noticed his unique love of words and writing and books. The consensus: a literary life would suit him better than sheep or any other type of farming. Richard concurred with the judgment of his friends and masters. 'I am just beginning to realize that in some ways I am not suitable for farming ... To be absolutely candid, I am far more interested in books than in rams.'

In his diary, read by all at Broomcroft, Richard had seeded the idea of skimping his way back to England by travelling as a steward or as a 'tweendeck passenger. Allen cabled twenty pounds to the Bank of New South Wales: 'BEST WISHES – NO OBJECTION TO WORKING PASSAGE – CABLE IF INSUFFICIENT.' He also sent a reply-paid cablegram that contained a simple question: 'WHEN ARE YOU COMING HOME?'

Richard reserved 'tweendeck accommodation on a French ship – the 'Ville de something or other' – and left Coonabarabran, New South Wales and Australia. He set sail for England having climbed Lion's Head at Cape Town, jackerooed at Bective, marvelled at Sydney Harbour, careered through Mallee scrub, and strutted vines at Renmark: the Empire youth *par excellence*.

At the beginning of his Australian experiment, Richard Lane had had several ideas in mind. He would find adventure and experience enough to help him ride the wave of New World growth and, perhaps, accumulate a modest fortune; he would return proudly to Broomcroft. To begin with, he viewed Australia with detachment, through the eyes of a tourist or a nascent anthropologist. Slowly, he came to see the southern continent for what it was: a trap. The prospect of riches? Hopelessly slim, especially in Moorook and at Bective, where soldier settlement was a slow-motion disaster, and in Renmark, too, where even the most established farms were folding. Dogged entrepreneurship had lost him money: he was in a fix. Back in England, unemployment was running high. Worrying prospects of economic dislocation loomed. Richard's parents entertained hopes that he would fill, not drain, the family's coffers. He had been determined to make the best of things; he was anxious not to be a burden on Samuel and Camilla. The tighter the Australian trap, however, the stronger was Richard's will to escape.

On the *Ville de Strasbourg* the cheapest accommodation was *entre-pont*, one class lower than steerage. Richard left Sydney in a cabin with twelve passengers, eleven of whom spoke no English. With schoolboy French he approached the maître d'hotel and secured, for a gratuity, an upgrade. Though officially still *entrepont*, Richard moved to a four-berth cabin occupied by a Swiss and a Norwegian-Belgian, both of whom spoke English. Among all the second- and third-class passengers Richard Lane was the only Englishman, the only man to wear a collar and tie, and very nearly the only one to bother with socks.

When the *Bendigo* crossed the equator, there had been such a fuss on board that Richard half-expected the moment to be announced by a tectonic break, or, at the very least, a tactile bump. The crossing on the northward journey was full of soberer meaning, and represented a dividing line between his life in Australia and his return home. After the *Ville de Strasbourg* left the southern hemisphere, Richard was certain for some time that he could still see the Southern Cross. But his eyes also scanned the skies for another constellation, the Great Bear, the appearance of which would declare that he and his family were seeing the same stars.

*

The Richard Lane who sailed back to England had changed in many ways. Conned and cheated in the Barwell scheme and in the Renmark-to-Adelaide car service, Richard had learned hard lessons from his own experiences but also from the entrepreneurs, professionals and pastoralists he'd met along the way. The best of these was Thomas Rowlands, a Merino man without peer. Richard knew now the importance of trust, integrity, capitalisation and experimentation in business. He understood debt and the real worth of money. In testing the values Richard had brought from Bristol, Australia served to cement them – acting on one's word, humility, resilience, generosity. In Australia, Richard's caring and egalitarian nature blossomed like an irrigated Doradillo vine.

Returning to England, he knew much better his own mind and preferences and capabilities; he knew a lot more about cars and people and life; and he knew a little more about women and love.

Richard's feminine ideal was not a track driver, nor the Renmark girls who played 'idiotic games' such as 'coffee pot' and 'the priest of the parish', nor Babe Cox of Coonabarabran (about eighteen years old, shingled hair, skirts above her knees, smoking and swearing 'when the occasion demands it'), nor Miss Dobie, the young New Zealander seduced by Joseph, the Capitaine d'armes of the *Ville de Strasbourg*. The ideal was much closer to Miss Esme Rowlands, and perhaps even closer to the beauties of Sydney:

> All shingled bobbed or bingled, with close fitting hats, short dresses and half of them wearing flesh coloured silk stockings . . . as fine a specimen of womanhood as could be found in any part of the world. Generalizing they are very well developed and exceptionally good looking, they dress smartly and in fairly bright colours, if you want to see if they really are well proportioned go to Manly for they walk about there in bathing costumes with wraps or overcoats lightly thrown over their shoulders and may be seen so clad at almost any hour in any street walking to or from the surf. And on Saturdays or Sundays the Ocean Beach itself is one mass of lightly clad young female Australians with young males in attendance.

As Richard sailed into the North Atlantic, the economic failure of his Australian venture grated, but not his decision to call it a day. The spectacular unburdening invigorated him: there would be no more riding the horse rake or the cultivator, no more emptying the pig bucket, or the dunny can. Australia supplied many role models but some of them trod paths that were to be avoided, like that of the 'swaggie' – cursed with wanderlust and a taste for gambling – whom Richard met at Renmark; or the late Tom Nunn; or everyone at Bective. Time spent with these people determined what kind of man Richard would be and taught him caution. He saw the obvious: that his trip was poorly planned, and poor planning had thrown him in with the reckless and the damned. Richard approached England feeling older, wiser, more destructible.

Bective had proved one book desert and *entrepont*, on the *Ville de Strasbourg*, was another. With nothing to read, and no one to talk to about authors and literature, Richard felt acutely his thirst for books and culture and writing. Surrounded by chaos, he continued to write in his diary. He had become a student of character and a connoisseur of human types. In his migration diary, he created a vivid, observant chronicle of daily life and an important document of antipodean social history. If Australia was Richard's coming of age, then the diary was his bildungsroman.

Practically Everything

When Allen Lane first moved to London to start work at The Bodley Head, he spent a short period – a kind of probation – boarding with his father's sister, Lily Smith, and her husband, Ted. The Smiths lived in Raynes Park, a London suburb so far from the city's chic precincts that Annie Lane accepted its existence only in theory. When Allen got the nod from his new uncle and aunt, he moved to Lancaster Gate Terrace, near Hyde Park and Kensington Gardens. The extraordinary house boasted a fifty-foot-long reception room, a dining room, a breakfast room, elegant bedrooms and bathrooms, an exceptional library and a distinctive collection of art and antiques. A far more satisfactory arrangement for young Allen than Raynes Park, though there were teething problems. Allen's 1921 diary is peppered with glum entries: 'Was lectured for hours by Annie about my lack of seriousness'; 'Uncle John says he will be writing to my father to tell him I am not working hard enough and he is thinking of sending me home.'

Samuel's other sister, Florence, married an Irishman, George Puxley, and had three children: Richard, George junior, and Dorothy, whose middle name, Oceana, memorialised her birth at sea. Everyone called George junior 'Pat', and Dorothy 'Ducka'. On a childhood visit to the Puxleys' home, Allen, dressed in a 'lovely tunic', had found a little girl called Doris in the underground kitchen. The whole family remembered how he went up to her and said, 'I want to kiss you.' Now a teenager resident in London, and finding many more girls to kiss, Allen reconnected with the Puxleys. On the way to a dance, Pat and Allen downed their first glasses of beer at the Victoria Station cafe. Pat became Allen's spree-buddy and the two teenagers explored the city's pubs and nightlife. With a ne'er-do-well streak inherited from George senior, unconventional Pat was two years older than Allen, and within the family he would later be known as 'the world's oldest living virgin'. When Pat first met Annie Lane, he made an impolitic remark about preferring ships to books. Annie, protective of her new ward and concerned about his future, decided that the Puxley boy was a bad influence. The sprees went underground and, on at least one occasion, Pat had to hide in a cupboard at Lancaster Gate Terrace to avoid detection by his cousin's famous aunt.

Uncle John baulked at becoming Allen's keeper. In the 1890s, he had happily let his stable of randy poets run riot, and life at his firm these days was much less dangerous for young men: Oscar Wilde was long gone and the firm had settled into a respectable rut. Good sense, and possibly Annie Lane, persuaded him to find for Allen a youngish man who would be a better role model than Pat Puxley. Before the First World War, Ben Travers had been the senior junior at The Bodley Head. During the war, he excelled as an air-force pilot, surviving nineteen crashes before his superiors judged him indestructible and sent him to teach others. After the war, he found success as a popular novelist and playwright. Uncle John enlisted Ben as Allen's chaperone, but the neophyte quickly took the lead in navigating London's evening attractions and night-time fun. A friendship blossomed, and Allen and Ben were soon getting into trouble together. One night, they crashed the annual dinner of the Worshipful Company of Fishmongers. Bored by the speeches, the pair escaped in search of a bar. Instead they found, reserved for the piscatorial guest speaker, a sitting room well provisioned with brandy, whisky, gin, port and cigars. Allen and Ben helped themselves royally until they were discovered and asked to leave. The pair returned fully cut to Lancaster Gate Terrace for a nightcap. Sheepishly, Allen opened the front door, anxious not to wake his uncle and aunt. Slipping on the mat, he reached out for an anchor, grabbed the seven-foot-tall, eighteenth-century William Barnard grandfather clock, and brought it crashing down on himself. Bells and chimes rang out. At times Uncle John no doubt wondered what kind of maniac he had let into the house.

Though Lane regarded his nephew with affection, he had less and less patience in his mature years for the enthusiasms of youth. Allen for his part promptly graduated from stamp-licker and dogsbody to play-boy and social butterfly. Looking like the young Ewan McGregor, he was handsome, charismatic and well turned out; he had a desirable address; and, to cap it all off, he was John Lane's nephew. These were enviable foundations on which to build a sociable reputation and life-style, even if 'nephew' stretched the true genealogy somewhat, and even if Allen's salary – only marginally above the wage for an apprentice jackeroo at Bective – failed to live up to his address and his appetites.

Putting aside these few cracks in the facade, Allen set about building on opportune foundations. He did duty in a series of shop-floor roles at The Bodley Head – packer, picker, sales rep, trade counter jockey, printer herdsman, royalty trimmer – and worked his way into the outer circles of his uncle's trust. When John Lane senior travelled to Paris to see Anatole France at the Villa Saïd, Allen came along as interpreter (his knowledge of French was 'unequal to explaining yeast'), before holiday-ing with W.J. Locke at the bestselling novelist's villa on the French Riviera. Allen counted seven bathrooms and reported as much to Rich-ard. Further trips would follow – to visit André Maurois, and to attend Anatole France's funeral, for which Allen had to borrow Pat Puxley's black coat. Crossing the Channel for work and pleasure would soon become quite normal for the boy from Bristol.

In England, he met other famous literary figures – encounters that were still such a novelty he kept mementos of them. When he had tea with the octogenarian Thomas Hardy and his friend John Drinkwater at the Dorchester, Allen made sure he kept the miniature chalice that Drinkwater had idly sculpted from biscuit foil. On another occasion, Allen visited Hardy at Max Gate, his home in Dorset. Drinkwater was again present, along with his wife. The novelist searched room to room for transcripts of the old Dorset folk songs he had heard at the village fêtes and dances of his youth. When he found the transcripts, Mrs Drinkwater played Hardy's favourite tunes, and he 'was as excited as a child, and listened with rapt attention'.

John Lane junior visited Allen in London and they attended a lecture by George Bernard Shaw. After the lecture, Allen and John walked down Piccadilly and spotted Shaw about fifty yards ahead of them. Pulling out their autograph books, the brothers 'tore after him'. Older and faster, Allen won the race 'by a good few inches', so John hovered behind to see how Allen fared. 'Excuse me, sir, but would you autograph my album?' 'Young man,' said Shaw, 'if, instead of wasting your time asking people like me to give you their autographs, you were to spend those valuable moments learning more about your own business, you would soon find that your own signature would be as much sought after as mine appears to be.' Later that evening, Allen and John hurled their autograph books off Westminster Bridge, drowning them in the Thames. Despite this dramatic gesture, however, Allen would ignore at least half of Shaw's advice by amassing a unique collection of literary signatures.

Though Bodley Head author Agatha Christie would soon sever her connection with the firm, she and Allen became friends and would remain so for many years. To lubricate this and other friendships, in a web of book-world contacts, Allen collected and shared liberally a repertoire of gossipy stories. Some were off-colour; many were injurious to the self-important; and nearly all of them were R-rated, like the ones he borrowed from Uncle John about the poet William Watson 'fiddling around with Mrs Watson's twat', and indeed Oscar Wilde fiddling around with an office boy at Vigo Street.

The board of The Bodley Head invited Allen to attend their meetings as an observer. When Uncle John embarked on a reorganisation that would turn the firm into a limited company with an injection of capital from outside shareholders, Allen, though unschooled in the finer details of accounting and corporate structures, watched over the old man's shoulder. John Lane found three men who possessed the gravity, experience and, most importantly, money the firm needed. Hubert Carr-Gomme, Lindsay Drummond, and a dabbler in socialism and sexology, Ronald Boswell, invested £10,000 each and joined the board. Allen joined too, in 1924, though his investment was entirely genetic and in-kind. Allen's promotion to the board, and to the role of company secretary, would be among John Lane's last acts at The Bodley Head.

*

On John and Annie's return from America, on which trip they had met Tom and Netta Rowlands, they spent a wet weekend in Brighton. After a damp wait on a train platform, John Lane fell ill. An aggressive pneumonia took hold and hastened his end. Uncle John's death in February 1925 shocked Allen as much as it shocked the other Williams-Lanes, but the impact on the great publisher's wife was of a wholly different order.

A widow for the second time, Annie entered a deep and extended period of mourning. The household at No. 8 Lancaster Gate Terrace changed markedly. Though the longstanding butler, Costin, might have disagreed, Allen was now the man of the house, and Annie Lane's connection to the Williams-Lanes – especially their three sons – strengthened noticeably. Several forces were at work here: the increasingly elderly widow needed and wanted familial support; and the awkward ancestral distance, which the Williams-Lane name change had papered over, became with John Lane's death irrelevant. John bequeathed to Devon institutions some pictures of regional interest. A few important non-Devonian paintings went to institutions in London and Brighton. A selection of books from the library were gifted to friends. But, in a final act of love and devotion, Lane left the overwhelming bulk of his estate to Annie. Already wealthy in her own right, Annie Lane was now a very well-to-do lady.

At The Bodley Head, Lane left behind a mess. Outside the firm, rumours of its insolvency swirled. Inside, there was unease among the new directors. Allen Lane, the new boy fast-tracked into their midst, was a lightning rod for their nervousness and ill-feeling. Only the protection of Annie, his affluent patron and the majority shareholder, prevented the rest of the board from putting Allen back in his place. At Bristol, the Williams-Lanes moved from Cotham Vale to Coombe Dingle, where Samuel built a new home and called it, once again, Broomcroft – he could achieve continuity of house names, if not family ones. Worn out by the stresses of work, Allen came down with scarlet fever and was quarantined at his parents' new home.

Richard Lane, meanwhile, returned from the wilderness eager to see everyone again but apprehensive about rejoining the family circle. He reached London on the last day of March, 1926, and walked from Paddington to Lancaster Gate Terrace. Overjoyed to see her long-absent nephew, Annie Lane showed her pleasure in a practical way by giving him a fiver. When Richard arrived at the new Broomcroft, his father was out, his sister was boarding at Saffron Walden and Allen was in his bedroom in isolation. But the welcome from Camilla and John equalled Annie's in its warmth. Mother and brother were alike struck by Richard's new stature and maturity. Here in person was the strapping young man they had read about in those remarkable notebooks. Samuel and Camilla had proudly shared extracts from Richard's diary with a journalist, who praised them in Bristol's *Western Daily Press*, turning the former boy migrant into a local celebrity.

In one of his last Australian letters to Annie, Richard had shared his hopes of returning to England.

> I will not mention the names of those I long to see, the list would be far too lengthy, but there is one above all others that I would give years of my life to see, and I do not think it necessary to tell you his name, you know as well as I do who it is. But even though I love my brother so greatly, none the less is my affection for my parents, all the family and many other relations and friends.

In the intervening years, Allen had grown up, not on the land or behind the wheel of a track car, but in an office. Publishers' intrigues and gossip were threaded through his formative years. As a result, two very different men spoke through the door of Allen's isolation room, but the brotherly bond soon revived and their conspiratorial planning resumed.

Allen and Richard had many things in common, including affectionate memories of the birth and infancy of their younger brother, John. Before he was born, they were both told that the family doctor would deliver the baby. When Camilla went into labour, the doctor arrived at Broomcroft with a medical bag, which he left on the staircase on his way up to see Camilla. Having taken somewhat literally the snippet of information about the doctor's role, Allen and Richard crept up to the bag and gingerly opened it. They were shocked to find a custard tart inside.

Richard had left for Australia when John was fourteen and still at school, his choirboy voice unbroken. Now, as the eighteen-year-old manager of Coombe Dingle's mill, John travelled the district gathering feed orders from farmers. With his friend Stanley Chivers, John had built a flat-bottomed boat to explore the mill waters. John also made a wireless radio set and loved searching for new stations to the sound of radio-static howls and 'extraneous noises'. These pursuits evinced an interest in movement and long-distance communication, so perhaps it is not surprising that the youngest Lane brother became a bird of passage who craved travel by land, sea and air. To the delight of his brothers, John mastered efficient transportation and logistics: 'He always knew how to understand timetables and he had an uncanny sense in knowing from which platforms trains would go and which end of the train was likely to be least crowded. He had a way with guards, porters and commissioners that always resulted in getting the best seats or accommodation.' On some of his first trips, he took Mr Ball, the miller, to London, and sailed around Land's End in a tugboat.

Though Uncle John had passed away in February 1925, his ashes remained unburied until April 1926. They were to be interred at St Nectan's church, Hartland, in John's beloved Devon. Annie Lane wired Broomcroft asking Richard to join her at what turned out to be a beautiful service on a beautiful sunny day. Appreciatively Richard joined the kernel of admirers who paid their respects as Lane's ashes were lowered into the grave. Stanley De Courcy Ireland unveiled a commemorative tablet and gave an affectionate eulogy.

In the days and weeks after this poignant interment, Richard toured the green fields of England and Wales, blissfully unlike those of ring-barked, pea-struck Coonabarabran. He went by motorbike to Llandrindod Wells, where Allen had been staying. The brothers rode the bike through Leominster and Worcester to Stratford-upon-Avon to see Shakespeare's monument; then on through Northampton to St Neots, where they 'discovered an ancient monastery which nobody seemed to know anything about – the old building had been converted into a farm, Abbey Farm, and was surrounded by a wide moat'. At Saffron Walden the brothers picked up Nora, and all three rode the bike to Cambridge, where they punted on the Cam. After returning Nora to school and Allen to Bristol, Richard went to Burnham to dine with Ben Travers and his wife, then accompanied Allen back to London, and finally enjoyed a pleasant reunion with Keith Garvie, his friend from the *Bendigo*. After all that, he took a long and refreshing bath.

Elder brother introduced younger to the authors, publishing contacts and associates who formed the upper and middle ranks of literary London. Richard met Mr Sunniors and A.J.A. Symons of the First Edition Club, the Bristolian novelist Beverley Nichols, his brother Paul Nichols,

Muriel Hine (The Bodley Head's 'number one female author'), Annie Haynes, Miss Lamb, Agatha Christie ('great fun and very shy') and other notables. The crime novelist Mrs Philip Champion de Crespigny arranged for the brothers to meet the aged Sir Arthur Conan Doyle, who had known Uncle John and cautioned him on some of his riskier and more risqué publications, like *Song of Songs*, by the nationalistic German novelist Hermann Sudermann.

The meeting with Conan Doyle was baffling and intriguing. A believer in the Cottingley Fairies and other doubtful marvels, Conan Doyle had become, after his son Kingsley passed away, absorbed in thoughts of spiritualism and conversing with the dead. When Conan Doyle noticed that a large vase in his study had been moved, he interrogated everyone in the household, but no one admitted to moving it. So he invited a medium to broker a paranormal conversation between father and son. Conan Doyle told Allen and Richard what happened next: Kingsley had confessed to moving the vase in order to let his father know that he 'was with him in flesh as well as spirit'. When Conan Doyle soon after joined his son entirely in spirit, Allen sought out – through go-betweens, booksellers and the writer's family – the autograph of the man who created Sherlock Holmes.

During his time in Australia, the best Richard could have hoped for was to mark his twenty-first birthday at Millamolong. To celebrate it, now, with family at the new Broomcroft was bliss. Samuel spoke in Richard's honour at a champagne supper, and the honoree received a Rolls Razor from John, three golden sovereigns from his grandparents, and a gold watch from Samuel, Camilla and Allen. Allen also found Richard a job, not at The Bodley Head but at the Willings Denton Library on Finchley Road. Richard moved in with Annie and Allen at 8 Lancaster Gate Terrace, where the mourning had ended and dinner parties were once more being held. Months out of jackerooing, Richard bought a dinner jacket and tails, from Pleydell & Smith in Cork Street, and joined Allen's schedule of carousing on a budget. The two brothers went to the Chelsea Arts Ball, where one reveller was dressed as Mephistopheles in a skin-tight scarlet catsuit with wicked horns and a long, solid, sinister-looking tail that wriggled and swished uncannily. In the course of the night, Richard visited the lavatory and discovered the devil's secret: a five-foot conger eel sewn into the suit.

Evenings such as this were the wriggling spine of Allen's life in London. After his own period of grieving and adjustment following Uncle John's death, Allen began socialising to such an extent that his recreational and professional activities often clashed. When they did, work took second place. Agatha Christie noticed that Allen's status as a budding publisher was as much an alibi as an occupation. She and other members of his circle thought he might be overdoing it. At the same time, an opinion developed in the firm, and perhaps also in the family, that Allen needed looking after, especially as Uncle John was no longer around to guide his protégé.

*

Allen without a minder was an accident waiting to happen, and the accident arrived in the person of the actor and author Hesketh Pearson. Soon after Richard moved to Lancaster Gate Terrace, Pearson delivered a manuscript to The Bodley Head. *The Whispering Gallery: Being leaves from a diplomat's diary* purported to be an anonymous tell-all memoir by a leading light in Britain's diplomatic service. It consisted of weightless vignettes on world leaders – Lord Kitchener, Cecil Rhodes, King Edward VII, Tsar Nicholas, Lenin, Mussolini – along with implausible pen-pictures of literary lions – H.G. Wells, G.B. Shaw, Thomas Hardy, Henry James, Kipling and Twain. Encouraged by favourable assessments of the manuscript, The Bodley Head's board agreed to publication on the condition that Pearson would tell one of their number the name of the author. The board chose Allen, and Pearson named Sir Rennell Rodd, the former ambassador to Italy, delegate to the League of Nations, classical scholar, memoirist and poet. By way of research, Allen consulted *Who's Who* and traced lightly a correlation between an incident in Rome and Rodd's tenure there. 'He checked a few more episodes and was quite happy to accept Pearson's word.' On Allen's assurances, The Bodley Head published the book in a large print run, anticipating strong sales.

The backlash from the press and the establishment was immediate; Rodd furiously disowned the book; The Bodley Head withdrew it and sued Pearson for fraud. J.W. Lambert and Jeremy Lewis have published detailed accounts of the trial and the ensuing scandal. The episode was a disaster for Allen, who was left looking credulous, incompetent and tricksy, and for The Bodley Head, which was almost brought down. When Allen appeared as a very uncomfortable witness at the trial, he drew criticism for not having read the whole book. Allen's relationship with the other directors soured irretrievably into acrimony and mutual suspicion. Though they could not remove him from the board, they sacked him from the position of company secretary. With news headlines labelling the firm 'disreputable', and articles branding the book a slanderous fake and a shameless forgery, the board issued by majority decision a series of humiliating apologies that cited the unilateral and erroneous actions of 'our junior director'.

The stress of the *Whispering Gallery* affair had an equally destructive impact on Annie Lane's health. She fell gravely ill and her advisers engaged a private nurse. When the trial was at its height, the nurse stood too close to a gas fire and her dress caught alight. She suffered appalling burns and both women were soon in hospital, each in a critical condition. In January 1927, shortly after the trial ended with Pearson the victor, Annie Lane passed away. Following her cremation, a memorial service was held at St James, Piccadilly. Annie's death was a shattering blow for Richard, for whom she had a special affection. In Australia, Annie's letters – Richard described them as 'perfect' – had been a great comfort to her nephew when he most needed it, and she had supported him in many other ways. Less than a year after his return to England, Richard was again on his way to the family grave at Hartland, this time carrying the ashes of his beloved aunt.

The *Evening Standard* obituary mourned her loss to society. 'Mrs John Lane . . . was for a quarter of a century a vivacious figure in the publishing and literary world of London. Few houses were pleasanter to drop in at than the Lanes' for both her own and her husband's tastes covered wide fields, and both had a genius for friendship.' Richard and Allen continued, at the expense of the estate, to live at Lancaster Gate Terrace for half a year, until the lease and contents were sold. In July 1927, Messrs Jackson Stops auctioned 'the library and the collection of autographed letters from distinguished men; early French, Chippendale, Sheraton, Heppelwhite and other period furniture; ornamental *objets d'art*, bric-a-brac, tapestries, samplers, fans; and the fine collection of early china, porcelain and pewter'. The sale catalogue included a precious letter from Aubrey Beardsley, illustrated with a self-portrait and a hangman's noose.

'My Dear Lane, I shall most assuredly commit suicide if the fat woman does not appear in No. 1 of the *Yellow Book*. I have shown it to all sorts and conditions of men – and women. All agree that it is one of my best efforts and extremely witty.' Richard competed with determination and success at the auction for items that his aunt and uncle had prized, and that evoked memories of them: a brass Cromwellian lantern clock, a finely carved oak bust of a gentleman, a pair of pierced steel antique spurs, an engraved metal fish, and other treasures full of meaning.

Once the executors determined the extent of the estate – a drawn-out affair as some disputed paintings at Lancaster Gate Terrace evidently belonged to The Bodley Head rather than the Lanes directly – they read Annie's will to the beneficiaries. This proved to be an extraordinary turning point for the Williams-Lane family. Annie had left 'practically everything' to Allen, Richard, John and Nora. Made up of Annie's own savings, her wealth inherited from her parents, and the vestiges of two marriages across two countries, the 'everything' was considerable. With portfolios of cash, shares and annuities, the Williams-Lane children were suddenly financially secure. The largest investment, in the Boston Safe Deposit Trust, gave each of the children a steady income of £400 a year. Richard and John also received sizeable lump-sum cash payments, while Allen, by inheriting a handsome majority shareholding in The Bodley Head, fulfilled a destiny that began awkwardly with two girls and a rabbit hutch. In addition to British pounds and American dollars, Annie's beneficiaries also received more than £1000 in German marks.

The manner of Annie Lane's death may have been tragic, but the generosity of her bequests was a bolt of good fortune for all the Williams-Lanes. The family decided that buying land was the best way to preserve and grow their capital. Samuel and Camilla moved to a grander house, at Falfield in Gloucestershire, called The Gables; a pleasant Tudor-style, stone-built sprawl with five bedrooms on seven acres (and now a Best Western hotel). From the French doors in the large sitting room, the acres could be viewed appreciatively. John acquired another twenty-seven acres across the road to use for pre-breakfast walks and as another land bank. The family also bought a succession of cars, and John took his parents to Paris by air. Nora left Saffron Walden for a school in Lausanne, Switzerland.

Despite their new wealth, the family retained a strong strain of frugality. Instead of boarding, Nora lived with a Swiss family; instead of an elite finishing school, she enrolled in the local high school, where she befriended an American girl. But that was the limit of Nora's personal economising. The two girls discovered that 'no-one at the school minded if they didn't turn up, so they found a tea shop called Niffneggers where they consumed enormous quantities of hot chocolate and cream buns. When Nora returned home for her first holiday, she hardly spoke a word of French, was very fat and had a pronounced American accent.' It took all the Williams-Lanes some time to adjust to their new prosperity.

THE LORD OF ALEXANDRIA

When Allen and Richard were at Bristol Grammar School, they performed in the annual concert. Richard sang, in Hubert Parry's setting, John Milton's quintessentially English 'Blest pair of Sirens, pledges of Heaven's joy'. Fittingly for the subject, Richard loved the music as much as the poem, and soon there would be more Milton. As an 'impot' for 'going on det', Richard the mischievous schoolboy had to copy out lines from 'Il Penseroso'. This poem, another from his beloved *Golden Treasury*, remained a favourite despite its punitive associations, and at Bective in Australia he would copy it out again as a comfort and a reminder of home. When John was at the All Saints Choir School in Clifton, Allen and Richard went to see a school performance not of Milton but of Shakespeare. In *The Tempest*, John sang with sundry choristers, 'Where the Bee Sucks, There Suck I', to his brothers' amusement. In concerts such as these, and at the old Broomcroft in the Bingham–Williams Concert Party, Allen and Richard and John all experienced the frights and thrills of performing before an audience.

For the elder Lane brothers, London offered more opportunities for stage fright and stage thrills. Through The Bodley Head and the late Mr and Mrs John Lane, Allen and Richard knew the author and translator James Lewis May. He and Annie had both translated Anatole France, and May would later write a reverent biography of Uncle John. In the weeks after Annie's death, May invited Allen and Richard to join

a production of *Hamlet* at Mill Hill School in North London. May had
top billing as Hamlet; the Lane brothers were stage-dressing at the
opposite end of the bill; and everything that could go wrong did. The
dinner-gong clock chime binged when it should have boomed; in a
scene that was supposed to be semi-dark, the lighting man turned on
the floods; May's slight stutter had a lengthening effect on the Prince's
soliloquies; and the Lanes wrecked the funeral of Ophelia. The stage
sides were steep so the funeral procession used a central gangway. By
this time, the play had been going for more than five hours; the audience consisted solely of people waiting to drive cast members home;
and Allen and Richard had thoroughly enjoyed the 'free liquid refreshments' available to the cast. Carrying Ophelia up the ramp – the dead
heroine was played by 'half a dozen cushions' on a stretcher – the
brothers 'got into a bit of a swing', with the result that she was dropped
and had to be 'reassembled'.

Now very much in charge of their own schedules, Allen and Richard
upped the tempo of their nocturnal fun. When Muriel Hine held her
annual 'bunfight' party at the Rembrandt Hotel in Knightsbridge, the
brothers made for the room with the bar waiter. There they met Muriel
Hine's cousin, the actor Hubert Hine. Richard and Hubert became
friends. Hubert was performing in *The Cabala* at the Royalty Theatre
and on the last night the brothers went backstage to see Hubert in his
dressing room, where they heard that a new nightclub had opened with
a special offer. People in tails would be admitted free and would be
served free champagne. Returning home at midnight to shave and
change into his tails, Richard was struck by how radically his life had
altered in the twelve months since leaving Australia.

Hubert Hine shared a basement flat with Neil Curtis, who in turn
knew the enterprising actor and producer Robert Atkins. Through
Hubert and Curtis, Richard met their famous friend in 1927, the year in
which Atkins had a brainwave. With his wife he began to assemble a
theatre company that had an unlikely ambition: to perform Shakespeare's plays in the land of the pharaohs. The nucleus of the company
would be a group of refugees from the Old Vic; they had grown up performing Shakespeare and would be safe hands in a risky venture.

In the shadow of his Australian debacle, Richard had vowed to
make more careful decisions in future, and generally to play it safe and

close to home, at least for a while. But, in the spirit that saw him leave England in 1922, and with a mind to muffle those rueful vows about better planning, Richard volunteered to join Atkins' company. He did so on the questionable terms of 'no salary but all expenses paid'. Hine, a friend in the mould of Mac McMinn, joined the company too, as did Neil Curtis. Twenty months after Bective, Richard was at Victoria Station en route to Cairo.

He records in his diary the crossing from Folkestone to Boulogne and the shaky train ride into Paris. 'From the Gare du Nord we rattled our way right out to the Gare du Lyon.' With Curtis, who had not seen Paris before, Richard went for a drink on the boulevard, then took the Metro to a cafe near the Opéra where they met Ernest Milton and Mr and Mrs Atkins. The party went to a restaurant: 'for the first time in the lives of some of the younger members of our company, we had wine supplied free and it was a rather hilarious company that made its way to the station at about nine o'clock.'

Overflowing with good cheer and *vin ordinaire*, the company reached the departure platform. The sleeping compartments of French trains had no sheets or blankets, and only one pillow, but the platform was busy with porters wheeling trucks of pillows and blankets that could be rented for three francs each. Two minutes before the train was due to depart, the company rounded on one of the porters.

> He, being French, immediately stopped issuing his wares and waved his arms about like a would-be windmill, shouting all the time, which of course had not the slightest effect on our company who just took what they required and gave him what they felt inclined to pay. Personally I had two pillows and two blankets for five francs which I considered to be more appropriate than twelve.

The company consisted of twenty actors, managers and crew. Atkins directed, H.R. Barbor was general manager, and Philip Harben assistant stage manager. The stars were Ernest Milton, Marie Ney, Wilfred Walter, Stanley Lathbury, and Harben's droll sister Joan, who would later find fame as Mona Lott in BBC Radio's *ITMA*. Hine had dual roles as an actor and stage director. Atkins also acted, playing Iago to Wilfred Walter's Othello. After the company left Marseille for Alexandria on the *Champollion*, most of them, Richard included, fell seasick. The ship passed Stromboli at night and Richard witnessed a small eruption.

> It was a very fine sight to see the dark mass of the volcano standing out from the greyness of the night, with just one or two lights at the base and a lighthouse blinking monotonously. Suddenly from the crater shot forth a bright red mass that curved like a fountain playing in a garden and fell back onto the blackness and poured down the sides until it was swallowed up. A distant rumble could be heard and the whole atmosphere seemed charged with a feeling of expectancy and one would hardly have been surprised if the whole mountain had suddenly slid down into the sea like the fabled Atlantis.

Rain greeted the company at Alexandria, but Richard still found the city to be 'a very dirty place, the docks, station, trains and people were all filthy'. The train to Cairo crossed dry flat country; he noticed the irrigation systems and was momentarily transported to Mr Withers' block at Renmark. The heat in Cairo was South Australian in its intensity, and 'all sane people' had a long siesta in the afternoon.

The grand Royal Opera House in Cairo was built, entirely from timber, to celebrate the inauguration of the Suez Canal. It opened in 1869 and could seat 850 people. There were no siestas for the members of Atkins' company when they settled in for the season. From the Cabinet du Directeur and the unventilated No. 18 Dressing Room, Richard wrote in his diary: 'This is undoubtedly a very marvellous theatre but I am seeing a little too much of it.' The company performed matinees but the main performances were at night, starting at eight or nine o'clock and often continuing to one-thirty or two in the morning. Dwelling on the flexible boundary between cast and crew, Richard had no official position: 'I am he who is in charge of the wardrobe, dresser, occasional call boy, office boy, barman, and general odd man of the company.' Under Hine he was notionally assistant stage manager, responsible for looking after the supers whom Hubert and Richard had recruited from Cairo and Alexandria's amateur theatrical societies to perform in crowd scenes. When the people of Padua condemned Petruchio's disgraceful wedding outfit, Cairo and Alexandria's bush-league actors came into their own.

Richard trained the supers and clothed them from the rich ward-robe at the Opera House. Working fourteen-hour days that ended well after midnight, Richard was also expected to act. The printed programs for the Opera House performances named him in the cast, as the Sailor in *Hamlet*. The part comprised a total of thirty-nine words, and more than once the Sailor scene was cut. With the other members of the lower echelon of Atkins' company, Richard stayed at the Victoria Hotel, 'quite a comfortable little hotel but not half as good as the Continental where the star half of our company is staying'.

> I have met a Captain Verner who is staying there and he tells me that his room with private bathroom is over two pounds a day exclusive of everything. In the season a bedroom, sitting room and bathroom fetch one hundred pounds a week also exclusive. Drinks vary from 2/6 to 5/- and a decent dinner for two costs from three to five pounds. It is the Americans who have spoilt the place by meekly paying what-ever prices are asked, in fact preferring high prices to low.

The whole cast and crew worked hard. 'One play was cast, rehearsed and produced in under a week', and other marathon feats were accomplished.

> One day Ernest Milton rehearsed Angelo in Measure for Measure in the morning, played Hamlet in the afternoon and Shylock ... in the evening. Another day Wilfred Walter rehearsed The Shrew in the morning, played the King in Hamlet in the afternoon and Oth-ello in the evening and this was on a Sunday too. Today we rehearsed The Shrew all day and are playing Measure this evening. Tomorrow there is a dress rehearsal of The Shrew and in the evening we play it for the first time. We have not yet had a free morning since we came here a fortnight ago last Saturday or to be accurate I should say a free morning afternoon or evening.

The company suffered triply from flu, food poisoning and the strains of the schedule. 'The whole company is beginning to crock up ... Temper-ament is far too common, gippy tummies are the rule, headaches and nervous breakdown are quite frequent.' Despite these trials, every per-formance sold out, in part because the local government made block bookings of 400 and 500 seats for schoolchildren. The King of Egypt came to one performance and, at another, Lord Lloyd, Britain's High Commissioner, took a box and arrived smoking a cigar. Smoking was forbidden in the all-timber building (years later, it would be destroyed by fire) but Lloyd 'was such a forceful character' that no one dared tell him to put the cigar out. The authorities stationed a fireman outside his box, with an extinguisher at the ready.

After Cairo, the company decamped to Alexandria's Mohamed Aly Theatre for five days of performances. When they had unpacked, Richard and Hubert went to a cafe where one item on the drinks menu sounded especially enticing. Neither Richard nor Hubert had heard of the Angel's Kiss before, so they ordered one each. Ten coloured liqueurs, poured painstakingly into a tall glass so the rainbow layers did not mix, and on top: a raw egg. Richard could stomach raw eggs but Hine could not. 'I enjoyed my drink and lasted it but Hubert couldn't cope with the egg, so he got a spoon and gave the drink a stirring, then he tasted it and promptly threw it away and ordered a beer.'

On the final night at the Mohamed Aly, Richard and Hubert worked for more than twenty-four hours straight. After a full day, the last performance ended at two o'clock in the morning, and the costumes had to be packed and ready for transport by 8 a.m. Richard and his friend recruited a team of helpers but, after a 'tea break' – actually beer and whisky – at 4 a.m., all the helpers fled. Apart from packing all the costumes, a manifest had to be kept of what was in each crate, and the costumes had to be delivered to the right dressing rooms, which were spread over three floors. Richard and Hubert, one of them merely a volunteer, kept going in order to prove something to themselves and each other about stamina and work and keeping one's word. Then they collapsed into sleep.

*

After one of the Alexandrian performances, Richard Lane had a fateful meeting. Richard Combe Abdy had made his fortune in Egyptian cotton and – at Barings Brothers and other banks – international finance. Once he had become rich, he set about hosting and socialising on a grand scale across three countries. For tax reasons, Abdy nominated his luxurious Alexandrian home as his primary residence, but he also owned a villa in Vevey, Switzerland, and a mansion in Essex. When the two Richards met, Abdy was struck by the tall, handsome, fair-haired youth who could talk authoritatively about literature and culture, and unguardedly about his life and prospects. The two promised to meet again back in England.

In Cairo and Alexandria, Richard confided to his diary his thoughts about life on the stage and its viability as a career. 'In this profession, "*The Profession*", one comes into contact with all sorts and conditions of people more than in any other save perhaps the law courts. The sad side of it strikes me far more than any other. "The glare and glamour of the footlights", I cannot see it.' The performers were as trapped as Renmark's fruit growers or Moorook's soldier settlers. 'It strikes me that a very large percentage of actors and actresses are people who have taken up the stage when they had nothing better to do and, having put their hand to the plough, could not turn back, and so are forced to walk in the furrow of discomfort up and down the rows of life. It must be admitted that the average actor's life is full of discomforts and disappointments.'

Such were Richard's reflections throughout the return Mediterranean crossing. But one source of comfort was the prospect of seeing again his new friend from Alexandria. Every year, Richard Abdy seasoned in Essex at Michaelstowe Hall on Dovercourt Bay, a few miles from Harwich. In the spring of 1928, Abdy invited Richard Lane for the weekend. When Richard arrived at Harwich station, his host pulled up to greet him in an immaculate Rolls Royce 40/50 Silver Ghost, driven by Halim, the Egyptian chauffeur-cum-valet. At the entrance to the estate's drive were colossal wrought-iron lodge gates flanked by lions. The head gardener, a Mr Rose, occupied the lodge. Half way down the drive, Halim sounded 'the deep throated horn' to alert the butler and the footman, who met Abdy and Richard at the front door.

Built in 1903 by the Garland family, in what Nikolaus Pevsner would later call 'the comfortable Neo-Georgian style of the day', Michaelstowe Hall was a grand pile in the great English country-house tradition. The rooms were large and airy. One side of the sitting room, all windows, overlooked a terraced garden. The dining room could seat fifty guests. Between 1928 and 1932 Richard stayed at Michaelstowe Hall on dozens of occasions, often for weeks at a time. He counted the bathrooms and studied the domestic arrangements, most of which were invisible to short-stay guests. The mansion and estate preserved many strange conventions. 'When anyone's case was unpacked, a note was made of the colour of his pyjamas or her nightdress and when early morning tea was served, the china would match the night attire. I don't know what would have happened if a married couple arrived with the husband in blue pyjamas and the wife in a pink nightdress.' Abdy presented every departing guest with a lavish bouquet of flowers.

The most magnificent feature at Michaelstowe was not the house itself but the gardens. In summer, Mr Rose supervised fifty-two gardeners, most of whom lived in bothies. 'On a fine day at least a dozen would be grass cutting, as apart from ordinary lawns there were also tennis courts and a cricket field.' Abdy famously offered a pound to any guest who could find a weed on the estate. The gardeners formed the Michaelstowe Cricket Club and Richard played for the MCC in a match against the Essex Constabulary. When the club had no fixture, the MCC A-team played the B-team. The estate's twelve enormous greenhouses maintained different temperatures, some for flowers and others for exotic fruit. Goldfish flourished in large concrete ponds. When Abdy commissioned an artificial lake and rock garden, the stones came in one complete train-load. 'R.C.A. never did things in a small way,' Richard wrote. When finally configured, the stones formed one of the finest rockeries in England. Richard loved promenading Michaelstowe's grounds in the evening, and rowing and fishing on the lake, where a large pike evaded a succession of determined fishermen.

Dinners at Michaelstowe surpassed the Devon meals of Richard's childhood. A dedicated farm kept the house in poultry and dairy products, and Abdy bought whisky by the barrel. The exceptionally strong coffee on offer was 'quite delicious', but Richard's favourite drink at Michaelstowe was gin, fresh grapefruit juice, ice and seltzer water – much better than Moorook's lime-flavoured frog brine. As High Steward of Harwich, Abdy enjoyed an honorary connection with the Harwich docks, and in that capacity entertained the officers and crew of an American cruiser, enlisting Richard Lane as *aide-de-camp* for the occasion. The staff erected a marquee on the cricket ground and served a meal of roast turkey, followed by strawberries and cream, to more than 600 guests in two sittings over consecutive days. Abdy contacted the Royal Academy of Music and invited a star pupil to the event. Only the two Richards knew that the pupil received 'a fiver and expenses' for the performance.

The Abdy connection and the Lane inheritance marked a golden period in Richard's life. Nora, meanwhile, still too young to have access to her wealth, was experiencing in Switzerland something of the destitution Richard had experienced while down and out in Renmark and Moorook. She sent her brother a letter postmarked 'Lausanne. Friday morning. After school'.

My dear Dick,

This is rather an urgent letter! The truth is I am stoney-broke! I hate having to always write home to Father and Mother for money. Do you think you could add it on to the account. I really must have some. Tomorrow I am going to Vers-chez-Perrin, and I shall have to beg-borrow-or-steal from Madame for the fare to get there. Besides I want a new chapeau. I only possess one winter one and that cost me five francs, and I can't wear that the whole time. Everyone in Lausanne knows it by sight I should think! There are umpteen dozen things I seem to want as well.

It has been raining so far all today and is still raining and doesn't look much like ceasing.

I hope you have had a decent time with Mr Abdy ... The chief reason I have written to you, is because Allen, well he's Allen, and he would put the letter down and forget all about it and John! Well! – he doesn't think anyone is short of money, when he stores his up! I started putting ten cents away every day and got to about two francs, but that has diminished down to about thirty cents and that is all I own. So PLEASE do send me some ... I get quite a lot of letters. Eight last week, and seven so-far this week. I have had another one from my French boy enclosing his photos. He is awfully ugly and soft looking. He starts off with first My dear!!!!

Love to All, Au revoir, Pip

*

Abdy paid Egyptian income tax, citing Alexandria as his permanent residence, but the English authorities argued that he was substantially resident in England and should pay tax there on the whole of his income, 'which was reputed to be in excess of £100,000 a year'. After an exasperating battle, Abdy sold Michaelstowe Hall, but kept, at La Tour-de-Peilz near Vevey on the north shore of Lake Geneva, Villa Claremont, which he lent to the Williams-Lane family. Samuel, Camilla, Allen, Richard, John and Nora moved in for a month. The villa was fully staffed and the family also had use of Abdy's motor-launch, *Gilliat*. Powering across the lake was for John Lane at least as much fun as taking his homemade boat out on Coombe Dingle's calm mill waters. Freddie Butler, another guest at the villa, introduced the Lane brothers to the eye-popping nightclubs of Montreux. Before breakfast, when they were not too hung-over, Richard and John explored the villa's walled kitchen garden, where they picked sun-warmed peaches and nectarines. Allen slept in. At breakfast, 'there was always a large bowl of eggs in warm water on the table just to help fill up any odd spaces that could be found'.

Abdy became President of the Land Bank of Egypt, and in 1898 helped found the National Bank of Egypt, whose British head office in King William Street was at the heart of London's financial district. Abdy told Richard there was a good future for him in banking, 'and especially an Egyptian bank'. With the blessing of the bank's principal, Richard started work at the NBE as a junior clerk on a monthly salary of five pounds, sixteen shillings and eight pence. He bought a business suit and joined the other ambitious young men who slogged each day into the City, where he learnt the dark arts of credit assessment, financial settlements and compliance. Though grateful to Abdy for the opportunity, after a year Richard decided he had had enough of 'jungle life east of St Paul's'. Office work certainly surpassed farming, but life as a banker clashed with the dream he had built in Australia and then gilded and crenulated at Michaelstowe. With the Lane inheritance, Richard now had a licence and a safety net with which to pursue his dream: to become a bookman.

Richard learnt a great deal from Robert Atkins' Egyptian theatre expedition, from staying at Michaelstowe, and from working at the bank. He studied actors and crew; audiences and guests; and the ethos of the City types with whom he worked and lunched. In Egypt, he had again noticed the price of everything. There, in London and in Essex he sharpened his appreciation for good friends, good food and the meaning of good value. At Michaelstowe – a household better even than Millamolong – and at the Villa Claremont, he saw what could be done when great powers of organisation were applied to great wealth.

Richard Abdy seems never to have married, and there are enough hints – the Egyptian valet and his deep-throated horn; sailors arriving en masse; male student musicians visiting for a fee; legions of itinerant gardeners; an attentive regard for floristry, and budding actors – to assemble one interpretation of his interest in young Richard Lane. Such an interpretation would be speculative. Certainly there is nothing in Richard's diaries or elsewhere that points to ulterior motives on Abdy's part. Another theory, propagated in the wilder corners of the internet, is that Abdy was a top *illuminato* who, in a cabal of bankers and sundry members of the Labour Party and the civil service and the aristocracy, orchestrated a Soviet plot to drive Germany into another world war. There is no credible evidence of Abdy leading either of these secret lives; a more plausible and economical conclusion is that Abdy was a rich man who enjoyed the company of intelligent people, and that he particularly enjoyed Richard's unguarded and disarming wit, and perhaps his connection to The Bodley Head and the late John Lane.

In Australia, Richard had built (with a nod to Dr Johnson) a system for classifying men according to character. In Richard's taxonomy, a man could be a flower or a weed, a schemer or an honourable doer, a safe driver or a corner-cutter. The honourable doer type was 'a real Englishman' for whom honour was everything: 'one could not imagine him doing a dishonest or shady action.' Mr Woods – secretary of the Renmark Racing Club, assistant returning officer for Renmark's elections, sometime postman and bridge player – exemplified this type, as did Samuel Williams-Lane, John Lane junior, C.R. Cudmore and the outstanding pastoralist Thomas Rowlands. Mr Withers exemplified the opposite type: the schemer, always less interested in honour than in cadging his way to profit. Following Richard's Egyptian detours, Robert Atkins and Richard Abdy joined the ranks of honourable doers in the young man's pantheon.

As a singular life experience, putting on Shakespeare for King Farouk was on a par with droving sheep at Coonabarabran. Some years after Richard left the National Bank of Egypt, he and his brothers gave a party on Shakespeare's birthday to celebrate a new edition of six of the plays. The Lanes invited actors, actresses, producers, and other theatre people, including Robert Atkins. In the course of the party, Richard claimed in conversation to have been a Shakespearean actor. The claim drew disbelief, so Richard took the doubter over to see Atkins and said, 'Please will you tell this gentleman whether or not I was or have been an actor.' Atkins, in his deep, booming voice, replied with a pithy summation of Richard's disjointed service to the dramatic arts: 'In my time, I have seen many actors and actresses, from stars to people just walking on, and in the whole of my stage career, never have I seen a better person than you at walking off!'

SWARMING BEES

T he dispersal of Annie Lane's estate sent Allen and Richard in search of new lodgings. After a spell in temporary digs, they moved to rooms above the practice of Dr Pritchard, a close friend of the late John Lane. Thirty-seven Southwick Street W2, four and a half levels of gloom, became the scene of a battle that revealed much about the Lane brothers' fearlessness and how they would comport themselves when fighting as a group. A map of the battleground: the housekeeper and her husband lived in the basement; Pritchard's surgery, waiting room and dispensary filled the ground floor; a bedroom and a sitting–dining room exhausted the first floor; and two top-floor bedrooms capped the building. Allen and Richard shared the larger of the top-floor bedrooms; when John started work at the London and Lancashire Insurance Company, he moved into the smaller bedroom; Pritchard's assistant, Dr O'Grady, occupied the first-floor bedroom; and the four men shared the sitting–dining room.

John's room had no power or light so he and Richard knocked a hole in the wall and rigged a length of dangerous-looking cable to the only electric plug in the large bedroom. The first and second floors had no plumbing so the brothers washed and shaved with one can of water. In Richard's words, 'we were rather pigging it at the time'. A tiny, desolate shared bathroom glowered on a landing between the ground and first floors. During the day, the only external light in the bathroom was glimpsed through a small ventilator, 'usually so dirty that it gave practically no light at all'. At night the tenants had to bring candles. Richard thought the bathroom the scruffiest, dirtiest, and darkest that he had ever used. A penny-in-the-slot meter activated a gas jet that heated the bathwater. 'The lid of the box where the pennies went was not locked and contained one penny, so all one had to do was take out the penny and put it through the slot four or five times.'

When Pritchard died, O'Grady bought the practice and cracked down on the tenants, with whom he had grudgingly shared the sitting room and the bathroom, and for whom he had developed a needling dislike. When he took over the building, one of his first acts was to pad-lock the bathroom's meter box. Rising to the challenge, Richard fos-sicked through his collection of old keys and found one that fitted, 'so we reverted to the one-penny system'. Relations with O'Grady quickly deteriorated and the Lanes decided to leave with a bang.

On their last night, the Lane brothers removed all the fittings: the cable from John's room, the pictures, the stair carpet (which was nailed down and only gave in after a fight), the stair rods and whatever else they could dismount, unscrew or jemmy up. Lifting the carpet made a racket and, accidentally on purpose, more noise was to follow. 'The stair rods which we had carefully gathered at the top of the stairs we had unfortunately forgotten to tie up securely, and soon after O'Grady had retired for the night someone, no doubt passing the top of the stairs in the dark, was unlucky enough to kick them down. They made even more noise than we expected.' Two pictures in 'rather unattractive frames' were smashed. 'Then when everything had quietened down, the three of us, who were attempting to dismantle John's bed, all lifted it upwards at the same time and peculiarly enough all let go at the same time. John's room was over O'Grady's bedroom, and this was too much for him.' The doctor put on his dressing gown and left in search of a policeman. Luckily for the brothers, 'the policeman was a reasonable type and refused to do anything about it'.

Allen, Richard and John went home to Falfield most weekends. When travelling by train, they would optimise. John knew how to get the best fare, Richard knew how to get the best food for the best price, and Allen enjoyed the fruits of his brothers' knowledge. To get the best fare: only first-class passengers could request a stop at the nearest sta-tion, Badminton; so, before buying tickets, John asked the guard if a stop had been booked; if not, he bought one first-class and two third-class tickets, then requested the stop. The best food: Richard befriended the restaurant car attendants so that, before serving lunch, they asked if the brothers wanted the outside of whatever joint was being served, as they knew this was the Lanes' favourite cut. The attendants also brought an unopened tin of Huntley & Palmer biscuits so the brothers could have first pick of their favourite digestives. Total price for the choice cut and sweets: two shillings and sixpence.

The brothers brought friends home, including the American printer Gaylord Donnelly, Hubert Hine, John's friend Cyril Peall from the London and Lancashire Insurance Company, and the strange duo of Wyndham Hazlett and a young man – called 'The Old Horse' – who galloped around 'making rude noises'. Sometimes John invited one of his girlfriends, but Allen preferred to keep his girlfriends to himself. The brothers and their guests spent Sunday mornings tinkering with the family's Sunbeam or its latest replacement, always finishing in time for a test drive to Stow-on-the-Wold. Calling in to see their friend Ivor Monckton, they would sample his homemade cider or brandy wine before ending up at the local pub, invariably getting back late for an enormous lunch prepared by Rachel the housekeeper. In shambolic tennis matches, John liked a net game and net points: 'it gave him great pleasure to place a ball just over the net where no opponents were, and watch their frantic and usually hopeless attempts to get it back.'

Richard had returned from Australia with his confidence shaken; alongside Allen and John and friends once again, his former sense of invincibility re-emerged. The brothers who had conquered Cotham Hill's gravelly descent now egged each other on to more dangerous escapades. On summer Sunday afternoons, bees swarmed at Falfield. Adopting a time-honoured practice, the brothers armed themselves with a bell and a pestle and mortar in the hope that the ringing and tanging would charm a swarm and cause it to settle. In this way, the Lanes disproved the well-known saying that 'swarming bees won't sting'.

After the battle of Southwick Street, the brothers moved into the top two floors of nearby 16 Talbot Square. There, the brothers' connoisseurship of bathrooms reached its apogee.

At Broomcroft, baths had often been cold. In New South Wales, after the 'very dirty job' of shearing sheep, Richard enjoyed a well-deserved dip in a tub 'half full of real hot water' which inspired thoughts of writing a lay sermon, 'In praise of a hot bath':

> to a person who has had a fairly strenuous and also fairly dirty time, what is finer than to lie down in a bath of warm water and laze, and think, not to worry about anything, just to splash the water occasionally, turn over occasionally to hear the soothing sound of running water, to watch the steam arising from the surface of the water and idly drifting upwards to the ceiling, then to sit up and vigorously play about with the soap and then to lie back again, the water covering you. When you turn the tap off, everything seems silent for a moment, then upon one's ears comes the sound of the wind whistling through the tall trees, and there you are lying in the bath.

At Talbot Square, the idiosyncratic bathroom became the centre of the flat and the Lane brothers' unofficial meeting room. Here they assembled each morning to discuss work, their plans, and the state of the world. At any moment in these hour-long gatherings, one brother would be in the bath, another would be shaving or washing, and the third would read out articles from the daily paper. 'It was a long bath and the califont gave really hot water. If the water was turned to low, there were likely to be popping and hissing noises, and more steam than water, but we soon got used to it and knew how long the water could be turned down without undue risk of explosion. There was a wide step leading up to the bath itself and in the first few weeks it was quite an experience walking up into the bath.' Richard saw poetry in the gas heater's instructions, which seemed to capture the spirit of the times: 'Swing out the burner to the full extent'!

The brothers hired a part-time home help to make their breakfast and clean up the flat while they were at work. Allen's revelry moved up another gear: most nights of the week, he would go to a cocktail party, return to the flat to change, often into 'white tie and tails', and go out again. Richard and John could not keep up, and anyway Allen sometimes preferred the company of others, especially his female conquests, so the younger Lane brothers usually had dinner together. After much trial and error, Richard and John arrived at the perfect circuit of places to eat: the Grill at Peter Cables, where the brothers stood to drink

Carlsberg lager from dimpled tankards and eat penny pork pies while their steaks sizzled; the restaurant on No. 1 Platform, Paddington; the meat shop in Praed Street, for sausages, bacon and eggs (and on the way back, why not call in at Ushers, the Spring Street off-licence, 'for a bottle of redders ... our evening requirement of hooch'?); any number of places in Soho, such as Dîner Français where seven courses cost two and six; De Hems, Driver's or Wheeler's for Cornish oysters or Blue Points, natural or mornay; the Shanghai next to the Pillars of Hercules for Chinese; Stones in Panton Street, or better still the Lord Belgrave a few paces further along, for steaks; and Simpsons in the Strand for lunch or dinner with a bottle of the three-shilling table wine. On this tour of the city's best kitchens, Richard and John forged a bond that would prove vital in the years ahead.

*

At the London and Lancashire Insurance Company in Chancery Lane, John diligently compiled and revised actuarial tables. Though this kind of complex and demanding work was beyond Allen, it appealed to the younger, brainier Lanes. Richard helped John in tasks they both enjoyed as intellectual puzzles, but John's feet were beginning to itch. His office overlooked a sorry patch of grass, which only served to make him feel more confined. Soon after moving to Talbot Square, he went skiing in Switzerland. 'As a holiday for exercise it was not a success, for on the first or second day he fell and sprained his leg and took no further part in active sports.' Still, he had a good time: holiday snaps show him cavorting with a girl called Nora (definitely not his sister), and after the trip he spent some weekends at her parents' house in the Home Counties. John meanwhile turned his mind to an even larger trip. The man who had sailed round Land's End in a tugboat would now travel around the world, visiting as many countries as possible, and – echoing Richard's Barwell plans – do it in a way that paid for itself.

After months of preparation, John arranged to represent scores of firms as a one-man British trade delegation. A blizzard of samples, price-lists, catalogues and letters of introduction filled the flat, and John's luggage consignment 'increased in proportion'. His twenty-first birthday had been such a booze-up that few who'd been there could remember the details. Now, with all the Lane brothers in residence, 16 Talbot Square became a party flat: publishing parties, Christmas parties, cocktail parties, annual Shakespeare parties (triply to celebrate the Bard's birthday, St George's Day and the anniversary of Allen's first day at The Bodley Head) and a 'lamp and lampshade breaking-up party' with their friends the Drummonds. But the most spectacular party of all was John's farewell bash, which started at Talbot Square and spilled out across London and into the North Atlantic.

Late in the night of drunken chaos, John's friend Paul Nichols was worse for wear. He stumbled over to John 'with tears in his eyes' and implored him to look up 'a former torch, or boat, bearer of his' in Shanghai. Richard noticed his favourite cut-glass fruit-bowl teetering on the part of the dining-room table that was kept in place with string and wire. He removed the bowl to safety just as another friend sat on the flimsy support, 'and ended up on the floor from where he refused to budge', like the drunken Scotsman from the *Bendigo*. 'Then for some reason . . . we wished to get Douglas Clarendon out of the way so we told him someone was phoning him from Bristol, and we pushed him into Allen's bedroom to phone from there. He was absent for a long time, but the joke was on us when the quarter's telephone bill came in.' Seventeen people slept in the flat that night, on four beds, one sofa, an armchair and an ottoman.

The party-goers reconvened at Driver's the next day for a long lunch that meant they missed the boat train from Fenchurch Street Station. Undeterred, everyone crammed themselves into three taxis, along with John's overweight luggage, and headed for King George V dock. Dumping the luggage on the quayside, the party boarded the *Carthage* – the first of the World Tour's forty ships – in search of a drink. Allen and Richard sailed with John on the inaugural leg and the farewell binge continued on board overnight. The next morning, they tied up at Southampton alongside the *Montcalm*, a Canadian Pacific liner on which the Lanes knew an officer, and they went on board for a gin. The officer and the *Montcalm* were sailing in under an hour, 'so the pace was fairly swift'. Returning to the *Carthage*, tea made way for brandy and soda. The drinking continued, and a departure delay of more than two hours proved to be Richard's undoing. When the new sailing time neared, Richard was last down the gangway, carrying a tumbler of brandy and soda in each hand. A P&O official stopped him and said he could not take ashore the line's property – the two glasses of brandy and soda – so Richard 'knocked them both back', returned the glasses, and continued on.

> I landed on my legs all right and saw John leaning over the rail offering me one for the road. I attempted to catch the glass – I didn't fall in between the ship and the quayside, but I know very little else save the ship behaving in a most erratic way sometimes being alongside then suddenly moving out into midstream. Eventually Allen persuaded me that she really had sailed and we got a lift back as far as the station in someone's car. There I had money but could not talk, and Allen could talk but had no money. We eventually bought tickets for London and got on to the train but I don't think the other occupants of our compartment appreciated our company. That was the last we saw of John for nearly two years.

On board the *Carthage*, the party continued at least until Gibraltar. During John's time abroad, Allen and Richard received from him an extraordinary series of letters, and many people reported by phone or in person that they had seen John in 'some outlandish spot'. From the Far East he reported on Japanese pedestrians, 'ten times worse than me on my way to school past rows of Wilwer's, Lanham's and such shops, and their pace or rather shuffle is at about the rate of one mile per hour'. And Japanese motorists, 'even worse than Nora driving along the main road on a bank holiday when she has espied one of her flames about a mile ahead driving a super sports Bentley'. At Bandung, high on the island of Java, John went to a restaurant where the waiter suggested *rijsttafel*, a Dutch word meaning 'rice table'. Without knowing what to expect, John ordered the dish.

> Take a very large porridge plate, place one dollop of rice in it and then proceed to cover it with curried fish, meat, chicken, roast fish, meat and chicken, boiled ditto, fried ditto, and then start adding flavourings of roast nuts, fried onions, chilli sauce, prawns, chutney etc, and you are allowed one extra plate for anything you want to take neat. You will naturally ask how it is served up, and the reply is that you have about thirty boys, lined up in a row, each carrying one plate, and

they file by one after the other, and it is extraordinary that the last ten in the line always have the most irresistible delicacies, and when the last boy brings you a plate of a dozen fried eggs, you just flick one on your plate, take a long drink of water or beer, undo the two top buttons of your trousers, pick up spoon and fork, and then weigh in.

For part of the trip, John had a boy of his own.

You may think that I am extravagant in taking a boy round with me, but for the journeys I use them it pays me hands down. I took this one on in Singapore and I am taking him with me to Sourabaya, and though his fares and wages will cost me a fiver, I shall emerge with more money in my pocket than if I went alone, the reason being that the cost of living is very high, and without him I should have to stay at least another week, at a cost of about 30/- a day for board and lodging alone, to say nothing of what I save in tips etc.

In French Indochina, John travelled with his 'harem': three vacationing American teachers from Shanghai, aged twenty-three, twenty-nine and thirty-something, 'the middle one being the most attractive, though I do not intend taking them or any part of my harem further than Siam, but, of course, one never can tell'. The foursome set out for the temple city of Angkor Wat. John thought the best way to proceed was by car but there were none for hire, so he bought one. In a remote part of Cambodia, the boggy road became impassable. Searching his letters of introduction, he found one to the governor of the district. John paid a carrier to deliver a message, then set up camp and waited. A few days later, the carrier returned with elephants, and the party continued on with their journey.

John also reported home on the progress of his love life.

For Nora's information, I have only had three affairs yet, and they all hail from Melbourne, so I am in for a thick time when I reach that part of the world . . .

I think, and hope, that you should send someone out to Australia to keep me out of mischief, as the samples that I have seen sound very interesting, but of course there is safety in numbers, and I shall have to become a polygamist if I fall by the wayside down there.

This predicament may help explain a now famous episode that occurred in Melbourne. The Bodley Head was one of the many businesses that John represented on his tour. Many people he met assumed he was *the* John Lane of The Bodley Head, somehow blessed with supernatural youthfulness. This led to a great deal of publicity: newspaper reporters sought interviews, literary clubs competed for his talks, and he was on radio in dozens of countries. A newspaper reported the moment in Melbourne when John spied an ancient battered car bearing the sign 'Melbourne to Perth'. According to the paper, 'The notion of crossing Australia in so bizarre a fashion appealing to him, he ran into the thick of the Collins Street traffic, leapt on the running board and inquired if the driver really sought passengers. "Yes," was the reply. "Very well," said Mr Lane, opening the door and dropping gracefully into the back seat, "Drive on." The driver nodded impassively. They drove on.' The ensuing car journey of 2500 miles took nine days and meant crossing the Nullarbor Plain. John and his driver slept in wayside shacks, under the stars and at least once in a shearing shed.

Apart from the overland trip, John completed a tour of southern and eastern Australia and the North and South islands of New Zealand. In regional Victoria, John stayed with the Purbrick family at their winery, Chateau Tahbilk. To help them spruik their wine, he called on every hotel within fifty miles of the vines. In South Australia, he went to Renmark to 'get the low down' on Richard's sojourn there. 'As far as I can make out, he broke more hearts than anyone has ever done before or since in South Australia (including myself!!).' Mr A.B. Withers had given up on fruit growing and opened a pub. In New South Wales, John called at Millamolong, where again much had changed. Tom Rowlands had passed away at home in 1933, bringing to an end a grand era. The Ashton family bought Millamolong the following year, and made it famous around the world as a polo venue.

On John's arrival in Sydney, a reporter asked if he was Mr Lane. When John said yes, the reporter referred to a piece of paper and said, 'I notice that you are connected with a publishing firm called the Bodily Head ... I presume that this means sex publications.' A newspaper in Wellington, New Zealand, reported an even more awkward episode during the approach of the *Rangitane* to Auckland. Mr and Mrs George

Bernard Shaw were on board, and in the ship's drawing room Shaw asked if he and his wife might listen to the wireless, which could only be turned on centrally. An officer left the drawing room for the switch-board, remarking as he left that the current broadcast was a lecture by Mr John Lane of The Bodley Head. Some minutes later, the officer passed by the drawing room again.

The words he heard coming from the loud speaker were enough to give him the impression that he ought to make a tactful entry. The lecturer, in reminiscence and comment, was showing that he had no great love for Shaw. The officer entered. 'I can't turn this thing off,' said a voice from near the floor of the drawing room. Mr George Bernard Shaw was on his hands and knees near the loud speaker working at the screws at the base of the wall where the radio flex was connected with the main. Then the words of the broadcast ceased abruptly. Mr Shaw had managed to turn it off.

BOOKMEN

A llen too assembled a harem of sorts, but trouble and contradiction plagued his search for love and attachment. In the early 1930s, he was anxious to marry and 'found a family'. As the heir, first apparent then actual, at The Bodley Head, he was becoming well known – a newspaper headline anointed him 'London's Youngest Publisher' – and there was no shortage of interested and beautiful women. One of his problems, however, was that he found it difficult to choose, and this had been so as far back as the furtive lapine meetings with Roma and Rosemary Gael, each sister by turns more attractive than the other. Uncle John had earned the nickname 'Petticoat Lane', and the example of his scattergun approach to female friendship only served to strengthen Allen's tendency to play the field. The rejection that followed Allen's premature marriage proposal, to a debutante in Hyde Park, probably solidified this tendency.

Peggy Beaton counted lots of girls with Allen at his local. If he was not charming a girl there, he was doing so at another pub, or the 400 Club, or Wheeler's, or the Café Royal, or somewhere off-grid. Among the scores of girlfriends in his address-book were two actresses, and Peggy Wood, and a girl called Hennie, and the four girls called Phyllis, and Miss Irvine, whom Peggy Beaton thought was Allen's favourite, until 'he attempted a caress and found she had false bosoms (not too firmly attached), that was the end of her – and so on', in a continuing succession of dalliances that heated up only rapidly to cool down.

Whether it was fake boobs or something else, a case for rejection always popped up. In Jack Morpurgo's words, Allen was 'quintessentially a bachelor who regarded the company of women as an enthralling pastime but never a career'.

Elsa Lanchester (Mrs Charles Laughton) and Ethel Mannin (Mrs Alexander Porteous) were also somewhere in the picture. Though married, the incendiary Mannin and possibly her husband had liberal ideas about the institution. She became especially close to Allen but befriended the other Lane brothers as well; when Richard called on her without a herald, she cautioned, 'it is never wise to call unexpectedly – I am so liable to be caught in a "compromising situation" . . . and that would be an embarrassment all round'. Some of Allen's affairs spiralled very close to embarrassment. A four-month liaison with a married woman from Manchester blew out the phone bill at Talbot Square – some of the calls lasted two hours – and Allen had to make himself scarce when the woman's husband staked out the Lane brothers' flat.

During that affair, according to Richard, Allen 'asked everyone's advice and took nobody's'. But, to help manage his rocky love life, Allen did seek the advice of astrologists. It is a curious fact of the Williams-Lanes that they took pseudo-science, mysticism and the occult as seriously as Sir Arthur Conan Doyle before them. One influential episode occurred in the early '30s. During a family lunch at the home of cousins, someone pulled out a Ouija board and the Williams-Lanes gave it a whirl. The message came: 'Beware Falfield 226'. This was their phone number and they drove home apprehensively to find that a bus had crashed into their driveway. In another episode later that decade, the three Lane brothers were staying at Windsor Castle, at the invitation of the Dean (Albert Baillie), when they were awoken at night by a creaking door. The brothers got up to investigate and saw a figure in the passage-way apparently walking along on its knees. The next day they reported the incident to Baillie, who told them the floor-height had been raised some years ago, and what they saw was a well-known ghost strolling along the old floorboards.

Allen's astrologer provided some very general paranormal feedback about his relationships – 'you will have some anxiety in connection with your love affairs', 'many of your little troubles will be caused by your own acts' – but also the answer to a specific question:

I think it is very likely that the lady you met in September will be your fate. But you must be very careful how you set about this whole affair, especially from now till the middle of April. From the middle of February you are likely to have bothers, nothing desperately serious but you need to be careful as they might affect your standing in your profession ... Certainly from what you have told me I feel that if you can manage to gain the lady of your choice without involving yourself in a scandal you will be very happy with her, but I do feel after looking at these maps that you ought to be more careful than most people. The map looks as if the child were going to complicate matters. Of course I know that everybody is getting divorced etc, but with your horoscope and in your position and with your ambitions it won't do you any good.

With such a busy personal schedule, Allen continued to prioritise fun over work. Joan Coles – possibly a distant cousin on the Williams/ Smith side – joined The Bodley Head as his secretary, an almost impossible job. Allen carried round a collection of notes on scraps of paper that epitomised his scrappy and chaotic working methods. Often away, he refused, even when in London, to keep regular hours. Try as she might, Joan could not persuade him to attend the office in the morning and deal with his accumulating mail. 'He used to come in late in the afternoon,' she said, 'and hope someone would stay to work late.'

One thing was constant. Richard Lane was his elder brother's best friend and closest confidant. Allen shared details of his amours, both seeking and ignoring Richard's advice about his most dangerous affairs. When Richard was in Australia and Egypt, Allen greatly missed him. Though he did not always take the younger brother's advice, he usually appreciated it and sometimes struggled to function without it. The *Whispering Gallery* fiasco had occurred at The Bodley Head before Richard was there to help and guide Allen. Richard would soon be by Allen's side as his colleague and principal counsellor at the firm.

In Australia, Richard had suffered as a book lover in a book desert. Now in London, a city challenged only by New York for literary preeminence in the English-speaking world, Richard was closer than ever to bibliophile heaven. He had savoured the library at Lancaster Gate Terrace, and had helped Annie sell some of Uncle John's books and manuscripts: 'Twelve chapters in the author's handwriting of *A Pair of Blue Eyes* fetched £1,500 and sundry other books £1,000.' Meeting and socialising with a wide network of book people, he began to build his own collection, and to refine his taste for good design and good writing. Alongside his pocket-sized prayer book from Camilla, and inscribed volumes from the Matthews of Moorook and the Rowlands of Millamolong, Richard's library now boasted presentation copies from Ben Travers and other Bodley Head authors, and a cross-section of fine books and the best contemporary literature. At Coonabarabran, Richard had kept his precious books in a suitcase; now, he put his prize specimens in a safe.

*

Shortly after Richard's return from Egypt, he met the ardent bibliophile A. J. A. Symons for a second time. At six foot three inches, Alphonse James Albert Symons was tall, dark, and almost handsome. Certainly he dressed impressively, wearing horn-rimmed spectacles and magnificent links four inches proud of his cuffs. A fine-press publisher, table-tennis enthusiast and music-box collector, Symons liked to be known as 'AJ', had a dandyish penchant for clubs and societies, and was active across many projects – including a long-planned biography of Oscar Wilde. With Desmond Flower he produced *Book Collector's Quarterly*; he was Brother Speculator for the Sette of Odd Volumes, an exclusive bibliophile fraternity; with André Simon he launched the Wine and Food Society; and he founded the respected First Edition Club as a niche enterprise for publishing and appreciating beautiful books. Riding Britain's inter-war wave of book love, and in competition with imprints like the Golden Cockerel Press and Francis Meynell's Nonesuch, the Club issued well-bound and well-printed volumes to several hundred subscribing members.

John Lane senior had been a member of the Sette, and had, like Allen, approved of Symons and his Club. When the Club's secretary broke her leg skiing, Symons put a proposal to Richard: would he like to take her place? Though unable to type or take shorthand, Richard was bewitched by the bookish possibilities, and agreed to give the role a try. Thus admitted into the enchanting world of bibliophilia, Richard started modestly – his first task was to produce the lunch menu for the Club's dining room – but he was soon shouldering the many tasks that needed to be done to make a small publishing house prosper.

Late one afternoon, Richard joined AJ in his office for a glass of sherry. Outside, in the haunting mist, the lights were coming on in Bedford Square. Symons asked Richard if he knew Wilde's 'The Sphinx'. When Richard answered no, Symons recited the darkly morbid poem in a deep, melodious voice, all the time walking about his office holding his sherry glass by the base. Richard's childhood chats with his uncle had both opened his eyes to the world of books and ruined his prospects as a farmer. Now, Richard felt as if he was finally conversing with the personification of his bibliophilic ideal.

Already familiar with some of The Bodley Head's finer editions, Richard learnt at the Club the art of the well-made book: beautiful hand-made paper; legible and appropriate typefaces printed crisply and evenly; handsome and robust bindings in buckram, linen and morocco. He made a close study of all the books he helped shepherd through, like H. Williams' *Book Clubs and Printing Societies of Great Britain and Ireland* (750 copies, printed at the Curwen Press and bound in floral cloth designed by Oliver Simon); G.S. Tomkinson's *A Select Bibliography of the Principal Modern Presses Public and Private in Great Britain and Ireland* (1000 copies, also printed at the Curwen Press, with an introduction by Bernard Newdigate); *The Ravenna Journal* by George Gordon Byron, Sixth Lord Byron (500 copies); and Graily Hewitt's *The Pen and Type Design* (250 copies printed by J. Johnson at the Oxford University Press in Treyfors Type on Barcham Green paper and elegantly clothed in an Art Deco binding).

Richard also studied the Club's business model and the economics of its style of publishing. Though the Club's name hinted at preciousness, the books it produced achieved a consistently high standard in both appearance and content. The Club's formula would be much copied in Britain and America. Richard could see the inherent limitations of a business predicated on high costs and a narrow client base, but he also divined the Club's strengths: a deep connection with its member-customers, and a sincere concern for quality. Richard also learnt much about the strange psychology of pricing. Like the American tourists who ruined Cairo's hotels, some people were happier if their books cost more, not less. This strictly irrational tendency was behind the Club's success, however limited. Richard sensed that there might only be two profitable price-points in British publishing, one of them measured in pence, the other in guineas. The Bodley Head's books were pitched at neither of these points; Richard and his brothers would soon experiment with both.

Richard and AJ shared an appetite for the absurd, and for good food. The two men joked and ate at the Wine and Food Society's Savoy dinners; at a Holborn pub – cut off the joint, two veg, half a pint of bitter; and at AJ's pleasant house at Finchingfield in Essex – cellar, large garden, table-tennis table and hundreds of music boxes. Once they became friends, Symons, a peerless door opener, inducted Richard into the arcane rituals of the Sette, and introduced him to the circle of fine printers, private press operators, exclusive booksellers and avant-garde authors who constituted the core of British bibliomania. When AJ wrote *The Quest for Corvo*, his ground-breaking quasi-biography of Frederick Rolfe, he presented Richard with an inscribed copy, 'For Dick Lane with memories of a brilliant period when he shared the responsibilities, as well as enjoyed the cordial goodwill, of his friend the author of this experimental work now offered as the memento of a long esteem. AJ.' Another treasure for Richard's expanding library.

Richard left the First Edition Club to plunge deeper into mainstream publishing, but he took away a deepened appreciation of fine books, and he remained friends with Symons who, ever the dilettante, called on the Lane brothers later in the decade to interest them in producing peep shows. Richard documented the meeting and the Lanes' serious consideration of the proposal: 'We went into it quite carefully but decided that there would not be a sufficiently large demand ... to make the proposition financially worthwhile. [AJ] was in poor health then, suffering from the effects of eating a bad oyster, but he would never say where he had been poisoned.'

After leaving the Club, Richard began reading freelance for The Bodley Head. Unlike Allen and Uncle John, he read every word conscientiously, and in one week reviewed and reported on twenty-one manuscripts, receiving five shillings for each one. Allen had also read manuscripts, to supplement his meagre income in his early years at the firm. After reviewing W.H. Rainsford's *That Girl March*, Allen singled out the 'rather odd names' of the characters, the large number of brackets and underlinings, and the glut of awkward adverbs. Allen's reports had traces of the superficiality, idiosyncrasy and equivocality that Richard deplored. 'A good reader,' Richard wrote, 'doesn't only read and report but also suggests alterations which, in his opinion, would improve the work.' If the book is in danger of being considered libellous, a good reader 'naturally mentions it'. Above all, the reports should be thorough and cogent, alert to style as well as content, and objective. From Richard's recreational reading, he developed a good appreciation of literary style and technique. Some years earlier, he had concluded that Margaret Kennedy's *The Constant Nymph* was 'certainly a remarkable book and written in a charming style'. After the 'intense mental pleasure' of reading A.S.M. Hutchinson's sensational romance *If Winter Comes*, he changed his own writing style as a compliment to the author. He was not so well disposed towards a parody of the novel. 'When I had finished [the Hutchinson], I read *If Summer Don't* by Barry Pain ... I did not think much of it. In fact I did not consider it worth reading. But I hate to leave a book half-read.'

As a reader for the firm, Richard followed his own advice to produce thorough and holistic reports, on the strength of which The Bodley Head invited him to read proofs. He began with *Andrée's Diaries*, a book about a nineteenth-century attempt by Swedish explorers to fly over the North Pole in a hot air balloon. In 1930, a Norwegian party found the Swedes' bodies near Spitsbergen. The explorers' diaries, letters and undeveloped film were recovered, and these provided the basis for the book, which at bottom was a mystery tale: the dead men had not run out of food and they had a working Primus. Translation of the diaries into English introduced a great many errors, which Richard spotted, much to the relief of The Bodley Head's management, who were so pleased with Richard's display of proofreading skill that they offered him full-time work as a bloodhound.

The Bodley Head's finances were in a poor state, and some staff were taking advantage of the turbulence that followed John Lane's death. Worried about the expenses submitted by some travelling book reps, the firm's managers asked Dick Lane to turn his dead eye in that direction. 'If a representative stayed at a commercial hotel that provided dinner, bed and breakfast (incidentally the price for this ... varied between 12/6 and £1) and on his expense sheet he put down a charge for dinner, this fact would be brought to his notice.' Perfectly suited to this role – puzzles and prices were among his obsessions – Richard performed it so well that the firm asked him to take a book rep's place. Just as his friend Keith Garvie had done, Richard became a book traveller. First, he covered the 'dreary' suburbs, before moving to the Travellers' Graveyard – the East coast. Richard would in due course call on every bookshop of note in Britain and Ireland. To become a good publisher, he argued, 'it is more than useful to get to know the people who actually sell your books'.

When Richard was again promoted, this time to the position of Greater London traveller, he blended a talent for mechanics – honed in the Australian bush – with an instinct for marketing – encouraged in those childhood chats with Uncle John about how to display and sell books. To promote a novel whose action took place on an intercontinental airliner, Richard approached the airline and borrowed some model planes. At Denny's bookshop, he piled copies of the book in the window and suspended an aircraft in front of them: 'there was a small gap between some of the novels and behind this I placed a fan. When this was switched on, although it was invisible it caused the propellers on the aircraft to move. This was a great success and almost caused a pedestrian traffic jam.' For Norman Hunter's *The Incredible Adventures of Professor Branestawm* (1933), Richard and Hubert Hine built a special display at Selfridges: a crazy eight-foot-wide Heath Robinson-esque working model of a pancake-making machine, which 'caused terrific interest among the Oxford Street passers-by'.

> When we published the Angus books, which recorded the adventures of a Scottish terrier, I approached the manufacturers of Black & White Whisky and they agreed to let me have a quantity of a model of a black terrier which they used to display this produce. Not only did the booksellers like this model but they had literally hundreds of customers who wished to purchase same.

The trade journal *Bookseller* announced that Richard was 'very popular with the trade in London', and that in sales he had had a lot to learn, 'but learnt it quickly'. Having quickly shown his worth to the firm as holistic reviewer, forensic auditor and mechanic marketer, and to Allen as principal counsellor, Richard was made a director of The Bodley Head. But he and Allen were not immediately in sync about how to lead a publishing house. On an especially hot day, Richard bought ice cream for all the staff at Vigo Street, with the firm's money, and 'Allen was far from pleased'.

Two years after the *Carthage* left East London, Richard went with Allen to Waterloo Station to greet John on his return. The elder Lanes found him somewhat aged, and 'getting a little thin on top'. Now an unassailable expert on the export trade, John joined The Bodley Head to manage foreign sales. He got to know London's exporters at their chief daytime haunt – Sherriff's Wine Bar under the railway arch at Ludgate Circus – the scene of an episode that recalled his epic Melbourne-to-Perth car trip. On New Year's Eve, John was drinking sherry and marsala with the manager of the French publisher Hachette, Monsieur Joubert, 'a Frenchman whose English became worse every year he lived in England'. Joubert said he had not seen his parents in Paris on New Year's Day for many years, so John said, 'Let's go.' Returning to the flat to grab his passport and a change of clothes, he left for a hectic week in France. The brothers abroad had their own informal banking system: 'when we ran out of money, we would proceed to the nearest bookseller and collect something on account, crediting the bookseller when we returned to the office.'

The shares Allen inherited from his aunt were useful ammunition in the intensifying power games at The Albany, a place of 'many disagreements and ill feeling all round'. Basil Willett had served John Lane for more than twenty years as a thoughtful manager and astute adviser; at the time of Lane's death, Willett was managing director of The Bodley Head. Allen, now the majority shareholder, moved suddenly – some thought brutally – against Willett and installed himself as chief. Allen exercised enough clout on the board and on the share register to fight off any reciprocal moves to oust him, but the more worrisome risk was that the whole enterprise would collapse, a real prospect given the firm's divided governance, high costs and struggling sales against the Depression-era backdrop of macroeconomic calamity. Allen took control of the firm's accountants (Smedley, Rule & Co.), directing them to send sensitive letters home to Talbot Square lest they fall into the hands of nervous and unsympathetic directors. To fend off the liquidators,

Allen and his brothers aggressively cut costs and took drastic steps to move the overvalued overhang of overstocks that had accumulated in the crypt-cum-warehouse at Holy Trinity Church. With personal liability for insolvent trading a real concern for the brothers, Allen also seized control of the relationship with the firm's solicitors (Bullcraig & Davis). Their legal armoury was insufficient to lever out the old guard but, by attrition and other means, all the hostile directors would soon be casualties of The Bodley Head's long march to liquidation.

There was also work to be done at Talbot Square. Though far superior to Southwick Street, the flat was getting rough at the edges just as Allen's tastes were becoming more refined (he had, for example, developed a passion for well-made suits). Soon after John returned, Allen served his brothers with an ultimatum: if they did not agree to a thorough redesign and overhaul of their flat, he would get a new one for himself, and they could carry on in squalor. One version of this story has Allen proclaiming that the flat lacked the dignity befitting the residence of British publishing's most distinguished family!

The younger brothers acquiesced, and with Allen they commissioned plans and chose a builder, called Coffin, to make the extensive alterations. The plans called for the bath and lavatory to be moved up a floor – a job made more difficult by the brothers' decision to continue living in the flat during the alterations. Thoughtful planning of the new bathroom was central to the project. At a showroom in Charing Cross Road, the brothers tried out a succession of bath suites for length and comfort. The baths were in the showroom window, and passers-by watched in puzzlement the serious deliberations among three young men about the merits of this or that enamel or porcelain. When the brothers insisted on trying out the lavatory, the store manager insisted on drawing the blind, and the fishbowl burlesque came to an end.

Elsewhere in the flat, there were new parquet floors, a bar with glass shelves and hidden lighting, and, a rarity, a gas refrigerator, in which Agatha Christie discovered the frozen corpse of a rabbit. Richard's old bedroom became the new bathroom, the old bathroom became the kitchen, and the kitchen–dining room became a much larger dining room. The passageway to Richard's room morphed into a decadent closet large enough for fifty suits. But the renovation was not all about decadence: so that he could tinker with machines and mechanisms,

Richard had a six-foot workbench installed, 'complete with vice and small lathe'. Still, Richard appreciated the fashionable furnishings of his new flat, none of them made from kerosene tins. Allen's room was decorated in eccentric green – the walls, carpet, and bed linen, even the telephone. The renovations cost the brothers £1000 and took nearly a year to complete.

In their newly fashionable flat, the Lanes could now hold dinner parties. They engaged a 'gentleman's gentleman', a tall ex-marine called Knight who stiffened noticeably when addressed. According to Richard, Knight claimed to be a teetotal non-smoking bachelor; over the years, the brothers found that 'not all these statements were correct'. To test their new helper, the brothers gave a small dinner party. The mission was spelled out thoroughly in advance. The brothers would fix their own pre-dinner drinks, while Knight would manage dinner, coffee and the washing up. 'Everything went well,' Richard later wrote, 'and he looked very impressive in a white coat and black bow-tie.' Having cooked and served dinner and completed his other tasks, Knight opened the sitting-room door and asked if anything further was required. Richard said 'No, thank you' and wished him good night, but Knight stood stiffly to attention and said, 'I beg to report, sir, we are one coffee spoon short.' To the relief of the Lanes and their guests, the spoon was found on the mantelpiece.

To prevent a different kind of embarrassment, the three bachelors established a system in the flat: if one of the brothers had a girl to stay overnight, he would place a towel over his bedroom's doorknob, signalling that Knight should not enter.

After John's grand tour, the brothers continued to travel. John and Allen went many times to Pontresina in Switzerland. Allen made six trips a year to Paris, and motored around the south of France with the 'burly, foul-mouthed' printer Raymond Hazell and his wife. Allen also travelled to Spain, which he came to prefer to France. Advertising this preference, he mounted posters for bullfights on the walls of the flat. Though not quite bullfighters, the Lane brothers saw themselves as the Three Musketeers: a tight brotherhood that would together take on their foes, as they had at Southwick Street. But the partnership was not without its tensions. All three saw it differently and expected different things from it. John was less inclined than Richard to idolise Allen or to excuse his growing egotism. Allen's flings, and his half-joking threat to leave Talbot Square, told his brothers that the partnership was not infinite in scope or necessarily permanent in duration. The sometimes trivial glue that held the brothers together became especially important, and the ritual of bathroom conferences even more sacred in the renovated flat.

Allen liked to bathe before shaving; his new tactic was to lie in the bath 'interminably discoursing on endless subjects to delay getting out'. Richard, accommodatingly, preferred to shave before bathing, while 'John couldn't care less which ablution came first'. The water was gas-heated, and filling the bath took fifteen minutes, so the brothers used the same bathwater, with frequent 'toppings up'. All manner of subjects were discussed at the conferences: fishing, travel, current affairs, the brothers' work. With all three brothers now at The Bodley Head, the chat about work – who was doing what to whom, in the office and beyond – took on a new intensity, which crystallised in the form of potent discussions about a new venture.

'At Length Did Cross an Albatross'

I n the early 1930s, the division of labour among the Lane brothers at The Bodley Head was as blurry as Richard's role in Atkins' Shakespeare company. Formally and publicly, Allen served as CEO. Richard moved from the role of London traveller to the editorial side, where he purged flowery adjectives, applied the precepts of Fowler's *Modern English Usage*, and became the firm's chief contact with authors and literary agents. John managed exports. These were the roles in theory, but in practice all three Lanes mucked in with whichever parts of the firm they could influence, and oversaw as a troika those parts they could control. All three took turns caring for the American branch; all three found and nurtured new authorial talent; all three cultivated wide publishing networks and lubricated them at pubs, restaurants and oyster bars across London; all three suggested and tested new ideas for the business through a process of creative opposition. The bathroom at Talbot Square became The Bodley Head's de facto boardroom, control centre and innovation shop.

In the years after Uncle John's death, The Bodley Head remained a household name and pulled off some notable publishing coups. But the firm's trajectory was downward. Company historian J.W. Lambert called this period a slide into chaos and enfeeblement. The imprint that once yeasted London's literary ferment was now crusty and inert. The causes were many: wrong scale, wrong priorities, and often the wrong books at the wrong price. Overall, an irretrievably tired business model weighed the firm down, and sloppiness and bad habits crept in. The plan for each new title rested on a multivariate equation that linked the proposed price, the likely sales, the fixed and variable production costs and the likely profit. Now as then, the art of costing a book is a search for the sweet-spot: the elusive combination of price, print run and investment – in editorial, design, marketing – that optimises expected profit, taking into account the publisher's overheads and any royalties due to the author. Fantasy can intrude at several points. Sales may be overestimated, costs underestimated, or the price may be set unrealistically high. Unreliable costings are fatal for publishers. At The Bodley Head, erratic and erroneous costings thrived in the unsteady aftermath of John Lane's death.

When Allen bought the British rights to a Walt Disney series of pop-up books called the Silly Symphonies, he was implicated in a spectacular costing fantasia. Caring little for hard-nosed calculations, even when they would guard him from easily avoidable losses, Allen announced to Richard and John an intention to sell the books for two shillings. Richard had an appreciation for the absurd, but this proposal for the Sillies was ridiculous.

> Dick raised first a sceptical eyebrow and then indignant and carefully argued objections. The successful implementation of Allen's theory, he argued, depended upon mass production, and Allen was proposing only comparatively short runs for these books; they could or would not be bestsellers. What was worse, the production cost, 1s 2½d, was so high that it allowed to the publisher only 1½d profit even on sales to smaller bookshops – not enough to cover overheads ... Allen listened carefully, put on his naughty-boy grin, gave no other answer but went off to over-rule similar objections from his sulky fellow-directors.

Richard would question the costings on many subsequent books and series, but it was too late for the Silly Symphonies; the books were a hit with customers, and the firm 'lost money on every copy sold'. Allen even talked of offering the books to the Woolworths chain of high-street stores, which sold 'Nothing Over Sixpence', and where losses would have ballooned.

The Allen–Richard nexus of creative opposition extended from the Talbot Square bathroom to the Vigo Street office floor. Allen made frequent visits to the sales department; Richard retraced each visit, discreetly toning down or countermanding his brother's extravagant and off-the-cuff directives. Though not always heeded, Richard became the professional minder Allen had sorely lacked during the *Whispering Gallery* affair and other debacles.

At The Bodley Head, the brothers faced a simple imperative: they had to turn the business around, or turn it into something else. The problem demanded new thinking. Though the outlook for their late uncle's firm was asymptotic, in hindsight the brothers could not have hoped for a better platform from which to launch a laboratory of publishing experiments. Here was a chance to innovate, to display Lane daring, and to shake up the publishing scene. From the fractured board of directors, the brothers won a licence to test different books, genres, formats and price-points. The books thus conceived would be produced and distributed through normal Bodley Head channels but would be underwritten by the Lanes, with all losses and profits landing with the brothers rather than the wider firm. In other words, Allen and Richard and John were now publishing at their own risk.

Just in time for Christmas 1931, the brothers' syndicate – now effectively a firm within the firm – published a book of sexy and irreverent cartoons. Despite trash-talking from sceptics inside and outside The Bodley Head, Peter Arno's *Parade* sold vigorously and the brothers 'made quite a bit out of it'. Having overseen the book's costing and production, Richard kept Arno's lively artwork as a trophy. *Parade* was a minor work, but the brothers' next syndicate publication would rank among the century's most important.

*

By the time it reached the Lane brothers in 1934, James Joyce's *Ulysses* had endured a bruising history in and out of print. Notoriously a red rag to the moral police, and the uniformed police, the book has a complex and contested publication history. In 1922, Sylvia Beach's Shakespeare & Co. produced a Paris edition of 1000 copies. In the '20s and early '30s, people who wanted to read the book in Britain or America relied mostly on copies imported from France, many of them printed by Maurice Darantière in Dijon. The authorities did their best to stem the flow: 499 copies from Harriet Weaver's 1929 Egoist Press edition were seized by British Customs and burned in the King's Chimney. The US Post Office went one better and burned 500 copies.

Bennett Cerf, co-founder of Random House, bought the United States publication rights in early 1932. Through a stroke of good fortune, the book was championed in America by Morris Ernst – the brilliant free-speech lawyer who would later become a friend of the Lanes. Cerf, Ernst and *Ulysses* won an obscenity trial in December 1933, and Random House published the book the following month. Between the trial and the appeal, in which the publishers again succeeded, sales of *Ulysses* were incendiary. Allen knew Cerf and saw first-hand in New York some of the *Ulysses* fever.

In England, Leonard and Virginia Woolf contemplated publishing the work at their Hogarth Press, but eventually turned it down, citing problems with printers. Faber & Faber was Joyce's preferred British imprint, but T.S. Eliot and his fellow Faber directors dragged their feet. Jonathan Cape, too, was reluctant to enter the fray. The Lanes were the first to make a concrete offer. Though determined to go ahead with a British edition, their fears of prosecution on the grounds of indecent publication were genuine. The book's printer would proceed only under the protection of a wide-ranging written indemnity. The Bodley Head's old guard set the bar even higher, demanding that the brothers stake a bond of £20,000 to insulate the firm against legal and other costs arising from the use of its imprint and distribution channels. The brothers (primarily Richard and John) assembled the onerous surety – a remarkable sign of their new wealth following the Lane inheritance.

Most of the imported French copies were dressed in cheap paper covers. As an insurance policy, the Lanes went in an altogether different direction: they limited the edition and gave it the deluxe trappings (good paper, bindings and layout) Richard had mastered at the First Edition Club in the 1920s. One thousand numbered copies were initially printed: 900 of them on Japan vellum bound in linen, price three guineas; and a hundred copies signed by Joyce, printed on mould-made paper and bound in leather, priced, for the most ardent bibliophiles, at six guineas. Eric Gill supplied an elegant gold block of an archer's bow for the cover decoration. The Bodley Head's extreme caution proved unnecessary – the book avoided prosecution, in part because the high price and luxurious format assuaged concerns about mass corruption – and *Ulysses* became a cash cow for the syndicate and for The Bodley Head. The brothers got their bond back, and Richard added one of the special six-guinea copies to his book collection.

The process of assembling the bond; foot-dragging among the Lanes' fellow directors; contractual issues; production delays attendant upon the deluxe publication – a surfeit of difficulties conspired to delay the Bodley Head *Ulysses*. The edition did not appear until October 1936, and in the meantime would be leapfrogged by another Lane venture, birthed at another bathroom conference: a series of affordable fiction reprints, to be launched and sold on the same basis as *Parade* and *Ulysses*.

Ever since the 1929 crash, all three brothers had been gathering string about the best way to make and sell such a series. Now, at their cloistered planning sessions, they dipped into reservoirs of ideas and precedents. Though ruefully aware of The Bodley Head's earlier experimentation with nine-penny paperbacks – a venture whose failure cost the firm a thousand pounds for every penny of the cover price – the brothers were also attuned to the contemporary book-trade debate about expanding the market by shrinking prices. In the 1930s, a typical new hardcover volume cost seven shillings and sixpence, a price that made such books a luxury for many potential readers. George Bernard Shaw championed the discounting cause, and can fairly be said to have fathered – or at least grandfathered – the Lane brothers' reprint venture. In a strident letter to the *Bookseller*, Shaw pushed for growth in the book-reading public, a cause for which he was prepared to put his own royalties on the line. Having already allowed an American book club to give away tens of thousands of his books, he confidently challenged Woolworths to send him a large enough order, which he would honour 'joyfully'.

Notwithstanding the sentiments John had expressed on New Zealand radio (and even though the playwright favoured Carpentier in the Dempsey–Carpentier boxing match), the Lane brothers aligned themselves with Shaw. A formidable group of established publishers, led by Sir Stanley Unwin, lined up on the other side. Cheap paperbacks would cannibalise sales of hardbacks, the heavyweights argued, or set customers' price expectations at a level that put the whole trade in the poorhouse. In publishing circles, Unwin did not hide his disdain for the new leaders of The Bodley Head, nor for the disruptive trends they exemplified.

Richard perched on a large pile of string. Though aware of the tenets and techniques of top-end publishing, he advocated for low-cost books on the grounds of reach and profit. He remembered his lightbulb moment at the First Edition Club about the two roads to profit in publishing: the high road of deluxe production and exclusive circulation, and the low road of large print runs and mass distribution. But his interest in cheap books was far from mercenary. His own formative experiences in the book desert of the impoverished outback had brought home to him the importance of making inexpensive books more widely accessible. Price-obsessed, he had an acute sense of what pennies meant in concrete terms – in wine, beer, chocolates and cigarettes. His whole life he would retain the vivid memory, from Mandurama, of that last thruppence worth of peanuts. And in thinking about high and low roads, he had another powerful thought: it should be possible to bring them together. Books could sell for peanuts *and* be well made.

John likewise had new ideas about winning in publishing. He studied the twopenny lending libraries that had recently arrived in London to cater for 'office boys, messenger boys, typists and similarly placed young people whose salaries would be well below the pound a week mark'. He returned from his world tour with a mastery of foreign markets and export strategy, a sharpened knowledge of book values and bookselling, and an awareness of the broadening of readers' interests 'in general literature' such as economics, politics, travel and biography. He got to know the wares of Harrap, Faber, Davies and other publishers whose titles he had represented alongside those of The Bodley Head. Impressed by the output of peer publishers, John had criticised from abroad the cost and quality of the run-of-the-mill books that came from his family firm:

I do not think that the [Bodley Head's 1933] novels are up to standard ... I have not been able to push a lot of [the Autumn list] as the greater demand in the East at the moment is for cheap literature of the Edgar Wallace type, and I shall have to see what can be done down South ... I shall have to write a soothing letter to Winnie [of The Bodley Head] and get her assistance. I am afraid that I have not been in her good books for the last ten months, as I have constantly been finding fault with their methods, making a lot of destructive and few constructive criticisms.

Richard had studied the books of other publishers, too, while Allen knew very well the successes and failures of The Bodley Head both under and after Uncle John. All three saw before them in the book trade a farm-table spread of opportunities and – though Allen seldom thought or acted in consultation – felt confident in their collective ability to dig in. All three could make imaginative and intuitive leaps, but the two younger Lanes were also good at arithmetic – at the kind of calculations that are necessary to make cheap books pay off. The Lane brothers were ready to demonstrate a flair that Jonathan Cape would later see as springing from a 'solid knowledge of what has gone on in the past, so that you can profit by people's mistakes and achievements, and you've got a smell for what can be done and what can't be done'.

*

A quaint parable of the origin of the Lanes' reprint series has since gained wide currency. Allen was returning to London after weekending with Agatha Christie and her husband, the archaeologist Professor Max Mallowan. Waiting on a train platform, Allen wanted something to read, so he visited the railway bookstall but found nothing to satisfy him. The anecdote first featured in Richard's 1973 recollections, before being repeated in Bill Williams' memoir of Allen Lane, and in the two more recent Allen Lane biographies, and in scores of other places. According to Richard:

On [Allen's] way back, he had to change trains and in doing so he had quite a long wait. Having run out of reading matter, he visited the bookstall but could not find anything he wanted to read at a reasonable price ... The only really cheap books were the Readers Library, which were smallish books with a pictorial cover. They were not particularly well produced and not particularly good titles, certainly not the type of book Allen wanted to read. Benns had published a series of books known as Benn's Ninepennies but these had rather a dull cover, were shortish – around 40,000 words … Also they were new books, certainly good authors but anyhow they were not a success.

So, the story goes, Allen put the idea to his brothers, and the new series was born as a means to fill the market gap exemplified by the books he could not find at the railway platform bookstall. The new venture would prove to be singularly important for the Lane brothers' publishing careers, so the details of its origins are of great interest. There is a curious sort of symmetry in the idea that railway platforms figured centrally in John Lane's end and the reprint series' beginning. Unfortunately, the railway genesis story is as implausible as it is famous, and it demands a thorough rebuttal.

First, the story itself is unlikely. Allen was never a hungry or fussy reader. Bookstalls stocked books (naturally) of various types and formats. Certainly some were unamenable, with their 'dull covers', but the stalls were enough to service a snacking reader, and Allen – who cultivated a special ability to digest books without actually reading them – was never more than that. In Richard's account, as soon as Allen's story is presented it is undermined: the inadequate bookstall was not so inadequate after all, as it still offered classics and quality contemporary works at low prices. Second, the details of the story changed more than once. The time of the visit was always unclear, and the location fungible: in one version, for example, the bookstall was at Exeter station, and in another, Newton Abbot. The vague sub-plot of visiting Agatha Christie looks like a simple attempt to drop a famous name into the story.

A third problem is that the story is too neat and well-pitched to be taken seriously. In it, Allen is presented as Everyman, waiting for the train and simply wanting a cheap, good book to read. Allen in reality was more playboy and budding tycoon than common man, and the platform yarn is too convenient for an entrepreneur who hoped to prosper from selling inexpensive books. Fourth, the story was documented many years after the event. In those intervening years, Allen demonstrated a talent for historical fiction and revisionism – a talent acknowledged by all who knew him. As early as 1973, Bill Williams branded Allen's railway story a myth. It was one of several creation stories – all of them based on no more than half or quarter truths – that Allen invented for the reprint series. One of the other stories involved an apple tree, and another a vicar, a table and a sofa-cushion.

Richard's personal recollections reveal that Allen had prior form in railway storytelling. Allen once told his family that when he first moved to London he could not afford the train fare to Bristol, but went regularly to platform No. 1 at Paddington Station anyway, to watch the departing Bristol trains. It is possible to imagine restless and unsentimental Allen telling his family this story about wistful trainspotting, but it is impossible to picture him actually doing it. If even half true, the story captures the only times in Allen's life when he sat still.

Two well-documented backstories provide nails for the coffin of Allen's railway-bookstall creation myth. Backstory number one: while the Lanes were incubating their syndicate, The Bodley Head's other youngsters were hatching their own ideas. H. A. W. Arnold was a junior on the accounting side, and Edward Young was at the same level in advertising and promotion. In 1933, the budding bookkeeper told the novice marketer of his conviction that the firm could undercut series like Everyman by issuing sixpenny paperbacks. Costs could be kept low by focusing on out-of-copyright titles. Abundantly bookish but meagrely remunerated, Young appreciated the idea on the same terms as Arnold who, with his friend's encouragement, presented the proposal to the managing director. Allen, though not giving much away, promised to think about it. Arnold would soon take his talent for cut-through insights to the British Museum. On the many future occasions when Allen spoke of the reprint series' origins, he seems not once to have mentioned his conversation with Arnold.

Backstory number two involves a colourful enterprise called Albatross Verlag. Founded in 1932, Albatross was owned by a South African and managed through an Italian chairman and a British holding company. From Germany, Kurt Enoch controlled marketing and distribution; in Paris, Max Wegner handled editorial and production matters; and the firm's German designer, Hans Mardersteig, was based in Italy. Such an international concern required an international frontman. Mysterious, multilingual, multifarious, John Holroyd-Reece was born Hermann Riess and had fingers in as many book-world pies as A.J.A. Symons. For tourists and Continental readers, Albatross published in

English, and in paper covers, the best of modern literature as well as popular genre fiction. Each category of writing in the Modern Continental Library had its own cover colour, so customers knew straight away what they were getting. Blue volumes: love stories; green volumes: stories of travel and foreign peoples; grey volumes: plays, poetry and collected works; purple volumes: biographies and historical novels; yellow volumes: 'psychological novels, essays etc.'; red volumes: adventure and crime.

Albatross issued its books in a format that Hans Mardersteig designed after reading Leonardo da Vinci's unpublished reflections on the 'ideal page size'. In 1933, Holroyd-Reece met Allen to discuss the possibility of an Albatross–Bodley partnership in which the firms would issue paperbound books in a common format and share printing costs. Powerful forces prevented this tie-up: problems with copyright; the rise of Nazism in Germany; and, inherited from his uncle, Allen's allergy to partnerships. But Allen gave an Albatross book, and one from its sister firm Tauchnitz, to Stan Olney, The Bodley Head's trade manager, and asked him to work with Arnold (before he left for the Museum) on a costing for the reprint series at the Woolworths–Shaw price-point of sixpence. For months, Olney and Arnold studied print costs and paper orders, poking and prodding figures until a profitable number popped out.

In the light of these backstories, Allen's picturesque railway tale fades away into the apocryphal. The 'garage myth' is a theme in the literature on start-ups, and especially IT start-ups that went on to greatness. The myth imagines a small group of founders – sometimes as few as one – labouring in rustic conditions towards something remarkable. Steve Jobs, Steve Wozniak and Ronald Wayne creating Apple, for example, or Bill Gates and Paul Allen creating Microsoft. The garage entrepreneur is pictured as slogging away like a poet in a garret, through isolated and inspired moments of creation. The myth characteristically downplays the influence of factors outside the garage – other collaborators, the wider milieu and earlier innovations. Allen's railway story provides the garage myth for the Lanes' reprint series.

The series' real origins were more democratic and less romantic: the Arnold–Young and Albatross–Tauchnitz currents flowed into the bath at Talbot Square where they were filtered and channelled by the Lane brothers' own toe-dipping deliberations. Made more urgent by the decline of their uncle's firm, the brothers' own thoughts and plans coloured and scented the blended currents, which were warmed up by Shaw's public call to action. The brothers also sought advice from their friends, such as Ethel Mannin and Ben Travers, and from trusted industry colleagues like Harold Raymond, Robert Lusty and Raymond Hazell. The idea, when it solidified, was this: the Lane syndicate would produce a series of books in the Albatross format – bright typographical paper covers, the da Vinci–Mardersteig page size, colour-coded genres – at the price of six pork pies from Peter Cables, and with a mixture of out-of-copyright and in-copyright titles that would be sourced from The Bodley Head and other publishers. The brothers would create a new Albatross. A British Albatross. A Lane Albatross.

GETTING HOME

P lanning for the reprint series electrified the Lane brothers and the younger staff at The Bodley Head. Pivotal to the plan was a brand name or trademark that would engage booksellers and the reading public, distinguish the reprint series from routine Bodley Head titles, and create something new that the brothers could call their own and – if things got too bleak at the old firm – take away. The brothers' branding discussion extended from the Talbot Square think-tank to Vigo Street, where it spilled out across the office. To bring the discussion to a head, the brothers convened a final conference around a meeting table. Edward Young was there, along with other members of the editorial and sales staff. Underneath a lot of back-and-forth and round-and-round that lasted several hours, this seminal session was two things: a wide trawl to gather a long list of potential names, and a rugged process of creative opposition to determine the survival of the fittest mascot – to find a winning brand.

Holroyd-Reece's Albatross was naturally the starting point for the long list. What comparable creature – real or imaginary – might best serve as title, logo and emblem for the Lanes' new venture? First on the list was dolphin, borrowed from Bristol's municipal crest. Phoenix was also suggested, along with kiwi, camel and great auk. Allen came up with woodpecker. Richard fossicked around in his mind for other suitable creatures. From Leigh Woods he plucked rooks, wrens and starlings. From the voyage on the *Bendigo*, he remembered flying fish, whales and petrels. Cape Town connoted warlike grey squirrels, peace-loving brown squirrels and, at Lion's Head, beetles and giant grasshoppers. Blue-tongue lizards, goannas and magpies leapt from the roadside at Renmark. Richard Abdy's lake offered up its cormorants and, finally, its giant pike. And then there was the uncanny fox, sitting on the bough of a tree, that Richard and John had seen on the Lane family plot at Falfield.

For many reasons, penguins were in several minds at the meeting. Like the albatross, they flourished in the Southern Ocean. The ultra-modern penguin enclosure at the London Zoo had opened in 1934, its affable inhabitants featuring prolifically in the press. In 1925, The Bodley Head had issued Anatole France's *Penguin Island*. Tudor published Stuart Palmer's *The Penguin Pool Murder* in 1933 with a striking black penguin blocked on the cover. As the supposed 'missing link' between birds and fish, penguins were also a mainstay of bogus palaeontology. There were penguin-branded chocolate bars and sports teams, and 'Squeak the Penguin' was one third of the much loved comic-strip *Pip, Squeak and Wilfred*. In various other forms, penguins had colonised the popular imagination, and around the conference table at Vigo Street they were on the tips of several tongues. Numerous people later claimed, or were claimed, to have come up with the idea. Allen maintained that his secretary, Joan Coles, first suggested the flightless swimming bird, but Richard put that down as another of Allen's myths, remembering instead the collective process of trial and error. One thing is certain: Allen Lane did not think of the penguin himself.

After finalising the long-list, the conference scrutinised the candidates for positive and negative echoes. This process of free association – familiar now to all big industrial firms and advertising agencies – bridges marketing and psychoanalysis. Step one: look blankly at the potential brand name. Step two: play with it. Freely associate. Document phonic and syntactic resonances. With a few stretches, it is possible to reconstruct how the thinking might have progressed at Vigo Street.

Dolphin was quickly out; it had already been used. Phoenix too was out; it had risen at Chatto. Woodpecker, kiwi, camel and great auk were all easy to dismiss as flaccid, obscure, unfriendly or extinct. What about penguins? They were better suited than dolphins to reproduction in black ink. The creatures themselves are gawky, comical, inelegant (on land) and highly vulnerable to predators. Certainly polar, but warm nonetheless, and much friendlier than camels. British interest in penguins was shared across the Atlantic, where American animators and commercial artists had rendered the stylised black-and-white plumage as an indelible tuxedo. This lent the bird a permanent formality that was immediately undermined by its lateral flippers, a waddling gait and the delightful absurdity of an Antarctic bird riding – in fashionable attire befitting a Lane brother – the metropolitan cocktail-party circuit.

A blank look at the word itself. From the prefix pen-, follow pendragon on an eventful writerly journey through penury to the penitentiary and ultimately penance. Emotional resonances: sanguine, and also pensive. Syllabic: from a Sino-phonic beginning in peng, ping and pin, into murkier gu-goo and ui-wee, and on to a winning terminus.

Most resonances were good but there were some infelicities. Parrot, a short alliteration away, suggested screeching and thoughtless mimicry. There were hints of whine and pidgin in the alphabet soup, and – though the name was easy to remember – for some reason people would insist on spelling penguin as 'penquin' (and later pelican as 'pelikan'). But, in 1934, the word did not yet have its Australian flavour of youthful iconoclastic anger, nor its American connotations of super-villainy. (Two other famous Hollywood penguins of the future were even further off: *Toy Story*'s lovable and fretful Wheezy the Penguin, and *Fight Club*'s icy, inner-cave-dwelling penguin power-animal.) The Vigo Street committee agreed unanimously that penguin's resonances were, on balance, strongly positive. From the same word-map of homonyms, synonyms and other associations, imitators would soon catch mermaid, bluebird, falcon, bantam, cygnet (signet), toucan, pan, panther, paladin, hippo, jackdaw, brolga and many other book-worthy game. The Lanes and their staff would themselves find porpoise, puffin, pelican, peacock, peregrine and ptarmigan.

The rhyming echo in 'penguin' of the antithetical 'Unwin' would have brought smiles to the brothers' faces. What better way to answer the staunchest critic of the Lanes' mass-market paperbacks? And what better name for a venture conceived in a bath? The brothers sent Edward Young to the zoo to sketch penguins. It was a hot day and Young complained loudly that the birds 'stank'. Returning from the malodorous mission, he presented the Lanes with his drawings. Only then was the name for the series finally settled upon.

Young was one of several chroniclers of these foundational moments and Allen's role in them:

> Allen was a man who didn't think of ideas himself but was very quick to latch on to somebody else's suggestions. He was always very persevering in following up the notes he made, usually on the back of an envelope, and of course he would look at all ideas and start things moving, and then on most of them he would go cold and then other people had to unscramble things for him. People would ring up and try to get hold of him, and he wasn't in, and other people had to do the apologizing. But certainly he was very quick to pick up ideas and look at them from a publishing point of view, to see whether they suited him, and whether there was any money in them.

Throughout the 1930s, Richard was Allen's principal unscrambler. In 1934, Richard checked Olney and Arnold's costings, and produced more of his own. He drafted a contract that offered authors a low royalty: a farthing per copy or a pound per thousand, with the total royalty bounded between twenty-five and fifty pounds. With these royalties, Richard reasoned, a cheap reprint series could be made to work by exploiting the simple calculus of print runs: as the number of copies increased, the cost of printing each book fell, and other costs like overheads and advertising could be spread more thinly over a larger number of units. With Richard's royalties, Penguin would operate within the copyright system and sell into British and American territories, unlike Continent-bound Albatross. This gave Penguin a larger market and, with the benefit of larger print runs, the ability to undercut Albatross. Like an old two-way highway newly paralleled by a four-laner, Albatross would soon see its market disappear.

*

The timing of Penguin's hatching was important. Readers had already seen reprint series – such as Dent's Everyman Classics, Grant Richards' World's Classics, Bohn's Shilling Library and Collins's Pocket Classics – which offered varying degrees of cheapness in price and production, and achieved varying degrees of success. But 1934 was a year of change.

Though Britain was inching its way out of the Depression era, the economic slump had softened-up printers, booksellers and authors to accept terms they would have baulked at a decade earlier. Old relationships and powers were breaking down. The middle class was growing, and along with it the reading public. In many industries, there was an openness to new products and business models, many of them influenced by American capitalism. Technical as well as social factors were important. Achieving legibility in small books had been a problem since Caxton; the proposed Penguin cost structure was only possible because of book-world innovations such as machine typesetting; more precise and economical black-and-white printing; the ability to print durable card covers cheaply in bright colours; and new paper stocks that used pulp and grass instead of relatively expensive rags. Near-universal literacy was another enabler.

In an act of what S.H. Steinberg called 'commercial heraldry', Edward Young worked up his penguin drawings into a logo to be used on a dummy book that the Lanes could show to booksellers. The first Penguin logo looked unfinished, like a student rough. The left-facing, potato-shaped bird is hunched, furtive, almost sinister, its beady eye avoiding the viewer's gaze. In contrast, the polished Albatross mark had a clean stylish symmetry. Only after several years of fast and loose experimentation – in which penguins appeared variously rampant, statant and sejant erect – did the Penguin logo reach its elegant potential: with a crisper and clearer eye, and a cleaner, more symmetric profile – more pear-shaped than potato-like. For the mock-up's cover, Young produced a simple layout with vexil blocks of colour and bold titling in a serifless font designed by Eric Gill, the artist and typographer who had supplied the cover decoration for *Ulysses* and had collaborated with Edward Johnston to signpost London's Underground. The new books adopted an Albatross-style colour-code: orange covers for novels, green for crime, blue for biography and so on. (Red made more sense for crime, but would have taken the copying of Albatross to an uncomfortable extreme.)

For the books' insides, the brothers selected ten safely saleable titles from ten safe authors – Agatha Christie, Susan Ertz, Ernest Hemingway, Eric Linklater, Compton Mackenzie, André Maurois, Beverley Nichols, Dorothy L. Sayers, Mary Webb and E.H. Young – several of whom were personal friends of the Lanes. Another friend, the publisher Jonathan Cape, cooperated by allowing Penguin to use the paperback rights for six of the ten titles. Though privately he wished the venture well, Cape's public line was that Penguin would certainly fail, and 'I thought I'd take four-hundred quid off you before you did'. Chatto and Benn provided a title each, and the remaining two came from The Bodley Head. According to Richard's costings, the brothers needed to sell 17,000 copies of each of the ten titles just to break even; he called this quantity his 'getting home' figure. Sales at that level were a massive ask, however, as most new books at the time were lucky to sell a few thousand copies, and the first Penguin titles had already been offered to the public in different clothes. But, in the spirit of 'go hard or go home', the brothers went in hard, commissioning Hazell, Watson & Viney to print 20,000 copies of the first titles – a founding colony of 200,000 Penguins. To fund the gamble, Richard negotiated a loan with the London Cocks Biddulph branch of Martins Bank.

Certainly there were glitches (problems with copyright and production) and flaws (the unfinished logo and the cobbled typography with too many changes in typeface, point-size and orientation). But the Penguins' bones, flesh and plumage harmonised into a pulsating whole. Clean and modern titling; bright covers ideal for mass display; household-name authors. The dominant impression of the package was one of cheerfulness, and if anyone was responsible for injecting good cheer it was Richard Lane. For the first Penguins, Richard was editor, sales manager, production adviser and chief financial officer. John continued to manage exports, and he and Allen did a bit of everything. In this environment, Richard's reserves of cheer were deep: he was working alongside his brothers; thanks to Annie's legacy he was, financially, in clover; he was building an engaging and promising career that suited him infinitely better than growing Doradillos or droving sheep; and he was living his bookman dream. Towards the planning and the management of Penguin, he directed the upbeat informality he had learnt in Australia. Richard's casual good cheer buoyed the brothers' deliberations and nourished the fledgling imprint.

Low-cost production of the reprint series had one important proviso: the low costs would be irrelevant if most or all of the books could not be sold. Mass production demanded mass distribution and mass retailing. New sales and distribution channels would need to be dug, and the most would need to be made of each brother's expertise in display, marketing, promotion, sales and logistics, so that the imprint's contagious good cheer could reach bookshops and readers. Using the contacts he had made on his World Tour, John built an efficient export department, powered by a precious Rolodex of cards and a subscription order system. Knowing all the export houses and foreign booksellers personally, he sent each of them the quantity of Penguins that he was sure they could sell – or so he told them. This bluffing method succeeded brilliantly; Richard could not recall a single complaint that too many books had been sent.

Allen toured England and Scotland, seeking orders from British booksellers, many of whom were highly sceptical about the new series and its proponents. Richard again concentrated on London, where booksellers knew and trusted him, but still the books met with a mixed reception. The most wary booksellers feared that the venture could destroy the book trade. How could retailers of sixpenny paperbacks retain their profit margins? How could they keep selling other books at the old prices? But enlightened booksellers like Wilson of Bumpus and Eliott of Selfridges grasped the core of the concept, and saw what offering high-quality literature at a highly accessible price would mean for readers and for the future size of the reading public. The shop window that once hosted the mesmerising pancake machine now displayed a raft of Penguins.

When Allen returned to London, the brothers tallied their orders. Richard had had more luck than Allen and John in securing orders, but the total came to only 70,000 copies, far below the target of 200,000. The first titles went on sale just before the August bank holiday, which Richard spent with friends and a summer cold at a Norfolk farm, miserably pondering the failure of the reprint venture and drowning his sorrows, and his cold, in audit ale. He readied himself to consign Penguin to the file of failed experiments that now housed cider-making, fruit growing, Shakespearean acting and the Renmark–Adelaide car service. Allen, too, was outwardly dejected, telling his closest friends in the trade that Penguin had flopped.

Failure was not assured, however. The brothers hoped customers might warm to the books once they saw them in shops, and furthermore that reader enthusiasm would drive bookshops to order more. On that wet holiday in August, readers did indeed come to the rescue. 'As soon as the books went on display, the public wanted them. Orders were just fantastic.' People were not just buying Penguins, they were collecting them. The Lanes also had another secret weapon. E. Clifford Prescott was the fancy-goods buyer at Woolworths, Britain's largest chain-store. Unlike the Silly Symphonies, the reprint venture was tailor-made to suit Woolworths' sixpence price-point. Prescott had an open-door policy for new products; Allen called on him at his Mayfair office and showed him the first ten Penguins. Prescott in turn showed them to his wife. 'She studied the authors and titles carefully and announced that she had not read a single one but that, at a price of sixpence, she would have no hesitation in buying the lot.' Prescott trialled the books at a few of his stores, before coming back with a 'consignment order'; Allen did not know what that meant but, always quick on his feet, said he and his brothers could accept any order.

Back in the office, he telephoned a friendly sales manager at Collins – Sydney Goldsack – and asked him what a consignment order was. Richard recorded the answer: 'Sydney explained that it was an order that was sent to practically every one of their stores. "About how many books would it be?" asked Allen. "It's hard to say," replied Sydney. "It could be anywhere between fifty and a hundred thousand."' The order turned out to be for just over 60,000 copies and Penguin was not a flightless bird after all.

The single Woolworths consignment very nearly matched all the previous Penguin orders combined, including exports. The main danger now was not a lack of subscriptions but a failure to fulfil them. If the Woolworths order was not supplied by the looming deadline, it would lapse. In total, the brothers had sold-in about 140,000 copies but, out of prudence, had sent only about half that number to be bound. Frantically they press-ganged another printer to help Hazells with the binding. Soon, the brothers were ordering second and third printings, and planning the second and third tranches of titles. Sales reached the heady velocity of one Penguin every ten seconds.

To house the hectic new venture in a space away from The Bodley Head, the brothers leased a small office at 204 Great Portland Street, above a car showroom, but 'all the serious work' was done nearby in the crypt beneath Holy Trinity Church on Euston Road. After taking over the lease from Dunlop Tyres, The Bodley Head had stored its overstocks in the crypt. Now Penguin used the premises for storage, packing, despatch, invoicing and nearly everything else. Richard ensured no cubic inch of room was wasted. 'Around the walls of the crypt were bricked-in coffins with a brass plate in front giving the name and particulars of the occupant. One of these spaces was vacant so we used it to store the firm's books and petty cash.'

*

The crypt at Holy Trinity became a Penguin totem but not an Allen totem. He seldom went there, preferring instead to hobnob with his contacts and receive visitors at Great Portland Street. In those early years, during the most intensive periods of work in which every available hand was enlisted to help out, Allen tended to be overseas, or touring in the country, or on a health retreat, or otherwise unavailable. But his brothers threw themselves into the venture. John on his World Tour and Richard in Australia and Egypt had built stamina and learnt follow-through. In the first Penguin years, the younger Lane brothers did the heavy lifting, supported by fewer than twenty employees – a blend of new recruits and borrowed Bodley Headers. In the crypt, Richard and John worked shoulder to shoulder with an all-male staff with whom they built a strong bond; they went to weddings and came to know the men's families. Bill Rapley, Peter Kite, Bob Maynard, Stan Olney, Ashton Allen, Jack Summers and Eric Muspratt were some of the men who kept up with Richard and John and who would feature prominently in the new imprint's history. Liveliness and optimism collaborated with nude pin-ups to brighten the dark crypt. The newly assembled Penguin team more than surpassed the records for non-stop work set in Egypt by Richard and Hubert Hine.

At the start of each day, the team entered the crypt via an unsafe electric hoist – controlled by a piece of rope – that had previously lowered coffins. 'If pulled hard, the hoist went up, and when let go it stopped, but if pulled lightly it went down, so if one was taking up a load of books and on reaching ground level one slackened the pull on the rope, the load would immediately drop back. There were two metal ends to the hoist but no front or back and controlling it took quite a lot of getting used to.' A curtain could be dropped to cover the glamour-girl pictures should Holy Trinity's vicar ride the creaking hoist down for a visit. The packing bench was beneath a metal grille directly in front of the altar. Loud noises tended to escape through the grille. During an afternoon wedding, when the priest asked the bride, 'Wilt thou take this man to be thy lawful husband,' a packer hit his thumb with a wooden mallet, and the groom received an unexpectedly blunt and masculine response. 'The language ... was very profane and very loud and could be heard by the priest, bride and bridegroom, and, in fact, most of the congregation.' A verger hurried down, the girly pictures disappeared behind the curtain and the packers moved their bench.

Shaped like an inverted squarish doughnut, the crypt stored coffins in its outer walls and in a central brick column. With space at a premium, the team had to stack books on the column. When Bill Rapley, a 'staunch Catholic', climbed to the top to move some books, the bricks gave way and 'he fell right on top of a coffin with sufficient force to smash it open'. In a cloud of dust and the bones of a West Indian official, Rapley crossed himself frantically. Mice were another problem. Richard sent the office boy to buy a dozen mousetraps. The next morning, 'the first trap examined was empty, the next ten each had a mouse and the twelfth had two'. Working at night was difficult enough in the creepy crypt surrounded by coffins and moaning pipes, but the mice added another dimension of disgustingness. The rodents would appear 'in the middle of the night when you were writing invoices or something. Rapley used to cross himself like mad!' Books stored among the coffins for any appreciable time 'got a crypt smell that lasted for years'. The first Penguin books smelt of rubber, mice and death. Sanitation was another drawback. The crypt had no water or toilet facilities. A bucket was provided for ready use, and 'was emptied every night, preferably after dark, on the churchyard'. The nearest WC – another penny-in-the-slot affair – was at the underground station on Great Portland Street: Richard gave each staff member each week the price of a Penguin as lavatory money.

In preparation for the next big push, the Lanes installed a fairground slide so that book parcels delivered at street level could reach the crypt floor in seconds. Richard and John and other members of the core team again worked around the clock for several days – hard work in mousy, rubbery, airless conditions. 'We did everything – invoicing, packing, stacking, and if in the early hours of the morning we started to get drowsy, our remedy was to try and run up the wooden slippery slide.' When Nora Williams-Lane came to help out in the crypt, the packers dropped the curtain again and she rolled up her sleeves. On the occasions that Allen visited, he made clear to everyone that he would rather be somewhere else. The office boy, Bob Davies, described Allen on such a visit as 'dark, slight, clipped and very, very abrupt, as if he hadn't got a second to live'. During the month that all records were broken for hours of work in the crypt, Allen decided that he was getting 'corpulent' and arranged to spend a fortnight at Tring, 'living on water with, as a special treat once a day, a slice of lemon'. This diet made him even more cranky.

He also continued to seek astrological advice. Evangeline Adams told him, 'There is little to indicate that you should go into business for yourself.' But Kate Murray of Decoy Avenue seems, with all the perspicacity of a good analyst or life-coach, to have divined his essence.

> You appear to be much more fixed and determined than you are ...
> You are rather inclined to waver and be indecisive ... You will meet
> with many changes in your life, and you will generally find that you
> will be assisted by someone at all important moments in your career.
> Although you are exceptionally forceful and energetic, you seem to
> need the stimulation of another person's mind and character to do
> your best work. And there will nearly always be someone to afford
> that. Hence you will not stand alone and create your own destiny but
> the help and advice of some other person will be of great service to you.

Concluding that Allen was inclined to be reckless and impulsive, she also noted his competitiveness and his winning ways in business. 'The termination of your transactions will always be for your good.' Allen found disconcerting the astrologer's advice about stimulation from another and not standing alone. Could he never be a great leader in his own right? Murray wrote to elaborate, delivering not quite the answer Allen had hoped for.

> Now in this question of not working with others, it is better for one of
> your temperament to be to a certain extent in command but united

with someone who has the internal definiteness that you lack. You see, you sound much stronger than you are, therefore you want in business to be allied with someone whose opinion is very definite, even if it is not always the same as yours.

In command only 'to a certain extent', and only if 'united' and 'allied' with another? Not as strong as he seemed to be? All very worrying. Murray finished by saying, 'I do not think you will ever get very stout, but people with your signs generally have to be rather careful in their diet.' At least Allen was on the right track with all that fasting.

Within four days of the bank-holiday launch, the firm had sold 150,000 Penguins; within four months, sales reached one million; within a year, they surpassed three million, equivalent to more than six hundred tons of paper. On New Year's Day 1936, the brothers formed a new company, Penguin Books Limited, with three owner-directors: Allen, Richard and John Lane. In Penguin's first two years, Richard drew no salary – the same as in Egypt, less than in Moorook. John, too, drew no salary, while Allen received £1000 in each of the first two years. In his third year at Penguin, Allen would draw £10,000.

AN AIR OF FRIENDLINESS

Penguin was, of course, not just a Lane venture but a Bodley Head venture as well. Words printed on the covers and title pages of the first Penguins claimed them for the firm that had published *The Yellow Book* and Oscar Wilde. By 1936, the three Lane brothers were the sole directors of both The Bodley Head and its feathered progeny. The parent firm might have been an ideal platform on which the young publishers could experiment, but in the mid-1930s the platform was rapidly giving way. Understandably, the Lanes directed their efforts and attention to the new imprint; the new chick needed their help, it was something they had created, and it held more promise than the tired enterprise they had inherited. In May 1936, the brothers took the inevitable step of placing The Bodley Head into voluntary receivership. On the rare occasions that Allen as managing director had to handle the old firm's business, he steered clear of Vigo Street – there was the real and present danger of being served with an unpaid invoice or, worse still, a writ – so Joan Coles resorted to meeting him at his club.

Though the shares Allen inherited from Annie had strategic value in his fight with the old guard, their financial value was zero. In its final years, the unprofitable firm could pay no dividends, and when ultimately it was liquidated all its shareholders lost out (as did its creditors). For this reason, among the three brothers, Allen benefited least – in strictly monetary terms – from the Lane inheritance.

An Unwin-led consortium of the Lanes' competitors would soon revive the Bodley Head imprint. For Allen and Richard and John, though, there was no time to shed tears over the loss of Uncle John's firm; readers and the publishing industry buzzed over the sprightly, successful Penguin. The brothers bought a yacht and naturally called it *Penguin*. Richard wrote a short story, 'The Maiden Voyage of the *Penguin*'. ('We slipped our moorings and, as there was no wind, we started the engine and chugged our way out to the open sea. The tide was on the make, the sun shining, it was beautifully calm and everybody was cheerful – the skipper, the navigator, the cook and I.') And just as the Lanes had copied Albatross, so the steroidal success of the new imprint attracted a flock of imitators. Knock-offs sprang up in Britain, Italy, France, India and in North and South America. Hutchinson's Pocket Library copied Penguin's stripes, format, binding, dust jackets, typefaces, layout and price. Secker and Warburg's Searchlight Books copied everything except the stripes and the price. The brothers worried that the imitators would get so close that they might eat into Penguin's market. The as yet unclaimed name 'pelican' was a particular vulnerability: people were misaddressing correspondence to 'Pelican' and asking for 'Pelicans' in shops when they meant Penguins. The brothers would jump on the Pelican brand as soon as they had an opportunity to use it.

George Bernard Shaw was pleased with the thriving Penguin he had helped father. He sent the Lanes a postcard saying they ought to publish an Antarctic book under their Antarctic imprint. Written by Shaw's next-door neighbour Apsley Cherry-Garrard, *The Worst Journey in the World* told the story of Scott's last expedition to the South Pole. Allen again demonstrated his quickness on his feet. The brothers would happily pursue the rights for *Worst Journey*, he replied, but what they especially wanted was Shaw's *Intelligent Woman's Guide to Socialism and Capitalism*. True to his words in the *Bookseller* about jumping at the chance to be on sale in Woolworths, Shaw accepted the proffered low royalty and went so far as to enhance the book by appending two topical sections on Sovietism and Fascism. Such timely non-fiction would be ideal for a sister imprint to Penguin, called Pelican. Richard recorded the birth. 'We decided to make a new series, all non-fiction, gave them a new colour light blue, very different from the biographical blue, and appointed an editor.'

In the dying days of Ronald Boswell's Bodley Head directorship, he had hired serious-minded and serious-looking V.K. Krishna Menon to read manuscripts and advise on the non-fiction Twentieth Century Library. Ascetic to the point of emaciation, Menon reputedly slept on a bed of nails, appeared 'as if he had stepped out of the tomb of Tutan-khamen', and maintained throughout his life the disconcerting habit of announcing his imminent death. In addition to Menon as Pelican editor, the brothers also appointed three editorial advisers for the new series: William Emrys Williams, Secretary of the British Institute of Adult Education; Professor H.L. Beales, Lecturer in Economic History at the London School of Economics; and Sir Peter Chalmers-Mitchell, recently head of the London Zoo!

The revised edition of the *Intelligent Woman's Guide* became, in two volumes, the first and second Pelicans, and an immediate success: 'book-sellers were arriving at the Penguin stock rooms in taxis, filling them up with Shaws and rushing back to satisfy the insatiable demand for the new Pelicans.' Cherry-Garrard's book also appeared, in two volumes, as a Penguin in 1937. The author wrote, 'I am glad the *Worst Journey* is com-ing out in Penguins: after all it is largely about penguins. How it can be done at this price with three maps is beyond me.' The *Daily Worker* lik-ened the arrival of 'really cheap' Pelicans to 'the discovery of printing . . . Slowly the best of modern literature will be coming into the hands of any man who wants it, and in the process man himself is going to be changed.'

Pelican's cost structure may have been a mystery but one thing was obvious to everyone: Allen and Menon were very different men, who would soon lose patience with each other's manners and methods. When Allen's tolerance ran out, he resorted to a tactic of freezing. He stopped answering Menon's letters and made decisions even more gla-cially and casually than usual. After this experience and a final bruising exit – the 1938 edition of Sigmund Freud's *Totem and Taboo* would be his last Pelican – Menon famously came to dislike anyone who reminded him of Allen: English publishers; Englishmen; English speakers; Euro-peans; whites. Menon figured prominently in the geopolitics of the coming decades as a key thinker and adviser in the Indian independ-ence movement, and from one point of view it could be argued that Allen's operating style had had its own curiously significant impact on the future of the Empire and the history of the world.

The Lanes' burgeoning sixpenny venture soon faced problems of supply and demand. On the demand side, the imprint hungered for more books to sell. On the supply side, it suffered from a glut of ideas. Readers deluged the firm with suggestions and requests, while authors pressed their own publishers to negotiate their books' appearance in Penguin plumage. Authors received only modest royalties from such appearances, but sales figures in the tens and hundreds of thousands for individual Penguin and Pelican titles offered writers a terrific boost.

To reconcile hunger and glut, Richard initiated a series of literary meetings at a Spanish restaurant in, of all places, Beak Street. Though they covered Penguin and Pelican titles, the meetings at the Barcelona were always called 'Pelican meetings'. Over a lunch highly recommended by A.J.A. Symons, the literary trio of Richard Lane, Lance Beales and Bill Williams started with sherry before moving on to flagons of Spanish wine. The flagons had a long narrow spout from which the drinker was supposed to pour wine into his mouth. 'We nearly always attempted this but ended by using glasses,' Richard recalled. In a system that quickly became a tradition, the committee arranged for a van to drop off at the Barcelona the week's intake of books, manuscripts and letters suggesting titles and ideas for books. 'We would work our way through these during lunch and I should think the fate of many books depended on at what stage of lunch they came up for discussion. I am certain our amiability increased with the amount of tinto we had consumed.' Allen and other senior colleagues – including secretary-cum-editor Eunice Frost – would soon join the meetings which, despite their informality, established the editorial policies and character that defined the new company.

Edward Young joined Penguin's small staff at Great Portland Street to manage design and production. Jean Osborne signed on as secretary and quickly fell in love with Richard – 'a dear' – and John – 'twinkly'. Allen, though, was frequently 'heartless' and made her feel dowdy and uncomfortable. Jean would only be with the new firm for a little while; the turnover of secretaries was high in the first Penguin years. Most work continued to be done at the crypt, where the rent was cheap – £200 a year and no rates – but the cramped, scary, verminous, airless, toiletless conditions could only ever be temporary. When Richard and John approached the Marylebone Town Hall for permission to install a bathroom, the council sent an official to investigate. 'He made a thorough inspection and spoke to several members of the staff. When he came into the office he told us it was impossible to install sanitation and, but for the fact that the staff were happy, he would have no hesitation in condemning the premises. He finished by saying that he had never heard of Penguin Books, had never inspected the premises and had never spoken to us, but do please get out as soon as possible.'

*

The Lanes decided they would purpose-build new premises outside London. Covering thousands of miles, Richard drove the brothers' Morris Cowley in search of suitable land for a new office and warehouse. This he eventually found at Harmondsworth, about fifteen miles from London, and he arranged to buy 'three and a bit acres for just over £2,000. The land was growing cabbages at the time and we had to pay an extra £200, being the estimated value of the crop. This really hurt me: not only could I not sell the cabbages – I couldn't give them away!' Samuel Williams-Lane laid the foundation stone on his birthday in 1937.

In the meantime, Richard and John established a new routine in which they would work all night at the crypt, find somewhere for breakfast at six in the morning, return to the flat for a shave and a bath, then row around Regents Park Lake for half an hour of fresh air before returning to the coffins and Penguins. Allen avoided this regimen and the crypt. Richard explained his elder brother's absence: 'Allen did not join us on these expeditions as he had decamped to Champneys for three weeks' slimming. The first day he had two salads, the second, one fruit dish, the next seventeen, nothing, the twentieth, one fruit dish, and the twenty-first, two salads. The result was that he lost over twenty-one pounds, but when he returned to work he couldn't cope with the hours that John and I were working.'

The brothers were running Penguin under the new corporate entity when their accountants pointed out an oversight: the founding capital was stated as £100, but this sum had never been paid. When thieves broke into the Gables at Falfield, they stole just over a hundred pounds' worth of Richard's things; he used the cheque from the insurance company to pay up the new firm's capital with his own money. 'So it can truthfully be stated that the finances of Penguin Books were founded on the proceeds of a burglary,' he wrote.

Perversely, the insurance proceeds came at a useful time. The demands of the new firm and the construction of its new premises had squeezed the brothers' finances. As the squeeze intensified, Richard called regularly on Mr Shankland, the firm's bank manager at Martins, to raise more cash. Shankland shared a large office with another manager; 'after they had dealt with the morning's mail, they liked to glance at the *Times* crossword, so on days when I had an appointment at the bank, I would spend as much time as possible on the crossword'. Richard's usual opening gambit was something like, 'Have you got one across yet?' He hoped this would inject 'an air of friendliness' into what were often awkward discussions.

Good relations with Martins owned much to Richard's Australian car-service days. Another outlet for Richard's casual good cheer, the meetings with Mr Shankland depended on expertise first developed on an Adelaide layover spent solving crosswords. At the time, Richard wrote to his family, 'I have still to find out "a golden eagle", four letters, with YL in the middle (-YL-) or it might be (-LY-). [The puzzles] are the craze now and everybody is "crosswording". They certainly are very instructive and bring fresh and unusual words to one's notice.'

To bring more fresh words to people's notice, the brothers commenced a series of Penguin Specials – shortish books on topical issues, such as Hitlerism and communism. More akin to journalism than typical book publishing, Specials had to be produced even more rapidly than normal Penguin and Pelican titles, and they stretched still further the team in the crypt. In February 1938, the brothers commissioned a French journalist, Geneviève Tabouis, to write a Special called *Blackmail or War*. When she came to London to discuss final points about the book, Allen was unavailable but Richard arranged to meet her, arming himself with a plan for what he hoped would be the perfect expense-account lunch with a sophisticated French woman of letters. Venue: Hyde Park Hotel. Drinks: 'Perhaps not a Dry Martini if we were going to have some really good wines so we might settle for a Tio Pepe, my favourite dry sherry.' Dinner: Oysters or smoked salmon, 'better wait until we had looked at the menu'. With coffee: 'I would have either a Kummel or Brandy Benedictine and of course a cigar and I would offer her either Turkish or Egyptian cigarettes but perhaps being a journalist she would prefer Gauloise Bleu.' The plan failed when Madame Tabouis turned out to be a teetotal non-smoking vegetarian. After lunch the final text of *Blackmail or War* was agreed, and the book went from manuscript to set type in record time. Richard sent a member of the production staff to the printer near Bath to read the galleys and page proofs as they came off the press. The book was in shops before the end of the month. Selling 250,000 copies, it became Penguin's first really big bestseller.

A sister series – Pelican Specials – would soon follow in the mould of Penguin Specials, and both series would continue to set production records. To inaugurate a series of Penguin corporate Christmas events, the brothers hosted a dinner at Talbot Square. Richard did all the cooking: turkey, ham, roast potatoes, Brussels sprouts, Christmas pudding and mince pies. Then the party moved to Edgware Road. During the variety show at the Metropolitan, nearly every performer had been primed to mention the firm or its staff. Each time they did, 'this brought roars of applause and a good time was had by all'.

The first Penguin company visit to Paris set a new benchmark for ebullience.

We went via Newhaven–Dieppe. The firm paid the fare plus sleepers on the ferry plus one night's accommodation in Paris and one formal dinner ... One of our printers, I think it was Jackson, had printed posters to stick on the carriage window 'Reserved for Penguin Books' and also provided every member of the staff with a small round cardboard disc about the size of a penny to hang in our lapels. It depicted a Penguin but had no wording. During the course of the evening one Penguinite decided to visit a house of ill repute and when the girls were lined up for his inspection, one girl's clothes consisted of a pair of high heeled shoes and, around her neck, a Penguin medallion.

Swatchway and Kingfisher

I n 1937, the Williams-Lane family seat moved again, this time to a smaller and quieter home called The Warren (a name it shared with the Witherses' farm in Renmark) near the village of Ipsden in Oxfordshire. Though not a 'military family', the Williams-Lanes knew their way around the fringes of the fighting services and were not slow to step up when the occasion demanded. Samuel had fought in the Boer War, and during the First World War, in his fifties, he had joined the Special Constabulary and the Local Volunteers, in which capacity he guarded the Filton Aircraft Works and recorded the crews of ships arriving at Bristol. As Boy Scouts, the two elder Lane brothers promised, in the event of a night-time air raid, that they would shin up lamp-posts and turn off the gas, but they only ever did this in drills: they never saw a raid. Between the world wars, Allen joined the Surrey and Sussex Yeomanry before accepting a commission in the Essex Artillery. At Buckingham Palace for the commissioning ceremony, he lined up to be presented to the King. When Allen's turn came, his spurs locked, possibly due to that old weakness in his foot, and he skated six feet forward before stopping to salute the monarch.

Early in the summer of 1938, the Second World War loomed. Richard, then aged thirty-three, positioned himself for a suitable role in the services. The Navy was the obvious choice: he loved ships, his ancestors had been seafarers, and he took his middle name 'Grenville' from Sir Richard Grenville – the famous Devonian privateer and maritime explorer, cousin of Sir Walter Raleigh and Sir Francis Drake, who defended Devon and Cornwall against the Spanish Armada. Richard knew that, in the event of hostilities, members of the Royal Navy Volunteer Supplementary Reserve would be offered commissions in the Volunteer Reserve proper. He applied to the Admiralty and was asked to present at HMS *President* for an interview. As soon as he was on board he realised his 'appalling ignorance' of naval rank. 'I was quite willing to say "Sir" to a Chief Petty Officer wearing a couple of rows of medal ribbons and to be offhand to a Lieutenant Commander who was not displaying any ribbons.' A sceptical and serious Commander chaired the three-officer panel that conducted the interview.

> First I was asked why I wanted to join the R.N.V.S.R. and I replied quite truthfully that I thought that in the not-too-distant future there might be a war and that I preferred a blue uniform to a khaki one ... The Commander thought I was trying to be funny and said so. He had my application form in front of him and in looking through he noticed that I had mentioned that I had done a small amount of yachting.

'Do you own this yacht [the *Penguin*] in which you occasionally sail?' the Commander asked.

'Not exactly, it belongs jointly to my two brothers and myself,' said Richard.

'How big is it?'

'It's a ten ton cutter, 4.41 tons registered.'

'If the three of you go sailing together, how do you split up the work?'

'My elder brother Allen looks after the sails and ropes and all those kind of things. My younger brother John is the expert on navigation and charts and the engine, and I cook and catch fish, but I really like fishing best.'

'If your younger brother was not there, who would do the navigation?'

'Oh, Allen would, if there was no one else to do it.'

'Don't you ever?'

'No, I should be hopeless at that and anyhow I prefer fishing.'

'Can you take a bearing?'

'Well, yes, I have done that.'

'How do you take a bearing?'

'Well, you have a kind of compass thing, I suppose it really is a compass, and you look through a small hole on the side of it at a light-house or church or something and at the same time you can see what the compass reading is – then you look at the chart and see where the lighthouse or whatever it was is and you draw a line on the chart giving the same bearing that you saw on the compass, then you find another lighthouse or something and do the same thing again and where the two lines meet that's where you ought to be.'

'You seem somewhat vague about it. What would you do if you couldn't see any lighthouse or thing, and if neither of your brothers were there.'

'I really don't know as I would never go out without at least one of them, but I suppose if you sailed on long enough you would come to some kind of landmark that would be shown on the chart.'

'Do you know anything about buoys?'

'I am afraid not, at least not very much.'

'Where do you normally keep your yacht?'

'We have a mooring at Buckler's Hard.'

'Very nice too. Do you know the Needles?'

'Yes.'

'Good. Now if you were going back to Buckler's Hard from the Needles and you saw a black conical buoy, what would that signify?'

'I suppose some kind of channel or swatchway.'

'What would you do if you saw one?'

'Normally I suppose all I should do would be to tell my brother.'

'Now really, Lane, you are not being very helpful. What would you do if neither of your brothers were there?'

'I think I should look at the chart, it's quite likely there would be something there about buoys.'

'What would you do if you hadn't got a light and therefore you couldn't see the chart?'

'I doubt very much in that case if I could see the buoy, and certainly I shouldn't be able to see what colour it was.'

'Fair enough,' said the Commander, who agreed to pass Richard on the dubious strength of his answers (Richard was rather pleased with his use of 'swatchway'), but advised him to ask one of his brothers for lessons in navigation and pilotage.

On most weekends in the summer of 1938, John and Allen took the *Penguin* out for a sail. John sailed like he played tennis – too violently for Richard; 'the more alarming the angle at which the yacht heeled over, the more he enjoyed it, and taking in a reef must not be considered until the very last moment'. After the Munich crisis, Allen said to Richard, 'I guarantee you twelve months from today we shall be at war with Germany.' Though Allen could tolerate John's sharp tacks, he lacked his brothers' stamina. Now, with war around the corner and faced with the pressures of a front-line role in a hectic new enterprise, Allen's instinct was to flee. He would put publishing fully out of his mind for six months. Richard and John had the business in hand and should be more than capable of keeping Penguin on track. With Nora as a respectable travelling companion, Allen would explore the East, perhaps write a travel book (this he started but never finished) and visit countries that might soon be put out of reach.

His inner circle reacted to these plans with disbelief, but Allen was serious. The father of one of his girlfriends knew the Governor of Aden, who knew in turn 'nawabs, rajahs and maharajahs' in India. Late in December 1938, Allen and Nora boarded a P&O liner for Aden. After celebrating the Crown colony's centenary, they sailed to Bombay and from there toured the Subcontinent. Delhi, Lahore, Peshawar, Khyber, Darjeeling, Cochin, Colombo. For part of their stay in India, they were given use of a palace with a front-gate sentry, 'who turned out the guard and presented arms every time they left or arrived'. Allen saw the trip not only as a holiday from publishing and the threat of war but also as an escape from England and the Three Musketeers.

Talbot Square had been for ten years a Lane sacred site, but in 1939 the brothers' lease was running out and the journey from London to Harmondsworth was becoming a grind. Richard and John searched for a residence near Penguin's new headquarters. On Stanwell Moor, about two miles from the office, they found and bought Silverbeck, a large and dowdy Georgian house with seven bedrooms (Allen's was huge), two bathrooms (the Lanes naturally added a third), a sitting room, a dining room, a library-cum-billiard room, a cellar (where they installed central heating), nine acres of fields and gardens, an ornamental pool, an aviary, an oversized greenhouse (heated by a coke-fuelled boiler), a mushroom shed, giant walnut trees, a garage, a workshop, a potting shed, a tame kingfisher and nearly half a mile of frontage on the River Colne.

Chuffed with their new mansion, the two brothers scraped and polished the floors, redesigned the kitchen, and installed a four-oven Aga and a new hot-water service. They wrote asking Allen and Nora to buy Indian rugs. Richard and John moved in on a Saturday and gave a dinner party on the Sunday, 'just to show that it could be done'. During the brothers' first weeks at Silverbeck, they often disappeared to tinker with the hydraulic ram – a fascinating pressurised pump that fed the ornamental pool. For the ram to work efficiently, 'we had to get the water in the river as high as possible. This was controlled by a sluice which was operated by a very large wheel, but the snag was that if there was a decent stream of water flowing and we closed the sluice, then the water would flow over a pedestrian right of way on the other bank of the river, which upset the populace considerably, especially those who were taking this short-cut to the railway halt at Poyle.' The name of the halt was Poyle for Stanwell Moor, 'a magnificent description for a very small halt'.

Despite the books' astronomical sales, Penguin's cash situation was still tight, as was lending in the lead-up to the war. Frequent cables from Allen – 'HAVING A LOVELY TIME, PLEASE SEND FIVE HUNDRED POUNDS, BANK OF INDIA, RAWALPINDI' – did not help.

Well into 1939, Richard and John ran Penguin with energy and verve. 'We had tons of interesting work to do, seeing authors, literary agents, printers, booksellers, exporters.' There was no falling off in quality or speed, or in the Lane charm or their social schedule. The Penguin engine purred as smoothly as Richard's immortal Douglas. New titles and series bred even faster than the amorous budgerigars in Silverbeck's aviary. Without Allen around to overbear, or overshadow, the staff could better gauge the other brothers' characters and abilities, and better see the dotted line where one Lane stopped and another started. Despite the threat of war, the period of Allen's absence was a palmy time for the brothers and for Penguin. During the spring, Richard and John hosted their friends and authors at Silverbeck: 'being only a couple of miles from the office, it was just as easy to bring friends back for lunch instead of taking them to The Berkeley Arms', the nearest up-market pub.

Before Allen left, the three brothers had agreed to develop a series of pretty, colour-illustrated, non-fiction titles, modelled not on Albatross Verlag but on another Continental series, Insel Verlag's small-format, hard-bound monographs. Many in the Penguin team were sceptical that books of that kind could fit the mass-production, mass-distribution model the Lanes had engineered. Could they really sell 20,000 copies of titles pitched primarily at art enthusiasts and bibliophiles? Amid this scepticism, Allen asserted – with a disturbing lack of evidence – that the books would certainly succeed. Then he disappeared, leaving Richard and John and the staff and their printers with 'a plethora of minor and major technical problems still to be solved'. In 1937, after Victor Gollancz's Left Book Club turned down her application for administrative work, Eunice Frost had joined Penguin as another in a long line of secretaries. Tubercular, fractious, inenubilable – everyone called her Frosty, except to her face – she quickly demonstrated broader talents and, while still notionally a secretary, picked up senior responsibilities on the editorial and production sides of the firm. In Allen's absence, Richard Lane formed with Frost, John Lane, Bill Williams and Elizabeth Senior (a young and promising editor who had recently joined Penguin from the British Museum) a coalition to stop the new King Penguins from dying in the rookery.

The coalition chose two highly esteemed nineteenth-century works to be the first titles in the series: Pierre-Joseph Redouté's *Roses*, and John Gould's *Birds of Britain*, excerpted and recast under the title *British Birds on Lake, River and Stream*. Despite many necessary compromises in format and printing, the books achieved an unlikely success and formed the basis for one of the most loved and long-lived Penguin series. The first volumes sold so well in the United States that Penguin's manager there, Ian Ballantine, had to restrict their sale to New York City. But the King Penguin team would still suffer an unexpected tragedy early in the Second World War: the death, during an air raid, of Elizabeth Senior.

*

In late May 1939, Allen and Nora returned from Asia with forty bags and suitcases, dozens of rugs and ebony elephants, and a chest full of tea. When Allen again turned his mind to publishing, he was quickly thinking about America. Two years earlier, Richard had set up Penguin's first New York office, not in a subterranean crypt but a skyscraper – at 245 Fifth Avenue – and had taken other small steps to find a sustainable way to sell Penguins into US retailers. (Allen's biographer Jack Morpurgo claimed Richard went because Allen did not know enough about American sales techniques.) To protect the local industry, US trade authorities limited imports of books to 1500 copies of any given title, a level drastically too low for Penguin to work any kind of magic there. Copyright was another barrier to direct selling of British-made Penguins. Richard began feeling around for ways to leap over, or swim under, these barriers. One option, of course, was to make books inside America's borders – a costly exercise, and one with its own share of copyright difficulties. Another problem was taste. Promoting the Lanes' offspring to booksellers, Richard found that Americans did not immediately share Britain's enthusiasm for the birds' plain printed covers. Penguin in the US faced a fork in the road leading to two very different futures. In one of them, Penguin Inc. would stay small and perhaps become a bit-part player in a partnership or licensing agreement. In the other future, Penguin would have to go big, with its own staff, investors and sales network. In anticipation of a big American Penguin, Richard took the pulses of labour, capital and retailing in the US book trade, and studied the complex rules for trade and commerce in the headquarters of capitalism.

That was all in 1937; by 1939, things were moving very quickly in America, 'and not necessarily in a good direction' for Penguin. With a friendly kangaroo logo and striking full-colour covers, Robert de Graff's Pocket Books Inc. had started at the time of Richard's previous visit and was now coming on in leaps and bounds, with rival paperback imprints Avon and Dell not far behind. The Lanes decided they needed to return to America, to advance and formalise what Richard had started, and put the American Penguin on a sounder footing. The brothers agreed that John should be the one to go, on the strength of his international contacts, which had been further fortified by his work on the firm's export side.

Nora Lane was absorbed in an altogether different branch of ornithology. Frank Bird, of the armaments manufacturer Armstrong Whitworth, had suffered during Nora's absence in the Middle East and India. On her return, he proposed marriage, and she accepted. This was a significant event for her brothers. Not only did it bring an end to her time helping out with the young Penguin, it was also an end of sorts for the Lane children. Since their childhood in Bristol, the four had been an exceptionally tight crew. They had worked together, gossiped together, and enjoyed joint pleasures whenever they could. To many outside observers, the Lane foursome looked impenetrable and unbreakable. Now, by becoming engaged, Nora had somehow left the crew, and at the same time she had brought a non-Lane into its ranks. For years to come, Frank Bird, the man who broke up, and broke into, the Broomcroftian foursome, would be treated like a common burglar and (from Allen and John especially) would have to put up with an offhandedness that bordered on hostility.

John's first concrete response to his sister's engagement was to invite Nora to accompany him to America. She accepted, and John and Nora were there when war was declared in Europe. During the first days, the passenger steamer *Athenia* was tragically sunk, and Frank Bird worried about getting Nora back home. Competing and contradictory cables shot to and fro daily. 'COME BACK ON FIRST BOAT.' 'DON'T COME BACK UNTIL YOU HAVE FIXED UP CERTAIN BUSINESS.' 'AM COMING BACK AS SOON AS POSSIBLE.' Securing return passage was difficult, and it was not until the beginning of November that John and Nora returned to a Britain suspended in a blacked-out state of phony war. Frank's view of the brothers was as dim as London's nights: Allen had snatched Nora away for six months, and John had stranded her in the United States, then subjected her to a dangerous sea passage in wartime. After reuniting with his fiancée, Frank moved quickly to tie the knot before whisking his bride away to Newcastle upon Tyne. In 1941, they would be blessed with the arrival of their first child.

Expecting wartime petrol rationing, Allen and Richard bought bicycles to ride between Silverbeck and Harmondsworth. A government ministry asked them if, in the event of hostilities, they would be willing to let the government use the new factory. 'We asked what were the alternatives and the answer was that if we agreed we would be given as much notice as possible as to when it would be required. If we said no it would just be taken, so naturally we agreed.' Christmas 1939 passed 'quite happily' – the war was still largely phony. Allen and John left early in the New Year for a skiing holiday in France and Switzerland. Through government friends they obtained permission to visit the two defenders of France: the Maginot Line and the Allied Headquarters at Arras.

In the absence of his brothers, Richard Lane pulled off a remarkable coup. When he sold to an oil magnate 50,000 copies of David Low's cartoon book *Europe Since Versailles* – for the magnate to present as gifts to his 'friends' – the press applauded the transaction as Penguin's biggest retail sale to date and, probably, 'the largest retail sale ever made in the book business'. On returning to London, Allen whispered to Richard that John had not solved New York and that Richard should go and straighten things out. Richard asked the RNVR when he was likely to be called up; the Admiralty gave him a window of three or four months, so he applied for and received a permit to visit the States.

Sailing on the *Athenia*'s sister ship *Athenic*, he left for a two-month trip to do what could be done. John had set up a subsidiary entity, Penguin Books Inc., under US corporate law. Working long days, Richard took John's entity forward by formalising its governing policies and establishing the systems that would guide it, hopefully for the benefit of the English parent. Richard Lane liked America, and America loved Richard Lane. In the evenings, he joined New York's social set, and he played a midnight game of tennis with an heiress. After revealing his knowledge of firearms and gunpowder – tuned on the tramline outside Doug Gael's house – he was called on to give expert ballistic evidence in a court case. Returning one night to his hotel after a long day, he received a telegram asking him to contact 'Lothian' at his earliest convenience. Richard assumed 'Lothian' was Penguin's Australian distributor, Lothian Press, and he put the telegram aside. The next morning, he realised it was from Lord Lothian, Britain's Ambassador to the United States. Richard phoned the Embassy and arranged to see Lothian in Washington the following day.

In 1940, Richard Lane was recognised as a successful publisher, closely in touch with many tiers of British society (including, through personal contacts, British military intelligence) and one tier of American society. Penguin was famous, and Richard's David Low sale had received hyperbolic publicity in New York's *Sun*, *Times* and *Herald Tribune*. In Europe, the phony war had ended, France had fallen and 'things looked just about as bad as they possibly could'. Lord Lothian asked Richard what he thought of the situation in England, what the average person thought of the war, whether Richard thought America might join Britain in the conflict, and a host of other questions that revealed the Ambassador's own thoughts and worries. Richard answered with candour and optimism, and Lothian expressed his gratitude.

Strolling in the pleasant gardens, Richard overheard one Embassy official say to another, 'Things look pretty grim ... It looks as if we are almost certain to lose.' Richard tried not to listen – he 'didn't want to hear any State secrets' – but the troubling conversation demanded his attention. A few minutes later, the same official returned with what sounded like even worse news. Richard's concern was obvious until the official said, 'There's nothing secret about our talks, we are only trying to rake up a team for a cricket match next Saturday.'

Richard returned to London at the end of June, after the evacuation in which Bob Maynard and Allen had briefly contemplated joining, in the brothers' yacht *Penguin*, the fleet of large and small craft that rescued hundreds of thousands of soldiers from the French beaches at Dunkirk. Richard and John received their call-up papers. First John then Richard went to HMS *King Alfred* at Hove in Sussex for four weeks of training. The brothers shared a billet at a small hotel nearby, and it was there they heard their first bomb of the war. After training, John joined HMS *Mollusc* as a navigation officer and Richard was posted to HMS *Excellent* for ominous-sounding 'battalion duties'.

PENGUINS GO TO SEA

I t turned out that Richard was to command a platoon in an under-equipped anti-invasion company for coastal defence in and around Portsmouth. He reported for duty at the north-west Bastion, where the commanding officer's cabin was also his office, and the officers' bathroom. 'One had to be careful in walking about this room as the C.O. had just found a small lizard of which he was very fond and which had been given the run of the place.' HMS *Mollusc* – a converted yacht used for escort work – was lying in Portsmouth at the time, so Richard and John saw a lot of each other. Richard made up a bed so John could sleep at the Bastion. One night, they had just turned in when a flustered officer appeared and said, 'Well this is it chaps, the church bells are ringing.' The signal for an invasion. Fully prepared to repel whatever the Nazis had in store, the Lanes hurried into their clothes. Richard readied his service revolver and gave his loaded spare automatic to John. For several anxious minutes, the C.O. and his lizard tried to find out by telephone what was happening, but they could learn nothing. 'It eventually turned out to be a church clock whose chimes had been mis-taken for bell-ringing, so we all turned in again, but it had been quite an exciting half hour.' Soon after, the *Mollusc* moved to the east coast and Richard and John were separated.

In March 1941, Richard was given leave pending a sea-going appoint-ment. John too came home, on what he said was a few days' seasonal leave. 'This was not quite the truth as while he was staying home one night the BBC announced that the *Mollusc* had been sunk. Mother looked at John and said, "How lucky you were to have been on leave and not on board," and John replied, "Yes I certainly was lucky." But of course he had been on board.' Near misses from a dive bomber had caused the yacht to fall apart and sink within minutes. The last person to leave the vessel, John had endured a cold swim in the North Sea before a Canadian corvette picked him up. The Canadians gave him a shot of rum, and once safely on shore he kept drinking. John called on Nora and Frank at Newcastle upon Tyne for a few days and the bender continued. Frank was relieved when John went home to The Warren for more survivor's leave.

During his own period of leave, Richard received a telegram from the Admiralty telling him to report to the Naval Air Division for what was 'the beginning of any sort of organised Fighter Direction in the Royal Navy'.

> We were told that the Admiralty were very disturbed by the losses of ·
> ships in convoy by enemy action from the air. Our particular enemy
> was to be the Focke-Wulf Condor which, although being mainly used
> for shadowing convoys and reporting their movements to subma-
> rines, was also in the habit of attacking stragglers not close to land,
> where they would be under the protection of our fighter aircraft, but
> up to distances of nearly a thousand miles from the nearest land. The
> Admiralty was in the process of converting five merchant ships into
> one auxiliary carrier, the *Empire Audacity* ... and four fighter cata-
> pult ships, the *Ariguani*, *Petia*, *Maplin* and *Springbank*.

The instructors introduced Richard and his fellow officers to radio telephony, wireless telegraphy and radar. Appointed to 'His Majesty's Auxiliary Anti-Aircraft Fighter Catapult Ship *Springbank*' as Fighter Direction Officer, Richard was ordered to report to Royal Air Force headquarters at Rudloe Manor near Bath, where he spent another week in training: 'from eight o'clock in the morning till midnight, with intervals for refreshment, we watched attractive WRAFs with even more attractive legs move counters over a large map of the district'. There were lectures and demonstrations on 'filtering' and estimating aircraft speeds; at frequent intervals the attractive WRAFs 'were replaced by even more attractive ones' and the sessions passed amenably. Richard sent positive reviews to John, who applied to the Admiralty for an appointment on the same ship. The Admiralty assented, perhaps judging that, in the light of Richard's first naval interview, pairing the brothers would be prudent.

The brothers met in London and were told the *Springbank* was at Scapa Flow in the Orkneys. This was the cue for a monumental party with Eva Knottenbelt, drinking whisky tempered with milk – in a doomed attempt to ward off hangovers – in a cocktail called Camel's Milk. Then came the night train to Thurso, on the north coast of Scotland, and the morning ferry to the Flow. A drifter took them alongside the *Springbank*. 'She looked very solid as we approached her, painted grey and her four twin four-inch turrets and her two multiple pompoms gave her an air of security.' A rope ladder dropped over the side, the brothers scrambled up and their suitcases were hoisted on board. Having been tutored by John on naval rank and protocol, Richard knew the *Springbank* was a 'proper' HM ship, not a Catapult Armed Merchant ship, and that the brothers should salute as soon as they reached the deck. They were taken to the ward room to meet 'Tubby' Martin, the cheerful Commander who smoked seven straight-grained Dunhill pipes, one for each day of the week. 'Well, have you come to join us?' he asked. 'We are the Lane brothers reporting for duty, Sir,' the brothers said. The Commander roared with laughter at this unconventional introduction, repeating it several times. Richard and John, thereafter known on board as Brother Dick and Brother John, joined their new friend for a breakfast of chopped kidneys in thick brown sauce. (John, who was older and somewhat hairier than the average sailor, would earn another nickname on board: 'Hirsute Harry'.) Tubby gave the brothers a day to sling their hammocks and get their bearings.

HMAAAFCS *Springbank*. A converted Bank Line ship. Extra armour plating (to protect the engine room); four turrets, each with two four-inch, director-controlled guns (if all four turrets could bear on the same target, the eight guns could fire simultaneously); two four-barrelled pompoms; two twin-point fives; ASDIC; radar; depth-charges; and, most important of all, a two-seater Fairey Fulmar aircraft mounted athwartships, abaft the funnel, on a catapult. The catapult system looked like a giant Meccano crossbow – an improvisation as madcap as Richard and Hubert's pancake machine. The plane perched on a car that

slipped along rails; in the event of a launch, an explosive charge rock-
eted the car to flight-speed with an exhilarating thwack. In all daylight
hours, a duty pilot sat in the cockpit ready to fly off. After a launch, the
pilot had few options. If land was not too far away and not too hostile,
he could attempt to return to an aerodrome. Or he could bail out and
lose the aircraft. Or he could attempt to set the plane down on the sea
and scramble out before the plane sank, a hazardous operation especially in heavy seas. As a fragile and unique line of defence, the plane
was precious and would only be launched in a confirmed emergency.

With Brother Dick as Fighter Director Officer and Brother John on
'Additional Watch Keeping Duties', the Lanes worked hand-in-hand.
John was also Pigeon Officer, 'his duties being to catch and examine any
bird that happened to alight on our ship, but as none ever did, this was
not very hard work'. Richard and John equipped the Fighter Direction
office on the *Springbank*'s main deck. Their priority: a plotting chart
that could record the progress of the Fulmar after launch and any
unknown aircraft nearby. On the back of an old Admiralty chart, they
drew pencil circles with dividers, then inked them meticulously by
hand. They cut out and painted cardboard discs: red for hostile or
unknown aircraft, blue for friendly. To 'filter' the plots, Richard made
arrows like toy soldiers and glued silver paper flags to them. After
dummy runs, Richard and John carried out their first interception exercise with two real aircraft, one pretending to be hostile, the other
friendly. This was to coincide with the *Springbank*'s first full-calibre
shoot. At the climax of the exercise, according to Richard, 'the plots of
the two aircraft were coming in well from the radar, my plot ratings
moved the coloured discs on the chart – it all looked rather like a super
game of Tiddly Winks – while I moved the silver arrows and occasionally told "our" aircraft to make some alteration of course or speed'. All
was going well until the *Springbank* fired a broadside. The blast blew
open the door of the Fighter Direction office, and Richard 'never saw a
single one of the counters or lovely silver arrows again'.

*

The *Springbank* went to sea in the North Atlantic as part of the Western
Approaches Convoy Organisation. The ship's low speed – usually seven

knots – meant it could only be attached to slow convoys. Many of the runs were conducted in constant northern daylight; the Fighter Direction plot had to be manned around the clock, and three Fulmar pilots covered each twenty-four-hour day in shifts. The convoys passed close to Iceland, and the *Ariguani* was the first of the group to direct her Fulmar to Reykjavik after it had been catapulted; 'this was on an outward bound convoy so on her way back she called there herself and picked up the aircraft.' It would be some time before the *Springbank* launched its own Fulmar in anger, but the ship had its share of excitement before then.

Accompanying a convoy to a rendezvous with Canada-based escort vessels, the *Springbank* was in turn to take back to England the convoy that the Canadians had brought out. Suddenly the radar picked up an unidentified object. The Fulmar pilot fired the engine; the catapult engineer performed the pre-release routine; the Commander took up his Catapult Release Action Station and prepared to wave the flag that signalled the order to fly off; while, in the Fighter Direction Office, Lieutenant Lane calculated the unidentified object's course and speed. 'It didn't take the radar staff and my organisation long to realise that it was static, it eventually turned out to be Cape Wrath, but by now some special release pin had been removed and could not be replaced.' On the catapult car, the Fulmar, the pilot and the gunner slowly rolled backwards and forwards with the movement of the *Springbank*. 'Any extra-large roll of the ship would have caused the aircraft to slide very ungraciously over the side.' The Commander took charge of Operation Lassooing Aircraft; 'the only tragedy that occurred that day was that he lost, over the side, his one and only Brass Hat.'

The *Springbank* was the senior escort vessel of a particularly slow convoy when the crew received grave news: the Kriegsmarine's state-of-the-art super-battleship was out on the hunt. The latest advice had the *Bismarck* sailing south through the Denmark Strait. By the next morning she would be within four hours' steaming time of the convoy which, averaging only four and a half knots (to the *Bismarck*'s thirty) and defended only by four-inch guns (to the *Bismarck*'s fifteen-inch monsters), would be a sitting duck. 'That night we prayed for a fog or the Home Fleet.' At dawn the next morning there was no fog but a magnificent sight appeared in the east: HMS *Hood* powering flat-out into a rough sea, leading the Home Fleet in pursuit of the *Bismarck*. Safe for now, the *Springbank* headed back to Belfast but soon heard the devastating report that the pride of Britain's fleet, the *Hood*, had been destroyed. Then came even more incredible news: the unsinkable *Bismarck* had been sunk. The *Springbank*'s captain joined a jubilant celebration in the ward room and led a series of toasts. John gave a toast too: 'To the *Bismarck*, her officers and men who died gallantly fighting to the very last.' The toast was drunk in silence.

Richard and John deepened their friendship with Tubby. In Northern Ireland, he and his wife Peggy frequently made a dinner four with Brother Dick and Brother John. The friends stayed at a hotel in Bangor, and their favourite place for dinner was the inn at Crawfordsburn. One afternoon, they arrived at the inn and found it in chaos. There had been two wedding receptions that day and 'proper sit-down meals for about 150 guests'; the stragglers were still partying on, the staff had not started washing up, and the inn expected a dinnertime rush. Richard and John and Tubby and Peggy took off their coats, rolled up their sleeves and set to work on hundreds of plates and glasses. After this, the Lanes and the Martins were treated as VIPs at the inn and had 'very jolly parties' there. In a time of rationing, generous improvised dinners were a delight; 'we would take turns in providing some speciality for dinner': snipe the Commander had shot; small lobsters bought in Belfast; a bucket of peaches from an unnamed source. On these spree-nights, the Commander was referred to as 'Commander Sir, if we wished to make a formal request to have another bottle of wine', or otherwise just plain 'Tubby'. Peggy kept a careful watch on him to see he did not drink too much, 'and was not led astray by the Lane brothers'. In town, the Commander wanted to buy her a present, 'but he said that if he did she would know that it was a peace offering and that he had been up to no good'.

In Belfast, just as the bar was opening on the *Springbank*, a dog arrived in the ward room; the crew named it Gin and adopted it as the ship's mascot. When the ship later docked for a refit, Richard and John arranged for a week's leave in Northern Ireland. Near Newtownstewart in County Tyrone was a magical place called The Rocks, where the brothers had once spent a weekend fishing. For their leave they rented a lodge there, invited Nora, and arranged for a man called Francis and his wife to look after the visiting party. Following long preparatory conferences, 'as to what were the best flies, spinners and lines to use', John went searching for provisions at a time when alcohol was hard to come by. On arrival at the lodge, Nora was enchanted. 'The water, the trees surrounding the house, the railway line less than a hundred feet away.' Richard and John told her about Peter, the Commander's son who always waved at the engine driver; 'if he did not wave back, Peter had been a bad boy but if he did wave back, Peter had been a good boy.' The Lanes waved frantically at the next train and the driver waved back. 'Nora has been a good little girl,' said Nora, 'and I think deserves a drink.' John had managed to get gin, whiskey, brandy, rum and four bottles of Pimms No. 1. 'We all decided on Pimms and, standing in front of the house looking on to the railway line, we drank to a pleasant week's stay.' John also arranged for Francis to lay in supplies of beer, stout and ginger ale.

As a true Williams-Lane, Nora became intrigued by the sanitary arrangements. 'A small stream ran past the house and it had been diverted to pass underneath what was very definitely a water closet. There was certainly a draught at times but also a pleasant sound of running water. Nora thought there might be fish in it and never repaired to this particular room without taking a gaff with her.' Following a tree-lined path up river, the visitors found wild cherries, and displayed another Williams-Lane trait. The cherries were 'somewhat difficult to pick . . . but we found some children who, in exchange for chocolate, were willing to do this for us.' Chocolate was strictly rationed, but on board ship it was freely available in cartons. The same form of barter worked for the wild raspberries that grew along the railway line. Every morning for breakfast, the Lanes had wild raspberries or wild cherries, along with cream that came from a 'very unofficial' source, in one clandestine pint bottle per day. After this idyllic retreat, the brothers really had to force themselves to say goodbye to Nora and return to duty.

A Question of Timing

In Richard and John's group of Fighter Catapult Ships, the *Maplin* made the first kill. Piloted by the Australian R.W.H. Everett, winner of the Grand National in 1929, the *Maplin*'s Hurricane aircraft shot down a Focke-Wulf Condor. Too far away from land, Everett had to bail out but was picked up. Soon after, the *Petia* with a fighter escort was returning to Scapa for working-up trials. At dusk the fighter pilot sent a farewell message, 'Am leaving you now. Good luck.' The ship replied, 'Thank you. Good night.' About two minutes later, the plane returned, 'at least that is what everyone thought'. It turned out to be an unfriendly aircraft, which bombed and sank the *Petia*. The *Springbank* would soon see real action too.

On a dull, cold, breezy dawn, a friendly Hudson from Coastal Command approached the convoy in the correct way and started to circle round. Then radar spotted on the starboard side another plane hopping in and out of the clouds; the *Springbank*'s lookouts called it friendly, but a destroyer identified it as a Condor. The Fighter Direction team sent, by Aldis lamp, a garbled message to the Hudson, which went off in the wrong direction looking for the enemy aircraft. The convoy's screen destroyers opened fire, and then came the great moment: the Captain gave the order and the *Springbank* catapulted its Fulmar. 'With a terrific roar and a colossal bang, off she went.' The pilot plugged his headphones into the wrong socket, causing chaos for Richard in the Fighter Direction Office.

I was shouting into my microphone and there was the pilot stoodging around shouting into his and of course we couldn't hear each other. And the pilot couldn't see the enemy but the Captain could and the Captain could also see me and I was the person who should have been able to direct the aircraft. In fact, that was the one and only reason I was on board and what was I doing about it, nothing, absolutely nothing. All this and much more did the Captain say to me.

Then the pilot found the right socket and the radio came on loud and clear.

'Where is it now?' the pilot asked, searching for the Condor.

'The other side,' Richard replied.

'The other side from where?' the pilot asked.

'From you.'

'Do you mean the other side of the convoy?'

This was a disaster: saying 'convoy' on radio was an elementary mistake and obviously forbidden. The chaos continued. 'The Captain was fairly dancing with rage as the enemy, the Hudson and our fighter all flew around and apparently none of them could see each other.'

When the Fulmar eventually found the Condor, the German pilot immediately dropped his bombs and shot up into the clouds. 'Our pilot did have a shot at him but the range was too great.'

Then what to do? Keep our fighter with us in case the enemy came back and when out of petrol tell him to bail out, or send him back to Ireland ... Finally we decided on the latter and he was given a course and off he went. As the distance from the nearest land was over 200 miles I had a nasty five or six hours waiting for him to make it and for news of his arrival to be sent to us. Had I added on the variation or should it have been deducted and had I added or subtracted the wind and was the wind correct.

To calm these doubts, Richard visited his plotting office, where he checked and double-checked the course he had given the pilot. John and the navigator reassured Richard that he was right, and he was. The pilot landed at an airstrip, though not the one to which Richard had directed him. Unsure of his landfall, the pilot had coast-hopped, 'until he saw an aerodrome!'. He only had enough fuel for ten more minutes of flying. When he reported to flying control in Ireland, claiming to have been launched from a catapult, they would not believe he had flown in from the Atlantic.

The *Springbank* received a signal from the Admiralty: on the ship's return to Belfast there would be a Court of Enquiry on the circumstances of the deployment of her aircraft. Lieutenant Lane would attend and swords would be worn; Richard did not have a sword and the proviso was amended. On the ship, he and John made a critical addition to their equipment: a large yellow arrow, mounted on top of the Fighter Direction office. In case of radio failure, the arrow could be pointed in any direction to indicate the enemy's position. The Court of Enquiry proved to be 'a dull affair' in which no one was praised or given any 'bottle'. When Richard and John returned to the *Springbank*, they found a terrific party well under way, with visiting Wrens in attendance. 'The two most attractive Wrens were being shown our Line Books and, unluckily for their escorts, they had so seated themselves on the built-in divan ... that [they were] next to each other with their escorts on either side. John did not hesitate for a moment. He did not gently edge his way between them but just plomped down on them and left it for them to make room ... It was a grand party.'

The Admiralty sent the *Springbank* to escort convoys to the Mediterranean. Richard and John usually went ashore together, but at Gibraltar the Commander ordered them not to do so during working hours. There was also a standing order that anyone going ashore must leave keys with the Keyboard Sentry. Before the *Springbank* sailed from Gibraltar, the local Admiral (Vice Admiral Commanding North Atlantic) was scheduled to inspect the ship. In a double breach of protocol, Richard and John went ashore together after breakfast with their keys (and the ship's doctor) to collect charts and to buy a few cases of sherry and other unobtainable luxuries, like perfume and silk stockings. The sherry cost two-and-six per bottle, which the brothers and the doctor planned to sell at threepence a glass for the benefit of the ward-room wine committee. Having sampled many varieties of sherry and made their choice, 'we then thought it a good idea to have a long John Collins, as it was a warm day, and then as one can't fly on one wing we had the other half, then as there were three of us we had one for the road'. Richard and John, their pockets stuffed with stockings and Chanel No. 5, led a porter with a handcart loaded with the sherry to where they hoped to find their boat, but it had left. The time was around 11 a.m. and the Admiral was due on board the *Springbank* in half an hour. The Lanes found the officer of the watch, explained their trouble and asked if he could get them back on board. Spotting the Admiral's standby barge, they asked if they could borrow that. The officer agreed and supplied a crew.

As the brothers approached the *Springbank*, under the influence of Tio Pepe and John Collins, they had a dangerous thought: 'wouldn't it be funny if we kept ourselves hidden in the cabin, the Captain might think it was the real Admiral arriving slightly early.' Richard and John concealed themselves in the barge until it approached the *Springbank*'s gangway. Hearing the shrill notes of the Bosun piping the arrival of the barge, Richard and John sprang from their hiding place; 'and there on the top of the gangway was our Ringed Captain saluting us. The Commander was even more furious than the Captain as, apart from having to break the lock on the Fighter Direction Office and try and make the place look operational for the Admiral's inspection, he had just gone to the Heads when he was informed the Admiral was coming alongside.' Before Tubby could give the brothers a real bottle, the Admiral arrived. 'The inspection went off well and the Admiral was pleased and gave us a pep talk but John and I did not make an appearance in the ward room until things had quietened down a bit.' Tubby and the Captain briefly considered a Court Martial for the Lane brothers, but events overtook them.

A day out from Gibraltar, shortly after noon, the lookout spotted a Condor. The *Springbank* lacked an air escort so immediately the Fulmar flew off, piloted by Petty Officer Shaw with Leading Naval Airman Tilley as observer. It was a clear day, the fighter got just within range and managed to damage the Focke-Wulf, which dropped its bombs and fled. Shaw and Tilley returned safely to Gibraltar while the *Springbank* continued on its voyage without air defence, 'hoping that we would not see any more enemy aircraft but, knowing that a sighting report had now reached Germany, the chances were that we should not have a peaceful time'. Early the next day, a second Condor arrived and circled the convoy just out of gun range, before being relieved by another which stayed until dark. 'Occasionally, if there was any cloud about, the aircraft would try and use it as cover and approach within bombing distance but they never succeeded. That was not their main job, which was to shadow us and report our position, course and speed. This information, of course, being given to any submarine that happened to be in our vicinity.'

Soon the Admiralty reported U-boats close to the convoy. 'We had not got the speed to get away and however much we altered course, we could not shake off the shadowing aircraft. It was a most annoying situation as we knew that sooner or later we were for it.' Perpetually on alert, as there was always a chance of getting a shot at the Condor, the gun crews opened fire every day, 'but it was always at extreme range'; armed with intelligence from spies in Ireland and elsewhere, the Germans 'knew very well' what the ship's armament consisted of, and therefore how to stay at a safe distance. At the end of each day, the Condor left and the *Springbank* made sharp changes in course. Through pitch-black moonless nights, the crew hoped these zigzags would shake off the menacing U-boats; 'but this was not to be. It was now estimated that we had at least six subs after us.' The first ship to be sunk – the Commodore's ship, carrying nurses and Wrens – was about 200 yards from the *Springbank*'s starboard side. Through powerful binoculars, Richard and John had watched and admired the nurses and Wrens, 'walking around the deck in shorts, a very attractive bunch of femininity'. The women were lifted from the water but a terrible tragedy was to follow: 'the next night the ship that had saved them was sunk and, although the Commodore was rescued, not a single [woman] was saved.'

The U-boats attacked nightly. They sank one ship one night, another the next, and four the night after that. Soon the convoy had lost twelve ships and the weather turned bad; 'one hell of a gale' whipped up forty-foot waves. For several nights in a row, John had the night watch. In the rough conditions he sat cold and stiff in saturated clothes. Richard visited him throughout the night, bringing fruit and chocolate and company. The brothers made plans that as soon as the ship was hit they would find each other and stick together.

The end for the *Springbank* came suddenly. About an hour after midnight, a torpedo hit astern and another hit just forward of the engine room, blasting a hole in a hold filled with empty forty-gallon barrels that escaped into the sea, making an eerie noise in the darkness. Richard and John rendezvoused on the bridge, where 'anything that could fall down had fallen down'. The *Springbank* listed alarmingly to the port side and the Captain gave orders to abandon ship. Carrying out the order was not straightforward, however. The ship was equipped with two lifeboats, which held twelve souls each; plus four Carley floats that had to be man-handled into the water – another thirty souls filed into the floats; and Denton rafts, which were tied to one another and thrown over the side. The barrels from the hold smashed into the rafts and rendered them useless. 'There were still about 200 of us on board and to jump into the sea would have been most unpleasant and the chances of being picked up very small, so we just waited.'

The Lanes were in their working uniform when John, who had already been sunk on the *Mollusc*, pointed out a Naval rule that prompted a legendary episode: 'when we came to claim on all our possessions, it would be assumed we lost our number-ones ... so when there was a lull, we went into our cabin and by the light of a torch we changed into our best uniform. The whole works: suits, shirt, ties, shoes and socks.' This way, they would escape with their best (and most expensive) clothes, and still be entitled to the maximum compensation. A proud Allen later relayed this instance of Lane enterprise to anyone who would listen.

While awaiting rescue on the *Springbank*, a strange reversal confronted the crew. Richard and John realised that the ship's wine store had been broken into; nearly every man on board had looted one or more bottles of spirits. 'John and I knew how serious this could become. The ratings were only used to their one tot of rum a day and if they filled themselves up with whisky and gin, the chances were they would pass out and quite likely go into the nearest cabin and fall asleep and that would be the end of them.' When the bow of the ship sank lower in the water, the wine store entrance was sealed off. Richard and John, known to the crew as good fellows and competent drinkers, patrolled the decks and asked every man they met to give them a drink; 'and once we had possession of the bottle we promptly heaved it over the side. We certainly were not popular but we did what we thought was the right thing.'

In rough seas quickly filling with forty-gallon barrels and lobbed bottles of hooch, a corvette came alongside and sailors began jumping from the tilted deck of the *Springbank* to the deck of the corvette, which was smaller and sat lower in the water. The difference in height between the two decks was considerable and every man who jumped 'broke one or more legs'. In the swell, the corvette bashed against the *Springbank* and the Captain of the smaller ship started to move off. A rating jumped but missed the corvette and fell into the water between the two vessels. 'As the ships crashed together, a lifebelt with a green flare attached was wrenched off our ship and fell into the water with him. As the ships separated we looked down expecting to see his mangled body but there he was, floating alongside the lifebelt and green flare, a sight everyone who saw it will long remember.' Sailors from the corvette leant over and hauled him safely aboard.

This was about two hours after the torpedoes hit the *Springbank*. Those remaining on board waited till dawn when they saw the sloop HMS *Fowey* nearby. 'Instead of coming alongside us, she positioned herself about a cable's length away ... on the lee side and waited until we drifted on to her.' The *Fowey* was much bigger than a corvette, and its deck not so far below that of the *Springbank*. From sailcloth and codline, the Lane brothers made a sling for Gin the ward-room dog. Gently lowered over the side, Gin 'to everyone's joy' joined the survivors. The men remaining on the *Springbank* were told to jump. 'It was all a question of timing, one had to wait until the rise of the sloop was at its maximum and the distance between the two decks at its minimum.' The paymaster jumped with more than a thousand pound notes, and other sailors jumped with their most prized personal possessions. 'One rating had been making his son a sailor suit and this was saved, and another had been making his girlfriend a handbag out of boot laces.' Tubby saved his beloved seven Dunhill pipes.

John made the jump but Richard landed badly, fracturing a bone in his heel – the os calcis. He later received a hurt certificate that stated he was sober at the time of the accident. The *Fowey*'s shipwright made him a walking stick. Accommodation on the sloop was scarce. In the ward room, which was as crowded as Talbot Square on the night of John's World Tour party, the injured Richard took over the sofa, two men slept on the table, and seventeen men slept on chairs and the floor. The ward room was immediately below one of the *Fowey*'s guns and shook every time it fired. Despite the stick, Richard found it difficult to walk or even stand, but 'marvellous' John tended to all his brother's needs. Apart from throwing Brother Dick and Brother John even more closely together, the sinking of the *Springbank* had another consequence: the 'colossal black' they earned at Gibraltar in the Admiral's standby barge was forgiven and forgotten, so, Richard remarked with considerable irony, 'all was well for the Lane Brothers'.

After a difficult voyage, the ship docked at Liverpool. An ambulance took Richard to a bookless hospital.

Apart from the clothes I was wearing, I had nothing and there I was left for two or three hours, nothing to eat, drink or read. I was separated from John and really felt miserable. Then the door opened and in came John. He had found out that I was to be x-rayed but that these operations were only carried out first thing in the morning. I was to be kept there for twenty odd hours. Somehow, he found out that he knew one of the doctors and had wrangled for me to be examined at once. The result was that I had a presumed fracture and after strapping up one foot, I was discharged. Within minutes, John and I were in the bar at the Adelphi and I felt very much better. John arranged everything, got railway passes to London on the night train, and even got adjoining first class sleepers.

Pecking Order

S
ix of Penguin's first ten years were years of war. The war tested the still-young imprint in many ways. Like the great majority of British firms, Penguin saw an exodus of personnel into the military machine. In the first year of hostilities, two young Penguiners were killed in France. By 1943, most of Penguin's pre-war staff and management would be serving in the armed forces. Bob Maynard joined Richard and John Lane in the Royal Navy Volunteer Reserve. Another five Penguiners served with the Navy, seven served in the Army abroad, seven served in the Home Forces, one joined the Auxiliary Territorial Service and one joined the WAAF. The war challenged and transformed Penguin's philosophy and operating model, and in some surprising ways was a boon for an enterprise still shaky on its feet: the demand among soldiers, sailors and airmen for pocket-sized paperbacks was very high. Though the war brought Richard and John close as never before, it also estranged Allen from his brothers.

To understand the impact of the war on the Lane brothers and on Penguin, we have to backtrack a few years. Before the war, the brothers worked together for the first time in their professional lives. At The Bodley Head and then at Penguin, the characteristic familial bond transmogrified into occupational collaboration. Richard's memories of Australia were fresh in his mind – memories of isolation, loneliness and poverty. The contrast between that time and this new period of business partnership was stark. In the lead up to the war, the Williams-Lanes enjoyed a satisfying prosperity, and Richard was blissfully happy to be working in London with his brothers and his books. He assumed Allen and John felt more or less the same way about things, and that the augmentation of their relationship would carry on smoothly.

Each of the brothers was a formidable talent in his own right. Bringing them together at work promised much more than a humble lane towards success: they were building a broad thoroughfare, even an expressway. But, to extend the metaphor, each lane on the freeway had its own speed limit and destination. Allen in particular was intent on going his own way. From his actions and contemporary documents, it is possible to glean much of what was going through his mind during this period. Richard's sanguine hopes for fraternal harmony proved to be misplaced. Most of Allen's mental traffic was out of sync with his brothers' plans.

The astrological reports that Allen commissioned in the 1930s are fascinating documents, and a surprisingly useful source of information about Penguin and the Lanes. Like the advice of a more conventional analyst, the reports were based on interviews; they engaged with the subject's thoughts, feelings and priorities; they adopted a psychological vocabulary of ego, libido and instinct; and they provided guidance for Allen in both his personal and professional life. That Allen studied these reports and took them seriously is certain. He asked the astrologists and psychics follow-up questions, he sought repeat advice, he engaged the 'best' practitioners from Britain and America, and he brought the tools of their trade into his work at Great Portland Street and then at Harmondsworth and Silverbeck. No one doing business with Allen could escape having his or her handwriting analysed by a graphologist, and Allen procured full horoscopes as part of the screening of executive candidates.

Ominously, one report from Decoy Avenue warned Allen that he would fall out with, or even lose altogether, 'a brother or male relation'. 'But I should be very careful not to be the aggressor if I were you,' Kate Murray wrote. 'Don't start the quarrel or you will be very sorry afterwards.' Murray's advice was astute and timely. Several factors undermined the brothers' partnership, and a series of tremors portended the earthquakes that would rock the Lanes in years to come.

*

Without meaning to be divisive, Annie Lane in her will had driven a wedge between Allen and his brothers. The competitive eldest brother, notorious for seeking the advantage in every transaction, was always alert to perceived slights and injustices. Though the difference in the brothers' Penguin salaries quickly reversed any disparity in their wealth, the inheritance became for Allen a sore point. Crowding at work was another source of tension. Allen had grown accustomed to his own show, his own rhythm, which Richard and John often found uneven and unpredictable; surprisingly ruminative, or at least procrastinatory. At The Bodley Head, where Allen had worked for well over a decade before his brothers joined him there, he had been in charge of how he spent his days, more or less. Most of the time, his distant uncle had been a distant mentor, and Allen was able to socialise and work when and how he pleased. After Uncle John passed away, Allen of course had even more freedom, including the freedom to make disastrous mistakes of the *Whispering Gallery* variety. Now, he had to share.

At Penguin, the brothers built their interaction around creative opposition. They stress-tested and challenged each other's ideas, and in so doing improved and strengthened them. Allen was in two minds about this approach. He could see its practical value, but he was also wearied by the process of scrutiny, and cramped by the strictures of decision-making by committee. At The Bodley Head, he had had patrons, mentors, managers, staff, flunkeys, critics and enemies, but no true peers apart from his brothers, who arrived at the firm just in time to witness its death throes. At Penguin, Allen was in a partnership but unused and unsuited to being a partner. He continued to set his own pace and do his own thing. He was often out of London, with friends or girlfriends in the country or on the Continent, and then he was mostly not thinking about business. Hedonistic 'vice parties' were as enticing for Allen as the uninhibited Thames Valley gin parties that he attended with Ethel Mannin and her bohemian buddies.

When in London, Allen kept neither regular hours nor a diary. His unconventional working style seldom saw him in the office. He was more likely to be at a restaurant or a cocktail party than at his desk. People hoping to meet with Allen were always made to wait. Whether Allen would show up at meetings at all was often a matter of chance, and always one of speculation. He cultivated other non-CEO-like habits. Indecision. Havering. A fickleness of mind. A disdain for business procedures and conventional corporate governance. These attributes sat unhappily alongside Allen's innate interpersonal discomfort (he admitted that he was 'reluctant to allow other people to get too close'). As a way of distracting himself from his own work or delaying decisions, he meddled in others' tasks and intervened unhelpfully in details for which others were responsible. Allen was the least intellectual, the most capricious and the least reliable of the Lane brothers; these differences came to life in his managerial missteps. More than once, Richard chipped Allen for his 'escapism', his chaotic methods and perverse priorities.

Despite these unbusinesslike attributes, Allen was ambitious to be a CEO and fully, viscerally expected to be one. It was ingrained in him that he would lead – hence the shock when his astrologist equivocated about his leadership abilities. Famously the chosen heir at The Bodley Head, he was the first and eldest of his brothers, and he saw himself as the obvious choice to be principal at Penguin. So obvious, in fact, that no alternatives needed to be considered. The press painted Allen as 'London's Youngest Publisher' and a £10,000-a-year publishing wiz. He was intent on living up to the image. Notwithstanding his corporate idiosyncrasies, he wore the CEO's mask, on to which people projected their own expectations of Uncle John's successor, filling in the gaps with myths and legend, impressions and gossip.

There was a paradox, however, at the heart of Penguin's frontman. Always ready to put himself forward, Allen nevertheless struggled to cope with too many people, too many things on the boil, too much responsibility. When he spoke and wrote publicly about Penguin, it was usually with words that others – like Beales, Frost and Williams – had written. All his best off-the-cuff comments were exhaustively rehearsed. Though not an innovator or 'ideas man', he frequently claimed and ran with the ideas of others – and he did so typically in a half-competent, fast–slow manner. He craved change and novelty – the projects that most appealed to him involved urgent telegrams and travel and a surplus of drama or intrigue – but he was put off by the intensity to which this naturally led. He seesawed daily between the urge to escape and the desire to be in charge; the impulse to flee and the need to lead. Always wanting to give an emphatic 'yes', and an equally definitive 'no' – with staff, book projects, corporate manoeuvres and women – Allen was over-endowed with contradictions.

Though he had never done more on a farm than take a holiday, his self-image was that of a Devonian yeoman somehow transported into the life of an extraordinary publisher. Outwardly affable, he could turn cold and vindictive in an instant. The publisher Robert Lusty memorably captured his friend's conflicted nature: 'One might be gossiping with him of this and that and he would be attentive and involved. Some word, some name, some project might strike a certain chord and on the instant Allen would be neither attentive nor involved. Cold little shutters would close upon the light of his eyes'; 'some sort of skulduggery was suggesting itself at the back of his mind [and] someone, something, somewhere had had it.' Lusty identified one cause of Allen's predilection for masks. Like Lusty, Allen entered publishing with no qualifications. He would only ever pass two exams in his life, one to enter grammar school and one to obtain a driver's licence. 'No A-levels, no O-levels, no degree in literature, none of those educational attributes without which today a citizen can hardly scramble from his pram,' Lusty wrote. 'The deprivation, so Allen Lane and I discovered, gave us both an inherent uncertainty we did our best to conceal from others.'

In the years before the war, John Lane junior took Allen's fame as 'London's Youngest Publisher' much less seriously than the young publisher himself. John could match Allen for charm, charisma, toughness and judgment, and was building rapidly his own network of contacts at the middle and top levels of the industry. The youngest Lane was smarter academically (he studied Latin in his spare time and nursed plans to study at Oxford), he was equally ambitious, and had more stamina and machismo. He drank and partied hard, but was better able to balance work and play, and in work he lacked Allen's habit of disappearing when the going got tough. Tension between the eldest and youngest brothers was inevitable. A greater age difference separated them, while fewer shared experiences bound them together. For many years, Richard had led the Allen fan club, but John refused to join. Inclined to bridle when Allen put himself forward as king penguin, John maintained the view that, if Allen was first, it was only as a first among equals. John willingly conceded to Allen a status as the natural external contact point for Penguin – given his experience and connections in the industry – and as the main spokesman, given his public profile. Hence, from about 1937, Allen's name appeared bracketed at the foot of the inside front flap of Penguin dust jackets: 'Penguin Books Limited (Allen Lane)'. (The first Penguin flaps had referred to 'John Lane The Bodley Head'.) But John junior was adamant that the substantive relationship between the three Penguin directors was one of equality, and the decision-making process one of debate leading to consensus.

The period from 1935 to 1940 was Penguin's start-up phase: a sink-or-swim time in which the hard work was done to establish the company. Though sales were exceptionally good, the low cover price meant that big sales did not equal big cash; the break-even point on some books was as high as 20,000 copies, meaning that handsome sales could still result in losses. Money flowed unevenly between surging peaks and worrisome troughs – the firm's profitability was paper-thin. Allen, who 'never quite grasped the niceties of budgeting or the tidal mysteries of cashflow', did not help matters. Set against the high-amplitude cycle, the hefty costs of Harmondsworth and Silverbeck – and his fat and unpredictable withdrawals – created enormous risks for the business.

Richard loved how his normally buoyant, energising, inspiring elder brother would muck in with fun projects; it was a quality he had cherished since their vegetable plot competition in Bristol. But now, during Penguin's crucial consolidation, Allen was missing in action. Separating himself from the fast and gruelling work that needed to be done to make the venture a reality and a success, Allen maintained his incendiary social schedule, and the compensating routine of health retreats when his waistline and the stresses of life became too great. (Allen's favourite book was F.A. Hornibrook's 1924 handbook on *The Culture of the Abdomen: The Cure of Obesity and Constipation etc.*) His frequent short desertions from the office turned into medium-length holidays and absences at weight-loss retreats, then the long disappearance in the Middle East and India which was an extreme example of his pattern of escape, and tantamount to an experiment with leaving Britain and publishing altogether. Jack Morpurgo called the holiday an episode of lunacy, and it could indeed have been one of several foreshadowings of the breakdowns Allen would suffer both during and after the war.

Allen dropped the ball, but Richard and John picked it up and ran with it in the formative years of their new imprint. After the little bird's early and unlikely splash, it was the younger brothers who worked around the clock to fulfil orders and do all the things that needed to be done to keep their bird afloat. While Richard and John were busy saving Penguin, Richard noticed Allen's aloofness and worried about his state of mind.

After six months away from Penguin and his fellow Musketeers, Allen decided to return. He was determined to do so on his own terms, but his Asian sabbatical gave him further reasons to worry. Perhaps Allen had secretly hoped that his brothers would struggle in his absence, but the opposite was true. Richard and John managed Penguin efficiently and effectively, and the new imprint thrived under their leadership. Sales of Specials averaged 100,000 copies a title and 'ordinary' Penguins 40,000. Richard initiated the Beak Street Pelican meetings which were to prove enormously important and productive on the editorial side of the business; John applied his logistical skills to improve Penguin distribution; and in many other ways the brothers brought a streamlined maturity to the running of the company. Possibly they did a little too well. The younger Lanes were more level-headed and strategic than Allen, and they earned the respect of staff and peers for their knowledge and judgment and their less erratic style of management. Rumours circulated in the office and beyond that Allen relied more on his brothers than he let on – even that Richard and John were the heart and brains of Penguin.

John, in particular, had looked very comfortable in the CEO's chair. It was never a good idea to let Allen sense rivalry, but rivalry brewed between the eldest and youngest Lane brothers. When Allen returned to England, his first move was to lever John out of the seat and, for a while, out of the picture altogether. John went to the United States in 1939 with a rationale – to use his international experience to kick-start the American subsidiary – but there was an ulterior motive for sending him. For Allen, John's visit to Penguin Books Inc. was more important in London than it was in New York.

Though on the face of things Richard Lane looked less threatening to Allen, he too displayed many qualities of the typical CEO: adeptness with contemporary commercial management; technical mastery of the business side of publishing and the financial side of Penguin; a capacity to plan and lead. Richard was respected and even loved by his employees, authors and fellow publishers. He had boundless personal resilience and commitment. And he wished with all his being to preserve and enhance what he and his brothers were creating. Allen Lane was a literary publisher who was not very interested in literature, whereas Richard lived for literature and literary culture, and of all the Lane brothers he had the strongest appreciation for the 'book beautiful'. Another difference was that Richard did not share Allen's allergy to partnerships. The middle brother entered happily into normal bilateral business arrangements for mutual profit. Colleagues and competitors described him as straightforward, honest, open, easy-going, humble, lovable, convivial, reasonable; 'an apple-cheeked countryman' and 'a larger, less mercurial version of Allen'. In his calm, friendly, collegiate manner, Richard Lane kept the Penguin engine running; he steered home many of the biggest successes of Penguin's early years, such as King Penguins (one of the most successful new series), *Europe Since Versailles* (the biggest retail sale) and *Blackmail or War* (the most successful Special and one of the most successful Penguins of any kind).

He also lacked some of the traits of a conventional CEO. He could think and talk convincingly, even inspiringly, about publishing and Penguin, but was generally reluctant to do so publicly. By nature he was shy and self-effacing. He refused to put himself ahead of his brothers. Richard Lane did not have enough moxie, enough ruthlessness, to become a full-time, full-energy CEO of Penguin. It is an oversimplification to say that the guy who tried to save Loopy Bourne and Tom Nunn, who rescued the *Springbank*'s ward-room dog, who brought wildflowers and grapes to the little girl near Gumeracha, and who bought ice-cream for the overheated staff at The Bodley Head, was just too nice to lead, but there is some truth in the allegation.

This reality was invisible to Allen, however, who saw Richard through a distorting lens of competition and threat. Allen decided that, one way or another, he was going to put an end to the old Athos–Porthos–Aramis act. If it was going to be 'first among equals', he would have to amp up the primacy and tune down the equality. Richard had been the other half of the very effective CEO duo; he had received disconcertingly extensive and positive press coverage following his landmark David Low sale; so now, like John, he needed to be levered out of the managing director's chair. When John came back from the States in 1939, Allen persuaded Richard in turn to leave for New York, on another trip that had its true rationale in London, not America. (Allen would later use Australia in a similar way, to put rivals on ice or in exile, and to give absence a chance to make his heart fonder.)

Allen flirted with other ways to recast the partnership. The brothers had shared Southwick Street and Talbot Square, and were now co-resident at Silverbeck. Allen again contemplated separate living arrangements but was again of two minds. Despite his competitive feelings, and a weariness with his siblings, he valued what Richard and John could do (and was happy that they did it on below-market salaries). Not yet ready to discard the bonds of family and musketry, he appreciated the efficiency that came from extending business life into after-work life, which was especially important for a CEO who hated paperwork, avoided putting his true thoughts in writing, and could stomach neither office routine nor office hours. Allen's ambivalent ruminations continued unresolved before being cut short when Richard and John received their call-up papers. In more than one way, the war would grant the Musketeers' bond a reprieve. But, during the first years of the conflict, there would be other strains on the partnership.

*

Allen, a man with a Phyllis for every point of the compass, maintained an elaborate love life that needed careful management. His astrologers continued to counsel him on his relationships with women as well as with his brothers. Noting the stargazers' advice about when would be an auspicious time to marry, Allen did a Nora: he brought a non-Lane into the fold. For more than a decade he had consulted Richard (in particular) and John on his love affairs; he even involved his brothers in several messy clean-ups, such as when Richard had to mind a lady's husband at Talbot Square for eight hours in order to prevent him from vengefully trashing the place. But this time, Allen decided not to seek his brothers' advice, and presented his engagement as a fait accompli.

For Allen, official diplomatic and colonial circles offered easy access to attractive young women. He dated the daughter of Sir Sydney Barton, the former Consul-General to Shanghai who knew the Governor of Aden; and now Allen was to marry the daughter of the Governor of the Bahamas. Pretty, intelligent, serious, Lettice Orr had the right pedigree, the right left-wing politics, and in her career as a psychiatric social worker could be unexpectedly useful for Allen. The pair met at a party hosted by H.L. Beales – Lettice knew some of his London School of Economics and Cambridge friends – and, from their first conversation, Lettice seems to have treated Allen as a puzzling psychological case study. Fascination with his unusual personality was a key part of the attraction she felt for this 'short powerful-looking man' dressed in country tweeds. On Allen's side, the attraction was effortless. He had always talked more easily with women than men; here was a beautiful young woman, formally schooled in listening. In Lance Beales' living room, with a tongue loosened by gin and sherry, Allen poured out his sorrows, his fears and his paranoiac thoughts. A five-month courtship followed, in which Allen clocked up several two-hour phone calls. He and Lettice married at Harmondsworth in June 1941. A famous photo shows the newlyweds leaving the church through an honour-guard of paperboard penguins.

When Richard and John came home on shore-leave, they met their sister-in-law for the first time. According to Jack Morpurgo, John made clear through his words and his behaviour that he regarded Lettice as 'an inconsequential interloper who had acquired the name Lane by subterfuge'. The marriage catalysed a heated confrontation at Silverbeck. John, who transparently had never believed the mythology of Allen Lane, unloaded his grievances and laid out a series of accusations and charges against his eldest brother. Allen had exploited his brothers' absence 'to take undisputed control' of their firm, John alleged. While Richard and John had been serving with the RNVR, Allen had made unilateral changes to management and had initiated new titles and series without even the pretence of attempting to reach a consensus. Most galling of all, Allen had repositioned his name on the new Penguins. No longer buried and bracketed on the jacket, his name now appeared at the foot of the title page:

ALLEN LANE

PENGUIN BOOKS

At that time, in the world of books, dust jackets were regarded as ephemeral but title pages enjoyed a monolithic status. The implication of the move was clear: Allen Lane had made a play to become synonymous with Penguin; to be at Penguin what Uncle John had been at The Bodley Head. For John Lane junior, the change was a betrayal, and the iceberg-tip of a broader attempt to take over; an Allen Lane coup d'état; the Bay of Penguins; the Night of the Long Beaks. And then came the most stinging charge of all: marriage to Lettice proved, according to John, Allen's incompetence and his inability to manage without his brothers.

Though Allen was gravely put out by John's accusations, he followed his astrologer's advice and refused to rise to the fight his youngest brother was clearly picking. Allen was conflicted: he knew he'd shown considerable cheek in putting himself forward as the personification of Penguin; he had his own mixed feelings about his marriage; he understood that the manner of his betrothal broke several commandments of the Lane brotherhood; and he was reluctant to do battle with either brother, both of whom would soon be returning to a real and much more dangerous fight with Fascism. Moreover, avoiding direct conflict and open warfare was in Allen a deep-seated trait; he kept his most personal thoughts to himself – and his astrologer – and preferred to act slowly in the cold rather than speedily in the heat. (Oddly, Allen later blamed Richard and John's Naval service for his marriage. 'If the three of us had stayed together,' he wrote to Eunice Frost, 'I very much doubt if I would ever have married.')

So the battle of Silverbeck was more a one-sided skirmish than a Titanic clash. Richard too felt conflicted, but in a quite different way. Allen Lane was the exceptional egotist in the family; John Lane had a healthy ego, too; but Richard, where his brothers were concerned, scarcely had one at all. Allen remained Richard's champion and idol, but the war cemented a special bond between Richard and John. Like the child of divorced parents, Richard responded to the unleashed tension with dismay and an instinct to broker peace. For him, the idea that the brothers could be competitors was ludicrous. He loved and empathised with both of them; in the glow of Penguin's early success and the darkness of wartime, he just wanted them all to get along.

Throughout his life, Richard Lane had had the time and freedom to choose a career. In his teens, twenties and thirties, he tried several roads and disappeared down many rabbit holes (and one very big wombat hole) in his search for the path that might suit him best. The eldest Lane brother, by contrast, had been plucked straight from school and duck-shoved into publishing to follow a path already laid out for him. Richard knew his brother better than anyone else on the planet; he could see Allen's inner confusion, and how he was trying to live up to an image that others had made for him. But the sincerity of Richard's empathy, and his efforts at reconciliation, were lost on Allen. Perversely, the new closeness between Richard and John was another spur to his insecurity. He could not prevent the suspicion that his brothers' intimacy 'not only excluded him but was in some sense directed against him and threatening of his interests'. Richard and John returned to sea leaving behind a darkened atmosphere at Silverbeck.

Bedroom problems compounded the bad start to Allen's marriage. Lettice was perfectly energetic and willing, but her husband remained, in his own words, 'a rather self-contained and aloof being, and although at the beginning Lettice and I had relations of a sort, they were never of the intensity which I now know they should be in a happy union'. Allen engineered a short escape from the 'claustrophobia' of England and Silverbeck. In 1941, he sailed to the United States, where he would prove, by appointing as Vice-President of Penguin Books Inc. the former Albatross manager, Kurt Enoch, that life really is a great wheel.

During the outward voyage, which Allen shared with RAF officers and a Hungarian sculptor, he wrote to tell Nora that he had instructed the company lawyers to make her a director of Penguin Books in Britain. He asked that Nora keep the appointment secret from their parents, and from Richard and John, and particularly from Lettice, as there was 'no reason why she need know'. Several people would later claim that, on this trip to America, Allen gave serious consideration to making a more permanent move to New York. Whether or not that is so, Allen returned to England shortly before the Japanese bombed Pearl Harbor. The war turned in the Allies' favour, and the optimism that Richard had expressed to Ambassador Lothian received its answer in a new and promising reality.

17

In Armour

fter the sinking of the *Springbank* in September 1941, Richard and John made a short stop at Silverbeck, for a bath, then travelled to The Warren for a fortnight of recuperation with their parents. Though autumn had arrived, the trees were still in leaf. Richard and John unfolded deckchairs and sat under the chestnut trees, where they drank Samuel's homemade wine and sleepily counted their blessings. John had been sunk twice, Richard once, and between them they had sustained only one minor injury. During the brothers' first week at The Warren, they followed the pattern of the *Mollusc* and did not tell their parents about the *Springbank*'s sinking; they wanted to break the news gently – to savour the peaceful interlude. Then John told Samuel, and Richard told Camilla, and the interlude was soon over.

John went to the Royal Navy Air Station at Yeovilton in Somerset for a Fighter Direction course, after which he was promoted to Lieutenant Commander, appointed to the RAF station at Speke, in Liverpool, and placed in charge of the Naval personnel manning Spitfire-equipped Catapult Armed Merchant ships. After a check-up at the Royal Navy Hospital at Chatham, Richard too was sent to Yeovilton for training. After his course, the Admiralty appointed him as Fighter Direction Officer, Force H, and he proceeded back to Gibraltar.

In the intervening months, the *Ark Royal* had been sunk and Force H now consisted of the flagship HMS *Malaya*, two carriers (*Eagle* and *Argus*), a cruiser (*Hermione*) and destroyers. The *Argus* was 'almost a museum piece' and the *Malaya* not much better; more than 40,000 tons, with eight fifteen-inch guns, and a secondary armament of six-inch, low-angle guns unsuitable for modern warfare. At the Battle of Jutland during the First World War, the ship had sustained heavy loss of life. Richard now occupied a cabin next to the chapel where the names of the dead were recorded.

Force H escorted a convoy of eleven ships (seven of them fuel tankers) from Gibraltar to Malta. When the convoy was attacked, it became a hellish flaming wreck; 'to see a tanker go up in flames is a horrible sight as one knew that the chances of there being any survivors was very slight.' Only two of the seven tankers reached port. Force H then regrouped and assisted the successful amphibious invasion of Madagascar by escorting the Allied battle fleet to Cape Town. After returning to Gibraltar in September 1942, Richard received a cable from Allen: 'JOHN ON LEAVE – WENT TO HINDS HEAD FOR LUNCH – WENT TO FARM SALE AT READING – JOHN SLEEPILY NODDED – HAVE BOUGHT FARM – TELLING BANK MANAGER TOMORROW.' The Hinds Head pub at Bray was where the brothers had enjoyed 'a slap-up meal including some liquid refreshment', before, riskily, bidding at the auction. (Now a Michelin-starred establishment owned by Heston Blumenthal and serving hash of snails and kidney pudding, the Hinds Head was the illustrious venue for Philip Mountbatten's bachelor party in 1947 on the eve of his marriage to Princess Elizabeth.)

Curiously, farming was another means of escape for Allen in the 1940s, and an increasingly important part of his self-image. With John in tow, he had searched for a farm that the three brothers could buy and, theoretically, operate as a joint interest. That is how the brothers came to buy Priory Farm, less than an hour from Silverbeck. The articles of association of Penguin Books were explicitly redrafted to include the business of farming as a permitted purpose of the corporate entity. At Long Ashton, Moorook, Renmark and Coonabarabran, Richard Lane had had more than his fill of farming – he was still 'far more interested in books than in rams', or any other livestock – and he had no desire to escape from Penguin or from London or publishing. But, in spite of these feelings, Richard supported the purchase. He liked the idea of brotherly collaboration and anything that could make things better between the Lane boys.

Left to right: Richard, John and Allen Williams, August 1912.

Richard and Allen as choirboys: 'Allen for his voice and Dick for his appearance.'

Richard Lane's batch of Barwell Boys, shortly after their arrival in Adelaide, 1922. Richard stands at the right end of the third row.

Richard with Nellie and Jimmy, Renmark, 1924.

The Williams-Lane family. *Left to right*: Richard, John, Camilla (seated), Samuel, Allen, Nora (seated).

Early Penguin delivery van.

Richard on the Lane brothers' yacht, *Penguin*.

The Lane brothers skylarking, photographed by Nora.

Richard Lane in Naval
uniform, 1941.

Richard Lane and
fellow officers on
board HMAAAFCS
Springbank, 1941.

Allen and Lettice with their wedding-day guard of honour, 26 June 1941.

Betty and Richard visiting Renmark on their honeymoon, July 1948.

Betty, Richard and colleagues celebrate Penguin design, London, early 1950s.

Richard Lane's daughter, Elizabeth Lane, and her children, Richard, Louise and Alexandra Paton.

Despite their military commitments, Richard and John stayed in tune with the affairs of their firm throughout the war and worked on Penguin projects while on leave and during the many stretches of down-time. From port and aboard the *Mollusc*, the *Springbank*, the *Malaya* and, later, the *Avenger*, both brothers continued to help run the Penguin machine. They reviewed manuscripts and wrote scores of business letters dealing with matters such as royalties, paper, printing, distribution, discounts, new titles, new series and New York. Once, when the *Springbank* docked at Methil, the pair called on Mr Frazer of John Menzies, the Edinburgh wholesaler that owned most of Scotland's railway book-stalls, to advance the sale of Penguins at Scottish train stations. Like Allen, the younger Lanes were always on the lookout for new authors and titles, and they maintained their vigilance in the Navy. At Gibraltar, they dined with an earnest chaplain who had written an earnest book and wanted to discuss its publication, and on many other occasions they heard and scrutinised ideas for new Penguin titles. The documents destroyed with the *Springbank* were not just Naval – they included literary manuscripts, publishing proposals and Penguin correspondence. After the sinking, Eunice Frost wrote to apologise to C.S. Kent. Lieutenant Lane 'was particularly interested in the idea of making a selection of your *Times Fourth Leaders*', she wrote, and 'had the material with him to work on. Unfortunately these went down with the ship.' Allen expanded: 'I am glad to say that both of my brothers got away from HMS *Springbank*, although one of them broke a couple of bones in his leg in the process. They are really more concerned over the loss of your cuttings than any item in their belongings.'

Perhaps unexpectedly, the Lanes' paperback venture assumed a new vitality in the depths of wartime. The Penguin model of standardisation and economisation exactly suited military logistics and wartime austerity. Leonardo da Vinci's format, suitably jerry-built by Hans Mardersteig, was perfect for a soldier's pocket or pouch, and massive numbers of Penguins were carried to the frontlines. On the home front, the appetite for reading – an ideal wartime entertainment – swelled, and all publishers found that readers cleared bookshops as fast as they could.

From 1940, Britain's commercial publishers came under a strict wartime regime of paper rationing. Each firm had an enforced quota that was measured in tons and based on the publisher's paper demand in the year preceding the war. For Penguin, 1938–1939 had been the year of the production record-breaking Specials, so the ration allocated to the Lanes was 'plush beyond the wildest dreams of any aspiring competitor'.

Notwithstanding this plushness, Morpurgo and Lewis both recount the story of Allen arranging to meet a black-marketeer (Lewis calls him a 'paper spiv') as part of a crazy plan to circumvent the quota. When Bob Maynard and Stan Olney unearthed the plan, they mounted vocal and cogent objections, in the face of which Allen 'took himself off for a holiday and left Olney and Maynard to extricate Penguin' from an unnecessarily risky scheme that would have jeopardised good relations with the military authorities.

In an altogether sounder deal, Richard negotiated with the Canadian government to barter Penguins for Canadian paper. This had an unexpected sweetener attached: 'The agreed calculation had been made in North American tons, but the Penguin account was submitted, and met, in Imperial tons, giving Penguin an unmerited bonus of 10 per cent.' The firm made the best use of its paper allowance by printing on thinner stock with narrower spacing and margins, and by discarding those ephemeral dust jackets.

Penguin was able to further expand its paper ration by collaborating with the authorities to produce patriotic and militarily useful books. A Pelican committee meeting between Bill Williams and Richard and Allen came up with a way to turbo-charge distribution of quality paperbacks. In front of Brigadier General Morgan, Colonel Jackson and other War Office warriors, a Penguin delegation (Bill and Allen) hustled, pitched and manoeuvred the idea of a book club targeted specifically at members of the armed forces; in effect, a supercharged and ruggedised version of the First Edition Club. When ultimately the Forces Book Club was born (the first books appeared in October 1942), Williams and Allen used overt and covert tactics in a rearguard action to undermine Guild Books, a rival sixpenny imprint sponsored by Walter Harrap and the Publishers Association.

The Forces Book Club issued a selection of Penguin, Pelican and Special titles, bearing the Penguin imprint, in hefty quantities – up to 75,000 copies of each title – at the welcome rate of ten titles per month. To enable Penguin to supply the Club, the paper controllers augmented the firm's paper ration generously. Penguin's authors received an additional royalty, and a warm inner glow, when their books appeared as Club titles. A marketing coup that promoted the Lanes' imprint on a gigantic scale at a critical time, the subsidised initiative also channelled public funds into Penguin's coffers, and allowed the company to reduce the cost of its normal non-Club titles: the firm 'could write off most of the print costs of publishing against the subsidised edition and run on, at comparatively low cost, copies for the public market' – effectively a second subsidy from the government.

Richard's calculus of big print runs and small unit costs thus reached a marvellous crescendo during the war, and Penguin's good cheer found its largest and most receptive audience. That two of the Lane brothers were active in the fighting services (and one of them, Richard, maintained strong ties with military intelligence) enhanced Penguin's standing in the eyes of officialdom and helped smooth the way for initiatives like the Club, which Morpurgo called 'without doubt one of the most successful public relations campaigns of the century; this conditioning of a whole generation to a sense of gratitude for Penguins, to a degree of autobiographical identification with Penguin achievement'. Allen, too, maintained connections with the fighting services. Though he obtained an exemption from being called up, he held as a formality throughout the war the rank of Captain in the Territorial Army and served briefly as a corporal in the Home Guard.

For Penguin, perhaps the most important benefit of the Forces Book Club was a deepening of collaboration between company and state. Richard, John and (when he was thinking straight about wartime austerity and compliance) Allen saw what benefits could flow from bringing Penguin into the sphere of wartime officialdom. They cultivated current and prospective politicians left, right and centre, and made the most of their own military and bureaucratic links. Apart from working at Penguin, Bill Williams maintained a parallel career as a member of public cultural and educational boards and, in wartime, as Director of the Army Bureau of Current Affairs. Through Williams, the Lanes connected with the Bureau and other administrative agencies, and brought into the Penguin fold other people who would further bolster good relations with the government. This strategy succeeded brilliantly. The Lanes and their firm became an integral part of the war economy. Against a global backdrop of extreme uncertainty, Penguin's war effort gave the imprint local certainty, and high profitability. Penguin sold everything it published, and had achieved by war's end a near monopoly in the British paperback market. It is only half an exaggeration to say the war made Penguin. It is no exaggeration at all to say Penguin, by war's end, would be established firmly as a national institution.

*

The war years were enormously productive: between 1939 and 1945, the firm published more than 600 new and reprint titles and launched nineteen new series, including the temporarily successful literary magazine *Penguin New Writing*, and the permanently successful children's imprint Puffin. With America entering the war, Penguin issued a well-timed monthly journal, *Transatlantic*, and an oddly timed series, on Modern Painters. The launch of French and Egyptian Penguins saw the Antarctic bird colonise new territories in the northern hemisphere.

Allen shared in Penguin's triumphs on the business front, but things were less positive at home. For Lettice Lane, her husband proved no Superman, and Silverbeck was more a Fortress of Solitude than the *Daily Planet*. Allen refused to admit his wife to the Penguiners' clubbish bubble, or to share with her his own immersion in a business and a lifestyle that, for him, went together. She also felt, quite reasonably, that she had been spurned by Allen's brothers, and pushed away by Allen himself in the bedroom. Triply disappointed with married life, Lettice reactivated an old affair with a Cambridge academic. Allen, aware of the affair and more used to being the cuckolder than the cuckold, fell into a sulk that could only be cured by spectacular news. That news came when Lettice fell pregnant. Clare Lane was born in April 1942, and Allen embraced wholeheartedly a new role, that of the proud and doting father.

In October 1942, Richard's ship returned to England and he went again to Yeovilton for more training. John was meanwhile appointed to the escort carrier HMS *Avenger*. When it docked at Greenock, the younger Lane brothers were able to rendezvous and spend a memorable night at the Central Hotel in Glasgow. Then John and the *Avenger* left on a mission to support a critical operation that would become a turning point in the war: Operation Torch, the Allied landings in French North Africa.

Richard went on leave. Just outside a village, he heard church bells ringing for the first time in years, not to announce a German invasion but to celebrate the successful landings that would help evict the Axis powers from the desert. Richard stayed at Silverbeck for a few days. One afternoon, he received a telegram: 'THE ADMIRALTY REGRET TO INFORM YOU THAT LT. COMMANDER JOHN LANE IS MISSING, PRESUMED KILLED.' Allen was out with Bill Rapley when he received the same message.

Holding on to the possibility that John might have survived – as he had the sinking of the *Mollusc* and the *Springbank* – Richard made enquiries through his Naval network and went the next day to White-hall. There he learnt that 'presumed' meant 'definitely'. On the morning of 15 November 1942, the *Avenger* went down with more than 800 souls on board. John Lane was not among the four survivors.

The impact on the Williams-Lanes, and especially on the two older brothers, was enormous. John and Richard and Allen had been a close-knit fraternal unit since their first meeting in 1908, when Allen and Richard mistook their baby brother for a custard tart. Friends now noticed the new seriousness, like armour plating, that surrounded Allen and Richard, manifestly dimming their brightness.

Though for many years Richard and John shared a home, friends, meals and bathwater, the war had brought them together as never before. For much of their Naval service, their daily movements, and sometimes the occupations of each and every hour, were held in common, and it was rare for one of them to go ashore without the other. Richard now wrote bleakly of the 'lonely days ahead':

> Possibly I am being selfish ... when I think that [John's] death has meant more to me than anyone else. Father and Mother have the family as a whole to cope with, its daily additions and alterations help, I think, to keep them young in spirit and interested in life generally. Allen and Nora, being married, have their own individual problems and joys and both can watch the daily growth of children, unfortunately denied John, who would I think have made a good and amusing parent – whereas I have nothing individual to look forward to.

In his grief, Richard remembered childhood exploits at Cotham Vale and Coombe Dingle; John's precious World Tour letters describing his harem and elephants, and that epic journey by taxi from Melbourne to Perth; the invasion scare at the north-west Bastion near Portsmouth; the moment John and Richard boarded the *Springbank* ('Lane brothers reporting for duty'), and other indelible episodes on board, like John wedging himself between the Wrens on the ward-room divan. Richard thought of the brothers' time at Scapa and Kirkwall; Loch Ewe, where they fished and John caught his first trout; idyllic times near The Rocks with Nora; surviving the sinking of the *Springbank* with the ship's mascot and their best clothes intact; the return journey on the *Fowey*, then recuperation in England, where John had cared for his brother so thoughtfully.

Richard's injury separated Brother John from Brother Dick; afterwards, Richard hardly saw John again. On the *Springbank* they had supported each other and protected the ship's company, as when the Lanes discovered the wine store had been broken into and took extreme measures to prevent further casualties. But Richard was filled with regret that he had not been on the *Avenger* to support, protect or suffer alongside his brother.

Allen, too, felt the loss terribly, though his reaction was characteristically uneven. In his grief, he would swing from calm withdrawal and near paralysis to violent outbursts and wild displays of emotion. One observer told how Allen was talking to a colleague when they were interrupted by the telegram that first brought the sad news: 'Lane received the telegram, read it, folded it up, put it in his jacket pocket then, without saying a word, went on talking to Bill Rapley, the London rep, about an order from Bumpus.' Later, in a less controlled moment, Allen, quickly forgetting the rivalrous tensions that had flared at Silverbeck, and deciding that John had been the best and closest of brothers, said something hateful and wounding: in the Navy's fight against Britain's enemies, the wrong brother had been killed.

POWER AND GLORY

A few days after notifying the Williams-Lane family of John's death, the Admiralty appointed Lieutenant Richard Lane as Fighter Direction Officer on the battleship HMS *Duke of York* and told him to report for duty in a matter of hours. He sought instead a shore posting so he could settle his brother's personal affairs. The Admiralty agreed and told him to remain on leave pending another appointment. Solemnly, Richard saw to his brother's will and estate, and the deeds John had signed to establish Penguin Books Inc. in New York.

In the weeks and months that followed John's passing, Allen had a full breakdown. He withdrew from friends and colleagues, drank alone, refused to eat, and avoided his daughter, Clare, who reminded him of John as a baby. At night, Allen cried himself to sleep. Agatha Christie said her old friend was inconsolable and that his character had changed completely. Eunice Frost witnessed an unprecedented disintegration; it was, she said, the 'only time I ever knew Allen to be uncalm and unconfident'. He would soon augment his astrologer's advice with that of a mainstream psychiatrist.

When Richard's new Naval appointment came through, he proceeded to the Royal Navy Air Station at Hatston in the Orkney Islands to supervise construction of a homing beacon and the Fighter Direction School at Hestar Geo. The posting, in a remote and unspoilt location on the rugged coast of Mainland, was perfectly timed and a tonic for Richard; 'the sea came to within a few feet of the main block, and in one direction, west, the nearest land was about three thousand miles away.' At the most difficult time in his life, the bracing wildness of Orkney and the friendly hospitality of the Orcadians helped him immeasurably. He came to love both the place and its people. In solitary moments at Skara Brae and among the mysterious standing stones and barrows of Stenness and Maeshowe, Richard contemplated his brother and his loss. Alone with his thoughts and ancient ghosts, he felt such pride for his brother-Penguin, the Pigeon Officer and bird of passage who had nobly toasted the sunken *Bismarck*, excelled in the Navy, and died serving a righteous cause. In every remaining year of his life, Richard would retreat into quiet reflection around the time of John's death.

Richard's wartime service had started in Fighter Direction and would end there. At war's end, he left one thing behind in Orkney: the radio call-sign of the Fighter Direction School, 'penguin'. As soon as he was demobbed, he went straight back to an office still largely occupied by Air Ministry personnel. When eventually the Ministry moved from Harmondsworth, it left standing the buildings that had been added on during the war: a Seco hut, which became Penguin's accounts department; a hanger, to be used as bulk storage for Penguin's standing stock of more than eight million books; and a canteen, cold and unamenable, whose leftovers fed the pigs at Priory Farm.

Just as post-war Britain differed markedly from its pre-war incarnation, so too the Penguin that Richard Lane rejoined in 1945 was very unlike the 1939 model. The Forces Book Club and other wartime collaborations had turned the firm into a national institution; its output was a part of the public good. Some time would pass before a new routine could be established; throughout 1945 and 1946, the firm's staff and management were in flux as demobbed Penguiners returned while others, like Edward Young, confirmed they would look for work elsewhere.

Despite the flux, Richard Lane transitioned easily into full-time Penguin business. From the *Springbank* and Hestar Geo he had stayed in touch with the affairs of the firm, and now he re-immersed himself in work he loved. Full of energy and ideas, he reviewed the firm's publishing program and its overloaded list. He analysed the state of advances, contracts, production costs and ledgers. In the royalty accounts, he discovered Penguin was paying an above-market royalty to the long-dead author of *Alice in Wonderland*. Other problems were equally glaring.

Perennially the bibliophile inside the paperback publisher, Richard had brought to Penguin a concern with good design and the physicality of book-making. Now, in the production department, he encountered sloppiness and scattershot methods that reminded him of The Bodley Head after Uncle John's death.

Editorial standards had slipped. Readers accepted that wartime economising had thinned and darkened paper, shrunk type and squeezed spacing and margins, but sacrifices had also been made in the quality of fact-checking, copy-editing and proofreading. Now, typos and howlers and sloppy blurbs were among the many indicators of a persistent carelessness and poor coordination that could no longer be passed off as wartime exigencies. Richard planned a campaign to restore and enhance Penguin's standards, and at the same time to set the business on a sounder footing. The books would look better, readers would be treated with greater respect, and the Penguin business would be run along more professional and efficient lines towards greater profitability.

Apart from mapping out a strategic push towards higher quality and performance, Richard fought tactical skirmishes in the name of improvement. The proofs of a new illustrated Puffin picture book, Phyllis Ladyman's *About a Motor Car*, were full of the kind of errors that even Don Mount of Renmark could have spotted. Richard Lane, former track driver and bush mechanic, scrutinised the draft illustrations and 'produced a detailed critique of sodium valves, gudgeon pins and cylinder heads'. When corrected, the book sold handsomely and was translated into more than twenty languages. Channelling his inner jackeroo, Richard made similarly improving comments on another Puffin, *On the Farm*, whose illustrations featured a plough 'without tripping gear' – even more old-fashioned than the one he had wrestled with at Bective.

In the 1920s, Uncle John had rejected a manuscript from a young author named Graham Greene. Now, in the 1940s, Greene was recognised as perhaps the best novelist of his generation, but he maintained an uneasy and precarious relationship with the Lanes. In 1945, he complained that the author biography in the Penguin edition of *England Made Me* was 'horribly chatty and personal and the photograph was wildly out of date'. Penguin tried to do better with a new edition of *Brighton Rock* (first published in 1938) and sought his consent to republish *The Power and the Glory* (1940) and *The Ministry of Fear* (1943).

Greene refused, arguing in the case of *Power* that appearing in Penguin covers 'would damage the sale of the five shilling edition', though he green-lighted publication of *The Lawless Roads*, the travel book on which *The Power and the Glory* was based. In early 1946, Allen sent Greene two Penguins – *England Made Me* and *Brighton Rock* – for their author to sign and return for the publisher's burgeoning collection of autographed copies. Greene promptly replied: 'I return the two books with insulting comments on your awful publicity matter on the back of *England Made Me*!' Soon after, Greene's agent David Higham wrote to Richard Lane to say his author was now even more upset: 'on the spine of your edition of *The Lawless Roads* his name is misspelt. Anything that I can tell him?'

Problems with biographical notes were not confined to Greeneland. The bio on an edition of Virginia Woolf's *The Common Reader* called *Orlando* an outstanding example of the 'stream of consciousness' technique. In reply, Leonard Woolf wrote with a revised version, saying the original bio was 'rather absurdly inaccurate, for *Orlando* is notable among my wife's books for having no "stream of consciousness technique" in it at all!' Vita Sackville-West objected strongly to being called, in the biography for *All Passion Spent*, 'the wife of a diplomat', an expression 'which evokes a dreadful type of person, only too familiar to me: the social, bridge-playing woman, who writes a little in her spare time and turns her foreign experiences to good account in the pursuit of publicity and pocket money!'

Nor was the error on the Greene spine the only one to evade Penguin's scrutineers. Captain W.E.D. Allen wrote to Eunice Frost from Beirut about *Guerrilla War in Abyssinia*; 'there are a certain number of misprints, the worst of which was a reference to Colonel Wingate in a "shapeless wet toupee" instead of topee! . . . PS: We are in the midst of a *coup d'etat* here at the moment.' A selection of other Penguin errors from the 1940s and later shows the pitfalls that publishers sometimes face: 'pit-bottom' became 'bit-bottom'; 'Gwyn Jones' became 'Glyn Jones'; in *Henry the Sixth Part One*, 'prostrate' became 'prostate' ('Meantime, look gracious on thy prostate thrall'); in a Penguin Special on *Housing*, 'pretty standardized blocks of flats' became 'good-looking standardized blocks of flats'; and 15,000 copies of *Exile and the Kingdom* were printed with the author's name on the title page given as 'Albert

Acmus'. Dangerous errors in Penguin cookbooks caused amateur chefs and their families and guests to overdose on nutmeg and hashish.

Despite the production hitches, Virginia Woolf and Graham Greene would star in the Penguin orange livery and the firm would take their writing to millions of readers. George Bernard Shaw was another popular pillar of the list. Allen and Richard both held him in the highest regard, and both had received many postcards (Shaw's preferred means of correspondence) rich with mischief and acute touches. Richard, for example, had maintained a long and playful correspondence with Shaw about the publication of *Plays Pleasant and Unpleasant* and other volumes of his work. In 1944, when Allen tried to start Clare collecting autographs, he provocatively wrote to Shaw, who provocatively replied. 'I think it is perfectly wicked to start an innocent child wasting her time and worrying her neighbouring fellow creatures with the useless practice of autograph collecting (except at the foot of cheques). Why not buy her a Teddy Bear?' Shaw agreed to send his autograph, on condition that Allen took 'the moral responsibility'.

Richard had noticed in the contract files that Penguin owned an option on the cheap editions of Shaw's works. This discovery sparked in Richard an idea that would become one of the greatest Penguin publishing successes: a ten-book edition of Shaw's plays, each book produced in a run of 100,000 copies, and each copy selling for a shilling. Richard well remembered the stunning early success of the *Intelligent Woman's Guide*. In August 1946, he wrote to Allen about capitalising on the option, and the 'priority one' importance of calling on 'the old boy', at Ayot St Lawrence or Whitehall Court, to win his blessing for the edition. To convince Allen, Richard gave his brother's feathers a stroke: 'Shaw has a very very great personal regard for you,' he wrote. Allen agreed to visit the author, whose blessing was as readily forthcoming as his support had been throughout the Lanes' reprint venture.

Ostensibly timed to celebrate Shaw's ninetieth birthday (he was born in July 1856), the release of the Shaw Million captivated the nation's readers, who formed long queues outside bookshops and newsagents to collect their share of the Million. The edition was the most tangible evidence yet of Penguin's ambition to make high-quality books widely available. Steve Hare has called it 'an extraordinary publishing coup'. A jovial celebration followed at Silverbeck, in which the guests ate raspberries that Richard had caned and picked. Stanley Morison toasted 'the most significant event in publishing in our time'. Sales of the Shaws helped Penguin reach another milestone: the sale of its hundred-millionth book. Other 'Millions' would follow, including a Wells Million – to mark H.G. Wells' eightieth birthday – and, more than a decade later, a Lawrence Million that would have far-reaching consequences.

*

At the time of Penguin's inception, the Lane brothers ran the firm as a triumvirate, and held exactly equal shareholdings: there were three shares in total, and each brother held a single share. After John's death, Allen made a play for super-majority ownership of the firm. With help from his lawyers and advisers, he created tens of thousands of new shares, and set up a new ownership structure in which the surviving brothers would no longer hold equal shares. Instead, Allen would hold 75 per cent and Richard 25 per cent of the owner equity of Penguin.

Allen dangled sugar so that Richard would consent to the new structure, in which Allen effectively took over not only all of John's stake but also a quarter of Richard's. The eldest brother offered to make Richard the beneficiary of life-insurance policies that would theoretically pay out enough to fund the purchase of Allen's shares in the event of his death. This arrangement would entrench Richard formally as Allen's successor and Penguin's future sole owner – provided he outlived his brother. Richard for his part was less interested in the sugar than in reaching a formal understanding that gave his brother sufficient executive latitude, while carving out a significant but non-threatening role for himself. Richard hoped to curb the insecurity that had flared in Allen before and during the war. Otherwise, Richard feared, he would be an obvious target for Allen's corporate manoeuvring. Other thoughts were also in Richard's mind when he considered the offer. He wanted to calm the Penguin waters and protect what the Lane brothers had created by making the most of their complementarities. He wanted to maintain Penguin's philosophy of good cheer, and to inject some kindness and wisdom into Allen's approach to business, management and life. And, despite

Allen's escalating megalomania, Richard wanted the best for the brother he still revered. So he agreed, and began paying half the premiums on Allen's life policies. Richard Lane became the junior shareholder in Penguin, and the prince to Penguin's king.

During the war, Allen's control over Penguin had been only half legitimate. Thanks to Richard's accommodation of the 75/25 shareholding agreement, Allen was now no longer the de facto but the de jure head of Penguin. With Richard relegated, and John no longer present as a shrewd and sceptical counterbalance, Allen became even more tycoonish and dictatorial, the unchallenged leader he had always assumed he would be. There might have been a coup in Beirut, but at Penguin the autocrat was in charge. The celebratory Penguin publication of 1945 – celebrating not the end of the war but the end of the first Penguin decade – proclaimed Allen's supremacy in hyperbole he would not have dared to use while John was alive: 'Allen Lane is very much the head of Penguin Books Ltd. He is its principal source of inspiration and invention as well as its presiding genius. He has a pretty clear idea of what he wants Penguin Books to become, but it would require a whole Penguin Special to accommodate all the details of his plans.'

Growth and diversification figured prominently in those plans. Throughout the 1940s, Allen collected new series with the same energy he applied to collecting autographs, antiques and saucy anecdotes. Despite the growth of the company, he maintained his chaotic methods: he still carried around scraps of paper scrawled with notes and ideas; he was still 'prone to vanish suddenly and without explanation'; and he retained his dislike of meetings – if they could be moved to the local pub (the Peggy Bedford) or, better still, to a rowboat at Silverbeck, 'lubricated with lashings of gin', they became more bearable.

Richard set about advising his brother on how to run the ever-expanding Penguin. In November 1945, he presented his manifesto under the gentle cover of 'what I think should be our policy for the next few years'. He proposed putting an end to 'uncontrolled or unplanned schemes', tightening up the firm's international network, and purging 'slapdash' methods from editorial and senior management:

> Take the large atlas project for example. You write a couple of letters,
> see a couple of interesting persons, and go off for six months. Frosty

writes a couple of letters, including one which is now filed as a contract, but which in fact only stipulates that we pay someone some money, but doesn't mention what the person receiving the money is to do in return, she then goes off. The situation, one might say, had now arrived at a half-baked state. But half-baked before the ingredients had been decided on or mixed, and the cooks had not yet discussed whether the mixture should go in the hot oven or on the simmering ring.

Richard prodded his brother to define accurately all senior positions in the firm, and to reduce the burdensome amount of capital locked up in long-term commitments like half-started new ventures and juicy prepayments: tens of thousands of pounds sat out of reach in advances for unwritten books. The firm's management should cultivate friendly relations with cooperative publishers, and ensure that someone senior was in the office every day. Allen himself needed to keep more regular hours, and a diary, 'mentioning whom you have seen during the day, and what you discussed'. He should hire a personal private secretary, and do other things that normal CEOs do, like being polite to staff, and taking department heads and their spouses out to dinner. 'Any policies or contracts we should naturally discuss, so that in the event of either of us going away, no unnecessary hold-up [will] occur.' Richard said he disliked people who called themselves directors, but, 'as this is our job, we should aim to carry it out'.

Perhaps the most important change Richard recommended would involve the owner-directors themselves. Allen had to get out of the rough. 'How long do you seriously consider you intend to go on dealing with difficult people and difficult situations? No one enjoys their leisure more than you, but unless some more definite policy is worked out, I am afraid your periods of leisure are not going to increase unless at the cost of the inefficiency of the whole concern.' The 'definite policy' in Richard's manifesto was that the prince would serve as a roving Chief Operating Officer or Deputy CEO, who would keep things running smoothly, clean up loose ends and bring order to the whole enterprise. With support of that kind, the king could become a 'benevolent dictator' who made the uppermost strategic decisions, spent much more time at Priory Farm and on holiday, and generally extracted himself from the day-to-day.

There is really no serious need for you to have to cope with all the difficult people and situations you do. I think they are nearly all caused by your having led people on. Possibly you don't know how infectious your enthusiasm can be, and people not knowing you well are apt to consider that you mean everything you say.

Allen was, Richard said, 'apt to waste time following up unnecessary people and ideas'.

In your position, you should be able to push them on to someone else. Apart from the waste of time, it is a waste of effort, and it would do you more good wandering around the garden contemplating than burning up effort talking to tiresome nitwits.

Allen made appreciative noises – he told Rubeigh Minney that, when Richard worried about a particular problem, 'there's no need for me to worry too' – and accepted his brother's judgment on the sloppinesss and slippages in the firm, conceding that 'we are definitely not first-class in our production', and that 'much more attention' needed to be paid to the editorial side. 'At the moment, any number of things slip through merely for want of someone taking an intelligent interest.' They needed to do better: 'each book which goes to press should be as perfect as possible and carry with it the feeling that it is not just another paperback but a book on which considerable thought has been expended. We have so much of which we can be justly proud that without boasting, we can yet give the impression that to be published by us is indeed a hallmark.'

Allen agreed that new recruits 'ought to be vetted by both of us', and he also struck a positive note in response to Richard's proposal for a new executive structure. 'I feel that there is some truth in your benevolent dictator theory and I wonder if absence from the office isn't a good thing in order to bring out the best in others.' Agreeing with Richard that Allen needed to step back, Bill Williams flattered Allen with a military analogy:

The magnitude to which Penguins has grown involves, so far as you personally are concerned, the exercise of the habit of delegation. I am no lover of Field Marshal Montgomery, as you know, but I am certain he was able to handle his operations because he did not involve himself in the day-to-day detail but kept his mental energy for viewing his broad objectives. He picked a small group of men on whose advice he put great weight, and once an operation had been argued out in this little council of war, he let the event take care of itself. That is the only reality I can see in the much abused word 'leadership'.

When Williams suggested that a Gang of Five might run Penguin, Allen wrote to Richard saying he would he happy, 'in fact relieved', to hand executive control to Williams as 'chief editor', Harry Paroissien as 'a sort of general manager', himself and Richard as roving principals, and a fifth person to manage production. Under such an arrangement, Allen wrote, 'we ourselves should be able to spare more time for farming and other pursuits'. After saying he would like to devote up to half of his own time to Priory Farm, he countered Williams' idea with his own proposal: a Council of Six that included Eunice Frost.

A new member of staff, Tatyana Kent, would act as the council's general aide. The hexagonal committee could only be complete if Penguin secured a suitable production manager. The firm would do just that, in a sequence of events that changed irrevocably, and for the better, twentieth-century book design.

THE NELSON TOUCH

In Richard's words, the Lanes' plans for Penguin centred on showing 'the reading public that it was possible to have good taste in cheap books'. They were plans that needed a guiding hand – someone with fresh ideas who could crystallise Penguin's design integrity. At lunch, Allen mentioned these aims to the bookman Oliver Simon, who had known Richard as far back as the First Edition Club and John Holroyd-Reece as far back as Albatross, and whose work at the Curwen Press was highly regarded. (Simon's wife Ruth shared some of Allen's pseudo-scientific beliefs and had introduced him to graphology.) Simon said the best man for the job, 'without doubt', was the Swiss typographer Jan Tschichold.

Though Penguin had benefited from talented production staff, and its managers had collaborated at arm's length with some of Britain's best designers and lettering artists, Allen and Richard had never before thought of letting loose in-house an expert typographer. 'Having got his teeth into a problem, Allen was never one to waste time,' Richard later wrote, 'so after phoning Tschichold, he chartered an aeroplane' and flew with Simon to Switzerland. Allen and Tschichold discussed the terms that would entice the typographer to England and Penguin. They agreed a salary, subject to two conditions: Allen had to discuss the remuneration with Richard, and they had to obtain permission from the Bank of England's exchange controllers so that Tschichold could remit money to Switzerland.

Richard had confidence in Oliver Simon's judgment on matters of typography and book-making. But, when he saw the salary his brother had put forward, he fell off his chair. 'I was not against employing an eminent typographer,' Richard wrote afterward, 'but I did think the salary Allen had offered him was more than we could afford. It was in fact more than Allen's and my combined salaries. We had long arguments about it but Allen eventually got his way.'

Allen was on holiday when Tschichold arrived at Harmondsworth. Richard introduced the great typographer to the senior staff, and everyone was soon calling him Tishy. A few days later, the firm had its annual staff outing. Compared to previous Paris jaunts, the excursion to Brighton 'was rather a dull affair': a plain lunch, followed by wholesome seaside games. Richard drove Tishy and Frosty to the venue in his car, and returned with them via a circuitous route so Tishy could see the picturesque villages and countryside. Spotting a cricket match on a village green, the three Penguiners stopped to watch. Tschichold had never encountered cricket before, 'so we had to explain everything to him'.

'How many men are there in each team?' he asked from the back seat.

'Eleven,' said Richard.

A slight pause. 'I can only see fifteen,' said Tschichold.

'That's because, although the whole side of one team is fielding, there are only two of the other side on the field at one time. They are the batsmen.'

'How can you tell which are the batsmen?'

'One, because they have a bat, and two, they also wear pads to guard their legs.'

'Who is the man wearing pads but who hasn't got a bat?'

'The wicket keeper.'

'Which side is he on?'

'The same side as the other fielders.'

'Who are the players wearing white coats?'

'They are the umpires.'

'Two umpires, one for each side, I presume.'

This went on, back and forth, until there was a long pause. The typographer had fallen asleep, and Richard and Frosty shared a sceptical glance about their star recruit.

When Tishy settled in to work at Harmondsworth, he did not like what he saw. Penguin and Pelican's standard covers copied the serifless style of Albatross and Gollancz, but without any distinction or unity of design. The internal typography too was a mess: poorly spaced letters and poorly selected typefaces impaired legibility and beauty. And his verdict on the Penguin logo? 'Deformed' and 'corrupted'. Richard shared with the newcomer his plans for low-cost good taste, and the two spent a great deal of time together developing 'a better system than the existent one for production generally'. Richard's confidence in the typographer grew, and he wrote to Allen with a proposal: 'I think apart from being our chief typographical expert, he should be the real head of the Production Department.' If Tschichold were to remain at Penguin a mere typographical dabbler, his potential would be wasted and his salary would be too much to swallow; but if he led production overall, Richard would be content. Allen agreed, and the Gang found its sixth member.

Innovative and perfectionist, Jan Tschichold cultivated throughout his career a uniquely strange blend of freethinking and rigid conformity to fixed rules. Having escaped persecution by the Nazis, he settled in Switzerland and advanced groundbreaking ideas for both modern and classical typography. He shared Allen's interest in graphology, and in interior design: Tishy's flat in Switzerland 'was entirely white except for the shiny black floor'. After being wooed by Allen and scrutinised by Richard, Tishy would spend two and a half years at Penguin, paying close attention to every book and every series, and establishing exacting systems of quality control that spread from the office to Penguin's printers and even its competitors. He knocked into shape the standard Penguin and Pelican covers and conferred on them a typographical beauty. After dozens of attempts to pluck, tuck and lipo-suck the misshapen logo, he replaced it with a sharper and more elegant bird that would become an icon of global design and serve the firm for decades to come.

Tschichold waged a personal war on slow English printers, grey paper, bad typesetting and lazy design. He established the Penguin Composition Rules, which embedded his strict prescriptions for text composition, capitalisation, paragraph indentation, spelling, punctuation marks, folios, footnotes and figures. 'Between initials and names, as in G.B. Shaw and after all abbreviations where a full point is used, use a smaller (fixed) space than between the other words in the line.' 'The word spaces in lines either of capitals or small capitals should not exceed an en quad.' Other publishers adopted Tishy's Penguin Composition Rules. His insistence that printers be given detailed instructions on what was expected for each book became the norm in the industry. (If printers ever dared to deviate from his directives, Tishy would exclaim, 'Whom do they think I am? I am not somebody so-and-so, I am Jan Tschichold!') When sterling was devalued in 1949, he returned to Switzerland, where he designed 'leaflets for tranquilizers' and other pharmaceuticals, and a remarkable era at Penguin came to an end. Tishy's typographic legacy at Penguin would be ably protected and advanced, however, by the equally exacting Hans Schmoller when he joined the firm from Oliver Simon's team at the Curwen Press.

*

Tschichold had achieved Richard's goal of bringing to mass-produced books what Simon called 'the typographical care and experience that had been lavished on the *edition de luxe*'. At Harmondsworth, Richard Lane continued to advise his brother on improvements and dangers. One big risk was Penguin's overstretched international network of agencies and subsidiaries. Allen had visited South America in 1944 and met young Tatyana Kent of Uruguay. He recruited her to Penguin so that she could further its interests in Brazil and Argentina. Richard was sceptical: though Allen hoped that, with Tatyana on the payroll, the South American business would 'almost run itself', Richard did not think it would be 'quite as easy as all that'. And especially not alongside other foreign headaches like New York and the old empire. 'To do any good in Egypt will obviously require a fair amount of supervision. India ... could no doubt be a terrific project again if time and care can be given to it. Australia, New Zealand, South Africa and Canada all want attention.' For the foreseeable future, caution and consolidation should rule Penguin's realm. 'Regarding subsidiary branches generally ... soft-pedalling from now onwards should be the general trend.'

The news from Australia – 'Penguins few and out of date' – was especially discouraging. Within weeks of Bob Maynard's demobilisation from the Navy in 1946, he found himself en route to Australia to assess and advance Penguin's interests there. Maynard saw that great opportunities were being missed, and he told Allen he would like to stay and open a proper subsidiary. Though Allen agreed, he accepted Richard's advice that Penguin as a whole was over-extended, writing in 1947 that, 'much as it goes against the grain to say it, there seems to be so little inducement to spread one's wings, that one is inclined to say let's hang on to what we have and know about and save ourselves the headaches of branches in the US, Canada, Australia, the Argentine and Brazil. You can say "I told you so" and with some justification, but honestly the worries attendant on so many enterprises are beginning to tell on me.'

The relationship between Penguin's English head office and its American subsidiary was fraught with inherent tensions. America was a bigger market, and had forged its own literary taste and identity. The managers of Penguin in New York naturally wanted to publish their own books, American books, for the American market, while Allen pushed continually to sell more English books there: either titles initiated and edited in England or, better still, books made entirely in England and exported. Allen understandably saw America as a Penguin colony, but the Americans were constitutionally against colonial subservience. The nature of American bookselling was an ongoing irritation. Penguin Books Inc. sold its wares through 'about 100,000 magazine dealers and not on orders from professional booksellers'; Allen deplored the American practice of retailing on a sale-or-return basis, as often the sales were skinny and the returns very fat. Allen and Richard shared deep-seated concerns about the American branch. Could it ever stand on its own feet and be profitable, to the advantage of its parent, while staying within the bounds of US trade law? Could the brothers be sure of retaining control over the subsidiary and, most importantly, the Penguin brand in America?

Faced with the challenge of navigating this maze, the Lanes' first American manager, Ian Ballantine, threw up his hands and decamped in 1945 with most of the New York staff to set up his own house, Bantam Books. Allen looked to Kurt Enoch and Eunice Frost to help rebuild, and the Lane brothers would do their share of the rebuilding as well. During the war, Allen had befriended an energetic young man from the American Embassy. Victor Weybright could keep up with Allen's wartime drinking and partying. Though he lacked experience in book publishing, he had worked on literary magazines and could talk intelligently about literature and culture. After the war, when Weybright's London posting came to an end, Allen devised a vague plan to pair Weybright with Enoch in New York.

With an equally vague job description, Weybright arrived at Penguin's American office. Attempting a kind of spy-versus-spy or pea-and-thimble trick, Allen quietly told Weybright that he would act as Allen's personal representative in America and report confidentially to him; and he said the same thing to Enoch. In this atmosphere of espionage and intrigue, Weybright's diplomatic training stood him in good stead. He found Enoch humorless and authoritarian, but he valued the German's experience in production and distribution, and resolved to bring him into his confidence, even though Allen had said not to. Enoch for his part already doubted 'Allen's personal reliability and credibility'.

Having turned Enoch, Weybright began making noises and decisions that caused Allen to doubt his envoy's judgment and, worse, his obedience. When Weybright advocated publishing Erskine Caldwell, for example, Allen said sharply that a separate imprint – Porno Books – would be required. Allen feared that the pictorial covers favoured in America would drag Penguin into the company of what Richard Hoggart memorably spoke of as 'sexational' front-cover depictions of the 'gone wrong' girls whose 'blouses sag permanently where the last attempt at rape was beaten off'.

Things came to a head in the winter of 1945–1946. Allen wrote to Weybright with a secret ultimatum: Richard would travel to New York and liquidate Penguin Books Inc. unless Weybright 'could persuade Dick that the company had a future in conformity with the policy of Penguin Books Ltd.' Richard also had another mission: to make sense of the Penguin Inc. shareholdings, after Allen had promised Weybright a 40 per cent share, Enoch a 40 per cent share, and Eunice Frost a 10 per cent share, while at the same time stipulating that Penguin Limited in the UK would retain majority control!

Weybright shared Allen's ultimatum with Enoch, and Richard sailed for America, where he had long walking talks with Weybright around Garrison, New York. Invited for weekends at the American's Hollow Rock Farm in Maryland, Richard's inner jackeroo came out; according to Weybright, 'he moved among the workers and talked with the farmer in the manner of a beardless Tolstoy, never so happy as when his boots were muddy and his sleeves rolled up to the elbows as if he were about to perform a mighty task that never quite appeared to summon his ready muscles'. (Richard never lost the common touch while Allen never gained it. When the latter borrowed a hat from his gardener for a Jewish wedding, he 'asked the lady in the Penguin canteen to steam it clean' so he could wear it.)

Weybright painted a bright portrait of Penguin's American future and a dim one of its financial present. The firm had won the respect of readers, booksellers, critics and academics. America's population was booming, as were college enrolments. Quality publishers like Penguin were sitting pretty to ride the double boom. Though Penguin Books Inc. was under-capitalised and 'barely solvent', it had arranged for Fawcett to distribute its books, and for W.F. Hall in Chicago to print them on credit. After hearing Weybright's pitch and studying the market outlook – supported by Weybright's statistics on college matriculation and post-war demography – Richard agreed that the prospects were good, and sympathised with the delicate position in which the American office found itself. He sent a favourable report to Allen, who in turn wrote to Weybright thanking him for hosting Richard and expressing agreement with Weybright's 'theory of operations as relayed to him by Dick'.

In reality, Allen had strong reservations about the kind of books Weybright was publishing, and how he published them. Weybright seemed to aspire to kingship, to building an empire in America rather than being Allen's vassal; certainly he refused to be Allen's 'stooge'. Weybright sensed the king's displeasure, later writing: 'Allen Lane's Penguin correspondence soon after [Richard's visit] became very rapid and critical ... Some of Allen's criticism was most useful, some of it was remote and uninformed and some of it was calculated to build up a record of close supervision on all details.'

Then came the crunch. 'In 1946 a general glut developed on the American paperback book market,' Enoch wrote. 'Since we operated entirely on credits from the printers and the expectation of accumulated profits, and since Allen Lane could or would not provide proper financing with which to weather the storm, we were hard pressed by the situation.' According to Weybright, Penguin Books Inc. could no longer pay its bills to W.F. Hall on time, 'unless credit could be extended by the printer for a longer period than called for by our printing contract'.

> We stalled off the W.F. Hall Company by saying that all problems would be solved when Allen Lane came over personally in early 1947. The Hall people were not too disposed to patience, but their imaginative sales vice-president, Carl Braun, was persuaded that we would be a major company with substantial printing requirements and that Hall would be better off if we continued.

To help put Allen in a favourable frame of mind for his trip to the States, Weybright went to see him first in London. John Lane had mentioned in one of his World Tour letters the beautiful dogwood blossoms of the Hudson River Valley; Allen asked Weybright to find some dogwood saplings for the Lanes to plant at Priory Farm in memory of John. At his own expense, Weybright brought over, in the belly of the plane, 'a clump of fifteen-foot trees with about sixty pounds of frozen earth enclosed in burlap'. These he lugged through Dublin Airport, on to the Dun Laoghaire–Holyhead ferry, and transported by train to the Dorchester Hotel in London. Informed that the earth was too frozen at Priory Farm to plant the trees, Weybright had them delivered to Silverbeck instead.

On this visit, Lettice and Allen made Weybright the godfather of their new baby daughter, Anna, and Weybright felt that he had re-established his wartime rapport with Allen. But when Allen flew to New York, it would be more wartime than rapport. Allen had agreed with Weybright and Enoch that he would go to Chicago and confirm to W.F. Hall that Penguin Books Limited was responsible for the debts of Penguin Books Inc., but on the plane he changed his mind, and on arrival he dropped the bomb: Penguin Books Ltd, he said, 'could not stand back of the obligations of the New York branch'.

This pulled the rug from under Penguin Books Inc. According to Enoch, when Allen and Weybright met afterward for cocktails at the Hotel Elysée (known in some circles as Easy Lay), they quarrelled and Weybright 'made a personally critical remark which Allen Lane apparently resented'. Privately, the Americans began discussions with their lawyers with a view to 'orderly separation from Penguin Books Ltd and the acquisition of all their American assets'. This they hoped to negotiate when Enoch and Weybright flew with their lawyers to London in October, to meet Allen for another showdown in another hotel suite. The week before, Allen had bumped his eye. When he appeared at the meeting wearing an eye patch, Weybright made an impish gibe about 'The Nelson Touch' that left Allen unamused. Any personal warmth the men had once shared was now replaced on Allen's side by cold contempt.

The difficult negotiations, which lasted a week, also involved Williams, Frost and Richard Lane, whose undimmed regard for Weybright was reciprocated. The American described Richard as 'a lovable man, so accustomed to reflecting the buoyancy and energy of Allen Lane that he was generally accepted as a mysterious partner full of deep and unutterable wisdom'. Richard urged his brother to soften his approach and to step cautiously through negotiations that weighed heavily on Allen and sent Richard's own blood pressure to 'a record high of 220 plus'.

Towards the end of the week, Weybright went to a concert at Covent Garden with friends. After the performance, Weybright and his friends were walking between the concert hall and their car when they were mugged and he was beaten up. 'The next day,' Weybright wrote, 'I appeared at the negotiations with a black eye as if in some grim and monstrous attempt to ape Allen's eye patch.' Amid all this theatre, a full separation was agreed. Weybright and Enoch would operate the New York business under a new brand, and the Lanes would start from scratch in America. The ex-Penguiners insisted that the name for their new imprint, 'Signet', meant 'authoritative seal of quality', but others heard a homonym of 'baby swan' that hinted at another water bird, one that Weybright and Enoch perhaps thought was an ugly duckling.

Allen and Richard were satisfied that they had rescued their brand in America, and had executed a not very damaging split with former colleagues. In 1949, the Lanes would send Harry Paroissien to make a 'fresh start' for Penguin in the US. (The black-eyed, gun-slinging drama had a curious coda: Penguin would soon start publishing Westerns.)

Pictorial covers had been one of the sticking points between Britain and America. Enoch wrote of Allen: 'He did not sufficiently recognize or concede the peculiarities of the American market and the preferences of the American readers. He disliked picture covers which were a vital instrument of selling books merely by display in magazine outlets.' As early as the first Pelican editorial meetings, Richard Lane had raised the question of pictorial covers, and he had noticed and admired, on his 1946 visit to New York, how Pocket and Dell and Avon were clothing and displaying their books. Now, Pocket's kangaroo competed with Penguins around the world, and had even made inroads into the British market. Tastes were changing. Bright, four-colour, laminated wrappers appealed to post-war consumers in the New World and the Old. Pan paperbacks were among the first in the UK to exploit thoroughly the new preferences. At Penguin, full-colour promised to add another pleasing dimension to Richard Lane's philosophy of casual good cheer. In 1947, he became the first senior Penguin to take seriously the cheerful matter of illustrated covers. As a key plank of his own improvement manifesto, and Tishy's design program, Richard sought Allen's blessing to try out pictorial covers on a selection of titles. 'Although I know it will put up our production costs,' Richard wrote, 'I think we should still experiment with this style of production.'

The debate between pictorial and typographical covers had been and would continue to be won and lost on both sides, for one obvious reason: neither style is stably nor incontrovertibly better or worse. Different fashions and preferences would dictate which style was ascendant at any given moment, and those fashions and preferences would differ whimsically across time, across market segments and geographical regions. An unstable coexistence is the only equilibrium for pictorial and typographic covers. But the competition was delightfully productive: it threw off artful sparks, such as the illustrated cover designs of James Avati, Robert Jonas and Robert McInnes, and the classic typographical designs of Jan Tschichold and Hans Schmoller. Pictorial covers would become for Penguin the standard treatment, indispensable on key series such as Penguin Classics and Modern Classics. And then again, more than fifty years later, for a combination of nostalgic and economic reasons, Penguin would re-adopt for a major new reprint series its original cover typography and simple coloured stripes. (Penguin's first adoption of full-colour covers was not without hiccups. In the 1960s, Graham Greene reacted so strongly to Alan Aldridge's psychedelic pop-art-style Penguin covers, which Greene thought 'beyond belief', that he threatened to withdraw his books from the firm.)

*

After the war, Richard had moved into his old home, Silverbeck, which he now shared with Mr and Mrs Allen Lane. Tatyana Kent moved in, too (at, everyone stressed, Lettice's invitation), and an odd kind of domestic harmony reigned. Richard picked fresh produce from the garden, juiced the tomatoes and sauced the horseradish. Sometimes he cooked dinner, at least once serving badger, and Allen threw himself into practical chores around the house. Tatyana wrote to her mother in Uruguay, describing how Allen 'as likely as not' would be found 'scrubbing out the larder or cleaning out the tool cupboard'. In 1946, Allen celebrated his forty-fourth birthday with a party at Silverbeck. The guests dined not on badger but on caviar and roast goose. Richard invited a girlfriend; Tatyana was also there, along with Eunice Frost, Ifor Evans (the Provost of University College, London), Oliver Simon and his wife, Ruth, Bill Williams and his beautiful young mistress, Estrid Bannister.

The harmony would not last long. The year 1947 was a troubling one for Allen, and most of the trouble had nothing to do with work. Priory Farm's chickens fell ill, its inbred cows got VD, and the king penguin's interest in farming cooled. He also lost his appetite for parties, and struggled with alcohol, which he could no longer tolerate in the quantities he had lasted in his youth. Penguin author and art historian Nikolaus Pevsner wrote that Allen 'couldn't take the drink, he was so easily just slightly sozzled'. The brothers should 'drop spirits', Allen told Richard, and instead 'get in some wine and we can have our bottle midday or on the way home. [In France] I have a bottle mid-day and another in the evening.' As England approached one of the harshest winters in decades, in which fuel-starved printers closed down and the book trade endured a sales recession, Allen descended into a deep depression. 'I'm afraid,' he wrote to Richard, 'that the pre-war spirit is absent from me for good.'

The arrival of a child normally cured Allen's darkest moods. The birth of his second daughter, Christine, in 1944 – Agatha Christie was her godmother – had helped lift him out of the breakdown that followed John's death. But when, in 1947, Lettice gave birth to their third daughter, things deteriorated at Silverbeck. Anna Lane suffered from a mild form of Down's syndrome. During her pregnancy, Lettice had been in a minor accident with a taxi. After Anna was born, Allen lashed out, blaming Lettice for their daughter's condition and making other accusations about his wife's conduct and 'carelessness', even suggesting that Anna was not his child. At the time of John's death, Allen had said unforgivable things to Richard. After Anna's birth, he said unforgivable things to Lettice.

20

___

THE BEST MAN

After his 1942 breakdown, Allen had worries about Penguin, and the war, and the return of his surviving brother to contend with. But since John's death, Allen knew, something had come between himself and Richard. Reunited in peacetime, they would sometimes pretend that their relationship was as it had been in the old days of Broomcroft and Talbot Square. They reached their shareholding pact; they collaborated productively at Harmondsworth, where staff called them 'Mr Richard' and 'Mr Allen' or, even more simply, 'RL' and 'AL', like a pair of reliable bookends. Despite the unified front, however, both brothers acknowledged the obvious fact that things between them could never be the same.

Allen struggled most with the loss of Brother John, and Richard reminded him of the loss. Grief added one more layer to Allen's complex and conflicted character. His second biographer, Jeremy Lewis, wrote that Allen had, 'in the second half of the 1940s ... lost some of his old sparkle, matching restlessness on the home front with the intrigues and anxieties endemic to tycoonery. He remained as mischievous and subversive as ever [and] found himself devoting more and more of his time to the manipulation of his colleagues and employees, and to his dealings with the outside world, and less to the everyday workings of the firm.' Allen's secretary Margaret Clark observed how he 'worked impulsively and restlessly, walking up and down, looking out of the window, biting his nails (the only outward sign that his volatile temperament, often so injurious to others, affected him equally)'. Her boss 'seemed to crave affection and attention'. Allen's eyes indicated his mood; during dictation, they 'dropped the twinkle and were cold as cold'. To Margaret's predecessor at Penguin, Allen had been so cruel that the young woman reported the persecution to her father, who 'stormed into the office with a horsewhip, promising to exact revenge'. Allen was out at the time – he had a knack for being away at the right moments – and he escaped punishment.

In the late 1940s, Penguin employed 200 people. Its revenues were beyond the dreams of the Lanes' publishing rivals. As the company grew, it began to take on the shape of a more conventional corporate entity, and so, too, a sense of the corporate culture became more meaningful. In publishing – famously a 'human-scale' activity – the culture is especially important. The personality of Penguin's principals, and how they interacted from day to day, dictated the character of their imprint and the efficiency of their work. As the decade turned, a rift opened up between Penguin's internal corporate values and its friendly public image.

Ignoring his brother's advice about defining senior roles, Allen retained instead his preference for loose organisation and a philosophy of natural selection in the office, where projects and tasks were allocated almost at random. Competition and the duplication of duties were the rule among his senior staff, so that no single manager could become indispensable, or a threat: there would always be a surfeit of people to take the blame for mistakes. During the dying days of The Bodley Head, Allen had presided over a dysfunctional organisation. Now indisputably in charge at Penguin, he moulded the company's top-level culture to his own style and appetites. Byzantine, political, gossipy, treacherous. Penguin's culture revolved around hollow charm, ingratiation, insinuous manoeuvring, and fear.

According to Bill Williams, at Allen Lane's Penguin, 'you could be top dog one day – and in the dog house the next'. Staff tended to disappear, sacked for doing something to cause Allen's 'cold shutters' to come down; or because he decided 'a face no longer fitted'; or for some altogether unaccountable reason. 'Every now and then some luckless member of staff was sacked', and the mode of dismissal would follow a fixed pattern. In the words of the publisher Peter Calvocoressi from Chatto & Windus, Allen Lane 'was bad at hatchet work unless he could put the hatchet into someone else's hands'. Bill Williams blamed a 'lack of moral fibre' and 'a decided streak of sadism' for Allen's habit of getting others – like Richard, Paroissien and Williams himself – to do the CEO's dirty work. The chosen hatchet-man would invite the hapless member of staff to lunch at the Berkeley Arms, and Allen would make himself scarce: 'at the critical moment Lane let himself out of a back door, and Margaret Clark would catch a glimpse of his stocky, grey-clad, neatly suited rear view bustling through a gap in the hedge *en route* for the car park.' Allen's sacking of loyal Stan Olney, 'who had devoted his life to Penguin', was so devastating that it was said Olney 'never recovered'. (Bill Rapley was reportedly 'so shattered by Lane's failure to attend his sixty-fifth birthday that he died shortly afterwards'.)

Apart from Richard, Allen's two most powerful lieutenant-generals were Eunice Frost and Bill Williams. Frosty wishfully called the three of them 'The Trinity', but if that's what they were, there was little that was holy about it. Behind a civil front, Frosty and Williams campaigned against each other, taking every covert opportunity to pull each other down. To Allen, Frosty wrote that Williams was one of the 'sources of infection' at Penguin, while Williams wrote to Allen that Frosty got into people's hair in the office and was 'inclined to get jumpy and hysterical' when too close to the boss. For this and other reasons, Williams thought Frosty should be excluded from the executive council.

Allen quietly joined both campaigns, mercilessly playing off the two courtiers against each other. To Frosty, he wrote that Williams was 'a problem in a class by itself'. With Williams, he concurred that the nervy, twitchy, prickly Frosty was 'inclined to rattle the juniors'. And he confided in Richard about both combatants. Williams was 'weak' and 'rather lost when there is no meeting on and so he has nothing to do but hang around in my room'. Allen's criticisms reveal a distinct lack of self-awareness. He accused Frosty of hypochondria, and Williams of being temperamental – of basing decisions on hunches. Richard worried about the confidentiality of all the nasty correspondence and its potentially corrosive effects on Penguin. Some years later, after a night spent drinking with senior editor Tony Godwin, Allen lowered his guard and shared his views on his immediate subordinates. Godwin was shocked by Allen's 'terrible contempt' for his closest colleagues, whom he subjected to 'ruthless denigration'.

*

Baiting Billy and Frosty was good sport, but neither council–counsellor threatened Allen's new authority. Richard Lane was a different case altogether. Allen's medieval style of governing worked best if there was no one around who could lead a castle revolt. As the only other founder-owner-director, Richard was the one person who could challenge Allen's supremacy – the one possible claimant to the power Allen had enjoyed since crowning himself during the war, and which he hoped to go on enjoying for as long as possible. And there were other reasons for Allen to feel unsettled by Richard's presence at Harmondsworth. The younger Lane got on well with the younger staff, who confided their grievances about poor pay and freezing working conditions; the 'them and us' culture between management and staff, and between current and former favourites. More fundamentally, Richard was too much of a bridge to Allen's past, a past that clashed with the impression of a tweedy Devonian tycoon he strived to project. And Richard's very presence, as an experienced and capable co-founder, destabilised the core of the Allen Lane myth – that of the publishing genius and one-man phenomenon.

Though three years younger than his brother, Richard had built a broader, more fully rounded career. In addition to his book-trade experience, he had seen up close a range of industries and businesses as diverse as Samuel Williams-Lane's grab-bag of hobbies. On four continents, Richard had learnt tough lessons about capitalisation and contracts and cash flow. He wanted to share his experience with Allen and Penguin, to help guard their little bird from predators; but Allen treasured his own cut-through (and often cut-throat) entrepreneurial style, and disliked being told what to do, however politely, and however well-meaning and closely related the informant. Hearing from Richard too many 'shoulds', Allen became as cross as a thwarted and chastised toddler.

Richard Lane had looked behind the curtain, and knew how much of the Allen Lane phenomenon was real and how much a fabrication. He knew what share of Penguin's inception his brother could truly claim as his own. He had seen Allen's reader reports at The Bodley Head and knew the literary and editorial limitations of the man who had turned down *Lucky Jim* and frowned at *The Catcher in the Rye*. He knew what numeracy problems confronted the man who would make a twenty-year error in their mother's date of birth. He knew that Allen confused Aleppo with Aloso and *fromage* with *homard*, and had sent a book for Katherine Mansfield to sign, decades after her death. He knew what lies Allen had told Weybright and Enoch and dozens of other colleagues and competitors. He knew how awkward and lost Allen had been during the *Whispering Gallery* affair. All in all, he knew too much.

Like a broken chess computer with only one opening sequence, the senior Penguin adopted a strategy for achieving complete corporate control that would follow the pattern he had used at The Bodley Head. Gather an unassailable majority of shares. Become the undisputed CEO. Grasp the leash of the company's lawyers and moneymen. Wage a slow war of attrition to lever out untamed directors and any other remaining rivals. Purge any relics from the less powerful past.

Leadership brought out the worst in Allen, whose suspicious, superstitious, depressive mind had no room for sentiment. The things that should have bonded him to his brother – their memories of a bucolic childhood, the tight Williams-Lane family circle, the halcyon days at Talbot Square, Richard's seminal part in the Penguin story – all counted for nothing. Writing in the 1950s, Allen's graphologist left behind a vivid picture of a man who had 'developed a cold, competitive and combative outlook, which of necessity brings him to the front . . . His whole life is a hunting expedition, and although he is a successful hunter he is not satisfied – indeed, he is not satisfiable.' In agreeing to the 75/25 shareholding pact, Richard had hoped to avoid becoming the hunter's prey, but that was not to be. Allen dissolved the Council of Six and launched a malignant campaign against his brother.

When Jack Morpurgo joined Penguin's staff to help with public relations, Allen told him to 'pay no attention to that moron Dick . . . He doesn't know anything about anything.' To junior editor David Herbert, Allen said of his brother, 'He makes a better farmer. He'd be better off still in Australia.' Allen told Eunice Frost that Richard was 'making a mess of everything'. And in a hundred other conversations and messages, Allen chipped and hammered and axed away at his brother's reputation. Unable to make people dislike Richard, Allen set about making people ignore him. He 'let it be known that Dick was a director only because he was a Lane, but of the Lanes the least, that members of the staff need not trouble to consult Dick even when Allen was abroad, that

Dick's opinion was scarcely worth having'. Allen even undermined his brother in front of Clare and Christine, whom he regaled with 'unflattering and often slanderous comments'. Like the ghost at Windsor Castle, Richard Lane was cut off at the knees. Slow, stolid, impotent Richard became the biggest of Allen Lane's lies.

For ten years Allen had regularly contemplated living apart from his brothers, and then from Richard. Now, the equivocation ended: a tycoon could not live in a share-house. Richard had to be put somewhere, preferably far away from Silverbeck and Harmondsworth. Three years after his demobilisation, Richard Lane set sail again for Australia. Though it was never quite made explicit, Allen's plan was that Richard would appraise the situation and then, perhaps, sooner or later, reach some kind of arrangement with the firm's Australian manager, Bob Maynard, that would see both Richard and Bob gainfully employed by Penguin Australia. If that did not work, Allen thought, one or both of them could be dealt with. Fate, however, would intervene and make a mess of Allen's plan.

The last time Richard Lane had sailed for Australia, he was part of a cargo-load of Barwell Boys. This time, he sailed in style on the Orient Line's air-conditioned, wide-decked *Orion* and met an Australian beauty on board. Miss Betty Snow, aged twenty-seven, was the daughter of Sir Sydney Snow KBE and Lady Snow, the owners of Snow's Department Stores, 'the Sydney equivalent of Selfridge's'. As a member of a Voluntary Aid Detachment, Betty had spent the war in Sydney's hospitals caring for wounded soldiers. At war's end she joined the crew of HMS *Glory* (26 September to 12 December 1945), collecting former prisoners of war from Singapore and other Pacific ports. (When the Detachment met Australian Imperial Force ex-POWs in Manila, Betty's fellow volunteer Jean Mascord reported that the men were thrilled to see 'Aussie women'. The soldiers had worked on docks, railways and mines, had been systematically brutalised, and were now suffering from beri-beri. Their spirits remained strong. 'The first question they asked was, "Are all the trees at Manly really cut down?"') After delivering British and Canadian soldiers to Vancouver, Betty and the *Glory* brought the Australian servicemen home. Then, with her uncle Fred Davis, she travelled to Europe on Snows' first post-war buying trip. Richard met Betty during the return journey, on which she wore Dior's glamorous New Look, and, with Fred, made an impressive sight at the table of the Purser, Tony Scarisbrick.

The Best Man

In 1926, Richard had admired the well-proportioned young women of Sydney, all 'shingled bobbed or bingled'. Now, his admiration for Betty Snow was boundless. They struck up a friendship, which deepened over discussions about books and retailing and Australia and the state of the world. Richard's musings about his feminine ideal were suddenly no longer hypothetical. Betty, for her part, was smitten with this kind and generous, smart and affectionate pillar of society – a man who knew everyone in literary London and had co-founded a world-famous enterprise. When the ship docked at Sydney Harbour, Richard sought Sir Sydney's blessing for their formal engagement, and the couple made plans for a June wedding. Under 'Forthcoming Marriages', a notice in the London *Times* announced the engagement of the younger Lane son to the youngest Snow daughter. In the lead up to the wedding, Betty stayed in Sydney while Richard and Bob went to Melbourne before completing an eight-week tour of New Zealand. Long, smoochy letters – Betty called Richard her 'Riccardo Mio', and Betty was his 'Mostie' – weighed down the trans-Tasman mail. Richard's letters reveal a man who was head over heels in love.

Friday, May 14, 1948, The Australia Hotel, Melbourne
I don't know how to begin to thank you for last weekend, it was so perfect, it was just out of this world. Our first sunrise together really was something ... I am not certain how good the phone was last night but there's no harm in quoting Allen, 'It's four days now since your good news burst among us and we are still gasping in joyous wonderment.' Nora, 'how delighted and thrilled we all are – father and mother are particularly excited and father seems to have taken on a new lease of life – our fondest love and blessings to you both.' Mother, 'It's the most wonderful news and we are both delighted.' Frosty, 'This is fantastically good and exciting,' and later, 'TK and I are mad to be sent on a long boat trip if such happy endings can be guaranteed,' and there are lots more of a similar nature.

Aren't these gossip writers being a nuisance. In order to try and keep them quiet, Bob Maynard went to see a couple of them yesterday but they weren't satisfied and phoned me and almost tried third degree stuff such as, 'of course if you want to get all the publicity you can, you are going the right way about it', then being arch and saying that, as they had been told it was a Sydney girl, they weren't really interested at all, and they even went as far as saying that there was an Australian custom that if the bloke was feeling a bit diffident about saying anything, all he had to do was give them the name of the girl and they would approach her direct.

Saturday, May 29, Hotel Waterloo, Wellington
The bank manager took us for a drive to show us the beauty spots of Auckland. The only snag about this was the driving. Long before we left the city, he passed a red light in a thirty mile limit doing about forty-five and, though he was stopped by a traffic cop after much blowing of whistles, he got away with it, how I don't really know, his main excuse was that he had a Tasmanian license and was not well acquainted with Auckland regulations. Still, he was let off with a caution and from then on rarely dropped below 55/60 in the 30 limit, took most corners on two wheels and at the end of two hours had two completely shattered passengers who could hardly speak ... Then a short pleasant interlude while we had a hot bath, shave and changed our clothes, followed by a somewhat sticky lunch in the afternoon with our agent here. We are not at all pleased with what he is doing here and the tension generally was fairly great ...

I do hope the 29th is going to be a possible date. Is there anything I can do about it or can it all keep until I return? If it is really going to be a small family affair, will it be necessary to send out printed or engraved invitations? Also what about a cake, should we have one, are they rationed, if so do you want my ration book ... I haven't a clue about these things ... Don't forget darling that I do I do I do.

Thursday, June 3, Hotel Waterloo, Wellington
We had lunch with Ngaio Marsh yesterday and told her that we are doing a special publication next year of ten of her titles. She looks after an invalid father but hopes to be able to do a trip to England next year as one of her books is being turned into a play and she would hate to miss seeing it ...

Do look after yourself darling and don't forget I love you and life seems very grim when you are not around.

The Best Man

Sunday, June 6, Hotel Waterloo, Wellington
How have I got as far as page three without having told you that I love you very very much indeed and am missing you even more than I thought possible.

Monday, June 7, Hotel Waterloo, Wellington
Don't ever forget I love you and want to make it a life ambition to make you happy always.

Friday, June 11, Hotel Waterloo, Wellington
This is a strange country and I don't feel at home here, not like I do in Australia. I have just had a pleasant soak in a hot bath and during the immersion period I re-read your last two letters for the umpteenth time. Darling I do love you and think you are the most amazing person that ever happened. Why you should love me I haven't a clue and yet apparently you don't dislike me too much.

Sunday, June 13, Hotel Waterloo, Wellington
Oh by the way darling, you say you haven't solved the old 'caps' problem. It's a printing and publishing abbreviation for 'capitals', therefore 'caps the perfect weekend' reads THE PERFECT WEEKEND, rather weak I am afraid, but I did so enjoy it that, if the rest of our life is going to be like that, I for one shall have no grumbles.

You ask if there's anyone I should like to ask along for the 29th. At the moment the only person I can think of is Lettice's sister, the Wollstonecraft type and possibly her husband. I don't know anything about him except that he is very deaf. Then you ask if I think I am going to hate it terribly. That's a difficult one darling. As I love you so much, and as I feel I can face anything with you around, I suppose it won't be too bad, but I do think I shall be glad when it's all over and we are on our own, starting our own life together. It's just too good to be true.

Richard asked Bob to be his best man. After the ceremony – at St Mark's Church, Darling Point – and the reception, Richard was 'in no mood to sit and write long letters', but Bob wrote to tell Allen about the service and the pavlova and an occasion that would, he said, 'go down as one of my big days'.

217

On the eve of the wedding, Dick, Owen Clayton and myself dined quietly together, and indeed quite soberly. We saw Dick off to bed about ten. The service was timed for 11.30, but for fear of being late, we arrived at the church soon after eleven. If Dick was jittery, he showed no sign of it. I must confess that I was feeling the strain of the occasion a little.

However, the bride arrived on time, and the service was over in twenty minutes or so ... Luncheon was à la buffet, and what a meal! Even I caved in before the end. In case you are curious, we worked our way through oysters (lashings of them), asparagus, fish pie, roast chicken and turkey, roast beef and ham, more asparagus, a magnificent meringue, loaded with fruit salad and cream, chicken livers on toast rounded it off. It nearly broke my heart to fail on such a gastronomic task. Particularly as Betty had whispered that three helpings of each had been specially ordered for me. You are going to like Betty.

We started on champagne fairly early in the piece, then carried on a shuttle service between champagne and whisky bottles.

The parson conducting the proceedings is a good type. He gave a truly magnificent speech at the toasting of the happy pair. Although he probably played a little too long around the Orion for Dick's comfort. The qualities of the groom and the 'noble institution of Penguins to which he belongs', took quite a while. Dick replied, first with thanks for 'the best piece of publicity the firm has received in years'.

I cannot give you much news of presents, as I have not so far seen them. I believe that a special ship will be needed to get them all home. The newlyweds got away at about two thirty, when the whole reception slowly folded up. It was indeed a good wedding. I wish that all of you could have been with us.

One bright remark from Dick is worth passing on. At one of our many talks about the forthcoming marriage, he confessed to a little apprehension over the ceremony, as, he said, 'I have never done this sort of thing before.'

For the ladies who would like to know, the bride wore a darkish blue (delphinium, according to one paper) dress, with white trimmings, a small crowned white hat, with a big white bow affair across the front. She carried a navy blue hand-bag, with a spray of either white gardenias or camellias across its front. There are no photographs unfortunately.

Bob took his duties as best man seriously. The day before the wedding, Richard told him, 'I do think I'd better visit a chemist's, don't you?'

'Well, if I'm thinking what you're thinking,' Bob said, 'it might be a good idea.'

> And he did and I thought he'd supplied himself very liberally. But a week or so later I got a telegram – he'd gone up the coast of New South Wales for his honeymoon – it was rather cryptic. It read: RE PREVIOUS CONSIGNMENT PLEASE REPEAT AS NOT YET 231 AND RATHER FEAR INCREASE OF A174. The A174 was the clue – I thought that's obviously a Pelican. So getting out the Penguin list I deciphered his telegram, which then read: '... as not yet *All Passion Spent* and rather fear increase in *Population of Britain*.' So then, of course, I had to search through the catalogue ... I sent a reply which merely read: 'S55.' '*Good God.*'

Apart from coastal New South Wales, Richard and Betty also visited a place of special significance. Richard had left the Witherses' block in 1925, hoping 'never to return'. But now he was determined to share with his new bride his old stomping ground, so that she could see for herself the remote Australian places that had shaped his youth. In the middle of winter they walked down to the banks of the Murray at Renmark. Betty took Richard's word about the hot summers, but she saw first hand how quickly the land dried out away from the river red gums. The couple picked a few oranges and Richard was momentarily overtaken by a memory of cutting apricots.

On his return to Melbourne, Richard checked the local book industry's pulse, then took his bride to England. Richard and Allen had both married in their forties. Allen's marriage was a failure, but Richard and Betty's life together would indeed be a love affair in all caps. They continued to exchange effusive letters, as well as demonstrative gifts, such as books of poetry and heartfelt quotations, and custom-made jewellery that expressed love and devotion in diamonds and white gold. For the five-thousandth day of their marriage, in 1962, Richard would commission from the leading Melbourne jeweller W.M. Drummond & Co. a platinum and diamond brooch that featured a square-cut sapphire, and five capital letter M's.

Betty was Richard's equal as a wit and an intellect, and shared his playfulness and sense of the absurd. In letters and books, the couple exchanged love quotes from the great writers of Penguin's pre-history – such as Hardy, Twain and Anatole France. Some of the words they selected were tender, others an in-joke. From Shaw: 'It is a woman's business to get married as soon as possible, and a man's to keep unmarried as long as he can'; and, 'The ideal love affair is one conducted by post'. From Wilde: 'The worst of having a romance of any kind is that it leaves one so unromantic'; and, 'The amount of women in London who flirt with their own husbands is perfectly scandalous. It looks bad. It is simply washing one's own clean linen in public'. And from Richard's old favourite, Oliver Wendell Holmes, 'I should like to see any kind of man, distinguishable from a gorilla, that some good and even pretty woman could not shape a husband out of'; and 'Women are apt to love the man who they think has the largest capacity of loving'. Both Richard and Betty had an enormous capacity for love, and their unwavering mutual support would be invaluable in the most difficult of times.

∗

Though Allen had been slow to discover the southern continent, he would soon pay it a great deal more attention. In the meantime, he took a long holiday, again to the Middle East but this time to Iraq where he visited Mr and Mrs Max Mallowan on a dig at Nimrud. To fool Max, Allen bought and buried a 'bogus artefact', but the schoolboy trick fell flat. Agatha Christie's husband had no illusions about his wife's old friend. 'Allen was a man of boundless energy, an opportunist, a born pirate . . . who could ride rough-shod over his best friend.'

Mallowan was not the only one to see through Allen. A succession of staff pointed to his cruel streak, and bemoaned his readiness to claim others' ideas, and their glory. The Penguin employee and bookman Ruari McLean noticed how Allen's clubbable persona was a façade. Peter Calvocoressi noticed likewise 'a sense of reserve, an unforthcoming watchfulness which came close to suspiciousness. Even in a *tête à tête* he left you wondering what he was thinking.' Bernard Venables 'always felt there was some guard . . . another Allen Lane standing by, making notes'. The artist Richard Chopping, who illustrated a classic series of James Bond covers (and therefore knew all about super-villains), called Allen an inscrutable 'pocket Napoleon'. After Allen Lane and the printer Geoffrey Smith called on the Bloomsbury Group's Frances Partridge, she sketched the following portrait:

> Allen Lane, a stocky figure squeezed into a smart suit of palest grey, was purely and simply the millionaire in an American film. He appeared to be acting a part, an important part of which was mani-festing the 'common touch' by revealing a passion for choc-ices. Yet I'm sure he never ceased thinking of himself as the personification of power through money, benevolent but not to be 'had'. This for some reason made him rather pathetic ... As our visitors were driving off I couldn't resist saying to Allen Lane: 'We've met before, you know – more than twenty years ago when I worked in Birrell and Garnett's bookshop.' His millionaire pomposity crumpled just a fraction at this reminder of his boyish diffident self, travelling the books of his firm and making up to me in the process.

To some of the younger staff at Penguin, Allen was simply the mad king; the naked emperor; the boorish uncle at a wedding reception who drinks too much, makes outrageous remarks and takes undue credit for the proceedings. Outside the firm, there were many more detractors – people who had been bruised or burned by Allen's sharp and mercurial ways. When Ben Travers put Allen forward as a potential member of the prestigious Garrick Club, the king penguin received so many black balls that they were said to be like caviar in a spoon.

The voices of scepticism might have been growing, but they mattered little at Harmondsworth, where Allen Lane was in charge and Richard Lane was in his sights. Allen's dissolution of the Council of Six had been predictable. Why would a man who despised committees – and craved executive power – hand authority to a council? Richard was smart and sensitive enough to know what was going on. He had seen the same tac-tics play out many times before, over the span of more than two decades, and as early as 1945 had feared that he himself might become a target. Now, tellingly, Frosty and Williams no longer consulted Richard in the way they once had. They had heard Allen undermine Richard so many times, and had, for the sake of ingratiation, been so complicit with that undermining, that they could now no longer look the younger Lane brother in the eye. Richard sensed, too, the erosion of his reputation among the whole of Penguin's staff. According to Jeremy Lewis, Richard 'was well aware that, with his brother's active connivance, he had become an embarrassment and a laughing-stock in Harmondsworth'.

SMALL FRY

Much more than the greatest playwright of his age, George Bernard Shaw won respect as a sparkling wit, essayist, social philosopher and reformer. His death in November 1950 marked the end of an era not just for Britain but for Penguin, too. He had helped the firm from the beginning, paving the way for its acceptance as an authoritative imprint and a transformative force in the book trade. Shaw's loss was a blow for both of the Lane brothers, but Allen was already in a bad way before he heard the news. Earlier in 1950, he had suffered another breakdown – Eunice Frost called it a 'crack up' – after another death.

The loss of Samuel Williams-Lane was a tremendous source of sadness for the whole Lane family, not just for the fact of his passing, but for its manner, and the dark colour of Samuel's thoughts at the time. During his last days, Samuel had felt his life ebbing away. In January 1950, with Rachel the housekeeper as witness, he updated his will, adding a reflection on his achievements in life. He appointed Allen and Richard as executors, and left 'all that I may die possessed of to my wife Camilla Matilda Williams Lane, and only regret that it does not amount to more, as a slight return for her patience, help and love during the period of our married life.' Then he composed a 'farewell note', and passed away after a final strenuous walk up Hottie Tottie Hill.

> I have not made any bequests to anyone but have left everything to
> one who has been my cheery helpmate for so many years, and to

whom I owe everything – not only in making my life a happy one but in giving me a family of whom anyone could be proud, and I feel confident they will do their utmost to compensate her for her loss.

One thing in particular gives me reason for satisfaction and that is the knowledge there will be no bickerings as to the disposal of my estate – what there is of it, and such as it is. There is however a sum of £230/2/8 due to John and £215/19/7 to Nora being the balance owing them during my guardianship.

I should wish however that some slight reminder of me should be given to Gladys Williams, say fifty pounds, which is not however to be spent on any foolish mourning attire.

My desire is to be cremated at the appropriate time, and the ashes scattered over some of the unknown people's graves in Ipsden Church, in the hope that in time to come the ground will be levelled and the site used for making a garden of remembrance.

And so I take my leave of you – God bless you all.

Daddy

No flowers or mourning attire

The estate included a beautiful silver cigarette box – in the shape of a beehive – that the Lane brothers commissioned for their father before the war, from the Bond Street jeweller Asprey & Co. And another gift that the brothers bought from the same shop: an exquisite miniature library finely bound in goatskin and gold.

As an addendum to the 'farewell note', Samuel scribbled a message attending to a last matter of family business: 'Nora has agreed to defray the cost of alterations to the new passage and lavatory out of the cash she has received from John's estate and has already paid £100 on account. As there seems no prospect of her finding the balance (£116) which Mother has paid, I suggest that the amount be deducted from what is due to her from that received by me during the period of my guardianship.'

Richard never revised his opinion that Samuel Williams-Lane was the best man he would ever know. Allen also greatly respected the man whom happenstance had made the patriarch of 'British publishing's most distinguished family'. Frosty suggested that feelings of 'anticlimax' at the loss, compounded by tension at work and on other fronts, had caused Allen's latest breakdown. But Allen was clearly also shaken by Samuel's will and farewell note, and especially stung by the remarks about the size of his legacy. At the same time, Allen noticed, too, the decline in his own health, and was struck by an awareness of his own mortality. Having become, in his words, 'strained of face and twitchy of finger', he left for a long rest on the Continent.

After he had recuperated somewhat, he wrote to Camilla:

My dear Mother,

I have naturally thought a great deal of the events of the last three months and particularly of Father, and the purpose of this letter is to set down some of these while they are fresh in my mind.

I was rather perturbed to read in his good-bye letter, I don't remember the words but the sense was, 'I am sorry I haven't more to leave you, but I'm afraid I wasn't very good at making money.' I had a feeling that perhaps he might have had this on his mind.

I hope that this was not the case as if anyone had cause for regret at the use they had made of their lives or of the smallness of the legacy they had left, it was certainly not him.

Of the making of money itself there is not much to be proud, especially if, as is so often the case, it has been done at the cost of suffering and hardship to others.

The maximum use to which anyone can put their life is in service to the community, either in a large and spectacular way as done by Churchill in saving a group of nations from physical and spiritual destruction; or in the more modest but not less relatively important role of being a good citizen, giving help to others when it lies in his power and above all in being a good husband and father.

During the whole of my life I don't remember ever having heard Father criticise you or any action of yours. He supported you in every act with I am sure at the back of his mind a full realization of the importance of a solid front being shown to the outside world and in particular to the family, which is the first to perceive any rift however slight.

Although sometimes when aware of the short-comings of one or other of your grand-children you compare their upbringing with ours, inferring that what they get away with now would have merited and obtained a walloping for us, I am sure that we none of us looked on father as an avenging god, and what character forming he did was done more by example than precept.

That our upbringing was a good one there is no denying. Like you, I have received numbers of letters on his passing. I have answered nearly two dozen since I came away, and a feature of nearly all of them has been a comment on the closeness of our family ties.

Such solidarity could only spring from a happy and secure home life such as we enjoyed, and I can think of no better legacy to leave than that.

We know to what pains he went to ensure that there would be a minimum of display at his going, and that not only was there to be no stone or other monument, but no grave either on which sentiment could be focused; he has however left a reminder of himself and of his life and work for us which will always remain green in our memory to the end of our days.

Your ever loving son,

Allen

Allen disparaged the accumulation of wealth, but of course it was an achievement in which he excelled. His personal fortune amounted to £215,000, almost 90 per cent of which was held as Penguin shares. Wealth, however, was no cure for Allen's depression, nor for his physical decline. He developed a pronounced stoop, and suffered, as Uncle John had done, from gout. Shocked by Allen's grey and balding head, and bent and gouty figure, Agatha Christie said that Allen, aged about fifty, resembled 'a tired old man of seventy'. Allen Lane's knighthood in 1952, for services to literature and literacy, confirmed Penguin's status as 'an estate of the realm', and Allen's as publishing royalty, but it went only a small way towards making him feel better. On learning of his elevation to Sir Stanley Unwin's exalted level, Allen returned to bed, where he stayed all day and complained of feeling 'bloated'.

An ageing knight in possession of a good fortune must be in want of an enormous group portrait. From the Slade-trained realist artist Rodrigo Moynihan, Allen commissioned a painting that would show an editorial meeting with all the key members of Penguin's team – a physical emblem of the team's collective achievement. Allen set the parameters for the portrait, gave his instructions to Moynihan, then went overseas, leaving Richard to make it all happen.

At the same time, other more important things were happening. In November 1952, Betty Lane gave birth to a daughter, Elizabeth. Richard embraced with gusto the role he had been born to play: that of father, and family man. Commander Ralph 'Tubby' Martin of the *Springbank* had the honour of being Elizabeth's godfather. Tubby would serve alongside two godmothers: Margaret Tink (Betty's cousin) and Sylvanie Higson.

Since Richard's 1948 visit, Australia had been on Allen's mental backburner. During the war, Lothian Press made and sold Penguins in Australia under licence – in a style and to a standard that would have horrified Tschichold; and with content – like the jaunty advertisements for Communist Radio in Nora Waln's Penguin Special, *Reaching for the Stars* – that would have shocked Allen and Richard. In 1946, Lothian made way for a wholly owned, controlled and controllable Penguin subsidiary. Veteran Penguiner Bob Maynard set up the new entity and operated it from an office in Melbourne, the capital of Victoria, and of Australian publishing. Maynard had started his career as an invoice clerk at Chatto, before joining Penguin in the early days of the crypt. He knew all the Lane brothers, had worked alongside them and shared their adventures and fantasies – planning, with Allen, to sail the *Penguin* to France to help with the Dunkirk evacuation; convincing him not to break the wartime paper quota; concocting with D.B. Wyndham Lewis a bogus bio for 'Timothy Shy', the pseudonymous author of articles collected and published in 1942 as *Beyond the Headlines*. To illustrate a wartime advertisement for Penguin pens, Maynard drew a picture of a soldier bayoneting Hitler's behind; it was this picture that prompted Germany to ban Penguins in POW camps.

The Penguin Australia 'office', in an industrial part of South Melbourne, was actually one half of an uninsulated tin shed, with a standard of accommodation not unlike Richard's annexe at Moorook. The shed's interior oscillated between bracing cold and enervating heat. Bob and his wife, Edith, did all the work – ordering, sorting, packing, despatching, invoicing – just as Richard and John and Bob had done in the crypt. In the hot Australian summers, Bob and Edith packed and sent home food parcels for their 'half-frozen and under-nourished colleagues' in England. Bob wrote to Frosty in July 1949:

You may be interested to know that, in the first six months of the year our turnover was as big as our first complete year here. I am tickled pink. It is now showing the fruit of the first couple of years hard grinding and I think is some indication of what the US market can be worked up to. It has struck me that you might like to come here for a year. The sunshine and change of scene plus two long sea voyages would do much to put you completely back to full health, youth, vitality and what have you.

Allen would see the southern sunshine before Frosty. Although he wanted to check up on Maynard's beach-head, there was another reason for Allen to visit Australia. Mr and Mrs Bird had migrated, settling more than 500 miles from Melbourne, in Sydney. Allen would call on Nora and Frank, and 'combine business with pleasure'. Richard, too, now living at Priory Farm with his Australian wife, still had strong connections to Australia. So, in 1953, Allen Lane made his first tour of the Antipodes – seven years after Maynard set up the Melbourne office, and thirty-one years after Richard Lane arrived at Moorook.

*

Like many Englishmen before him, Allen arrived in Australia with the feeling that he was the first to discover it. Though Allen had read Richard's Barwell notebooks, he had absorbed little of Australia's epic geography. Innocently, he asked Maynard to drive the firm's Vauxhall from Melbourne to Fremantle so the pair could meet at the quayside and drive back to the office together – the same mad journey of more than 2000 miles that John Lane had completed in the opposite direction in a taxicab.

Rather than endure a 4000-mile road trip, Bob instead drove almost 500 miles to Adelaide and travelled the remaining 1500 miles to Perth by air. When Bob greeted his disembarking boss at Fremantle, Allen insisted on making the journey to Melbourne overland, so he crossed the Nullarbor Plain by train and met Bob in Adelaide, where Allen gave a journalist a memorable line that was used as the theme of a newspaper cartoon. Allen's first impression of Australia, he said, was of the diamond-studded railway line: 'the track is framed by empty beer bottles and in the sunlight they glitter like gems. There's 1,500 miles of diamonds from Perth to Adelaide.'

Friendly, loyal, steady and unflamboyant, Bob Maynard had turned Penguin's Australian enterprise from nothing into something. Along the way, he had built close and rewarding links with the book trade, and gained an impeccable reputation. Harry Muir of Beck's Bookshop in Adelaide wrote in a laudatory way of Bob's 'personality, his approach to business, the service he has given and, above all, the faith which he has inspired in Australian booksellers'. At a time when 'every bookseller in Australia was being encouraged to buy paperbacks of every sort', Muir had increased the value of his annual Penguin order from thirty pounds to more than £1000 – as a direct result of Maynard's hard work.

Under Maynard's leadership, Penguin Australia prospered to such an extent that it outgrew its shed and was preparing to move to a larger repurposed office–warehouse at Mitcham, in Melbourne's outer east. In 1953, the plans were finished and the building works were about to start. The architect, Professor Brian Lewis of Melbourne University, asked Bob what wording he would like to display on the site's hoarding. Bob came up with a clever tease – 'A Sanctuary for Penguins and Pelicans is being erected on this site' – which caused no end of confusion and trouble. 'One firm wanted to tender for tiling the pools,' Bob later recalled. 'A bus company wanted to arrange tours and old ladies wrote to the press complaining of cruelty to birds.'

On Allen's first trip to Australia, he received the full celebrity-publisher treatment. Newspapers and chatterers called him a visionary publishing genius. On the southern continent, where wild penguins flourished, Allen's diva-like traits seemed to be magnified. He was late for every meeting; he accepted invitations to events he had no intention of attending; and he made promises he had no intention of honouring. In Britain, Allen's 'unmannerliness' was an expected part of the whole Allen Lane performance. The Australians he met, however, had not received the memo, and 'were more sensitive to slights, real or imagined, and especially to slights inflicted by a Pommie. They noticed, they were hurt and they did not forgive.' Bob and Edith suffered a hundred mortifications, noticing that Allen had become ruder and more erratic over the seven years since they last saw him.

His drinking was harder than they remembered . . . but he managed alcohol less discreetly . . . He urged them to invite to the house numbers of Victorians who had supported the development of Penguin, who might be willing to give the firm publicity or who were eager to add Allen Lane to their collection of celebrated names for dropping. [But] if his mood was black, if the company bored him and especially if the spirits took him, he glowered in a corner, silent and unapproachable. Not infrequently, he disappeared to bed even when a party was at its height, leaving the Maynards to fend off guests who had not yet met the star of the evening and to explain as best they could his disappearance.

Maynard showed Allen around the South Melbourne office (a very brief tour) and the local trade, outlining the subsidiary's achievements and presenting a proposal for modest growth. Allen looked on attentively, all the while forming unsympathetic views of Maynard's style, ambition, commercial acumen, salesmanship, and ability to build Penguin's presence in the educational market. And he shared none of these opinions with Bob. Allen's interest in Australia was now fully aroused. Having 'convinced himself that Maynard was not the man for the job that he now wished to have done', Allen returned to England where, little by little, he eroded Bob's confidence and authority.

Richard was enduring a similar erosion but, despite his diminished role and reputation at Harmondsworth, he continued to deputise for Allen, and to help keep Penguin swimming along. Around the same time that the firm intended to publish the complete *Canterbury Tales*, the Ballet Rambert planned a *Canterbury Tales* ballet, to be performed in Canterbury. Richard arranged for the publication date to coincide with the opening of the ballet, and Penguin hosted a 100-guest party in Canterbury to celebrate both occasions. Allen was away, so Richard met each of the 100 guests at the entrance. Frosty stood beside him and introduced each guest on arrival. Richard soon slipped into a rut of, 'Good evening, I am glad you could manage to come. My brother Allen is unable to be here to welcome you, but he asked me to thank you for coming.' On hearing this spiel, a 'very American' lady remarked, 'I've never heard of you or your brother or even of Penguin Books, but I heard there was a party going so that's why I'm here.'

While Allen was absent in 1953, Richard's tasks at Harmondsworth were many: shepherding new titles and reprints; dealing with sittings for the Moynihan portrait; and helping staff recover from working at Penguin under Allen Lane. He wrote to Allen in February in a tone that wavered between the aggressive and the defensive, and which betrayed a deficit of patience.

I had lunch with Moynihan yesterday as in the afternoon we were having another session with the editors. There were about eight absentees, but we all had our photographs taken again. I saw a photograph of the painting as it stands at the moment, and I really was appalled at its size. Naturally you must know all about this, but where are we going to put a picture which is fourteen feet by ten feet without a frame. Out of interest, I worked out that the cost of the picture is approximately one shilling a square inch, again without the incidentals or the frame. Moynihan told me it took himself plus two labourers a full day to put on the priming coat ...

Sometimes, I am rather under the impression that you think nothing happens here while you are away. Possibly we are not as efficient, but to balance this, we are much more cheerful and several types who had signs of gastric ulcers are now recovering slowly. In case you think nothing is happening, I should like to mention that plans have been prepared for an extension on top of the front offices; also an application has been made to put a 10,000 square feet building at the rear of the present one (plans for this have also been prepared); we are negotiating for the sale of the Mill and West Drayton properties; there have been many alterations to the publishing programme and before you come back titles will have appeared which had not been considered before you left. Naturally, I don't want to worry you about small details like this, as I am perfectly capable of coping with such things without any assistance from you ...

I am afraid I cannot give you very much news of the farm as apart from evenings I don't see much of it. I have just looked at my diary and see that I spent nine out of the last ten working days either at the office or in London on the firm's business, and it looks as if in the future this will be going up to ten out of ten days.

Allen replied that if the office extension included, as he envisaged, a grand entrance and stairway, then 'we could plan for the picture to be hung at the head of the stairs' – something like a football team photo at club headquarters.

When the finished portrait finally appeared, under the title 'After the Conference', it met with smirks and bafflement. An odd image of senior Penguins milling about in the Senior Common Room of the Royal College of Art, it was supposed to show a meeting of editors in their natural state. In fact, the people who were depicted had never met as a group, and several people in the picture had never met at all, and would never do so. The figures stand about bleakly, gormlessly, like scholars in a dreary university lounge, or an extended family waiting for news of a difficult birth. One of the people depicted remarked, 'Better a team photograph, all of us in rows with AL in the centre clasping a Penguin marked 1955 and the small fry of the team cross-legged.'

Only one person depicted in the painting was truly happy with it. Had Moynihan made Allen the largest figure, charges of egotism would have been too easy to make. Much better to cast Allen as the second most imposing figure, but one who stands in a uniquely flattering pose and is portrayed from a flattering angle. For a man concerned about his height and weight and posture – and who always wore impeccably tailored suits from Kilgour, French and Stanbury – the angle was important. Allen is one of the few figures painted front-on, and one of the first seen when the viewer scans from left to right. He looks spritely, nimble, alert, friendly. Everyone else looks stiff, dour and confused.

Allen's detailed instructions to the artist conveyed the relative importance – and therefore the relative prominence – of all those who sat for the group portrait. A calculated put-down for Allen's subordinates and rivals, the painting gave the 'small fry' of former favourites and marginally attached series editors especially short shrift. Jack Morpurgo's face hangs, 'like a gargoyle', from one pillar, and John Lehmann is half-concealed by the other. Richard Lane is dismembered then buried in the background alongside an anonymous waiter who has been painted in the same scale and with the same prominence – a strange time-travelling ricochet of Oscar Wilde's decision to insult Uncle John by naming a servant 'Lane' in *The Importance of Being Earnest*. Frosty, respectfully, stands in the centre of the group. On A.S.B. Glover's face, it is impossible to see traces of the tattoos that, in life, covered his cheeks and indeed the rest of his body.

*

In 1955, having abetted Allen's portrait project, Richard set sail with Betty and Elizabeth for Melbourne. There were echoes of Richard's Barwell days in this trip to Australia. He saw it as 'only a visit' and continued to think of Priory Farm as his home. Allen as usual had different plans, and saw the expedition as part of a long-term commitment that his brother would be making to Australia.

Allen had decided that Maynard was on the way out, whether he liked it or not. If someone else had to run Penguin Australia, who better than Richard? He was the only senior person at Harmondsworth with any real conception of the continent's epic geography. Moreover, he was married to an Australian. The Melbourne office had to be re-energised, a task that Allen would of course lead, but with Richard as his 'viceroy'. Despite everything that had gone on between them, thought Allen, Richard was still a Lane. The brothers shared an obvious family resemblance; in Australia, Richard could be 'a visible, audible and immediately recognizable representation of Allen's genius and vigour'. Richard was 'instinctively responsive to Allen's instincts'; had co-founded Penguin; and 'to have a Lane who was a founding-father in their midst must be for the Australians a powerful demonstration of the earnestness of Penguin's intention to enliven their Australian business'. Though reasons such as these were probably in Allen's mind, it is impossible to know how seriously he took them. Underneath all the obvious and spurious arguments, one imperative remained. A second attempt must be made to remove Richard from Harmondsworth, and to exile him in Australia.

When Richard arrived in Melbourne, he got down to business, applying the same discipline and versatility that he had demonstrated in London. Planting a Lane in Penguin Australia bore immediate fruit. Writing of the subsidiary, Bill Williams concluded, 'Finally it achieved some equilibrium when Allen's younger brother, Dick, took over in 1955, and it is now a flourishing partner in the Penguin Commonwealth.' Better-run than Penguin UK, Penguin Australia pioneered computerised stock management and became a cash cow for its parent. Richard and Maynard got on well – Bob said that Richard at Penguin UK 'had always been the strongest influence from the start' – and they reached an arrangement in which Richard operated as a sort of consultant-cum-chairman, with Bob as a sort of general manager. They recruited an assistant, and Allen wrote to Richard in November 1955:

> I think it would be very useful if you were to write to me pretty fully giving me your views of the time which you consider it would be neces-sary for you to spend in Australia in order to see that the organization there gets off to the sort of start which I feel it should. My own view I think is that you will require at least twelve months in the saddle, and if your new assistant Anthony seems at all promising, I think it might pay the firm to have him sent home to England for three months for training here and for returning to you before he is left on his own.

Despite Richard's presence in Melbourne, Allen continued to wear away at Bob Maynard in the same way that he had worn away at Wey-bright. From Harmondsworth, Bob received an intensifying stream of questions, about-turns, criticisms, countermands, objections, refusals; what Steve Hare called 'a series of humiliations that amounted to con-structive dismissal'. 'By his own admission,' Jack Morpurgo wrote, 'Maynard was slow to appreciate what was happening. It was two years after Allen's first visit to Australia before he woke to the knowledge that Allen was acting towards him in a manner which he had observed in his actions towards others.' Maynard told Frosty that things must come to a head. 'I am tired of being kicked around and I am coming home for a showdown.' If Allen no longer had confidence in Bob's leadership, his position was untenable. He telephoned Allen and proposed flying immediately to England for a face-to-face meeting. Allen – who hated any kind of meeting and avoided wholeheartedly the confrontations that inevitably flowed from his tactics – dodged Bob's proposal like a frightened rabbit: 'No, no, no. Don't do that on my account. I won't be here. Don't do that.'

Richard had been angered and saddened by the campaign against him at Harmondsworth. Now, he was appalled by Allen's treatment of Maynard. He made appeals in Bob's favour and started referring to his brother, 'with heavy irony', as the Noble Knight. Clare Lane added her voice to Richard's, urging fairer treatment for Maynard, and criticising Allen to his face for 'his ruthless treatment of his senior Australian staff'. Allen told her to mind her own business. In an act that infuriated the Australian book trade (Harry Muir, as President of the Australian Booksellers Association, conveyed to Richard his 'very deep and sincere regret'), Allen sacked Maynard and directed Penguin's lawyers to conclude terms such that he 'would not be paid more than was due to him'.

A Personal Letter

I n 1956, Allen told Richard he anticipated 'greater efficiency' from
Penguin Australia, now that Maynard was gone and Richard was in
charge. To lock in the efficiency, Allen offered his brother a deal. If
Richard would make himself 'entirely responsible for the Australian
company, remaining in Australia for the next five years', Allen would
authorise Penguin UK to pay for the one-way journey out. While Richard
feared he had been an inadvertent player in Allen's moves against Maynard, he was pleased to be out of the wearying cycle of erosion at Harmondsworth, and now in charge of an important and growing concern.

Though separated by a great distance and much more besides, the
two founder-directors continued to deal jointly with routine matters
affecting the global firm, like a flirtation with the remainder market
(Richard thought rushing into that market 'would be a very grave mistake'); the high volume of returns from Boots; efforts led by Paroissien
to rebuild in America; and the closure of the Canadian office. (Among
the many problems that Penguin experienced in Canada, one was zoo-
logical. When a skunk took up residence under the floor of the main
warehouse, the managers sought advice from experts and reported to
Harmondsworth. 'They think the skunk may stay under the warehouse
floor all winter, and every time there is movement in the warehouse, he
will discharge his odour ... The smell is very bad at the moment.')

Behind this cooperative front, Allen continued his campaign against
his brother. A few months after Richard left England, the campaign

reached a smelly low. The king signed an edict banishing the prince. As Richard's absence did not appear to have given the CEO any extra work, Allen wrote, he would not allow Richard ever to return to Harmondsworth. Seemingly barred from the business he had built and steered, and that he co-owned, Richard was shocked by this new turn, the grounds for which he knew were imaginary. Penguin's whole executive culture pivoted on overlap and competition, and the hiding of competitors' contributions. It was Allen himself who had most aggressively limited and concealed what Richard could do, and what he could claim to have done. Richard knew that Allen had made similar assertions after previous executive departures; he could not know, but might perhaps have guessed, that Allen would later make equally false and deprecating statements when he demoted Eunice Frost, Bill Williams and Harry Paroissien.

There is ample evidence, moreover, that Richard's exit had a tangible impact on Penguin. In the ensuing decade, the firm lost its discipline and committed the error that Richard had worried about from the outset when he first ran the costings for Penguin's large print runs. Mass production could lead to profitability only if readers bought the books. If, instead, the majority of a print run could not be sold, then the low unit cost was illusory and irrelevant. At Penguin, amid a great forgetting of the tenets on which the firm had been built, 'unbusinesslike' editors committed the 'cardinal sin': exaggerating potential sales in order to inflate print runs and make dud books look profitable.

Undermined by fantastical costings and overburdened by unsold books, the firm's profitability slumped. Over the next decade, there would be other signs of mayhem, too, such as the bumbling attempts to expand into new markets and fend off competition from new imprints. The firm adopted an arrogant and decidedly unfriendly tone with its authors, even in public. Advances fattened massively, and the 'incompetence' of the people who ran Penguin became a topic of wide discussion. Those people had little interest in the slogging work – like budgeting and stocktaking and balance-sheet management – that separated publishing from chaos. In the 1960s, the firm's cashflow entered a period of dangerous crisis in which, instead of food parcels, Penguin Australia would send remittances and loans to Harmondsworth, and the British firm depended on its colonies to stay afloat. Allen would be forced to hire a string of management accountants and logisticians to do what Richard had done reliably and quietly at Harmondsworth for more than a decade. The younger brother's absence left Penguin in disarray, and Allen unhinged. Without Richard Lane, Penguin lost its buoyancy, and its cheer.

Most of these troubles lay ahead. In the mid-1950s, Allen faced more immediate problems. Heinrich Maria Ledig-Rowohlt was credited with having introduced American-style paperbacks into post-war Germany. In July 1955, Allen invited him to spend a pleasant summer weekend at Silverbeck. Ledig-Rowohlt arrived with his tall and thin, young and sexy, pale and fleshy-faced mistress. Susanne Lepsius was eighteen years younger than Allen. Over the course of the weekend, one thing led to another, and Allen and Heinrich swapped partners. When Heinrich left for Germany, Lettice went with him, while Susanne remained at Silverbeck. Allen submitted a sample of Susanne's handwriting to his graphologist, 'accompanying it with a frank statement on what he had in mind'. The reply was encouraging, and Susanne became a fixture of Allen's life, even more so than the enormous leather armchairs he bought at auction and prized as having belonged to von Ribbentrop when he was ambassador to Britain. A German mistress would be another signifier of Allen's wealth and status. Allen bought Susanne a flat in Notting Hill, and she became a regular presence at Allen's own 'gaunt' and 'ugly' new flat, in Shaw's former building at Whitehall Court, where visitors were struck by a cold atmosphere not wholly compensated for by glimpses of Susanne's sexy underwear hanging in the bathroom.

Bill Williams already had a young Continental mistress – Estrid Bannister, a beautiful Danish journalist and patient of Karl Bluth, the German doctor who prescribed controlled doses of heroin. (Though she seems to have done little or no work at the firm, Bannister's name was for some reason on Penguin's payroll.) Now, Allen and Susanne and Bill and Estrid went on holiday together. Lettice soon split from Ledig-Rowohlt and returned to Silverbeck, but her presence there could only be temporary. Faced with Allen's erratic behaviour, and what he had said about their daughter Anna, and now the presence of Susanne, Lettice left Allen on 21 September 1955 – his birthday. Alone and short of money, the wife of one of Britain's most illustrious tycoons dressed herself in secondhand clothes and took a job at Harrods selling new handkerchiefs. Apart from one brief and awkward meeting at Lettice's sister's flat, Mr and Mrs Lane would not see each other again for three years.

Allen wrote to Richard that, with Lettice gone from Silverbeck, he 'didn't see that there was any point in keeping the Aga going', but that, with it off, 'the house soon began to feel a bit on the chilly side, both in temperature and emotionally'. Allen bached for a week or so, before asking Camilla Williams-Lane and Ducka Puxley to move in; 'they accepted with alacrity, and although adjustments have had to be made on both sides, I think that the plan is working out well.' But the new arrangements did not warm Allen's inner chill. In Ireland, during the summer of 1956, Allen fell into another deep depression. He lost interest in family and work, which 'all seemed so pointless', and confessed to Frosty that his marriage to Lettice had been an unhappy one; 'but for the children', he doubted it would have lasted as long as it did. 'I didn't love Lettice,' he wrote pointedly. Allen also shared with Frosty his doubts about Susanne, and his determination not to marry her. 'I am convinced that marriage would spell disaster. She is a complement to me in many ways, but in other ways we are vastly separated.' He told his cousin Joan Collihole that, while marriage to Susanne would drive him 'round the bend', a reunion with Lettice would also be a mistake.

Like most of the publishing industry, the younger Lane brother had heard about the big weekend at Silverbeck and Lettice's departure. Having also received worrying reports of Allen's declining health and mental state, Richard decided to embark on a mercy mission to England. Unable to fly for health reasons (pressurisation played havoc with his now fragile kidneys), he set sail on the *Oronsay*, informing his brother – in terms a parent might use with an errant teenager – that he was coming to Silverbeck and would spend a few months helping Allen to sort himself out.

> You may hardly believe it but one of the main things I want to do on this visit is to help try and solve some of your personal problems, but as you know only too well, you will have to be willing to cooperate for anything to be achieved. If you are going to dig in your toes and stick out your jaw and say that not only are you capable of looking after your own affairs but also those of all your family and relations, not to mention a couple of hundred employees – then we shall get nowhere.

You know very well you have given me a very raw deal during the last few years, on the firm's shares not only did you swipe all of John's but also twenty-five per cent of mine. You have always refused any increase in my salary, mine is the same as it was fifteen years ago, yours is roughly trebled. A few months after leaving England in 1955 you wrote and said ... if ever I did return to England I could not live at Priory Farm house as you had arranged for a manager to live in one half and you wanted the other half yourself. You didn't even invite my suggestions on this, you just said that that was what you were going to do.

Just before you went for your month's holiday to Ireland last year you said that one of the things you were going to do there was to write me a long personal letter and I thought it was these and other points that you were going to write about; as you know, no letter was ever written.

Now none of this has been very pleasant for me as it means that at an age of over fifty I have had to make arrangements for living a fresh kind of life. I don't suppose even now you fully appreciate what we put into the farm. From my point of view, the present state of the farm is absurd, making a loss of over £3,500 and I can't claim back anything against tax as I have no English income.

However, nevertheless, I still am worried over you. The last half dozen people that I have met in Australia who have seen you during the last few months have given me most disturbing reports, and I do honestly think that with your cooperation we can work out for you some better existence than I am led to believe you are having at the moment.

Allen would go to enormous lengths to avoid his brother on his trip to England. In the meantime, Richard received a reply that was half business letter, half break-up letter.

We had already been on to the Orient Line who told us that the *Oronsay* is due at Tilbury next Tuesday morning, but that passengers will not disembark until midday. I am therefore sending the Mercedes and the Dormobile down with Dorothy to be there by noon. I am sorry that I won't be able to be there myself, but I have got this wretched Publishers Association meeting at eleven and another meeting at three in the afternoon, after which I leave for Ireland, but I will be back on Sunday week, June 2nd. I look forward to discussing future plans with you in June, before I leave for Moscow and Peking in early July.

I of course have thought a good deal about a number of matters over the past eighteen months, and of one thing I am quite certain, and that is that it would be much better for both of us if we divided up the various properties which we at the moment share. We are entirely different characters, and when we run in double harness, it is rather like hitching two entirely different types of horse to the same vehicle. Each of us independently can pull our weight in the jobs for which we are best suited, but I am afraid that we will never be able to pull together without causing each other a considerable amount of friction and frustration.

You are by nature steady-going, conservative, and full of the sterling qualities; whereas I am more mercurial, much less reliable, and inconsistent; and for this reason, even before I got your letter regarding the farm, I had been thinking that we might well decide while you are over to sell this, which should realize sufficient funds for you to buy your property in Australia, and would also give me some money towards any other venture in which I might be tempted to stray during the next few years.

During the month or six weeks between my return from Ireland and my departure for China, I shall be staying in London, but we will have frequent opportunities of meeting at the office and at Silverbeck ... I am sorry that our mutual friends who have seen me during the last few months have given such sad reports on my general state of health. Actually now that I have come through the rather sticky period of the past eighteen months or so – which I think took its toll – I am now very much on top of my form – at least I think so, and ready and anxious to grapple with any problems ... You will I think find that there have been considerable changes in the office, which is now run on much less haphazard lines than it was a few years ago ... Unfortunately the place I am going to in Ireland is not on the telephone.

When the brothers finally met – civilly, uncomfortably – they made progress on the joint properties front, but fell short of making 'friendly decisions on the firm, farm and family problems', and putting Allen in 'a happier frame of mind'. In his biography of Allen Lane, Jeremy Lewis wrote that Allen offered Richard at this time an 'olive branch' in the form of Allen's Bentley, which Richard might take to Australia as 'passenger's baggage'. Lewis's claim is incorrect: the Bentley was for Frank Bird, who was to buy it from Allen. Richard received no olive branches, and there was no Bentley in his baggage.

*

Before Richard and Betty and Elizabeth set sail for Australia, there was very nearly a tragedy at Silverbeck. Three-year-old Elizabeth Lane almost drowned. She was found floating upside down in the swimming pool, and rescued in the nick of time by a quick-thinking cousin from Sydney. On the return voyage to Melbourne, possibly as a result of having taken water into her lungs, she fell ill. The ship's doctor came to see her four times a day, but she refused to eat or drink and lost all interest in her toys and books:

> the only thing that she enjoyed was being told stories, but these all had to follow a certain pattern and they had to start off with, 'Once upon a time when I was a little boy with Uncle Allen, Uncle John, Auntie Nora and Pussy Pickpaws' – the last named was a kitten invented by Betty . . . Several stories were based on fishing for sticklebacks with Auntie Evie [Collihole]. Newt gathering was popular, also birdnesting, especially if the egg carrier fell off a tree with the egg in his mouth and it was addled. We all, including Pussy Pickpaws, made many trips in paddle steamers from Hotwells to places as far away as Clovelly.

The doctor continued to treat Elizabeth in Melbourne, and stories of Richard's childhood – and Pussy Pickpaws – assisted her recovery. In his home on Melbourne's north-eastern fringe, Richard sought to replicate life in London's green belt. Pine Lodge, Templestowe, sat on twenty verdant acres. The working orchards grew apples, pears, peaches, cherries, apricots, plums and – rare in Australia at the time – Chinese gooseberries. Richard and his farmhands experimented with apple varieties and made other innovations. Lucerne and chickens helped improve the soil. Richard joined the Blue Moon fruit cooperative to export Pine Lodge's fruit overseas; the closing of the canal during the Suez crisis disrupted the farm's deliveries to Britain. The sunshine and fresh fruit helped Elizabeth return to good health.

As part of the sober division of properties between the Lane brothers, Allen shipped out to Pine Lodge Richard's personal possessions. From the *Springbank*, his Navy uniform and a shell-case from a multiple pom pom. From Lancaster Gate Terrace, a refectory table, the silver spurs and Annie Lane's Bechstein piano. From Coonabarabran, his pith helmet and bush-knife. And a Christmas carol of other treasures: six dinner plates, five pairs of trousers, four cufflinks, three powder horns, two silver porringers and a cigar case with accessories. Richard requested specifically his prized pair of duelling pistols, but twitchy-fingered Allen declined to send them, claiming they had been lost. The list of items that had 'gone missing' was long and included Richard's lathe from Talbot Square and his deluxe edition of the Bodley Head *Ulysses*.

In Melbourne, Richard himself fell ill. Kidney disease was diagnosed; his left kidney was removed; and 'three weeks and one day after the operation' Richard was again driving himself to the office from which he ran Penguin Australia. In England, a greater calamity struck the family when, in the drawing room at Silverbeck, Camilla suddenly passed away. The loss of the brothers' wise, devoted and steadfast mother brought to an end a familial era – she was the last of the Lane-Williams-Lane generation that brokered the family's name change and changed thereby the fate of her children. She had been an affectionate and stabilising influence, especially during John and Richard's war service and in the dark days after John's death, and had observed with pride the achievements of her children. After Camilla's funeral, Allen turned off the Aga once and for all, moved out of Silverbeck, and tried to make Whitehall Court more of a home.

The Lane brothers' 75/25 shareholding pact was meant to have enshrined Richard as Allen's successor. As late as 1953, Richard remained of the belief that, on Allen's death, he could complete the purchase of Allen's shares by means of the life insurance funds for which he continued to pay half the premiums. Now, Richard's banishment from Harmondsworth was just one of many signs that Allen had no intention of honouring the pact. In fact, he was determined to dissolve it. He set up a family trust to hold a third of his shares, and made other moves to increase his power over Penguin and, maybe, one day, to anoint a successor of his own choosing, from outside the family. The brothers took the pact to formal mediation, facilitated by Lewis Ward, but this got nowhere. Allen simply acted as if the agreement had never existed.

Despite Richard's illness, and the recent deaths of his mother and father, Allen turned up the heat at Penguin Australia. Reprising the Maynard erosion formula, Allen tormented his brother about travel costs and other expenses, as well as dividends, bonus shares, sales growth, corporate tie-ups, performance reviews and new personnel. Allen flip-flopped and overruled; he sent letters to Australian booksellers without informing his brother; and in secret he entered a joint publishing agreement with the Australian pulp publisher Israel Horwitz – an agreement which, when it came to light, Richard called 'possibly the worst single move the firm has made in twenty-five years'.

Although I quite like Horwitz personally, I think the paperbacks he publishes are of a very low standard both from a production and editorial point of view ... I have always regarded our own imprint as being the best in the paperback field and to share an imprint with Horwitz is sheer prostitution. The only possible reason for this joint enterprise must be money and if we have sunk so low that this is the only way we can make it, I think it shows a great lack of moral integrity.

I have always maintained that our sales both in Australia and elsewhere could be greatly increased with the aid of pictorial covers ...

As this venture will obviously have a bad effect on the reputation of the Australian company, I consider it only reasonable that I should have been informed of the negotiations and not sent a copy of the agreement after it had become a 'fait accompli' ... Just as one more personal moan. Whenever I have wished to publish even one title here, I was always given the brush off ... It appears that this difficulty will easily be overcome if Horwitz wishes to publish an edition here under a joint imprint.

Allen decided that Richard's colonial possession needed a shake-up. The subsidiary would embark on a sales drive, he decreed, and Allen would commission a review to map out an operational overhaul. In 1959, Allen despatched a cocksure management consultant, A.H. Reynolds, to report on Penguin Australia. And, as an example of Allenist duplication, he also engaged Brian Stonier to prepare simultaneously a financial report. In a short and sharp review, Reynolds considered the option of an agency deal with Longmans; a merger with Angus & Robertson or Horwitz; and Richard's plan to publish Australian paperbacks in cooperation with local hardback publishers, just as Penguin did in the UK. When Reynolds prepared his report, 'a masterly effort' from a three-week visit, Richard was flummoxed by commentary on his own remuneration – '"RL would continue at a reduced cost" ... I presume means that Reynolds considers that one of the best ways of making the Australian branch more profitable would be to reduce my salary' – and by comments on the possibility of asking Bob Maynard to come back! Richard told Allen that he found the report 'too destructive or alternatively not constructive enough', and awaited the second part of Reynolds' report, which Richard hoped would be 'the milk in the coconut and constructive. Naturally I am saddened by his remarks.' Richard made several attempts to compose an answer to Reynolds' criticisms, but the attempts 'have been so bitter that I have thrown them away'.

Impressed by Reynolds' work on Penguin Australia, Allen appointed him as 'personal assistant' to the chairman and CEO at Harmondsworth, with the idea that he would 'gradually take over a number of the chores with which I now deal'. Reynolds produced a series of penetrating reports about the parent company, even daring to criticise, in writing, Allen's leadership and 'the unhappy atmosphere which so often exists in the Company'.

> This problem of atmosphere is one you may care to think over, because you know of it yourself and it is impossible to over-emphasise its importance in the long term. Mostly it comes from the top – who would hasten to deny it – but it is now pretty deep-rooted as to become an accepted way of working. I consider this a fundamental weakness in the company and one aspect of it can be seen for example in the attitude now of most of the better younger people who have come in the last couple of years, compared with when they arrived. And it's a pity.

Anyone who knew Allen knew he had no appetite for this kind of advice. Reynolds was shown the door. The minutes of a Penguin board meeting in October 1959 note a resolution to take legal advice from Linklaters & Paines to terminate Reynolds' consultancy agreement. According to Geoffrey Dutton, Reynolds initiated his own legal action to force Allen and Penguin to honour the agreement.

The fight with Reynolds was quickly over, but other battles continued. Richard gave Allen further details of his health problems, imploring his brother to soften the attack and not to treat his plea 'as a business letter and send it to all your colleagues for comment. It is naturally a very personal document and what I have really tried to explain is that I do not feel up to an aggressive reorganisation myself because I am not too sure of myself physically.'

> Although I go to the office every day and to Melbourne once or twice a week and accept full responsibility for all that goes on, I am nevertheless not forcing myself as I had to, say, during the war or even in the early days of Penguin, when we worked for forty-eight hours or more without stopping. I have to force myself quite enough just to 'tick over'. I am not really sick but on the other hand I am not one-hundred per cent fit.

Nora visited Melbourne and was shocked to discover how unwell Richard had been in the weeks before his operation. She wrote to Allen about their brother, and Allen replied to Richard's personal letter.

> You will now have had a chance to study the Reynolds report in some detail. I have read it three times myself and it is obvious that the situation demands some re-thinking and reorganization. If I was faced with the job at my time of life I would have to admit to some alarm and despondency at the prospect.
>
> I am, despite my advancing years (sixty in three years' time) and my, at times, reprehensible way of life, in remarkably good form which has kept me from realizing before how much your recent operation has taken out of you. Both Nora and Reynolds helped correct my view and I wonder if it would be wise of you to attempt to tackle such a colossal job in your present state of health.

There is no question that the job has got to be done, quickly and with great energy and it seems to me that a clean sweep and a fresh start is indicated.

In the circumstances don't you think it might not be worth considering an early retirement, on terms to relieve you of financial anxiety and giving you time to enjoy the building up of Pine Lodge. For your information it is what I intend to do myself at Beech Hill when I retire in three years' time.

Allen in reality had no interest in his own retirement, but by 1957 he had hatched plans to retire Richard as a director and a shareholder. Allen had held himself back from a decisive move against his brother while either of their parents was alive. Now, with Camilla's passing, nothing stood in his way. He would accomplish the plan within three years of his letter. In the middle of that period, he would be at the centre of the most sensational publishing trial of the century.

Gamesmanship

The Italian publisher Giuseppe Orioli was the first to release *Lady Chatterley's Lover* without expurgation. His 1928 Florentine edition of 1000 signed copies wore the key trappings of an *edition de luxe*. Despite the elegant clothing, however, many opinion formers regarded the novel as one of D.H. Lawrence's weakest efforts. The fashionably influential critic F.R. Leavis, for example, numbered it among the author's least impressive works, while the more enduringly influential poet and publisher T.S. Eliot worried that it could appeal 'to the sick and debile and confused' and that its author seemed 'to have been a very sick man indeed'. Graham Greene's feelings were ambivalent, but he found parts of the novel 'rather absurd'. Evelyn Waugh agreed with Greene about its absurdity, and added charges of pretentiousness and dullness.

Regardless of its artistic merit, however, the novel was notorious in literary circles for its frank descriptions of adultery, female arousal, and sex 'in the Italian way'. Literary circles, though, were not Allen Lane's circles. He had only a passing familiarity with Lawrence's body of work and, for Allen, *Lady Chatterley's Lover* was just another title to be included in a ten-book edition that Penguin would release along the venerable lines of Richard Lane's Shaw Million. The Lawrence Million would be timed to coincide with the thirtieth anniversary of the author's death. By appearing in the Million, the unexpurgated *Lady Chatterley* would make the jump from a small-circulation, high-priced edition to a mass-market appearance, with a first printing of 200,000 copies.

In the lead up to the book's publication, Allen Lane's contradictions were starkly evident. When his colleagues warned him that the novel might run foul of Britain's recently renewed obscenity laws (embodied in the 1959 *Obscene Publications Act*), Allen gave a look of innocent surprise. Despite his own transgressions (embodied in his mistress and a still-lively tendency to play the field), his tastes in literature, to the extent that he had any, were more puritanical than libertine. He had no appetite for overtly sexy books, and had come down hard on Weybright and Enoch over Erskine Caldwell and the 'bosoms and bottoms' covers favoured in America (Allen also called them 'breastsellers'). Nor did he relish the idea of legal action. Memories of his roasting in the witness chair at the *Whispering Gallery* trial remained a source of terror. But Allen was never one to shy away from a fracas or imbroglio; he was cunning enough to know what impact an obscenity case might have on book sales and the freshness of Penguin's image; and, anyhow, he would look weak among his colleagues if he backed down from the plan to publish the novel without cutting out the rude bits.

Despite the enticing prospect of a generous print run, the firm had trouble securing a printer, eventually going with the company that had produced the brothers' Bodley Head edition of *Ulysses* almost three decades earlier. Bill Williams and Hans Schmoller delivered twelve copies to Detective Inspector Monahan of New Scotland Yard, who in turn passed them on to the Department of Public Prosecutions. The next move was in the government's court. The prosecutor, Mervyn Griffith-Jones, had a simple method for deciding whether or not to pursue an action. 'I put my feet up on the desk and start reading. If I get an erection, we prosecute.'

Allen was holidaying in Spain when Harmondsworth received word of an impending action under the new law. Schmoller and Williams sent a slightly panicked telegram to Allen's villa: 'LEGAL ACTION IMMINENT. ADVISE YOUR IMMEDIATE RETURN.' Lady Chatterley had worked her magic on Griffith-Jones, and Schmoller made plans to leave the country. To Richard, Allen wrote with determination: 'My own view has always been to refuse to give way on anything I have published on grounds of politics, religion, morals or what have you . . . I don't see myself in the role of crusader, but I thought that if ever a book had been designed to be a test book for the Act, this was it.'

The book was on the banned list in Australia, but a few proofs and copies found their way to Mitcham. Richard hid them in his office, where his daughter, Elizabeth, discovered them and read the novel, eagerly and furtively. In England, Clare Lane got her hands on a copy too, finding it 'all right, but a bit old-fashioned'. Other people had stronger views, about which Richard wrote to Allen.

> A Rev. Gordon Powell has recently returned from England and has stated both in the Press and on TV that because we have published Lady C. he will never again buy one of our publications and he has collected several followers. He has a book shortly coming out published by Peter Davies (it has been pointed out in the *Age* that Heinemann are bringing out a hard cover edition of Lady C.) so it might be quite amusing if we could get the paperback rights on his book, as long as it's a good one. It is a children's book I think and the word Bethlehem comes in the title.

Richard shared his brother's enthusiasm and excitement about the trial, and noticed an interesting reversal. 'You say you are studiously avoiding letting out the names of the witnesses you are proposing calling,' he wrote to Allen. 'Was the *Bookseller* way out in the list they gave last week? If this was anywhere near correct, I find it slightly amusing to find Stanley Unwin on your side and Basil Blackwell against you.'

Regina v. Penguin Books Ltd would become a milestone for Penguin, and a cultural watershed, the implications of which spread far beyond the corridors of Harmondsworth. During 'the most celebrated trial in publishing history', dozens of eminent witnesses lined up to use the occasion as a free-speech soap-box, thereby helping to pry open the door to the liberalism that would so strongly characterise the rest of the decade. Throughout the trial, though, Allen Lane 'was manifestly ill-at-ease'. He 'declined to face the fast bowling as an opening bat and went in much lower down' – appearing on the fourth day of the trial (the third and final day of witness cross-examination) along with the Reverend Donald Tytler, and the writer Stephen Potter – Founder of the Lifemanship Correspondence College of One-upness and Gameslifemastery. When, to the sound of cheering in the court and the press, Penguin finished one-up in what was generally seen as a test case for the legislation, a huge pent-up demand surged forth. People queued at bookshops, just as they had for the Shaw Million, and Penguin enlisted other printers to help produce three million copies of Lawrence's now notorious work. For Philip Larkin, famously, and many others of his generation, the interregnum between the end of the Chatterley ban and the release of the Beatles' first album was the time when sex began.

The victory and subsequent sales had an extraordinary impact on Penguin's bottom line. Between 1959 and 1960, the company's margins doubled and its pre-tax profit tripled. The effect on Penguin's desirability as an investment or acquisition target was equally striking. For three years, Allen had been working on a plan to take Penguin public through a share offer and listing on the London stock exchange. *Lady Chatterley* played spectacularly into his hands.

Allen had seen share floats before, including some in the book industry that went back to his time with Uncle John. More than once, he had thought about dipping his toe in the stock market. In 1947, for example, he wrote to Richard, 'Did you see in the *Times* that the Kenyon's firm, Esmés husband's, are floating themselves entirely on account of death duties in the future ... Their bankers are Martins.' The following week: 'If father wants a flutter, the share issue by Harris Lebus the furniture people should be a very safe bet. It was announced in the *Times* on Monday.' As early as 1950, Allen discussed the possibility of selling part of Penguin or executing some other major change of ownership.

As a founding shareholder, Richard Lane held a substantial stake (43,750 shares), though it had been somewhat diluted – from a third to a quarter of Penguin's equity – when Allen snaffled John's shares and some of Richard's. That move left Allen with three-quarters of the company, and he transferred just under a third of his holding (or just under a quarter of Penguin) to the family trust that he established and controlled, and that held assets notionally for the benefit of the founders' children. For Allen and his plans, Richard's shareholding was a nuisance, but also an irresistible opportunity. In 1955, Allen and Walter 'Whatty' Whatmore of the accounting firm Peat, Marwick, Mitchell & Co. discussed in a series of letters the possibility of Richard selling his shares, and Penguin raising 'permanent finance to the extent of, say, £150,000 to £200,000 or whatever sum is required'. The method of assembling this sum needed 'further consideration', but in principle included a public offering of shares.

Thomas Tilling Ltd was a bus company that had diversified into publishing by acquiring a large slice of Heinemann. In 1957, Tilling offered to buy Penguin for £400,000. The offer prodded Allen to look more seriously at alternative options, including a stock-market float. The Tilling proposal would be one in a long succession of offers. In fact, Penguin received as many visits from suitors as the stunningly beautiful Clare Lane, who juggled a series of overlapping boyfriends, and turned down three marriage proposals before accepting the fourth. In 1958, Allen wrote to Richard:

> Unfortunately rumours have got round the trade of a possible sell-out by the Lane family, and as a result I have been approached by Longmans Green, Cassells, The Westminster Press, Ansbacher through the Bodley Head, Collins, Odhams and last week two directors of Bantam Books came to see me to ask me if there was any truth in the rumour that I was thinking of doing a deal. I have kept Whatmore informed of these conversations, but it has been agreed that we can't do anything as long as the Tilling offer is under discussion.

The Economist, Harper's, Houghton Mifflin, Random House and various other businesses, institutions and magnates were also in the salivating mix of potential British and American bidders for much, or all, of Penguin. A conveyor belt of besuited delegations smiled and handshook and haggled their way through the corridors and conference rooms of Harmondsworth. Allen savoured the chance to receive these moneyed gentleman callers, and mercilessly to string them along. Throughout the many conversations, and especially those focused on the solidifying idea of a stock-market listing, two big questions were at the forefront of his mind: how to maximise his wealth without relinquishing control of Penguin; and how best to evict his brother from the company and the share register.

Though good at spending money, Allen found accounting mystifying and had had scant exposure to finance. Richard Lane was the senior

Penguin with the financial smarts and City experience. Allen 'seldom dealt directly even with Penguin's own bankers; that had been left to Dick. Allen's only part in the financial affairs at Penguin had been to decry and override the acute if conventional advice of his brother and other, even more cautious counsellors.' To safely advance the idea of the float, and answer the two big questions, the inexpert Allen needed expert advice. This he got in spades.

*

R.A. Machell of Martins Bank introduced Allen to a short, cunning, wide-mouthed lawyer from the City. Leslie Paisner specialised in financial law, and would become Allen's right hand in the float and subsequent ventures. In addition to Paisner, Allen engaged a legion of advisers: bankers (Martins); solicitors (Linklaters); accountants (Peat Marwick); two merchant banks (Helbert, Wagg & Co. and J. Henry Schroder & Co.); and, ideal for *Lady Chatterley*, the brokers Cazenove & Co. Allen enjoyed the prospect of issuing shares as much as issuing books, immersing himself in the float to such an extent that there were neglected and jealous ladies in Notting Hill and Decoy Avenue.

The task of putting a financial value on Penguin turned into an exercise in ballooning, or rocketry. In 1958, the Tilling offer had seemed to be right on the money. Whatty advised Allen in June 1958 that a valuation of £437,500 for the whole of the share capital 'does not seem to me to be unreasonable'. (The year before, Lionel Fraser of Helbert, Wagg & Co. had given a similar though marginally lower valuation to Richard.) In a year's time, however, the valuation would increase by a third, and in 1960 things would look brighter still.

In that year, the owners of *The Economist* offered £795,000 for Penguin, before lifting their offer to £875,000 – more than double the Tilling offer. In the very early years of Penguin, *The Economist* had been one of the first serious publications to praise the Lanes' effort, 'to bring serious, well printed books and genuine literature to homes where ephemeral trash has been the staple diet'. Now, though, Allen and Richard found plenty of reasons to turn down what was in fact a trashy attempt to buy Penguin with Penguin's money.

My dear Allen,

In reply to your letter of the 4th August, together with the draft agreement you enclosed regarding the proposed sale of the whole of the issued capital of Penguin Books Ltd to The Economist Newspaper Ltd, I should like to make the following observations.

The draft agreement is dated 1959 but altered in your own hand-writing to 1960. Although this is obviously the first sight I have had of the draft agreement, I presume you have been contemplating this sale for at least eight months . . .

Although at first the price . . . appears quite a good one, the fact that payment is to be made over ten years, and does not bear any inter-est, creates some nasty snags [the impact of inflation and death duties, late payment penalties, what would happen if the purchaser entered liquidation, and what would happen with a change of government].

I don't know anything about the financial status of The Econo-mist Newspaper Ltd. If they show a loss, the profit they would make on Penguin Books would have a useful 'set off' value, but even if they make a profit it would mean that, if our profit remains the same for the next ten years as it has for the last two years, the amount of profit available after taxation would pay for well over three quarters of the annual instalments.

Dick

My dear Dick,

You may have seen in your press something of the indignation which has been caused here by the sale down the river of the *News Chronicle* and *Star* to the extreme right-wing Tory paper the *Mail* . . . As you know, one of the main reasons why I was negotiating with the *Economist* was that I felt that this was as sure a way as could be devised of ensuring the continuity of the business, but from the events of the last few days it seems that we might have been doing exactly the opposite. I am now contemplating the possible flotation of a public company which I imagine would suit you quite well as you could then dispose of your shares on the stock exchange in the ordi-nary way.

Allen

As the float preparations advanced and the *Chatterley* momentum accelerated, Penguin's apparent market value rose still further. By January 1961, a £1 million valuation was looking realistic. After meeting with Paisner and Fraser and two of Fraser's co-directors, Allen wrote to Paroissien (27 January 1961):

> They were obviously very much impressed with the figures and after some solemn warnings against the dangers of floating a company on the crest of the wave (I think that they had LADY CHATTERLEY in mind but I was able to tell them that, as we had not published the book until 2 November, it was not included in the figures which they had seen), they hinted that the worth of the company might be something in the neighbourhood of £1,000,000 ... I am certain that a flotation is advantageous if not imperative, and I think too that in view of the fact that the financial boys seem to set some store on my agreeing to hang around for seven years, I suppose the sooner the thing is done the better ... This is obviously one of the most important steps I have taken in my business life.

The advisers set about rearranging Penguin's capital structure by capitalising reserves and lifting the number of shares to a total of two million, of which Richard Lane owned 500,000. Using accounting adjustments and reclassifications, Whatty dressed up Penguin's financial accounts for their big day. Allen told Paroissien in March that everything was moving smoothly on the float front. 'We had a Board Meeting yesterday at which we agreed to increase the capital to £500,000, and fixed an Extraordinary General Meeting for Friday to confirm this. It looks now, since Whatmore's intervention, as if the price will be considerably higher than we had at first envisaged, and I would not be surprised if it is not now in the neighbourhood of ten shillings.' A price of ten shillings per share would mean a total value for Penguin of more than £1,250,000. Later the same month, Gordon H. Gunson of Helbert, Wagg & Co. Ltd told Allen that the estimate had gone up again, and was now twelve shillings and sixpence per share, or more than £1,560,000.

The stakes were high and rising. The Initial Public Offering promised to be an economical way to inject new capital into Penguin, but for Allen there was one overarching attraction. By re-setting the value of the whole firm, Allen could re-set the value of his own shares – the majority of Penguin shares – that he intended to keep. (Excluding the new shares, Allen owned 1,000,355 shares directly, and controlled a further 499,645 shares through the trust – of which 100,000 would be for sale in the float.)

With the two big questions in mind, the float's managers implemented a strategy that enriched Allen, and, at minimum cost and maximum advantage, purged Richard from the share register and the boards of Penguin UK and Penguin Australia. In intensive and clandestine meetings, Allen and his advisers agreed their tactics. Richard's exit was, they would claim, an absolute must for the float. It was imperative that Richard should sell his shares to Allen before the public offer. This was of course nonsense; the company could list without selling Richard's shares (Allen's shares, the largest holding, were not for sale); and it could raise capital by selling new shares rather than existing ones. But the neat opportunity was unmissable. According to Jeremy Lewis, Allen 'used the planned sale of shares to acquire Dick's holding in the company, and finally sever his connection with it'.

If Richard Lane was to sell his shares before the public offer, however, there would be an obvious problem, as the bankers foresaw. And, to their credit, they put forward a fair solution. Richard, they proposed, would be compensated for the difference between the sale price of his shares and their market value: 'it would be better for the other shareholders to purchase your brother's holdings before any reorganisation of capital was effected. The purchase consideration should, of course, be calculated to give him, in effect, the same price as he would have received if his holdings were marketed in their new form.' Allen, though, would have none of that. Astrologer Kate Murray got it right: the termination of his transactions would always be for his good. He himself would profit from Richard's shares by buying them below the market price then selling them into the float.

The tortuous negotiations between Allen and Richard would last the better part of two years. To secure his brother's cooperation, Allen would tell lies, hide behind his advisers, and use them to create an artificial sense of compulsion and urgency. He would make hollow promises; continually change the rules; and, a stratagem he had used before, dangle the prospect of his own retirement and relinquishment of control.

Allen promised Richard continuity of employment ('you should remain on the Australian Board'), then reneged; promised him a pension ('we can accept as a question of principle that you will retire at the end of June or at the end of December and that the firm should continue to pay your present salary indefinitely'), then reneged; promised that Richard would be able to sell his shares at the market price ('you could then dispose of your shares on the stock exchange in the ordinary way'), then reneged; and changed his mind about his own retirement plans more than a dozen times. The negotiations would play out finally as a series of last-minute telegrams. As was often the case with mercurial and manipulative Allen, it would be hard to tell, in the confused traffic of letters and cables, where precisely the mercury ended and the manipulation started. With Paisner directing traffic, the needle pointed more often towards shrewd connivance. At the height of the frantic negotiations, several of Allen's most pivotal messages to his brother would be scripted by Paisner – whom Richard considered the personification of Allen's inner schemer, and for whom he developed an intense and uncharacteristic dislike.

SHOCK TROOPS

I n the early years of Penguin, Richard and John Lane had worked,
first pro bono and then 'low bono', to make their firm succeed.
Though they shared imprecise ideas about how their investment of
time and toil would give them and their loved ones a stake in the growing enterprise, and how it would eventually 'pay off', the defunct 75/25
pact was the closest any of them got to an explicit plan. Having come
through the series of family calamities that peppered the decades after
John's death, Richard Lane was unready for his Penguin endgame. It
began, innocently enough, with a conversation about the possibility of
both brothers retiring early.

> My dear Allen,
> The idea of slowing down at the office is in principle a pleasing
> possibility, especially in view of the fact that you state you intend to
> retire in three years' time and as much as I like Harry [Paroissien] it
> would be a very different situation for both of us if I as one of the
> founders of the firm had to accept him as my boss. But of course the
> big snag is going to be the question of scratch [i.e. money]. As you
> know, apart from dividends from the firm, my income has actually
> decreased in the last twenty years, not the purchasing power but the
> actual amount and for the last few years I have been living on capital.
> Dick (17 September 1959)

My dear Dick,

In order to help you in your thinking about your own plans, I'll tell you what I have in mind myself. I'm now fifty-seven as you know and I propose to be off the active list at sixty … There have been many discussions in various directions over the past year concerning the sale of my shares. These have included Odhams, the Amalgamated Press, Tillings again, and at least three newspapers … [Whatty] came to lunch at Silverbeck while Nora was here with Denman, Branscombe and Machell and all agreed that I must take some steps to divest myself of control before long. At the present time, my estate duty rate would be 60 per cent which would be ruinous both for the firm and my family. The picture therefore is that at some time in the near future, possibly this year, I will sell my shares, or most of them, and some of my children's trust as well with an undertaking that I will continue to run the firm for three years and possibly act in an advisory capacity for a further five.

Allen (22 September 1959)

At Penguin Books Ltd's October 1959 board meeting, Allen, Frost, Paroissien and Williams discussed 'Australia'. They entered into the minutes a cable from Richard to Allen:

HAVE DISCUSSED YOUR LETTER 22 SEPTEMBER WITH [CECIL] HYLAND [A DIRECTOR IN AUSTRALIA] AND I AM PREPARED TO RETIRE NEXT JULY AFTER TWENTY-FIVE YEARS IF ENGLISH COMPANY WILL GIVE ME YEARLY PENSION OF £3,000 STERLING OR ADEQUATE LUMP SUM PAYMENT ON RETIREMENT PROVIDING THIS IS TAX FREE IN MY HANDS. PENSION FIGURE BASED ON SERVICES RENDERED ESPECIALLY DURING EARLY DAYS AND FACT THAT I HAVE NOT HAD A SALARY INCREASE FOR TWENTY YEARS. APPRECIATE YOUR REASON FOR DECIDING TO DISPOSE LARGE PORTION OF YOUR SHARES. WOULD NOT WISH TO CONTINUE AS SHAREHOLDER MYSELF IF YOU SELL. WILL YOU PLEASE INCLUDE MY SHARES IN ANY PROPOSED SALE. FEAR NOT FOR FUTURE OF AUSTRALIAN COMPANY AS REORGANISATION ALREADY COMMENCED. WOULD APPRECIATE SECOND PART REYNOLDS' REPORT WITH SPECIAL REFERENCE TO PLANS FOR FORMATION OF EDUCATIONAL DEPARTMENT. PROPOSE ENGAGING MAN AS OUTLINED IN YOUR LETTER IMMEDIATELY.

DICK

In asking that his shares be included 'in any proposed sale', Richard had several thoughts in mind. He was anxious to avoid becoming a stranded minority shareholder, and he expected that, in the event of a float, he would be able, as Allen had indicated, to sell at the market price. Needless to say, he did not intend to sell before the sale at a substantially inferior price.

In a series of letters back and forth, Allen and the board rejected Richard's pension request, offered a lower figure and asked him to reconsider the terms on which he would retire. Frustrated by Allen's intransigence and evasion, Richard put his frustration in writing. 'I replied giving details and this you eventually turned down. So what next? Naturally I cannot afford to retire without an adequate pension ... Your letter of the 26th deals mainly with the possibility of Longmans buying my shares on which I have not heard anything from them so far ... You definitely state, 26th May 1960, that you are retiring in September 1962. As the Board has turned down my suggestion regarding a reasonable pension, I wonder if they have decided what to give *you*. If the Board cannot agree on my pension, I suppose whether I like it or not I should have to stay on as an assistant to Paroissien.'

Allen told his brother that, before retiring in September 1962, he would start transferring his responsibilities to Deputy CEO Paroissien from March of that year. Richard wrote again.

My dear Allen,

Naturally it was assumed that my retirement was to be on terms mutually agreed between us ... This is not a subject I enjoy writing about in the slightest, but at the moment I cannot see any other way out ... The amount you suggest as a pension is so low that I have no option but to refuse it so the position now is that at your suggestion of nearly a year ago I mentioned a figure which you turned down, and you have named a figure which I have turned down. To make it quite clear, I ask for a pension of £3,000 a year and you offered £1,250, both figures being Sterling. It rather looks from your offer that you consider the amount I mentioned as being on the high side and you have therefore made a counter offer on the low side in the hope that I might suggest a 'split the difference' compromise. This is not so. When I first mentioned the figure of £3,000 I did not consider it an amount on which to start arguing but what I thought a fair amount based on many factors and especially on matters dealing with the early days of the firm. But apart from the days when John and I worked for nothing, possibly the most difficult assignment I had was when just after the war I was sent to the States to try and clarify the situation then.

In case you have forgotten the details, you had promised Kurt Enoch a 40% interest in the American firm, later you promised Victor Weybright a 40% interest and then for luck you promised Frosty a 10% interest and all these figures were confirmed in writing. Then you insisted that Penguin Books Ltd must retain a controlling interest. During the negotiations I certainly had the benefit of excellent legal advice, but believe me Kurt Enoch's legal adviser was no nitwit. Had the outcome of my negotiations been unsuccessful there is little doubt that we should have lost the right of using our name in the States. So I do feel over the last twenty-five years I have contributed something of value to the organisation.

In 1955 I was sent to Australia to try and clear up the Maynard situation which had got completely out of hand, but had I stayed at Harmondsworth I imagine my salary would have increased quite considerably. I really do hate having to write like this, but having started I might as well be perfectly frank. I cannot help but take two other factors into consideration: one the famous share agreement [the 75/25 pact] and the other your own personal remuneration as compared to mine. I have already written to you at length over the agreement which was your idea and which you honoured in everything but the observance and incidentally I wonder if Lewis Ward [the mediator for the pact] ever pointed out to you the fact that, apart from not receiving any benefit from the agreement, I actually received approximately £1,000 less than I paid in and naturally never received any taxation rebate on my contributions. My own income is £2,500, the same as it was twenty years ago, yours I don't know exactly as there is apparently some contribution from the American Company apart from the £10,000 a year shown on the Penguin Books' Balance Sheet, and the perks are quite considerable, living in a house that stands in the Company's books at over £10,000, at a rent of £100 a year, plus the firm paying the subscription and expenses of three clubs plus Whitehall Court. You may remember that on my last visit, when as a working director of the firm I spent two nights at Whitehall Court, I received a note from the Accounts Department suggesting that I ought to pay for this privilege. Some of your perks may be expenses legitimately incurred in the interests of the firm, but I doubt if they all are.

You may think that I feel a little bitter about things, well I am. As one of the founders of the business, after twenty-five years' service you offer me a pension of £1,250 and yet some person or persons unnamed after one year's service are given £3,500 compensation. No, I don't feel a bit inclined to reduce the amount of the pension I first mentioned. In fact, I think that apart from the pension, I should be given a car ... also I think I am entitled to a return trip to England by sea for myself, Betty and Elizabeth and all reasonable expenses.

Dick (28 July 1960)

In summing up his achievements, Richard was overly modest. Across editorial and production and corporate strategy – and in bestsellers like the Shaw Million and stand-out Specials and series – his contribution had been decisive. Architect and engineer of a firm that now had 270 employees and sold seventeen million books a year, he received an unsatisfying reply from Allen, who wrote that Silverbeck had lost one of its giant walnut trees to make way for jet planes.

My dear Dick,

On the question of the famous share agreement, this is all over and done with and I don't think that either of us is going to get anything out of arguing it now. Neither do I think there is any point in going further into the details of my remuneration. These are all items which we could argue about indefinitely but, I feel, quite unprofitably ... P.S. Work is now proceeding on No. 5 runway at the airport which is being lengthened at our end by 1,400 feet to enable it to take the new 200 seater long-distance jets which are not yet in service. A line drawn down the centre of it, if extended, would meet the junction of the hedge between the garden and the field at Silverbeck at the river's edge and they are taking down the walnut tree nearest the house and the elms at the end of the long walk as a precaution!

Allen (12 October 1960)

Allen continued to equivocate and obfuscate about his own retirement, and Richard worried about a stressful and drawn-out negotiation: 'your letter to me of 22nd September . . . said, "The picture therefore is that at some time in the near future, possibly this year, I will sell my shares, or most of them, and some of my children's trust as well" . . . now what is the picture today? . . . I do remember the Victor Weybright–Kurt Enoch negotiations during which my blood pressure reached a record high of 220 plus and I want if possible to avoid the re-occurrence of any such state.'

Allen's bulldozer mind, fully engaged in the plans for the float, had one destination: 'it is hoped to be able to get everything tied up not later than the end of March, which means that we will have to work on a very tight program,' he told his brother. 'In anticipation of the thing going through, I have postponed my visit to Spain' (3 February 1961). 'I would like you to let me know what your plans are for the future. If you are going to cease to run the firm in Australia at the end of the year, I think it might be as well if you came off the board before the issue is made, rather than resign a few months later' (7 February 1961).

As a financial transaction, the float itself was a straightforward matter. Penguin's capital structure and the rudiments of its business activities (making and selling books, and farming) were easy enough for investors to understand. Since its inception with a hundred pounds of Richard Lane's money, and using staff and premises borrowed from The Bodley Head, it had grown into a highly saleable prospect. The float would be a picnic for Allen's legion of advisers. Gordon Gunson estimated that the 'total expenses to be borne by the vendors' would be £27,275. And how much happier would Allen and his advisers be if someone else footed the bill?

After setting in train a plan to cut Richard out by buying his shares before the public offer, and insisting on Richard's resignation as a precondition of the float, Allen took the incredible step of charging Richard for the bulk of the expenses.

My dear Dick,

A large amount of time at the meeting [with the float advisers at Helbert, Wagg & Co.'s offices] was taken up with discussion of the cost of the flotation which would have to be borne by the shareholders in relation to the number of shares which they are selling, in other words that it would fall most hardly on you and to a much lesser extent on the Trust which would be selling a few of its shares so as to make up the total number of shares offered to 30% of the equity.

The total amount looks like being something between £20,000 and £25,000. At the same time it is suggested that I should point out to you that the amount which you would be likely to receive for your shares, including this expenditure, would not be less than eight shillings. I thought that I should tell you this at the earliest possible moment so as to obtain your comments.

Allen (7 February 1961)

My dear Allen,

From a business point of view it may be correct to charge the cost of flotation to the owners of the shares being offered to the public but I do think it is morally wrong ... First of all I should think that you would be willing to admit that you are going to get more benefits from the flotation than anyone else, and under your suggestion, or suggested plan, this will not cost you one single penny. Considering everything, I should have thought that you would have been willing to pay the whole sum yourself or, if you thought this too much, to have offered to pay 75%. I should think that the most generous offer that I could possibly be asked to make would be a 50/50 one.

Dick (14 February 1961)

My dear Dick,

This is a very personal letter written frankly and to be answered as frankly too, I hope. The position is this. I own in my own name 50.018% of the shares in the company now. The children's trust 24.982%. In these days of take-over bids I consider that, to be 100% safe, I should hold a clear 51%. To do this I'll have to raise just on £10,000 by selling the few shares I held on to from Mother's estate, by cashing now my life policies and by further increasing my overdraft at Martins. This will mean that apart from Boston I will have no unencumbered assets outside the firm. What I am writing to ask you is if you get a clear £200,000 after every expense in connection with the flotation has been met, you will feel that you have been treated fairly.

If you say 'No' I'm of course content to leave things as they are. If you say 'Yes' I'd be that much more so. I don't need to elaborate on this. You have all the facts. It's true that I in fact control the children's trustees now but I have no legal right to prohibit any action they may see fit to take at some future time. I've just re-read this and I realize that I do of course have my Irish and Spanish parcels of property more than half paid for ... P.S. You may ask why I don't get the trustees to transfer .982% back to me but the trust deed specifically prevents me from ever deriving any benefit from it.

    Allen (19 February 1961)

My dear Dick,

    I feel that it would be advisable if you were to resign as a Director of the English company but that you should remain, together with Cecil Hyland, on the Australian Board. At our Board Meeting last week we agreed that the Director's fees should be £250, which I suggest should cover the Australian Board as well.

    Allen (20 February 1961)

My dear Allen,

    In reply to your very personal letter of the 19th, I hate to think of you having to sell up all your shares, apart from the firm, and cash in your insurances in order to acquire a .982% of the company, so in principle I agree to your suggestion that I should get a clear £200,000 Sterling after every expense in connection with the flotation has been met, but there are one or two points that I should like cleared up.

    You say in your letter of the 20th that at a recent Board Meeting it was agreed that a Director's fees should be £250 Sterling a year and that this should apply to the Australian company. You also said in your letter of the 16th, that if I wished to be relieved of the responsibility of running the Australian company but wished to remain as a Director that I should get this remuneration. Am I correct in assuming that this sum would be in addition to the pension you agreed that I should have of £2,500 Sterling, and can you let me know if both these sums should be debited to the Australian company or only the Directors fees and for the pension to be paid by the English company? ...

For sentimental reasons I should like to have some shares myself.
Dick (27 February 1961)

Allen discussed Richard's 27 February letter with Paisner, then arranged
to speak with Richard over the phone (8 March 1961). By going along
with Allen's plan, Richard was not just selling his shares – he was losing
his job and his income as the head of Penguin Australia. Falling outside
Penguin's 1946 contributing pension scheme, he sought to negotiate a
pension or a capital sum that would compensate for the loss of his
income and recognise his contribution to the firm. Allen offered £10,000
over and above the consideration for Richard's shares. The minutes
from the phone conversation have survived, along with Allen's emphatic
handwritten notes.

(1) If RL resigns as director of Australian company for the flotation,
can he be re-elected afterwards. (2) Alternatively can he be appointed
as advisor at the same salary, i.e. £250 p.a. (3) Can £10,000 compensation be upped to £15,000 [No]. (4) Will the firm stand RL wife & child
a trip to England this year. Last trip cost over £4,000 [No]. (5) Can he
have his present salary (£2,500 Sterling) for another year [No]. RL says
he wants to go on working. He says he's in poor shape & that a sea trip
would do him a bit of good. He would like cable to which he will cable
his acceptance. He asked why he was being asked to resign from Aust
Co. With reference to (4) that he'd even pay his own fare if necessary.

After the call, and more counsel from his advisers, Allen sent Richard a
telegram that brought everything to a head.

REORGANISATION OF ENTIRE GROUP AND ITS ACTIVITIES INVOLVES
ASKING YOU TO RESIGN AS DIRECTOR FROM AUSTRALIA. AM ADVISED
THAT YOU SHOULD NOT BE APPOINTED IN ANY OTHER CAPACITY PAR-
TICULARLY IN VIEW OF YOUR PENSION CLAIMS. AS LESLIE PAISNER
TOLD HYLAND IN NO CIRCUMSTANCES CAN TEN THOUSAND POUNDS
BE EXCEEDED AND EVEN THAT HAS NOT BEEN APPROVED BY ISSUING
HOUSE AND LINKLATERS. URGENT YOU RESIGN AUSTRALIA UNCONDI-
TIONALLY AND AUTHORISE PAISNER TO GET AS MUCH UP TO TEN
THOUSAND POUNDS AS HE CAN GET FOR YOU AS COMPENSATION FOR

LOSS OF OFFICE AND PENSION CLAIMS. ADVISORS WILL NOT AGREE TO
EXPENSES TRIP HOME AND SALARY FOR ONE YEAR. SPEED IS THE
ESSENCE AND ON YOUR CABLE ACCEPTANCE AND RECEIPT OF YOUR
SHARE CERTIFICATES WILL ARRANGE TWO HUNDRED THOUSAND
POUNDS TO BE REMITTED FORTHWITH.
ALLEN (8 March 1961)

At the same time, in a letter to Paroissien (9 March 1961) Allen revealed
his true plans for Australia.

I am in daily contact with Paisner and we seem to be moving towards
a settlement with my brother. The present situation is that I have
offered to take over his holding for £200,000 free of every expense on
his part, so that he gets this amount net net net. He is trying to make
some conditions. Paisner has spoken to Cecil Hyland, Dick has rung
me up, and there is a constant stream of cables. As soon as this is out
of the way, we will be able to go forward with energy.

Robin advises that it is essential that I get the shares in my possession and the money despatched to Dick before we proceed to
reorganise the capital, and he has arranged for Schroder to advance
me the necessary sum for a period of three months at 1% above the
bank rate. The duty on the transfer comes to about £4,000 which is
also being added to the loan ...

One of the conditions we are insisting upon is that Dick resigns,
not only from the English Company but from the Australian Company as well, and ceases to have any connection with it. This will then
enable us to push on with our own plans for the reorganisation of
Australia and although I have not discussed it with anyone else here
I think we might want to send out a two or three-man team to carry
out a shock troop operation.

Allen's claim that Richard had 'all the facts' was extraordinary. The offer
of £200,000 for Richard's shares was based on them being worth eight
shillings each. Jeremy Lewis has rightly called this assumption 'misleading'. It is certain that Allen knew, by the time Richard came to sell his
shares, that their market value had increased considerably. There was
evidence all around: Whatty was working his magic to report a higher

profit; every man, woman and child seemed to have bought a copy of *Lady Chatterley's Lover*; and people were lining up at the door or climbing over the battlements to secure their share of the Penguin float action. A week after confirming the price with Richard, Allen would be writing to Paisner to say that the market value was ten shillings or more per share. Before the float itself, Allen would send his brother a draft prospectus with an issue price of twelve shillings – a glaring fifty per cent higher than the price Richard received – and would say that the likely market price was even higher than that, with the advisers harbouring clear expectations of a 'stag' profit at the start of trading.

As Allen turned up the pressure, Richard, though dumbfounded by his brother's audacious tactics, fought back. The king penguin could shove his float.

OK LETS THROW THE WHOLE THING AWAY. I DON'T WANT TO SELL ANY SHARES OR RESIGN AS A DIRECTOR UNDER YOUR CONDITIONS. UNLESS MY CONDITIONS ACCEPTABLE IT WOULD BE TO MY BENEFIT TO RE-ESTABLISH ENGLISH RESIDENCE AND AS A SUBSTANTIAL SHARE-HOLDER RESUME MY RIGHTFUL POSITION AS DIRECTOR OF ENGLISH COMPANY. SCRIP NOT HELD HERE. WILL YOU AS MY ATTORNEY PLEASE ASCERTAIN ITS WHEREABOUTS AND ADVISE.

DICK (9 March 1961, 2.15 pm)

Allen responded less than three hours later.

AM WILLING TO AGREE TO A TOTAL OF TWO HUNDRED AND TWENTY THOUSAND POUNDS STERLING TO INCLUDE YOUR SHARES, COMPEN-SATION FOR LOSS OF OFFICE, SALARY FOR TWELVE MONTHS, AND COST OF TRIP TO EUROPE ETCETERA. I WILL PERSONALLY MAKE UP THIS SUM IF LINKLATERS AND OR ISSUING HOUSE CANNOT AGREE PAYMENT OF SUM AS QUOTED IN FULL BY COMPANY. ESSENTIAL YOU RESIGN AS DIRECTOR OF AND CEASE CONNECTION WITH ENGLISH AND AUS-TRALIAN COMPANIES.

ALLEN (9 March 1961, 5.10 pm)

Allen had learnt from Uncle John a technique of wearing down an opponent by fighting simultaneously on multiple fronts. Against Ronald

Boswell, Lindsay Drummond, Krishna Menon, Kurt Enoch, Victor Weybright, Bob Maynard and others, Allen had honed this skill and made it his own. Richard was well aware of Allen's methods and their impact. Moreover, for the younger Lane, the wear and tear of jousting with Allen brought to mind an equally hopeless and uneven dispute from long ago – with Daddy Ryan of South Australia's migration department. Allen had given ground slightly by upping his offer to £220,000. Resigned and exhausted, Richard sent a telegram – 'AGREE OUR CONDITIONS IN CABLE RECEIVED THIS MORNING' (10 March 1961) – accepting the offer that amounted to exactly one thousand pounds for every unit of his soaring blood pressure. Brother Dick was a Penguin no more.

CHATTERLEYS

A llen cabled Hyland in Australia with the news that Richard Lane's ties with Penguin were severed. 'FURTHER MY CONVER- SATION WITH PAISNER AT A BOARD MEETING HELD TODAY MR LANE RESIGNED AS A DIRECTOR AND EMPLOYEE OF PENGUIN BOOKS PTY LTD' (10 March 1961). He informed his chief collaborator Paisner that, with things 'now settled with Dick ... the stage will then be set for the final scene'. Hyland worried about Richard's wellbeing: 'Your brother appears to be over the initial shock of having to relinquish his connec- tion with the Company, but I do feel his health should benefit from his proposed trip to England in May next.' On 14 March 1961, Allen issued a half-true memo to all staff. 'My brother, who has been in indifferent health for some years, has now decided that the time has come when he will have to give up his duties in the Australian Company and he has therefore resigned from both the English and Australian Boards.'

Ten days before the closing date of the share offer, Allen wrote again to Richard to say that he would most likely not be able to see Richard in England on his upcoming visit, and that the expected share price was still rising.

> My present plan is to leave here on 19 June and to be back here again by about the same date in July via America ... I am enclosing the last draft of the Prospectus ... I am going up to London tomorrow for a meeting at Wagg's office at which Whatmore and my solicitor will be

present. As you know, their thinking started in the eight to nine shillings bracket and since then it has moved steadily upwards until I have reason to believe that their thinking at the moment is something in the neighbourhood of thirteen shillings. As soon as I hear the decision I will send you a cable.

A preliminary announcement – of an 'Offer for Sale by Helbert, Wagg & Co. Limited and J. Henry Schroder & Co. Limited of 750,000 Ordinary Shares' – appeared in the *Sunday Times* and the *Observer* on 23 April. The next day, the *Times*, the *Telegraph*, and the *Financial Times* all carried the full announcement. Allen sent another memo to staff, giving details of a milestone that happened to coincide with Penguin's publication of Machiavelli's *The Prince*.

> To begin with the two reasons which led to the decision to turn the firm into a Public Company were (1) to assure as far as is humanly possible, that the future conduct of the firm will be on the lines which we have followed since our earliest days, and (2) to protect my family after my death. Far from being an attempt on my part to sell out, I am in fact increasing my holding so as to give me a clear 51%, and this holding, plus that of the Trust, which I have set up for my family, will be 70% of the capital of the Company, the remaining 30% being now offered for sale to the public. The control thus will remain in my hands.
>
> The capital of the Company is £500,000 which has been split up into 2,500,000 four-shilling shares of which 750,000 will be available for sale at the issue price of twelve shillings. Of these 750,000, 8% (or a total of 60,000 shares) have been reserved for purchase by the staff, each employee being entitled to apply for up to 500 shares (£300) with a minimum of 50 shares (£30) in multiples of 50. If the total applications from all the staff exceed the number of shares reserved, then shares will be allocated on a pro-rata basis. (19 April 1961)

Richard Lane's shares made up two-thirds of those on offer.

By the time of the float, Penguin had sold a total of 250 million books across some 3250 titles, 1200 of which remained in print. The firm still depended on the Martins Bank overdraft that Richard Lane and the *Times* crossword had established and nurtured for three decades. The firm's record of profitability was mixed: 'in only five of the previous ten years had the profits for Penguin and its overseas subsidiaries exceeded £100,000 before taxation'; and in three of the years it was below £50,000. 'In but half of those same ten years had Penguin declared a dividend and only in the last two had the dividend exceeded five per cent.' The exceptional 1960 profit result (£364,588 before British and overseas taxation) owed much to the pre-float financial window dressing, and even more to Griffith-Jones's visceral reaction to Lady Chatterley and her gamekeeper.

Though high profits were a novelty and cash flow always a problem, the firm had long been rich in assets. Apart from an extensive stock of books and rights, the firm owned land and buildings enough to make a real-estate agent swoon. Over and above the company's principal offices and warehouse (51,000 square feet on three and one-third acres opposite London airport at Harmondsworth), Penguin owned 7.8 acres of adjoining agricultural land; another twenty-five acres nearby with a further 9000 square feet of warehouses plus five flats and two houses, one of them Silverbeck; buildings under construction; and the assets of Penguin Australia, including its 9000 square feet of modern offices and warehouses on a half-acre site, with a further four acres suitable for development. The balance sheet also featured the promising American subsidiary, and the cheerful, lovable, inimitable, invaluable Penguin brand.

With these specifications, and in the afterglow of the *Chatterley* windfall, the opportunity to float Penguin was, for London's merchant bankers, a gift. More important than the raw financials, the firm had become a treasured institution, and already a public property – something like a privately held BBC. People had come to identify with Penguin. Readers developed a strong sense of ownership after the opening splash and the rising demand of the war years; they even measured their own lives against the firm's books. Bob Maynard kept for many years 'a touching letter from a South Wales coal miner' that he received in the 1930s: 'Every Friday I spend sixpence on a green Penguin. Last Friday they only had a pale blue one [a Pelican]. I bought one called *Religion and the Rise of Capitalism* by R.H. Tawney. It made me think. Could I have a list of others please.' After Penguin began experimenting freely with pictorial covers, the mother of the future publisher Hilary

McPhee wrote to Allen personally, taking him to task for the American-isation of Penguin design, and the 'dangers of dumbing-down'.

*

When the deluge of applications arrived, it broke all records. The issuing houses received 150,000 begging and pleading requests. Nancy Mitford sent a personal appeal to Allen: 'I am not sure if I ought to do this as it is perhaps against all etiquette. I wrote and asked my stockbroker to get me some Penguins. He replied very difficult, but suggested that as I am in a sort of way (I'm proud to say) associated with the enterprise I might "write to the Company direct". He is applying he says for 2000 shares on my behalf (Mr Sharp of Warburg & Co). If it's too dreadful of me to have written please throw this away and FORGET.' Another applicant, D. Crawley of 116 Craddocks Avenue, Ashtead, in Surrey, framed his appeal in verse:

> Here's to the Penguins,
> Good Books by the score.
> May they help me from now
> Keep the wolf from the door
>
> And successful for ever
> I hope they will be,
> With many more gold mines like
> Old Lady C.
>
> My endeavour I trust
> Will meet with success,
> It's my one application,
> No more and no less,
>
> I'm a small-scale investor,
> By no means a Stag,
> So I'm hoping for luck
> When you draw from the bag.

One of the most remarkable letters to Allen (and one that drew a remarkably cold response) was from Lieutenant J.L. Gledhill RNVR: 'I am writing to you, assuming that you served as an Officer in HMS *Springbank*, which was torpedoed and sunk in 1941. I was at that time a very ordinary seaman, but later rose to the dizzy rank of Lieut. RNVR. I remember there were two Lane Brothers aboard, also a Lieutenant Wrigley. If you are not one of the Lane Bros, please ignore the rest of my letter. I am applying for five-hundred shares in your Company . . . I do not know if it will be possible for you to give my application your blessing, if it is I shall be very grateful, for Auld lang syne!' Allen wrote in reply: 'No, I am afraid that it was not me with whom you were in HMS *Springbank* but my brothers Richard and John. I am afraid too that I cannot help about your application for shares.'

At the height of the deluge, Harmondsworth received in one day twenty-six sacks of mail. No less than £100,000,000 was chasing the £450,000 of shares being offered. When the dust settled, the float managers calculated that Penguin's shares – which the merchant bankers had taken to calling 'Chatterleys' – were 150 times or 15,000 per cent oversubscribed. For the public (non-staff) part of the float, a ballot was held to select 3450 investors, who would be allowed to buy just 200 shares each. With that level of interest, it was inevitable that the share price would skyrocket once trading commenced. On the first day, the price rose from the twelve-shilling issue price to end at eighteen shillings, a jump of fifty per cent. All 3450 investors and the participating Penguin employees received a handsome debut profit. The staff at Harmondsworth could remember only one event that rivalled the float for excitement, and that was the launch of the Shaw Million.

As part of the sprucing up for the float, Allen had committed to serving for seven years as chairman and managing director of the listed company. Whether or not he wanted to leave sooner or later was entirely up to him: 'His position as majority shareholder was unassailable; he could trump the 750,000 shares owned by several thousand institutions and individuals with 1,250,000 registered in his own name and a further 475,000 held by trustees (all but one directors of Penguin and the exception Allen's cousin) for the benefit of his daughters.' At eighteen shillings per share, Allen sat on a pot worth £1,552,500 – a controlling interest in an enterprise that was now worth £2,250,000 in total. When, shortly after the shares' debut, Allen ran into David Herbert (not David Herbert Lawrence) at Whitehall Court, the king penguin could not contain his excitement, exclaiming, 'Do you know I'm a millionaire?' According to Herbert, Allen was 'enjoying every minute' of it.

They had drastically undervalued the company, but Allen's advisers too were all smiles. Whatty wrote on May Day 1961: 'The operation was a very successful one and the premium to which the shares went was somewhat in line with what I had thought and mentioned to you. I would think that the publicity gained from the Offer for Sale will add further to Penguin's popularity.' Allen and the advisers, along with a chosen few 'male members of the Penguin old guard', would celebrate the stag profit at a dinner that paralleled in a weird way the float itself. Penguin commissioned in advance the printing of a dinner menu that featured modest food – Steak and Kidney Pie, Brown Windsor Soup, Fried Cod and Baked Beans – and a modest wine list – Spanish Sparkling Wine, Yugoslav Riesling, Algerian Red and Applejack. Then the size of the stag became clearer, and modesty went out the window. Penguin's printers lifted the menu into what promised, for fourteen diners, to be a spectacular experience around an oblong table in the Marie Antoinette Room at London's Ritz Hotel. Schwenter, the Ritz's general manager, promised to pull out all stops for the dinner that cost £70 a head, plus a 15 per cent tip.

Le Menu
Caviar de Beluga ou Pâté de Fois Gras
Consommé Yvette, Paillettes Frangées d'Or
Homard Thermidor
Filet de Boeuf Bouquetière, Pommes Fondantes
Asperges de Lauris, Vinaigrette
Soufflé Grand Marnier
Mignardises

Les Vins
Lanson Extra Quality, 1953, (Magnums)
Vodka
Gewürztraminer, 1959
Château Cheval Blanc, 1953

Cockburn's 1935
Fine Champagne
Liqueurs

Allen stipulated that only Havana cigars could be served – no stogies or tobies. Lighting up some Cubans was one of several reasons for him to be jolly at the dinner. Apart from profiting through the appreciation of his own shares, he had booked a £100,000 cash profit from Richard's shares, having bought them for £200,000 net of Richard's share of the float expenses (the additional £20,000 was for Richard's pension and other entitlements) and having sold them into the float for £300,000. On top of this, the lucky people who in turn bought Richard's shares reaped an immediate windfall of £150,000. By missing out on both these profits, Richard doubly lost, receiving less than half the market value of his shares.

In 1935, the founding capital for Penguin had come from a burglary. Now, Richard thought his brother was the burglar. He tracked Allen down in England, the brothers went to lunch, and Richard demanded the hundred large that Allen had pocketed from the 500,000 shares. The man who Max Mallowan said would 'ride roughshod over his best friend' – and whose halo, in Richard's eyes, had long ago slipped – evaded and squirmed through the lunchtime meeting, and afterward wrote a mealy-mouthed letter to explain why he had bought from his brother 500,000 shares for eight shillings each when they were worth eighteen.

I have thought over two of the three points you raised at lunch on Thursday, the third has up to now eluded me.

Before arriving at my conclusions, perhaps it would be a good thing if I ran over the events which led up to the flotation. For years now we have realized that something would have to be done about the capital structure of the business if we were to avoid considerable hardship to all concerned on our deaths. You had stressed how much you wanted to be in a position to provide adequately for Betty and Elizabeth by making your assets more liquid and in addition having funds in Australia for rebuilding your house. You didn't want a bonus issue on account of its effect on your taxation. On the personal side, for health reasons, you wanted to be able to effect an early retirement and in view of the fact that you were a founder member of the firm you didn't like the idea of having to be under the direction of more recently appointed directors.

Bearing all this in mind, I had had a number of conversations with an assortment of interested parties including Cecil King, Roy Thompson, Odhams, the Amalgamated Press, the *Times*, the *Guardian* and the *Economist*. In addition I had been approached by numerous publishers and finance houses on both sides of the Atlantic. The only concrete proposals were those put up by Geoffrey Crowther [of *The Economist*], proposals which by the way had the support of both Whatmore and Martins but which, I am sure rightly, we turned down ...

Whatmore said 'OK you've turned down Crowther ... but you've got to do something soon.' Machell and Denman said much the same. I was approaching sixty and there were persistent rumours of a change of legislation aimed at collecting on capital which was being amassed without attracting taxation. Machell went further when at lunch with Dickson and me he said that ... we should take the advice of a really shrewd solicitor who was well versed in the ways of jungle life East of St Pauls and he offered to introduce me to Leslie Paisner. From that point onwards things moved with great speed and in the opinion of the financial world the timing could not have been bettered ...

As you know, Lionel Fraser's first estimate of the price was lower than that which was ultimately fixed but even this was better than the Crowther offer of a few months previously and I think I was right in thinking that you were well content with it until the question arose of certain payments having to be made by the vendors of the shares in proportion to the number being offered for sale.

At every stage I kept you informed of the state of the negotiations and I had no reason to think that you were not in agreement. During those hectic days of cables and telephone calls I was constantly in touch with Leslie Paisner and every step we took was taken with the greatest circumspection. I myself took a considerable risk which depended on which way the chancellor was going to jump in his budget speech. As it turned out the risk was justified and for the first time since I started my career I found black ink being used by the bank in making up my statement. I immediately paid off the farm overdraft which was over £15,000 and cleared my debt with you of £12,000 and put the balance on deposit pending getting my bill for my share of the flotation expenses, which will I think be somewhere in the neighbourhood of £20,000, and being able to consider an investment policy.

Before however I was able to deal with either of these matters the offer of Howard Samuel's shares in Methuen's came up ... We consulted the bank but they were not prepared to play to the full extent and I offered to put up in cash almost half of the required sum at 5% interest. This has to all intent wiped out my credit balance allowing for the flotation charge which has still to come and as far as I can see this will not be a short term affair so that even if I considered that there were any further sums due to you, I am not in a position to find them.

To revert to your other suggestion that you should continue to work for the firm in some capacity I feel that this would be unwise as by the look of things although I am tied by a seven year agreement to act as managing director, in view of recent events I feel that this is likely to be a remote control operation and the day to day running of the business will be in the hands of my co-directors and chief executives which would put you in exactly the position which you had said previously would be so distasteful to you ...

You are of some substance. Even if you lived on capital to the extent of £5,000 a year and you lived to Father's and Mother's age you would still leave an estate which would provide well for your dependents. You have your farming interests and are well settled in the land of your adoption and despite recent setbacks you are, as far as I can judge, in good if not rude health.

Scared that Richard might sue for the £100,000, or pursue an action for fraud or unconscionable conduct, Allen sought defensive legal advice from Paisner.

I am very concerned about my brother at the moment. I saw him last Friday at lunch when he said that he felt that material information had been withheld from him regarding the value of the shares and as a result he had been given a raw deal. He said that he had no intention of taking the matter to law but that he would feel satisfied if I undertook to leave his daughter the sum of £100,000. I said that I did not feel that I should do this, that she was in any case a very wealthy young woman, but I could assure him that if I felt at any time that she was in real need, I would consider it my duty to help.

This evening he rang up to say that he had been thinking it over again, and what he now wanted was 5% of the sum of £50,000 until his death or until such time as I had paid him the sum of £50,000, and in addition I would undertake to leave his daughter £50,000. We are going to meet tomorrow before I leave from Euston, and I propose to repeat what I told him on Friday – and that is that while I am conscious of my obligations and do my best to live up to them, I would not be prepared to undertake any legal obligations such as he envisages. (7 August 1961)

When Allen Lane, assisted by Paisner, drove Tony Godwin from the firm in 1967, Allen grudgingly offered him a handsome severance package. Williams remarked that Godwin left Penguin 'with a handshake which was indeed golden but otherwise very limp'. When Allen, assisted by Paisner, drove Richard out, the handshake was not golden but iron-clad, with spikes. In a candid moment of reflection on the float and the events surrounding it, Allen confessed, 'I'm not a very intelligent man, and I've really got away with murder.' After the share sale, Richard Lane's name no longer appeared on Penguin's accounts or its letterhead. When his old friends in England noticed this, many of them assumed he had died.

The Great Adventure

Allen Lane hugely enjoyed his first visit to Australia in 1953, and for the rest of his life he would fly there at regular intervals to issue half-baked and fully disruptive directives, initiate sales drives and shake-ups and purges, and stride about as the unassailable paperback king. When Clare accompanied her father on one visit, she refused 'invitation after invitation from willing hosts eager to give a good time to the girl whom the Australian press was for ever describing as Princess Penguin'. When Christine joined her father on another Australian trip, she laid the foundation stone for Penguin's new Ringwood offices and warehouse – a modern marvel of efficient publishing – which Australia's treasurer (and future prime minister) Harold Holt would formally open in 1964. On every trip that Allen made to Australia, he left behind bruised egos, disjointed noses and classic stories that have been well told by his biographers, and by Hilary McPhee and Geoffrey Dutton in their colourful accounts of Penguin Australia.

Jack Morpurgo records a famous incident from Allen's third visit to Australia. After touring around with Richard Lane's replacement and the new manager's deputy, Allen held a series of amicable meetings in which the three of them made positive plans for the subsidiary's future development; 'there had been comments on past performance but no criticism that might have aroused any foreboding.' The Australians took Allen to the airport so he could catch his return flight to England. 'They shook hands, Allen moved to go, and then Allen turned back, looking, as one of them said years later, "as if he wanted one last word with old friends". He pointed at the manager, "You're out." He stabbed his finger at the second-in-command, "You're in," smiled, said, "I'm off," and walked calmly through the door that separates travellers from well-wishers.' It was one of the few times that Allen held the hatchet in his own hands.

Australia, like America, was forging her own literary identity, and the southern subsidiary was determined to publish Australian writers. Culturally, Penguin had become as important to Australia as Penguin UK had long been for Britain. Local authors relished the idea of their work appearing under an illustrious worldwide imprint. And then Penguin Australia unveiled a new logo. Composed of Tschichold's enhanced bird plus a garland of Aboriginal hunting weapons, the modified logo rescinded instantly what Australian authors craved: internationality. As soon as Patrick White saw the logo, he telephoned Penguin's local editor–manager Geoffrey Dutton and said, 'Get rid of those fucking boomerangs!' Not until Hilary McPhee was appointed as Penguin Australia's first full-time editor in 1969 did the boomerangs go, and not come back.

Penguin Australia became a vital and successful part of Australian publishing and the Australian literary scene, so much so that it helped prop up its parent company in England. In 1969, for example, when intense competition from upstart paperback houses and other media made life especially tough for Penguin UK, Penguin Australia lent its parent $200,000 on top of the handsome profits it remitted to Harmondsworth. In the 1970s, without the financial lifeline of Penguin Australia, Penguin UK would not have been able to pay its own staff. By 1986, Penguin Australia accounted for almost a quarter of total Penguin group turnover. In 1996, the Australian company's sales topped $100 million.

Though Pine Lodge was not far from Penguin's new Ringwood offices, and though Richard Lane was always eager for news of the Australian firm's progress, he stayed away. He was determined not to disrupt the new management, nor to be seen to re-prosecute his painful exit. In the first months of his exile from Harmondsworth, Richard had felt as though he was again stranded in Australia. But he and Betty and Elizabeth built a new life in Melbourne, and he renewed contact with the friends and authors and fellow publishers who thought he had been pulped. Richard joined several company boards, including Jas Smith, a Ballarat-based engineering firm owned by Sir Sydney Snow and famous for making stationary agricultural equipment such as chaffcutters, corn-crushers and grain-grinders. Richard and Betty re-engaged the 'penguin sanctuary' architect Brian Lewis to design a circular guest house – the Rondavel – in which to accommodate their many visitors. Jack Morpurgo, Eva Knottenbelt, Emile Rieu and his wife, Nellie, were among those who experienced Richard and Betty's 'prodigious' hospitality. (Mr and Mrs Rieu had enjoyed great success as translators – she of the Babar the Elephant musical, he of Homer's *Odyssey*. The Rieu Penguin Classics edition of that work became one of the bestselling Penguins of all time; Allen memorably described Emile as 'bucked as a dog with two tails' over the book's unlikely but magnificent reception.) Ben Travers stayed at Pine Lodge whenever the English cricket team was in town. And when the legendary Australian cricketer Arthur Mailey visited the Lanes, he demonstrated his signature leg-breaks and googlies by bowling oranges in the living room. Elizabeth was amazed at how the uncanny spin caused the oranges to turn backward. In time, Allen Lane would also be welcomed at Pine Lodge.

The main house was a modest post-war timber construction, but Richard and Betty installed rare modern conveniences, such as a pair of dishwashers, a commercial-sized chest-freezer, and a swimming pool. A helicopter delivered a new greenhouse. Elizabeth went to nearby leafy Tintern Grammar; when her friends visited her home, they were amazed by the industrial quantities of ice-cream in the freezer. (In kindergarten, Elizabeth had composed a nonsense poem – 'At bedtime all good girls get hotties / Naughty girls get spanks on botties' – and it appeared in Penguin's *Yet More Comic Verse*, 1959.)

Since his childhood in Bristol and rural Australia, Richard had always been supportive of his friends and egalitarian in his friendships. As he had done in England, Richard continued to lend money to his neighbours and employees and their families, and to perpetrate anonymous acts of charity. When he read in the newspaper that thieves had stolen a tricycle from a disabled boy, Richard contacted the police and offered to buy the boy a new one. Applying Samuel Williams-Lane's principles of *sloyd* woodworking, Richard made and donated children's furniture and rocking horses and other toys. He also supported authors who fell on hard times. In 1964, James Ronald told Allen about Richard's support during a time of great difficulty.

The kindness of your letter, the cheque from Dick which comes just at my lowest ebb, and Dick's wish to be nearer so that he could thrash out my problems with me have all done a lot for my morale. I feel greatly heartened and less isolated. I have written to Dick to thank him, and I most sincerely thank you ...

My first novels were run-of-the-mill detective yarns, not because they were what I wanted to write, but because I had to learn my trade as I went and needed a strong plot framework to write in. The first indication I had that I could do better was when I wrote *Murder in the Family* which Dick accepted for Bodley Head ... I wrote another murder novel, *This Way Out* ... which appeared serially in *Cosmopolitan* magazine and was later filmed with Charles Laughton in the leading role. I had learned a lot from Dick who shoved my nose deep into Fowler's *Modern English Usage*, and who, before re-issuing a couple of my earliest novels, made me go back to them and prune the adjectives that flourished there as extravagantly as weeds. During the next ten to twelve years I did well with such novels as *A Medal for the General, The Night is Ending, The Angry Woman* ... I came down with a thump a few years ago when an associate persuaded me to put every penny I had into a studio for making television films which he was starting in New York. He turned out not to know half as much about the business as he thought, and for a nightmarish period I watched my savings go down the drain ... When the final crash came, I did not know it, for I was confined to a New York State Mental Hospital with a severe breakdown and I stayed there for seven months.

When I was discharged I found that the worst was yet to come, for I had lost all facility with words ... The United States Department of Immigration moved in on me while I was still dithering and deported me ... In the five or six years that I have been back in this country I have managed for the most part to earn a barish living writing serials and short stories ... I have two serious and promising novels in shape for writing, the major difficulty being that I have no means of support while writing them.

(The film of *This Way Out* was called *The Suspect*. Never fully recovering his old facility with words, Ronald would enjoy no further literary success. Eight years after this letter, he passed away in his home town of Glasgow.)

Without Richard around to act as Allen's counsellor and conscience, there were fewer unaccountable acts of generosity at Harmondsworth. Throughout the 1960s, Allen worried about the share float and whether his brother would take the matter to law. Whenever the brothers spoke, Richard continued to remind Allen about the £100,000 large, and Allen continued to dodge, string along and fob off. The younger Lane would not receive any compensation, and neither would Elizabeth, but the Lane vs Lane court case also never took place. Brotherly compassion held Richard back. In spite of everything that had happened, and even though he reserved a place for Allen alongside Mr Withers among the dishonourable schemers in life, Richard would try always to see the best in his brother, and to regard his transgressions in the best possible light. Allen, for his part, demonstrated for the hundredth or thousandth time his uncanny ability, aided by a mischievous grin, to win forgiveness. 'To work with him,' said Bill Williams of his former boss, 'one had to share his faith, accept his inspiration – and forgive him his trespasses.'

Even though Richard had made a large notional loss in the Penguin float, he did walk away with more than £200,000. This he invested in several canny places, including a mortgage for the prominent Melbourne businessman Everard Baillieu, who used it to buy a fine home in Kooyong Road, Toorak. But the most important outlay was made in memory of the youngest Musketeer. Richard established the John Lane Bequest as a trust for the Australian Red Cross to buy books for sailors, hospital patients and other people in need, and in need of books. Richard sought Allen's advice on who might design a fitting bookplate for the Bequest's books. Hans Schmoller wrote to Reynolds Stone, the distinguished engraver and artist who designed the Churchill Memorial in Westminster Abbey: 'Sir Allen suggested that an engraving incorporating the *Revenge*, which carried Drake's flag against the Armada and which was later commanded by Sir Richard Grenville (1542–1591), would please his brother. The words "The John Lane Bequest" should also form part of the engraving. Would you be willing to take this on?' Through Schmoller, Allen suggested a 'galleon' as the subject, but Stone thought that was 'too hackneyed a motif': 'It must be a little battered ship ... "the Little *Revenge* ran on" ... I love the small sailing vessels that I remember and which have only just died out – schooners and brigantines and barquentines.' The finished bookplate features a delicately beautiful rendering of the *Revenge*.

*

In the '60s, the Beatles might not have been bigger than Jesus, but Penguin was at least as big as the Beatles. Allen had become one of the important types he'd enjoyed lancing and lampooning in his youth. His corner office at Harmondsworth housed a desk, twice the size of any other Penguiner's, that was decorated, to recall his Talbot Square bedroom, in green leather. The green desk was arguably a bad investment, given that Allen spent as much time as possible away from it. He continued to holiday for long stretches abroad – especially at the Spanish home that he renamed 'El Fenix' in homage to D.H. Lawrence, for whom the phoenix was a personal emblem. Allen retained his other habits, too: he continued to consult psychics and graphologists, and maintained his slapdash and scattershot approach to business and administration. 'As he was an insomniac, he would get up at three a.m. and write countless little notes to himself with which to harry his staff and others on the following morning.' The notes were typically 'trivial, inconsequential jottings written on a flimsy sheet torn from a notebook'. In the supervision of his subordinates, Allen continued the ruthless exercise of executive power.

The obvious consequence of a cut-throat culture is that throats get cut. Chaos in senior management defined Penguin in the sixties. Old players like Paroissien and Williams jostled with a new breed of turks like Tom Maschler, Tony Godwin and Chris Dolley. Allen knew that eventually someone else had to take over, and he sought counsel from his graphologists, who advised him on a plethora of writing samples. 'It may easily be the most important one you have shown me for years ... I can imagine vividly what makes him attractive to you but also what you may not overlook ... He is cautious, genuinely timid and needs to proceed without drawing attention to himself. He is not aggressive but will make a good representative rather than a leader.' Every favourite was in turn built up and chopped down. Each time Allen settled on a successor, and each time he got close to a corporate alliance, a switch flicked in his mind: the successor was a bald usurper; the agreement was nothing more than a 'subtle plot to erode his power'. In flirting with succession, Allen faced the same problems of choice and commitment with which he wrestled in love.

Tony Godwin provoked in Allen the most dramatic mutinous fantasies, and caused the most violent behaviour. After disputing Godwin's decision to publish an irreverent volume by the French cartoonist Siné (Maurice Sinet), Allen broke into his own warehouse at midnight and destroyed the whole stock. No one at Harmondsworth dared mention the book thereafter. The destruction of the Sinés might have been covert, but Allen's final parting with Godwin was very public. Though he promised to keep his mouth shut after agreeing the terms of the exit, Allen in fact took every opportunity to speak of 'that shit Godwin'. At the height of the settlement negotiations, Godwin likened his former boss to 'a gentleman who has dismissed his butler'.

Susanne Lepsius remained on the scene throughout the '60s, and complicated the issue of succession. It was rumoured, for example, that Tom Maschler fell out of Allen's favour by becoming too close to the boss's mistress. When Chris Dolley was mooted as the chosen one, Susanne blurted out, in front of a group of Penguin executives, 'Not Chris! Not Chris to follow my little millionaire!' Allen and Susanne and Bill and Estrid had made a happy foursome on holidays and at parties, but the foursome split when Estrid fell in love and married an Irish fisherman she met at Rosscarbery in County Cork. 'Poor Bill,' Allen wrote to Richard. Bill's health suffered throughout the decade, and his relationship with Allen thinned, but despite the loss of Estrid he enjoyed a personal renaissance of sorts, writing to Allen in 1964: 'Yes, I've got my second wind all right, and I realise now what a psychological strain the Arts Council was, much as I loved it. As a free-lance I seem to have more fun and more varied opportunities, and the old stamina seems unimpaired. I hope it keeps on that way until the final summons arrives. One seems to come to terms with life, in time; the irony is that one reaches one's best so near closing-time!' In 1969, Estrid's fisherman drowned.

Allen's wheels fell off somewhat as he approached his own closing time. He had suffered serious mental collapses in 1942, 1947, 1950 and

1956, and his physical and mental health would be worse still in the 1960s. Early in the decade, he had written to Richard from hospital: 'Yes, your guess was right. I have had hepatitis and the after effects, as you say, are depressive and, having been in bed for a month, weakening ... Bill goes to Greece for a month before the end of this month. He has become increasingly unreliable and at times I doubt his loyalty.' The same year, Allen was hospitalised with virus-induced jaundice – a precursor to the cancer that would claim his life. He continued to suffer from gout; he 'ended up with a stye in one eye'; and he endured a reaction to poison ivy that was 'more an inconvenience than anything else. The doctor kept me in bed for ten days, mostly in order I think to keep me quiet and under observation, the latter particularly as poison ivy is virtually unknown here and he used the opportunity of fetching in a few of his buddies from St Thomas's to have a look-see.'

In October 1966, Allen told his brother, 'I have now entered into the first stage of a phase of retirement, having cut myself down to a three-day week at the office.' The year before, he had toned down his drinking. 'My drink intake is two rums before lunch and two before dinner with no wine and no evening snifters. The seventh decade is one of gradual withdrawal I find. I'll be interested to hear if you find it so too ... P.S. I bought a Turner for £100 at Sotheby's a few weeks ago.' After analysing Allen's handwriting, a graphologist had observed of his subject: '[this] mode of appearing and tackling things, although it is forceful, has become ... almost stereotyped ... others expect him to present himself according to an anticipated pattern. He feels the need to be a magnetic centre.' Though Allen had always been an unusual leader, this was the decade, from 1961 to 1970, in which his mask slipped and he lost the veneer of capable leadership. Decisions were no sooner made than unmade. Unnecessary conflicts broke out all around. The man who could only function with 'the stimulation of another person's mind and character' had no close collaborator, no close counsellors, not enough fetters.

On top of health troubles and problems at work, there was turbulence as usual on the home front. Clare Lane turned down a procession of suitors before falling in love with Jack Morpurgo's stepson, Michael. Allen displayed all the signs of jealousy. At Priory Farm, Allen 'ignored or humiliated' Michael; he 'just did not like young men', Clare later lamented. There was much in Michael for Allen to dislike: good looks, a generous and friendly character, an upper-class demeanour, strong prospects, entry into Sandhurst, a Sandhurst scholarship at King's College, and a habit of whistling the March of Scipio, the regimental slow march of the Grenadier Guards. Clare and Christine both chose their husbands 'without consulting Allen and without due consideration to the interests of Penguin'. According to Christine's husband, David Teale, who wrote from bitter experience, Allen would seek out a person's weak point 'and then blow them to smithereens'. For Allen, though, Clare's marriage to Michael was especially disturbing. In 1963, Clare fell pregnant. Allen suggested that, once the child was born, Clare and Michael might seek a divorce. Jack Morpurgo pushed Clare to abort.

During Lettice's separation from Allen, which lasted for the better part of a decade, she was rumoured to have had a series of affairs. In 1966 or thereabouts, she struck up a close relationship with the artist Dawn Sime. Lettice and Dawn toured Europe together, visiting Rome and Athens, and they lived together for a time in Australia, along with Dawn's flamboyant husband, Eric Westbrook, director of the National Gallery of Victoria, in Melbourne. It is not entirely ungenerous or inaccurate to say that Allen's unique personality turned Krishna Menon off Europeans and Mrs Lane off men. But, late in Allen's life, Lettice came back to him, and the couple established 'what all the world knew to be a somewhat ambiguous arrangement'. Allen did not make it easy for his friends, who were 'occasionally embarrassed by his unthinking, unapologetic habit of accepting invitations *pour deux* without giving notice whether he would be accompanied by Lettice or by Susanne'. Allen told Richard that Lettice had her own living quarters fitted out on the top floor at Priory Farm: 'her bedroom is the one facing the drive, the centre room is her studio as we are putting in a third bathroom in the room facing the farm buildings.' Husband and wife lived separately during the week but met up for most weekends.

Apart from the partial rapprochement with Lettice, there were other consolations for Allen: new book projects, and the honours attendant upon becoming publishing royalty. Allen wrote to Richard of a special lunch:

> I was in Julie Belcher's office one morning when her phone rang. She answered it and putting her hand over the receiver she said 'It's Sir

Mark Milbank.' I said 'Try and find out what he wants. I've never heard of him,' and scuttled back to my room. A minute later she came in and said that he wanted to know if I'd go to lunch with the Queen and Prince Philip. I waited for an hour and then called him up and said 'Yes please.'

Arrival time was 12.50 and then eight guests including James Robertson Justice who used to come to Silverbeck with the Genns, Tyrone Guthrie whom I used to see with Lance Beales, a man who had just been given the job at the Treasury to see that finance for the implementation of the Robbins report was forthcoming, Lord Halsbury who is in charge of the change to decimal currency, a consulting physician at Hammersmith hospital who cheered me up no end by saying that there was not much evidence that alcohol was harmful whereas cigarette smoking was fateful, and a couple of others. Oh yes I've just remembered that one was a partner of Glyn Mills the bankers.

We stood around having drinks and chatting until we were lined up in an informal way, the doors opened and in came three corgis followed by H.H., the Prince, Anne and Charles. We were introduced and went on standing around and chatting and drinking until grub was announced or in fact H.H. was told quietly, I was talking to her at the time, that it was ready.

We had been told where we were sitting. I was next to the Prince who sat opposite H.H. and the conversation was terribly easy. Among other things I told him about the dining table and the other furniture from Britannia with the result that they are going to the Maritime Museum at Greenwich in memory of John.

For Elizabeth's information we had prawns on a bed of rice with a pink sauce, breasts of chicken with little rolls of bacon and sprouts and *haricots verts* and a rich chocolate layer cake with cream. I had white wine and Philip had a lager.

After lunch we went back to the room we had started in and had coffee. There was port and brandy and Drambuie for those who were that way inclined and we stood around and talked in little groups for twenty minutes or so before the royal party withdrew and we pushed off – I to go to the dentist.

Allen wanted a souvenir of his celebrity lunch at the Palace, but the Windsors and their staff locked everything down so well that the only thing he came away with was a swatch of lavatory paper.

*

Though Allen had tactically withdrawn his name from the Penguin title pages in 1942, he had long nursed an ambition to return to full visibility and would do so, with mixed success, via a new imprint that deliberately echoed John Lane The Bodley Head.

My dear Dick,

The greatest excitement at the moment is still on the secret list but I thought you might like to know something about it. For a long time we have been allowing a certain number of our original titles to be published by other firms. The number of books available has now increased to such an extent that we feel we are dissipating our energies by allowing the list to be broken up in this way, and we have decided to set up a wholly-owned subsidiary to handle these.

When I came back from Spain to give evidence at the hearing against the Minister's decision not to allow us to develop the land alongside these offices, I went to lunch with Derek Hammett who has offices in Sackville Street. In going down Saville Row I noticed that the windows of the Bodley Head looked very scruffy and that there was a notice posted on the window. From this I learnt that Bertram Rota [the bookseller] had moved to larger premises. Before lunch I rang up Julie Belcher and asked her if she would start making enquiries as to the possibility of taking over the lease. This resulted in our doing this and we will be opening in the spring a new firm to be known as ALLEN LANE THE PENGUIN PRESS. I felt it was very fitting to go a full circle and end up where I began nearly fifty years ago.

Allen

The name of the hardcover imprint harked back not only to John Lane but also to the private presses of the '20s and '30s, like Golden Cockerel and Boar's Head. Richard replied generously: 'The news in your last letter about the Bodley Head premises is very exciting, do let me know how you are going to reconstruct the premises and will you still have the use of the couple of attic rooms. I don't suppose the Costin sky-blue ceiling complete with stars is there any longer.' But Richard and others would see the project for what it was: a self-indulgent departure from Penguin's ethos and business model. Though the Penguin Press realised Allen's ambition to be back on the title page, as a publishing exercise it was fraught, and ultimately an 'expensive failure'.

The approach of old age put Allen in a reflective frame of mind. 'I dwell often on our boyhood days and my memory is stimulated as I visit or pass by the scenes which made their background,' he told Richard. 'We did have a happy childhood and boyhood and I obviously think about my own family and wonder if they are going to be as fortunate in their memories.' On the thirtieth anniversary of Penguin's launch, Allen wrote to Richard from El Fenix:

> I wonder if you realize that July 30th falls this year on a Friday so that it is exactly thirty years ago today that the great adventure began. Then we were in our early thirties, now we are in our sixties.
>
> Lettice, Anna and I came down here on Tuesday evening and we are staying here for two months with the exception of ten days when I'll have to go back to give evidence at a hearing at Uxbridge against the Minister's decision not to allow us to build on the land behind the Buffer Depot.
>
> Lettice gets quite a bit of arthritis and it disappears as soon as she comes here so I think that we'll probably spend more and more time out of England ...
>
> I'm now working about half time at the office. On Friday evenings I go to Beech Hill and stay there until Tuesday morning and as you can see I take off quite a lot of time to come here. I'm hoping to be able to cut out all business trips, to keep any visits to Australia as purely personal and to let the younger chaps do the American run ... WEW has retired after his heart attack. Sir Edward Boyle the ex-Minister of Education has taken his place. Frosty is still far from well and I think she will retire within the year. The only two remaining members of the Old Guard are Ashton who is sixty and is going to retire at the same time as I do, and Jack Summers who doesn't seem to have changed over the years.

In 1966 and 1967, the firm entered a cashflow crisis caused by imprudent and short-sighted administration. According to Bill Williams, it 'shook Allen badly'. The firm's list had become as over-extended as its territories, its costings driven by wishful thinking. The quick fix was to take on a large debt by issuing corporate debentures, 'a step which Allen hated to take' because it weakened his control and diluted the mythology of his genius. In 1965, Allen had set up the Allen Lane Foundation as an eclectic charitable trust that would, among other things, 'fund archaeological expeditions and the publication of books by young writers'. Dismayed by Allen's management of the Foundation, Williams and others urged him to move funds into it before they became liable for Estate Duty. 'He used to say he was easily able to put another half-million or so into the Foundation, and he was always "going to see to it". But he deferred action until ten months before his death, and so the additional £521,000 was eroded by Estate Duty to a mere £70,000.'

In 1968, his health already in steady decline, Allen was diagnosed with bowel cancer. He spent most of his last two years bedridden, at home, and Lettice was often by his side. Marriage to Allen had left her jaded and emotionally battered. Whenever she referred to her husband, sarcasm was not far away, and when finally his illness confined him to hospital she struggled to express much sympathy, even confiding to Frosty that 'I sometimes think you must think I am very callous about Allen, but he is so much part of me that the cruel part of me exactly fits him – I can exorcize myself through him'.

Shortly before his death, Allen asked Richard to contribute some words to a book of Penguin reminiscences. Richard decided to travel to England so that he could meet Allen in person. From his hospital bed, Allen wrote, 'It goes without saying that I look forward enormously to your visit.' Richard arrived just in time to see his brother, who returned briefly to Priory Farm before a final deterioration in his health saw him again hospitalised. Sir Allen Lane died on 7 July 1970. After Allen's cremation, Richard took a fourth set of ashes to the family grave at St Nectan's in Hartland, North Devon. Some years before his death, Allen had told his brother: 'I am a very untidy man, and one of my consolations at the moment is thinking what a mess my executors are going to find when the time comes.' After Allen's death, Richard, Betty and Elizabeth lived at Priory Farm for a few months to help put Allen's affairs in order.

Both of Allen Lane's biographers agree that the '60s – a decade, for him, of 'unprecedented affluence' – were the least happy years of his life. Lewis describes an incident that serves as a sad, *Citizen Kane*-like emblem of Allen's later life. In 1967, he hosted a party for literary figures at Vigo Street. At the height of the event, Tony Mott, a Penguin employee, discovered Allen sitting on a stack of toilet paper rolls in the bathroom. 'Who are all those people out there?' the king penguin asked bitterly. 'But, Sir Allen,' came the reply, 'you invited them.' 'Why the hell did I do that? I don't know any of the fuckers,' Allen said, before draining a bottle of wine while still perched on the toilet paper.

The reading of Allen's will was almost as incredible as the reading of Annie Lane's, but for all the wrong reasons. Allen left nothing to Lettice, and nothing to Clare, Christine, Anna, Richard, Betty, Elizabeth, Nora or her family. Lettice, he feared ungenerously, 'could all too easily fritter away a fortune'. And his three daughters, he thought, were already provided for adequately through the Penguin share-trust. In the early '60s, Allen had claimed that the rationale for Penguin's float was 'to protect my family after my death'. How he wrote his will, and how he managed his estate in his final years, damaged that claim. Though most of his estate went to the Allen Lane Foundation, Allen did make some specific small bequests, and he left £10,000 to Bob Maynard's daughter, Leander, in Australia. There was something too for Ducka Puxley, but Leslie Paisner held back the funds when, ultimately unsuccessfully, Lettice contested the will – Bill Williams called her 'greedy'. Cementing Penguin's status as a national institution, Her Majesty's Treasury was Allen's single largest beneficiary.

The Master Builder

No one felt the impact of Allen Lane's death more keenly than Richard Lane. He was saddened equally by the loss of his remaining brother and – with no trace of bitterness – by how things had turned out between them. For most of their lives, the two men had been exceptionally close. That Allen in his will again reneged on the £100,000 he owed his brother was a blow but no great surprise; there were precedents. Richard rationalised Allen's final gesture as an unavoidable symptom of a conflicted nature – provocative but nervous; belligerent but timid; promiscuous but puritanical; inspiring but enervating; agile but obstinate. With the Noble Knight, Richard knew, there would always be a trace of toad in the lime juice.

Before John's death and the 75/25 shareholding pact, a triumvirate led Penguin, and to speak of 'Allen's successor' had no meaning. After the pact, which established Allen as the single undisputed leader, such talk became meaningful, but the pact itself explicitly solved the problem of succession by naming Richard Lane as the firm's future owner and future chief. Even before the pact was formally voided, however, Allen put on a great pretence of succession planning in which he looked far beyond the parties to the agreement. Proving that the planning was as hollow as the pact, there was, after his death, no clearly anointed leader who could step forward and make sense of what Allen had left behind. Penguin entered a period of heightened confusion that rivalled Allen's personal affairs for sheer messiness. As the business stumbled from crisis to crisis, Richard Lane watched ruefully, and from a distance, the tribulations of the business he had built and nurtured. Having sold his shares and formally resigned his directorships, he could not ride in on a steeple-chaser to restore order and Lane leadership. A Lane would never again lead Penguin. Order would only be restored when Pearson Longman Ltd, owner of the *Financial Times* and Longman's publishing, acquired the firm.

In the post-Allen era, Penguin's new directors supported the Pearson takeover unanimously, but there were dissenting voices from elsewhere. In addition to contesting her husband's will, Lettice Lane also questioned the acquisition, as did Clare and Christine. Allen's daughters remained the beneficiaries of the family trust that held a large number of Penguin's shares, but beneficiary status did not confer voting rights. Resistance was futile. The takeover would preserve the Penguin brand, and much of the Penguin spirit, but the Lane surname, opportunistically adopted by the Williams family in 1919, turned out to be a genealogical blip. John left no children, while Allen and Richard had no sons. Anna Lane would never marry, and Clare and Christine adopted their husbands' family names. Elizabeth Lane's marriage to Hugh Paton in 1974 at Melbourne's Scots' Church in Collins Street – near the spot John had caught his taxi to Perth – ensured that the Lane name would be lost to the next generation.

Elizabeth and Hugh's wedding reception was one of many joyful occasions at Pine Lodge. Richard and Betty made a happy home in which arguments were rare but visitors were not. Richard painted and fished, and continued to tinker with locks and guns and engines. (In her teens, Elizabeth had told Richard that she wanted to learn to drive. The former track driver agreed to teach her, but insisted that they must first take the car apart, so Elizabeth could see how it worked.) Richard adhered to a rigid daily routine: a glass of scalded milk in the morning, a gin at noon and, at 7 p.m., a whisky. He collected Black & White Whisky dogs, and wrote to Gordon's with an idea about how it could glue its labels upside-down on dispenser bottles; the company thanked him with a case of gin. For the federal Bureau of Meteorology, Richard maintained and monitored the Templestowe rain gauge. Determined to be on time whenever he and Betty travelled, Richard always packed his cases the day before departure.

In 1926, the year Richard left Bective, Sydney Snow had bought a beach house at Wamberal, near Gosford, on the central coast of New South Wales. In the 1970s, Richard and Betty and Elizabeth spent sublime summers there, walking down to the beach to sunbathe and collect oysters for shucking. The family spent other idyllic holidays on cruise ships in the South Pacific, and near an old whaling station at Tangalooma, on Moreton Bay in Queensland. At the height of one especially hot Australian summer, bushfires threatened Pine Lodge. The family gathered all their silverware in clothes baskets and sat them beside the swimming pool, ready to plunge them into the water for safe-keeping. Richard's precious books were shelved – double-stacked and alphabetised – in the office and sun-room of the main house. To stop burning embers from setting fire to the house and the Rondavel, the family blocked the downpipes with tennis balls and soaked the roof gutters. Another season, flooding rains inundated the main house. Richard rescued most of his prized books, but the floodwaters damaged some original Agatha Christie manuscripts, Richard's collection of Penguin Christmas Books, his Peter Arno pictures and other treasures from his Penguin days.

Richard would outlive Allen by more than a decade, and there would be much time at Pine Lodge and Wamberal and Tangalooma for quiet reflection about Allen, John, Penguin and a life well lived. His earliest memories were of the tight family circle in Bristol, and an idyllic boyhood rich in blissful moments – drinking Somerset cider, climbing in Avon Gorge, crossing the Clifton suspension bridge and exploring Nightingale Valley in April. From school, he remembered dear old Eggy Hutchings, dear old Fifty Fortey and dear old Billy Beames. Richard pondered the good fortune of Allen being chosen by a distant relative practising a distant form of nepotism. Uncle John selected the Williams son who had the seniority, but not the real love of books. Revisiting his extensive diaries and a collection of remarkable letters, Richard thought about his coming of age in Australia, and the daily texture of life as a boy migrant – doing dishes with Mr Withers at Renmark, avenging the pea-struck ewe at Bective, and falling in love at Millamolong. He retraced his first carefree years in London at The Bodley Head and Penguin, when there had been so relatively little at stake. Thinking about the hundred pounds he had stumped up as Penguin's starting capital,

Richard conjectured casually, 'I never got my money back. I wonder if legally I have any claim on the assets of the firm?'

In his Barwell notebooks, he found a surplus of beautiful moments, like the arrival of spring at Renmark.

> Small almonds may now be seen on the green almond trees. The weeping willows are now clothed in their luxuriant Spring mantles. Peach blossom can be seen everywhere. Already are the sultana shoots one and two inches long. The buds on the currant vines are either swelling or have burst into a tiny ball of red which is characteristic of them. Every time a gentle breeze blows through the apricot trees, white petals fall like snow to the ground ... The sultanas look very pretty just now. Their shoots are of the freshest green imaginable. And looking at a sultana block from a distance reminds one of rows and rows of Chinese lanterns.

Looking back on his career, Richard could point to a record of achievement as a bookman. Earning his way into The Bodley Head; jointly planning and founding Penguin as a transformative series of sixpenny paperbacks; overseeing the crucial London market, where his promotional displays fuelled the Lane brothers' take-off; collaborating closely with authors as Penguin's first editor, confidently in tune with contemporary literature; pulling off stratospheric wins like *Blackmail or War*, which sold a quarter of a million copies on the eve of the Second World War, and *Europe Since Versailles*, the largest single retail sale the book trade had ever seen; finding and settling the Penguin sites at Harmondsworth and Silverbeck; founding the Beak Street meetings that decided what to publish and established Penguin's editorial character; reversing the slippages and compromises of wartime production; celebrating George Bernard Shaw's ninetieth birthday with the Shaw Million; leading the successful adoption of pictorial covers; striving to protect Penguin's corporate values and philosophy of good cheer; maintaining the highest level of respect for readers, in the firm's tone of address and the quality of its output.

Small, legible typefaces, paper covers, the 'ideal' rectangular format, low prices, good design, ornithological branding, colour coding, mass printing, mass distribution – the Lanes did not invent any of the elements that came together in the making of Penguin; all were freely available in the public domain, and several had been there for centuries. But the Lanes melded and branded and delivered a compelling combination of the parts. And, crucially, they pioneered an approach to licensing that allowed them to use others' intellectual property. Their effort to convince hardback publishers to agree to a paperback appearance under someone else's imprint was a forerunner of the kind of copyright licensing that is now a mainstay of media and consumer industries, of (for example) film-making and toy manufacturing. In the early days, rival paperback competitors in Britain mostly stuck with their own authors, so Penguin was freer and more agile, with more potential for growth. Penguin's unique business model allowed it to profit from household-name authors such as Woolf, Greene, Christie, Lawrence and Shaw, but also from single-book authors no other publishers would touch, and multi-book authors who appeared with Penguin only once. Penguin's ingredients came together at precisely the right moment: the reading public was growing and they were hungry for good books; social norms and class barriers were breaking down; the Great Depression made printers and retailers readier to support a low-margin product on a very large scale, and it made hardback publishers more likely to subcontract a paperback licence. From the very beginning, experienced publishers like Stanley Unwin and Jonathan Cape were sure that the venture would fail. If the Lane brothers had had more experience – if, in the beginning, there had been more at stake for them – they might not have tried the experiment at all.

*

Richard Lane played a principal role in every major part of melding, branding and delivering Penguin. Bob Maynard was not the only observer to see 'unutterably wise' and 'extremely useful' Richard as the firm's heart, backbone and 'strongest influence'. Richard could rightly claim to have been Penguin's master builder: the champion of its visual integrity, editorial quality and commercial viability; and the necessary and effective counterweight to his mercurial and unreliable elder sibling. Adamant that mass production need not mean shoddy production, Richard was Penguin's cheerleader for good design, responsible more than anyone else for the imprint's signature synthesis of high circulation and high standards. He believed everyone deserved access to good books, and he knew that producing good books in large numbers would spread good writing and sound design principles much further than a conventionally restricted publisher ever could. His youthful experiences in rural South Australia and New South Wales influenced strongly the character, philosophy and price of Penguins. The firm's cheerful, optimistic and straight-talking essence owed more to Richard than it did to Allen Lane. Allen has been accused of many things, but cheerfulness and straight-talking are not among them.

The eldest Lane struggled with numbers but Richard could instantly dissect a book costing or a balance sheet. More than once, he steered Penguin away from the financial abyss, and many more times he cleaned up after Allen's mistakes. Good relations with the Cocks Biddulph branch of Martins Bank were the strut on which Penguin perched, and it was Richard who maintained those relations – and occasionally pulled them from the fire. Allen went missing in action during Penguin's start-up years. Brother John and Brother Dick worked around the clock – just as Richard had done when standing up sheep in Australia and packing up a sprawling theatre in Egypt – to fulfil the Woolworths order and other commitments that made the difference between ongoing success and early failure. A vital ingredient of Penguin's early days was follow-through, and this is what Richard and John brought to the fledgling company. Doing something, not just talking about it, was the essence of their entrepreneurship.

To aid his reflections at Pine Lodge, Richard recorded his memories of serving with John in the Navy, and he used that record, along with his diaries, letters and other reminiscences, to pen first a portrait of John and then a longer memoir of his own life. Writing the memoir was a marvellous exercise in recollection, reflection and forgiveness. After pouring his soul into the manuscript, he submitted it to Penguin, naturally, for publication – and Penguin turned it down.

Pine Lodge's verdant acres continued to produce and export fruit for many years, until the encroaching suburbs drove out the pickers and labourers, and the orchards became unviable. With Betty, Richard contemplated planting grapes and running a vineyard – he knew all about trellising, strutting, straining, irrigating and pruning vines – but there was not enough time left for that. Richard had always kept fit; he carried a pedometer at all times, and on cruise ships he walked an accurate pre-breakfast mile every day. At Pine Lodge, he regularly walked the five-mile perimeter, until he could walk no more.

In 1981, his doctors told him the tickle in his throat was cancer and he had six weeks to live. Elizabeth was pregnant at the time – a risky pregnancy as she was bearing twins and suffering from pre-eclampsia – and there was a desperate moment in which father and daughter, separately confined to bed, thought they would never see each other again. But Richard beat the doctor's timeline, living for another year and long enough to meet his baby grandson – Richard junior – and his baby granddaughter, Alexandra. Betty stayed at Richard's side throughout his radiation therapy, and comforted him as the advancing cancer made it impossible for her generous, candid, cheerful, loving husband to talk. Apart from Betty and Elizabeth, a few flimsy papers gave him the greatest comfort in his final weeks. A letter, from a nineteen-year-old boy to his sixteen-year-old brother, full of love and pride and encouragement about a trip to Australia. A copy of a letter about gathering birds' eggs. And a faded, dog-eared photographic portrait.

On 23 June 1982, Richard Lane passed away at Pine Lodge. His cases were already packed and he had had his twelve o'clock gin. Elizabeth was fortunate to have visited him earlier that day. At a small funeral, her father was honoured as the last co-producer of the paperback revolution, and the last of three brothers who had landed a great idea and left a superb legacy. In accordance with his specific request, Richard's ashes were interred at St Nectan's in Hartland, Devon, alongside those of Uncle John and Annie Lane, Camilla Lane and Allen Lane.

Betty and Elizabeth sold the beach house at Wamberal, used the proceeds to buy another at Somers on the Mornington Peninsula, to the south-east of Melbourne, and moved the bulk of Richard's book collection to a purpose-built library there. Betty's third grandchild, Louise, was born in 1983. Betty spent her final years at Templestowe and Somers, surrounded by grandchildren and the relics of Richard's publishing life. Never really emerging from the grief of losing her Riccardo Mio, she passed away three years after his death. When Pine Lodge was sold at the end of the decade, developers split the acres into a network of streets with names – Whitehall Court, The Priory and Falfield Place – that bequeathed a little bit of Penguin history to suburban Melbourne.

Epilogue

The myth of Allen Lane's railway-platform revelation is widespread. It features prominently on the back cover of every low-cost Penguin reprint in Australia and in the end-pages of many other paperbacks throughout the world. At the time of writing, the Penguin history page on Wikipedia names Allen Lane as the company's founder. Pranksters have added V. K. Krishna Menon as co-founder. Allen's real co-founders, Richard and John Lane, are relegated to a footnote. On the history page of Penguin Books' corporate website, the two brothers do not appear at all.

On Friday 6 March 2015, Richard's daughter, Elizabeth, revived the Lane surname in her branch of the Penguin family. As soon as she re-adopted her maiden name, she updated her details on Facebook.

ACKNOWLEDGMENTS

I am grateful to Hannah Lowery and her colleagues in the Special Collections of the Bristol University Library, who were unfailingly helpful in facilitating access to that priceless research resource, the Penguin corporate archive. Joanna Prior, Managing Director of Penguin General, gave that access her permission, and this book her blessing; its author will be for ever grateful for her kindness. (References for specific archival items are provided in the notes.) Special thanks are also due to Elizabeth Lane and Fiona Kells – my fellow editors of Richard Lane's Barwell diaries – and Louise Paton. Fiona and Louise helped navigate the corporate archive in Bristol, and scouted the numerous sacred Penguin sites there and in London. Louise also helped with the Lane family interviews, and throughout the project was always an optimistic and wise adviser. Fiona made the book possible through a multitude of direct and indirect gifts of support and collaboration, just as she has done on many previous projects, and I owe her – and our daughter, Thea – a great deal. Over a period of more than twelve months, Elizabeth Lane participated in interviews, collaborated with my search through the Lane collection in Melbourne – which features remarkable documents from the Bodley Head era, for example, as well as from Richard Lane's Penguin and post-Penguin eras – and in a thousand ways provided wonderful support and encouragement. Along with Elizabeth, Bill Leslie also shared memories of Richard and Betty Lane, and helped inform the evolution of the book. Alexandra Paton and

Richard Paton also provided welcome encouragement and helped with the Lane family archive. The support for the project that I have received from Elizabeth Lane and her family has been exceptional.

I am also grateful to the following people for encouragement, advice and information: Sheila Drummond, Ann and Geoffrey Blainey, Jacky Ogeil, Lisa Ehrenfried, Lorna Lawford, Maurice Hanratty, Paul Edney, Megan Cope, Tom Hudson, Hilary McPhee, Maria Katsonis and many of my fellow members of the Abbotsford Convent Foundation and the Australian and New Zealand Association of Antiquarian Booksellers. The team at Black Inc. – Chris Feik, Sophy Williams, Julian Welch, Peter Long, Jessica Pearce, Elisabeth Young, Imogen Kandel, Christina Cox, Anna Lensky and Siân Scott-Clash – took marvellous care of the book and its author. Will Eaves was the ideal editor, deftly bringing order, clarity and crispness while preserving the idiosyncrasy.

The author and publisher gratefully acknowledge the permission granted to reproduce the quoted material in this book. The extracts from Richard Lane's diaries and other documents are reproduced by permission of Elizabeth Lane. The extracts from *The Bodley Head 1887–1987* by J. W. Lambert, published by The Bodley Head, are reproduced by permission of The Random House Group Ltd. The author and publisher would also like to thank Penguin Books for permission to quote from Steve Hare, *Penguin Portrait: Allen Lane and the Penguin Editors 1935–1970*, and Jeremy Lewis, *Penguin Special: The Life and Times of Allen Lane*. Thanks are also due to History SA and the Migration Museum of South Australia for permission to reproduce the group photograph of the Barwell Boys who arrived on the Bendigo in 1922 (image number GN03238). Every effort has been made to trace copyright holders and to obtain their permission for the use of copyright material. We apologise for any errors or omissions in the above list and would be grateful for notification of any corrections that should be incorporated in future reprints or editions of this book.

The following institutions provided important information and assistance: the State Library of Victoria, the State Library of South Australia, the University of Melbourne, Monash University, the Australian National University and the Penguin Collectors Society. The staff of Sweet by Nature provided the fuel for the project. Parts of the chapters on *Lady Chatterley's Lover* were informed by studies I undertook at the University of Melbourne for the subject 'Art/Pornography/Blasphemy/Propaganda'.

Notes

Chapter 1: Williamses Before Lanes

'did all the chasing', interview with Joan and Evelyn Collihole, 12 Sept. 1970; Lane Collection, Melbourne ('LCM').

'the thrills . . .', Richard Lane Diary ('RLD'), Jan. 1924; LCM.

'Allen for his voice . . .', reminiscences of Ducka and Pat Puxley, 14 Aug. 1970; Bristol DM1294/14/1/41.

'This was quite . . .', R.G.W. Lane Memoir, Sept. 1973 ('RLM'), p. 11; LCM.

'produced her paint . . .', 'Nora challenged anyone . . .', RLM, pp. 35–37; LCM.

'always leading . . .', reminiscences of Ducka and Pat Puxley, op. cit.

'could be heard for miles', RLM, p. 13; LCM.

'Dear old Billy . . .', 'We would start . . .', RLD, Jan. 1924; LCM.

'a bit of lawn . . .', RLM, p. 27; LCM.

'As many eggs . . .', RLM, p. 5; LCM.

Chapter 2: The Jump Start

'of splendid build', RLD, 12 May 1925; LCM.

'under the superintendence . . .', letter from B.T.P. Barker, 11 Apr. 1922; LCM.

'Uncle John was . . .', RLM, p. 13; LCM.

'a gathering-place . . .'; from *The Bodley Head 1887–1987* by J.W. Lambert ('Lambert'), published by The Bodley Head, p. 3. Reproduced by permission of The Random House Group Ltd.

'a consuming passion . . .', Lambert, p. 27.

The Maria novels: *According to Maria* (1910), *Maria Again* (1915), *War Phases according to Maria* (1917).

'almost people ...', RLM, p. 13; LCM.

'always had an eye ...', transcript of interview with Joan Coles, 21 Nov. 1970; Bristol DM1294/14/1/11/1.

'You've had a good ...', RLM, p. 178; LCM.

'Can you milk ...', South Australian Farm Apprentice Scheme – Application Form for Migration, Richard Lane ('RL').

'thoroughly reliable ...', letter from B.T.P. Barker, 11 Apr. 1922; LCM.

'assist in pruning ...', South Australian Farm Apprentice Scheme – Application Form for Apprentice, Lenden Athelburt King.

Chapter 3: The Barwell Boys

The bare-knuckle boxer was William Abednego Thompson, aka 'Bendigo'.

'and quite a number ...', RLD, 11 Sept., 1922; LCM.

'soup, cut off ...', 'knocked up ... was put', RLM, pp. 24–25; LCM.

'at the rate ...', RLD, 15 Sept. 1922; LCM.

'very hard small ...', RLD, 10 Oct. 1922; LCM.

'galvanized seawater', RLD, 'Retrospect', Nov. 1922; LCM.

'do almost anything ...', RLD, 8 Oct. 1922; LCM.

'He was so violent ...', RLD, 1 Nov. 1922; LCM.

'like a Turkish bath', RLD, 15 Sept. 1922; LCM.

'He will not ...', RLD, 19 Sept. 1922; LCM.

'to oil his throat', RLD, 20 Sept. 1922; LCM.

'I am very ...', RLD, 19 Oct. 1922; LCM.

'soup, curried eggs ...', 'a kind of bun ...', RLD, 28 Sept. 1922; LCM.

'Every time he goes ...', RLD, 19 Oct. 1922; LCM.

'broad minded ...', RLD, 18 Sept. 1922; LCM.

'grand supper parties', RLD, 19 Sept. 1922; LCM.

'physical jerks', RLD, 15 Sept. 1922; LCM.

'a private secretary ...', RLD, 18 Sept. 1922; LCM.

'Around the world ...', RLD, 4 Oct. 1922; LCM.

'He was very interested ...', RLD, 15 Oct. 1922; LCM.

'Allen would have ... be right', RLD, 14 Oct. 1922; LCM.

'in a very poor state', RLM, p. 27; LCM.

'for personal use', RLD, 27 Oct. 1922; LCM.

'Attend to all ...', letter from State Immigration Officer, 3 Nov. 1922, to RL; LCM.

'The boys, being ...', letter from Immigration Department, Intelligence and Tourist Bureau, 1 Feb. 1923, to A.B. Withers; LCM.

'a sort of lean-to ...', 'This was nearly ...', 'a small wooden ...', RLM, pp. 27–28; LCM.

'a hefty swipe', RLM, p. 30; LCM.

'they know when ...', 'eyes and ears ...', RLD, 1 Nov. 1922; LCM.

'Whatever I earn ...', 'I am sure I ...', 'I quite understand ... Mrs Matthews', letter from RL, 30 Dec. 1922, to C.R. Cudmore; LCM.

'As far as I ... heart out', 'seems to be in ...', letter from Rev. Davis, 16 Jan. 1923, to Victor Ryan; LCM.

'was unfortunately ...', 'Your informant ...', letter from King, 8 Jan. 1923, to State Immigration Officer; LCM.

'Mr King is known to ...', letter from [W.M. Hellig], 16 Jan. 1923, to V.H. Ryan, State Immigration Officer; LCM.

'As the boy will ...', letter from A.B. Withers, 8 Jan. 1923, to Immigration Officer, Adelaide; LCM.

'When I signed ...', letter from RL, 5 Feb. 1923, to Victor Ryan; LCM.

'The original agreement ...', letter from Victor Ryan, 12 Feb. 1923, to RL; LCM.

'I am surprised ...', letter from Victor Ryan, 23 Feb. 1923, to RL; LCM.

Chapter 4: Cold Dip

'while I write ...', RLD, 5 Apr. 1925; LCM.

'soon grew tired of it', 'He became ... from this', 'private secretary ...', RLD, 4 Sept. 1925; LCM.

'was smallish ...', RLM, p. 30; LCM.

'no ceiling ... prunes', RLD, 22 Feb. 1925; LCM.

'for the first ...', RLD, 27 Jul. 1924; LCM.

'I asked him ... too much", he added', RLD, 27 Jul. 1924; LCM.

'there is a right ...', RLD, 8 Aug. 1924; LCM.

'The boss washes ... tomorrow', RLD, 5 Aug. 1924; LCM.

'We came up ... a tin', RLD, 8 Aug. 1924; LCM.

'he is a real 100% ...', 'now he is ... in town', RLD, 4 Jun. 1925; LCM.

'got the wind up', 'Of course none ... baffling', RLD, 9 Sept. 1924; LCM.

'They have run ... cannot', 'Renmark at present ... washing', RLD, 'Preface', Jan. 1924; LCM.

'from wagons ... block horses', 'From motor bikes ... picture', RLD, 6 Apr. 1924; LCM.

'I think ... equally well', RLD, 28 Dec. 1924; LCM.

'Oh they have ...', RLD, 'Preface', Jan. 1924; LCM.

'You know the ...', RLD, 29 Jun. 1924; LCM.

'complete with ...', RLD, 13 Dec. 1925; LCM.

'In the beginning ... artistic name', RLD, 5 Apr. 1925; LCM.
'did not discover ...', 'crawled underneath ...', RLD, 12 Apr. 1925; LCM.
'Some very fine ...', RLD, 8 Mar. 1925; LCM.
'So almost anyone ...', 'a great number ...'; RLD, 11 May 1925; LCM.
'I am now desirous ...', letter from RL, 4 Oct. 1924, to Victor Ryan; LCM.
'there were no made ...', RLM, p. 31; LCM.
'Don had to hold ...', RLD, 8 Feb. 1925; LCM.
'I suppose this ...', 'a little cripple girl ...', 'She was a very ... quite well', RLD,
    16 Jul. 1925; LCM.
'did us out ...', RLD, 8 Feb. 1925; LCM.
'rather slipped me up', 'in hard cash ... for him.', RLD, 22 Feb. 1925; LCM.
'I did not ... many days.', RLD, 28 Mar. 1925; LCM.
'If I had £850 ...', 'I wish my ... track driver', RLD, 29 Mar. 1925; LCM.

Chapter 5: Which Is the Englishman?

'never to return again', RLD, 30 May 1925; LCM.
'he is always ...', RLD, 4 Sept. 1925; LCM.
'always somewhere ...', James Lewis May, quoted in Lambert, p. 16.
'Lady Ramsay ... the Royal', 'Which is the Englishman ...', 'had a glorious
    time', 'a fine house ...', RLD, 1 Aug. 1925; LCM.
'We had dinner ... to bed', RLD, 1 Aug. 1925; LCM.
'one stormy night', 'just make a mess of him', RLD, 23rd Aug. 1925; LCM.
'If I could be ... school master', RLD, 16 Jul. 1925; LCM.
'I do not really ... jump at it', RLD, 2 Aug. 1925; LCM.
'On enquiring at ... peanuts', 'but Mr Rowlands ... many times', RLD,
    15 Aug. 1925; LCM.
'not a decent ...', RLD, 1 Nov. 1925; LCM.
'late Kerosene period', RLD, 4 Oct. 1925; LCM.
'always making ...', RLD, 1 Nov. 1925; LCM.
'one pulled ... my belongings', 'or else the brats ...', RLD, 4 Oct. 1925; LCM.
'When the Armistice ...', 'the General sent ... thousand men', RLD, 4 Sept.
    1925; LCM.
'the horse did ...', 'tried to break ... dear life', RLD, 15 Aug. 1925; LCM.
'At each leap ... to prevent', 27 Sept. 1925; LCM.
'I was holding ...', 'just as he started ... exciting day', RLD, 22 Nov. 1925;
    LCM.
'lighting the kitchen ... front gate', RLD, 1 Nov. 1925; LCM.
'a very dirty job', RLD, 19 Sept. 1925; LCM.
'The boss is not too ... at all', RLD, 1 Nov. 1925; LCM.
'besides losing ...', RLD, 10 Feb. 1926; LCM.

'butter oil', RLD, 10 Feb. 1926; LCM.

'Some sheep ...', 'In time ...', 'they walk ...', RLD, 19 Dec. 1925; LCM.

'but I expect ... has twins', 'making a mess ... flesh', 'I soon had ...', RLD, 27 Aug. 1925; LCM.

'All Crows Beware', RLD, 10 Sept. 1925; LCM.

'Here if by some ... thousand', RLD, 26 Sept. 1925; LCM.

'I am beginning ... reference book', RLD, 27 Sept. 1925; LCM.

'When I opened ... were done', RLD, 19 Sept. 1925; LCM.

'Not counting a ... crisis', RLD, 8 Oct. 1925; LCM.

'I regret that you ...', letter from Victor Ryan, 19 Nov. 1925, to RL; LCM.

'things are in a terrible ...', 'If I could possibly ...', 'everybody is getting ...', RLD, 25 Nov. 1925; LCM.

'for if they do ...', RLD, 9 Jan. 1926; LCM.

'Some of the sheep ... trampling on', 'like a blooming ...', RLD, 10 Jan., 1926; LCM.

'It looked as if ... and grey', RLD, 13 Dec. 1925; LCM.

'First one name ... talking about', RLD, 19 Jan. 1926; LCM.

'I am just beginning ...', RLD, 11 Feb. 1926; LCM.

'idiotic games', RLD, 29 Mar. 1925; LCM.

'when the occasion demands it', RLD, 24 Oct. 1925; LCM.

'All shingled ... in attendance', RLD, 25 Feb. 1926; LCM.

Chapter 6: Practically Everything

'lovely tunic ...', reminiscences of Ducka and Pat Puxley, 14 Aug. 1970; Bristol DM1294/14/1/41.

'unequal to explaining yeast', letter from AL, 17 Jul. 1947, to RL; Bristol DM1819/22/3/2/5.

'was as excited ...', *T.P.'s Weekly*, 5 Jan. 1929, 'London's Youngest Publisher, A talk with Mr Allen Lane of the Bodley Head'; Bristol DM1649/4/4.

'tore after him ...', transcript of John Lane (Jnr.) interview on Books Grave and Gay, 2YA (New Zealand), 12 Mar. 1934, p. 7B; LCM.

'fiddling around ...', letter from William Watson to John Lane, cited by Lambert, p. 82.

'I will not mention ... and friends', RLD, 30 Dec. 1925 (letter from RL to Annie Lane); LCM.

'extraneous noises', Richard Lane Memoir of John Lane ('RLJLM') p. 3, LCM.

'He always knew ... accommodation', RLJLM, p. 7; LCM.

'number one female author', RLM, p. 43; LCM.

'great fun and very shy', archaeologist Stuart Piggott; Nicholas Shakespeare, *Bruce Chatwin*, p. 90 (Harvill Press: 1999).

'was with him ...', 'He checked ...', 'practically everything', RLM, pp. 38–40;
    LCM.
'no-one at the school ... American accent', RLM, p. 52, LCM.

Chapter 7: The Lord of Alexandria

'free liquid refreshments', RLM, p. 41; LCM.
'no salary ...', RLM, p. 43; LCM.
'for the first time ... nine o'clock', 'He, being French ... than twelve', Richard
    Lane Egypt Diary ('RLED'), 17 Nov. 1927; LCM.
'It was a very ... Atlantis', 'a very dirty place ...', RLED, 28 Nov. 1927; LCM.
'This is undoubtedly a very ...', RLED, 18 Nov. 1927; LCM.
'I am he who ...', RLED, 20 Nov. 1927; LCM.
'quite a comfortable ... to low', RLED, 28 Nov. 1927; LCM.
'One play was cast ...', RLM, p. 46; LCM.
'One day Ernest ... evening', RLED, 21 Nov. 1927; LCM.
'The whole company ... quite frequent', RLED, 21 Nov. 1927; LCM.
'was such a forceful character', RLM, p. 46; LCM.
'I enjoyed my drink ... a beer', RLM, p. 45; LCM.
'In this profession ... see it', RLED, 21 Nov. 1927; LCM.
'It strikes me ... disappointments', RLED, 21 Nov. 1927; LCM.
'the deep throated horn', 'the comfortable ...', 'When anyone's ... nightdress',
    'On a fine day ...', 'R.C.A. never ...', RLM, pp. 49–50; LCM.
'My dear Dick ... Pip', letter from Nora Lane, [c. 1930], to RL; LCM.
'which was reputed ...', RLM, p. 51; LCM.
'there was always ...', RLJLM, p. 7; LCM.
'one could not ...', RLD, 4 Sept. 1925; LCM.
'Please will you ... walking off', RLM, p. 84; LCM.

Chapter 8: Swarming Bees

'we were rather ...', RLJLM, p. 4; LCM.
'usually so dirty ...', 'The lid of the box ...', RLM, p. 53; LCM.
'so we reverted ...', RLM, p. 54; LCM.
'The stair rods ... expected', 'rather unattractive frames', 'Then when ...
    about it', RLJLM, p. 4; LCM.
'The Old Horse ... noises', RLM, p. 58, LCM.
'it gave him great ...', RLJLM, p. 3; LCM.
'very dirty job', RLD, 19 Sept. 1925; LCM.
'to a person ... the bath', RLD, 19 Sept. 1925; LCM.
'It was a long ... the bath', RLJLM, p. 5; LCM.

'Swing out . . .', RLM, p. 70; LCM.

'for a bottle . . .', 'As a holiday . . .', RLJLM, pp. 6–7; LCM.

'increased in proportion', RLJLM, p. 8; LCM.

'lamp and lampshade . . .', RLJLM, p. 5; LCM.

'with tears . . . bearer of his', letter from John Lane (Jnr.), 9 Jun. 1933, to his
    father; Bristol DM1649/5/1/9.

'and ended up . . .', 'Then for some . . . came in.', RLJLM, p. 8; LCM.

'so the pace . . .', 'knocked them . . . two years', RLJLM, p. 9; LCM.

'some outlandish spot', RLJLM, p. 10; LCM.

'ten times . . .', 'even worse . . . Bentley', letter from John Lane (Jnr.), 5 May
    1933, to his father; Bristol DM1649/5/1/5.

'Take a very large . . . weigh in', letter from John Lane (Jnr.), 20 Aug. 1933,
    to his father; Bristol DM1649/5/1/15.

'You may think . . . tips etc.', letter from John Lane (Jnr.), 15 Aug. 1933, to his
    father; Bristol DM1649/5/1/14.

'the middle one . . . can tell', letter from John Lane (Jnr.), 20 Jul. 1933, to his
    father; Bristol DM1649/5/1/12.

'For Nora's . . . the world', letter from John Lane (Jnr.), 5 May 1933, to his
    father; Bristol DM1649/5/1/5.

'I think, and . . . down there', letter from John Lane (Jnr.), 27 Sept. 1933, to his
    mother; Bristol DM1649/5/1/19.

'The notion . . . drove on', RLM, p. 65; LCM.

'to get the low . . . (including myself!!)', letter from John Lane (Jnr.), 30 Dec.
    1933, to his mother; Bristol DM1649/5/1/25.

'I notice that . . . sex publications.', transcript of John Lane (Jnr.) interview on
    'Books Grave and Gay', 2YA (New Zealand), 12 Mar. 1934, p. 2; LCM.

'The words he . . . it off', RLM, p. 65, LCM.

Chapter 9: Bookmen

'found a family', 'he attempted . . .', letter from Peggie (Duke of York Inn,
    Iddesleigh, Winkleigh, Devon), 30 Dec. 1970, to Tanya Schmoller; Bristol,
    DM1294/14/1/52.

'quintessentially a . . .', J. E. (Jack) Morpurgo, *Allen Lane: King Penguin, A
    Biography* (Hutchinson: 1979) ('Morpurgo') p. 57.

'it is never . . .', letter from Ethel Mannin to AL, cited in Lambert, pp.
    242–243.

'asked everyone's . . .', letter from RL, 6 Jul. 1933, to John Lane (Jnr.); Bristol
    DM1549/4/3.

'you will have . . .', 'many of your . . .', 'I think it . . . any good', letter from Kate
    Murray, [1929], to AL; Bristol DM1819/21/4.

'He used ... work late', transcript of interview with Joan Coles, 21 Nov. 1970; op. cit.

'Twelve chapters ...', RLD, 18 Apr. 1926; LCM.

'We went into ... poisoned.', RLM, p. 48; LCM.

'rather odd names', reader's report by AL for W.H. Rainsford's *That Girl March* (published by John Lane, 1920); Bristol DM1819/27/4.

'A good reader ... the work', RLM, p. 54; LCM.

'certainly a remarkable ...', RLD, 3 Mar. 1926; LCM.

'intense mental ...', 'When I ... half-read', RLD, 23 Mar. 1924; LCM.

'If a representative ... notice', RLM, p. 55; LCM.

'it is more ...', 'there was a ... traffic jam', 'caused terrific ...', 'When we published ... purchase same', RLM, pp. 56–57; LCM.

'Allen was far from pleased', Lambert, p. 250.

'getting a little ...', RLJLM, p. 10; LCM.

'a Frenchman ...', 'when we ran ...', RLM, p. 73; LCM.

'many disagreements ...', transcript of interview with Joan Coles, 21 Nov. 1970; op. cit.

'complete with ...', 'not all these ...', RLM, p. 69; LCM.

'Everything went ... spoon short', 'interminably discoursing ... came first', RLM, p. 70; LCM.

'burly, foul-mouthed', Nikolaus Pevsner, cited in Susie Harries, *Nikolaus Pevsner: The Life*, p. 372 (Pimlico: 2013).

Chapter 10: 'At Length Did Cross an Albatross'

'Dick raised ... fellow-directors', Morpurgo, p. 62.

'lost money on ...', J.W. Lambert (with Michael Ratcliffe), *The Bodley Head 1887–1987* (The Bodley Head 1987) ('Lambert'), p. 252.

'made quite a ...', RLM, p. 74; LCM.

'office boys ...', 'in general literature', transcript of John Lane (Jnr.) interview on 'Books Grave and Gay', 2YA (New Zealand), 12 Mar. 1934, pp. 5–6; LCM.

'I do not ... criticisms', letter from John Lane (Jnr.), 6 Sept. 1933, to his father; Bristol DM1649/5/1/17.

'solid knowledge ... be done', Jonathan Cape, interview with Heather Mansell-Jones (1968).

'On [Allen's] way ... success', RLM, pp. 73–74; LCM.

Another example of Allen Lane's creation myths appears in Steve Hare (ed.), *Penguin Portrait: Allen Lane and the Penguin Editors 1935–1970* (Penguin Books: 1995) ('Hare') (p. 3). In a letter from Allen to E. Glanvill Benn, Allen wrote: 'I am particularly interested in these [Stead's Books for the

Bairns] as I was more or less brought up on them and I have always considered that they really gave me the first idea of Penguins.'

Chapter 11: Getting Home

'Allen was a man ... in them', talk with Edward Young recorded at Vigo Street on 10 Feb. 1971; Bristol DM1294/14/1/51.
'I thought I'd ...', Alex Hamilton interview with AL, *The Times*, 1969.
'As soon as ...', RLM, p. 79; LCM.
'She studied ... the lot', 'Sydney explained ...', RLM, p. 78; LCM.
'all the serious work', RLJLM, p. 11; LCM.
'Around the ... petty cash', 'If pulled ... used to', RLM, p. 79; LCM.
'The language ... was very profane ...', RLM, p. 80; LCM.
'staunch Catholic', 'he fell right ...', RLM, p. 81; LCM.
'the first trap ...', RLM, p. 85, LCM.
'in the middle ...', typescript, 'A Report on Penguin World' by Mass Observation, Nov. 1947, p. 249; Bristol DM1843/14/1.
'got a crypt ...', RLM, p. 85; LCM.
'We did everything ... slippery slide', RLM, p. 83; LCM.
'dark, slight ...', Bob Davies, quoted in Morpurgo, p. 280.
'living on water ...', RLJLM, p. 11.
'There is little to ...', letter from Evangeline Adams, 16 May 1929, to AL; Bristol DM1819/21/4.
'You appear ... to you', 'The termination ...', letter from Kate Murray, 'Tuesday' [May 1929], to AL; Bristol DM1819/21/4.
'Now in this ... as yours', letter from Kate Murray, 13 May [1929], to AL; Bristol DM1819/21/4.

Chapter 12: An Air of Friendliness

The Bodley Head was sold not long after the delayed edition of *Ulysses* finally appeared.
'We decided ...', RLM, p. 81; LCM.
'as if he ...', Shiela Grant Duff, *The Parting of Ways: A Personal Account of the Thirties* (Peter Owen: 1982), p. 102.
'I am glad ... beyond me', Apsley Cherry-Garrard, 'Author's Note' to *The Worst Journey in the World* (Penguin: 1948), p. 10.
'We nearly always ...', 'We would work ... consumed', RLM, p. 82; LCM.
'a dear ... twinkly ... heartless', letter from Jean McFarlane, 16 Feb. 1984, to Eunice Frost (Bristol), Eunice E. Frost archive ('EEF'); DM1843.
'He made a ... possible', 'three and ...', RLM, p. 83; LCM.

'Allen did not ... working', RLM, p. 85; LCM.
'So it can ... burglary', 'after they ... crossword', RLM, p. 86; LCM.
'"Have you got ...', RLM, p. 86; LCM.
'I have still ...', RLD, 7 May 1925; LCM.
'Perhaps not ... Gauloise Bleu', RLM, p. 88; LCM.
'this brought ...', RLM, p. 46c; LCM.
'We went via ... medallion', RLM, p. 46c; LCM.

Chapter 13: Swatchway and Kingfisher

'appalling ignorance ... ribbons', RLM, pp. 89–90; LCM.
'First I was ... Fair enough', RLM, pp. 90–92; LCM.
'the more alarming ... moment', RLJLM, p. 13; LCM.
'I guarantee ...', RLM, p. 92; LCM.
'nawabs ...', Morpurgo, p. 141.
'who turned ...', RLM, p. 92; LCM.
'just to show ...', RLJLM, p. 14; LCM.
'we had to ... Poyle', 'a magnificent ...', RLM, pp. 93–94; LCM.
'HAVING A LOVELY ... RAWALPINDI', RLM, p. 94; LCM.
'We had tons ...', RLM, p. 93; LCM.
'being only a ...', RLM, p. 94; LCM.
'a plethora of ...', Morpurgo, p. 145.
'COME BACK ... POSSIBLE', RLJLM, p. 15; LCM.
'We asked ... agreed', RLM, p. 96; LCM.
'quite happily', RLJLM, p. 15; LCM.
'the largest retail ...', *New York Times*, 3 May 1940; *New York Herald-Tribune*, 3 May 1940; and *New York Sun*, 7 May 1940; Bristol DM1819/28/2.
'things looked ...', 'Things look ... Saturday', RLM, pp. 98–99; LCM.

Chapter 14: Penguins Go to Sea

'One had to ... place', RLJLM, p. 19; LCM.
'Well this is ...', RLJLM, p. 20; LCM.
'It eventually ... half hour', RLJLM, p. 20; LCM.
'This was not ... board', RLJLM, p. 21; LCM.
'the beginning ... *Springbank*', RLM, p. 106; LCM.
'from eight ... district', 'were replaced ...', RLM, p. 107; LCM.
'She looked ... security', RLJLM, p. 22; LCM.
'Well, have ...', RLM, p. 109; LCM.
'his duties being ... work', RLM, p. 141; LCM.
The Fulmar was named after a tubenosed sea bird.

'the plots of . . . speed', 'never saw a . . .', RLM, p. 112; LCM.

'this was on . . .', RLM, p. 123; LCM.

'It didn't take . . . replaced', 'Any extra-large . . . Brass Hat', RLM, p. 113; LCM.

'That night . . .', RLM, p. 115; LCM.

'very jolly parties', 'we would . . . no good', RLM, p. 117; LCM.

'as to what . . .', RLM, p. 130; LCM.

'The water . . .', 'if he did not . . . drink', 'We all decided . . .', RLM, p. 131; LCM.

'A small stream . . . with her', 'somewhat . . . for us', RLM, p. 132; LCM.

Chapter 15: A Question of Timing

'Am leaving you . . . everyone thought', RLM, p. 122; LCM.

'With a terrific roar . . .', RLM, p. 119; LCM.

'I was shouting . . . each other', RLM, pp. 119–120; LCM.

'Our pilot did have . . . was the wind correct', RLM, p. 120; LCM.

'until he saw an aerodrome!', 'a dull affair . . . bottle', RLM, p. 121; LCM.

'The two most attractive . . . grand party', RLM, p. 125; LCM.

'we then thought . . . the road', 'wouldn't it be . . . alongside', RLM, pp. 139–140; LCM.

The inspection . . . down a bit', RLM, p. 140; LCM.

'hoping that we . . . peaceful time', 'Occasionally . . . our vicinity', 'but it was always . . .', 'knew very well', RLM, p. 143; LCM.

'but this was . . .', 'walking around . . .', 'the next night . . .', 'one hell of a gale', RLM, p. 144; LCM.

'anything that could . . .', 'There were . . . just waited', 'when we came . . . shoes and socks', RLM, p. 145; LCM.

'John and I knew . . . end of them', 'and once we . . . the right thing', 'broke one or more legs', RLM, p. 146; LCM.

'As the ships . . . remember', RLM, pp. 146–147; LCM.

'Instead of coming . . . on to her', RLM, p. 147; LCM.

'to everyone's joy', RLM, p. 148; LCM.

'It was all . . . minimum', RLM, p. 147; LCM.

'One rating . . .', 'marvellous', RLM, p. 148; LCM.

'all was well . . .', RLJLM, p. 22; LCM.

'Apart from the . . . sleepers', RLM, pp. 148–149; LCM.

Chapter 16: Pecking Order

'a brother or . . .', letter from Kate Murray, Tuesday [May 1929], to AL; Bristol DM1819/21/4.

'But I should ... afterwards', letter from Kate Murray, Tuesday [May 1929], to AL; Bristol DM1819/21/4.

'One might be ... his eyes', 'someone, something ...', Robert Lusty, 'Allen Lane,' *The Bookseller*, 22 Aug. 1970.

'Some sort of ...', transcript of part of radio broadcast 'Now Read On: Sir Robert Lusty on AL', 23 Jul. 1970; Bristol DM1819/20/2.

'No A-levels, no O-levels ... others', Robert Lusty, *Bound to Be Read*, (Jonathan Cape: 1975), p. 24.

'never quite ...', W. E. Williams, *Allen Lane: A Personal Portrait*, (The Bodley Head: 1973), p. 59.

'an apple-cheeked ...', Victor Weybright, *The Making of a Publisher* (Weidenfeld & Nicolson: 1968), p.180.

'a larger, less ...', J.E. Morpurgo, *Master of None: An Autobiography*, (Carcanet: 1990), p. 196.

'short powerful-looking man', Lettice Lane; Morpurgo, p. 175.

'an inconsequential ...', 'to take undisputed control', Morpurgo, p. 176.

'If the three ...', letter from AL to Eunice Frost, 10 Aug. 1956; Bristol, EEF; DM1843.

'not only excluded ...', Morpurgo, p. 178.

'a rather self-contained ... union', letter from AL to Eunice Frost, 10 Aug. 1956; op. cit.

'claustrophobia', Morpurgo, p. 180.

'no reason why she need know', letter from AL, c. 1942–43, to Nora Bird; LCM.

Chapter 17: In Armour

'to see a tanker ...', RLM, p. 151; LCM.

'JOHN ON LEAVE ...', 'a slap-up ...', RLM, p. 154; LCM.

'far more interested ...', RLD, 11 Feb. 1926; LCM.

'was particularly interested ...', letter from Eunice Frost, 10 Nov. 1941, to C.S. Kent; Hare, p. 75.

'I am glad to say ... belongings', letter from AL, 18 Nov. 1941, to C.S. Kent; Hare, p. 76.

'plush beyond ...', Morpurgo, p. 157.

'took himself off ...', Morpurgo, p. 161.

'The agreed calculation ... 10 per cent', Morpurgo, p. 162.

'could write off ... market', Morpurgo, p. 164.

'without doubt ... achievement', Morpurgo, p. 165.

'lonely days ahead', RLJLM, p. 1; LCM.

'Possibly I am ... forward to', RLJLM, p. 1; LCM.

'Lane received ... Bumpus', Jeremy Lewis, *Penguin Special: The Life and Times of Allen Lane* (Penguin Books: 2005) ('Lewis'), pp. 169–170.

Chapter 18: Power and Glory

'only time I ...', Eunice Frost; Hare, p. 26.

'the sea came ... miles away', RLM, p. 160; LCM.

'produced a detailed ...', 'without tripping gear', Lewis, p. 185.

'horribly chatty ...', letter from Graham Greene, 10 May 1945, to A.S.B. Glover; Hare, p. 161.

'would damage ...', letter from Graham Greene, 31 Jul. 1945, to A.S.B. Glover; Hare, p. 162.

'I return the two ...', letter from Graham Greene, 18 Jan. 1946, to AL; Hare, p. 163.

'on the spine ... tell him?', letter from David Higham, 3 Jul. 1947, to Richard Lane ('RL'); Hare, p. 163.

'stream of consciousness', Virginia Woolf, *The Common Reader*, 1938, Pelican A36.

'rather absurdly ...', letter from Leonard Woolf, 2 Jan. 1942, to Eunice Frost; Hare, p. 160.

'which evokes ... money!', letter from Vita Sackville-West, 14 Dec. 1942, to Eunice Frost; Hare, p. 159.

'there are a ... moment', letter from Cpt. W.E.D. Allen, 22 Nov. 1943, to Eunice Frost; Hare, p. 219.

'pit-bottom' etc.; Hare, p. 218; *The Penguin Collector*, Dec. 2003, p. 57; letter from Stanley Alderson, 28 Nov. 1962, to Dieter Pevsner; Hare, p. 219; *Fifty Penguin Years* (Penguin Books: 1985), p. 76.

'I think it is ... Teddy Bear?', postcard from Shaw, 22 Feb. 1944; Hare, p. 63.

'Shaw has a ... for you', letter from RL, 5 Aug. 1947, to AL; Bristol DM1294/3/2/9/4.

'an extraordinary ...', Hare, p. 96.

'lubricated with ...', Lewis, p. 226.

'what I think ...', 'uncontrolled or ...', 'Take the large ... ring', 'mentioning whom ...', 'Any policies ...', 'as this is ...', 'How long ... concern', letter from RL, 27 Nov. 1945, to AL; Bristol DM1819/1/1. RL's business diaries (LCM) also show him deeply engaged in daily Penguin business.

'benevolent dictator', letter from AL, 13 Jul. 1947, to RL; Bristol DM1819/22/3/2/3.

'There is really ... you say', 'apt to waste ... nitwits', letter from RL, 27 Nov. 1945, to AL; Bristol DM1819/1/1.

'there's no need ...', Rubeigh Minney interview within AL, *The Recorder*, 3 Sept. 1947.

'we are definitely ... side', 'At the moment ...', 'each book ... hallmark', letter from AL, 13 Jul. 1947, to RL; Bristol DM1819/22/3/2/3.

'ought to be ...', letter from AL, 7 Jul. 1947, to RL; Bristol DM1819/22/3/2/2.

'I feel that ... others', letter from AL, 13 Jul. 1947, to RL; Bristol DM1819/22/3/2/3.

'The magnitude ...', letter from W.E. Williams, 14 Jul. 1947, to AL; Bristol DM1819/22/3/1/2.

'in fact relieved ... manager', 'we ourselves ...', letter from AL, 13 Jul. 1947, to RL; Bristol, DM1819/22/3/2/3.

Chapter 19: The Nelson Touch

'the reading public ...', 'without doubt', 'Having got his ... aeroplane', RLM, p. 156; LCM.

'I was not against ... his way', 'was rather a dull affair', 'so we had ... presume', RLM, pp. 157–158; LCM.

'a better system ...', 'I think apart ...', letter from RL, 5 Aug. 1947, to AL; Bristol DM1294/3/2/9/4.

'was entirely ...', Lewis, p. 243.

'leaflets for tranquilizers', Hans Schmoller, *Two Titans: Mardersteig and Tschichold* (The Typophiles: 1990), p. 63.

'the typographical ...', Oliver Simon, *Printer and Playground: An Autobiography* (Faber: 1956), p. 106.

'whom do they ...', Erik Ellegaard Frederiksen, correspondence with Colin Banks, cited in *Jan Tschichold Designer: The Penguin Years* (Oak Knoll Press: 2006), p. 173.

'almost run ... that', 'To do any ... attention', letter from RL, 27 Nov. 1945, to AL; Bristol DM1819/1/1.

'Regarding subsidiary ...', 'Penguins few ...', letter from RL, 5 Aug. 1947, to AL; Bristol DM1294/3/2/9/4.

'much as it ... on me', letter from AL, 7 Jul. 1947, to RL; Bristol DM1819/22/3/2/2.

'about 100,000 ...', Kurt Enoch, autobiographical memo, 17 Jun. 1971; Bristol DM1294/14/1/15/3/2.

'Allen's personal ...', Kurt Enoch, *Memoirs Written for His Family* (privately published: 1984), p. 172.

'sexational ...', 'gone wrong ...', Richard Hoggart, *The Uses of Literacy* (Penguin Books: 1958), pp. 213–214.

'could persuade ...', Weybright, p. 179.

'he moved ... muscles', Weybright, p. 184.

'asked the lady ...', Lewis, p. 372.

'barely solvent', Weybright, p. 180.

'theory of operations ...', Weybright, p. 181.

'stooge', Weybright, p. 195.

'Allen Lane's Penguin ... all details', Weybright, p. 185.

'In 1946 ... situation', Kurt Enoch, autobiographical memo, 17 Jun. 1971; Bristol DM1294/14/1/15/3/2.

'unless credit ... continued', Weybright, p. 185.

'a clump of ...', Weybright, pp. 192–193.

'could not stand ...', Weybright, p. 194.

'made a personally ...', Kurt Enoch, autobiographical memo, 17 Jun. 1971; Bristol DM1294/14/1/15/3/2.

'orderly separation ...', Weybright, p. 195.

'a lovable ... wisdom', Weybright, p. 184.

'to a record ...', letter from RL, 10 Jan. 1960, to AL; Bristol DM1819/22/3/2/23.

'The next day ... patch', Weybright, p. 198.

'He did not ... outlets', Kurt Enoch, autobiographical memo, 17 Jun. 1971; Bristol DM1294/14/1/15/3/2.

'Although I know ... production', letter from RL, 5 Aug. 1947, to AL; Bristol DM1294/3/2/9/4.

'beyond belief', Charles Pick, letter of 11 Apr. 1967 [Bristol]; Lewis, p. 351.

'as likely as ... cupboard', Tanya Schmoller, 'First Impressions,' *The Penguin Collector*, Dec. 2009, p. 20.

'couldn't take ...', Nikolaus Pevsner, interview with Tanya Kent (Schmoller), n.d. [Bristol]; Lewis, p. 232.

'drop spirits ... evening', letter from AL, 7 Jul. 1947, to RL; Bristol DM1819/22/3/2/2.

'I'm afraid ... for good', letter from AL, 16 Jul. 1947, to RL; Bristol DM1819/22/3/2/4.

Chapter 20: The Best Man

'in the second ... the firm', Lewis, p. 221.

'worked impulsively ...', Margaret Clark; Russell Edwards and Steve Hare (eds), *Twenty-One Years*, Miscellany 10, (Penguin Collectors' Society: Jul. 1995), p. 37.

'seemed to crave ... as cold', Margaret Clark; op. cit.

'stormed into ...', Lewis, p. 224.

'you could be top ...', W.E. Williams, *Allen Lane: A Personal Portrait*, op. cit., p. 23.

'Every now ...', Lewis, p. 224.

'was bad at hatchet ...', Peter Calvocoressi, *Threading My Way* (Duckworth: 1994), p. 183.

'lack of moral fibre ... sadism', W.E. Williams, *Allen Lane: A Personal Portrait*, op. cit., p. 23.

'at the critical ... car park', Russell Edwards & Steve Hare (eds), *Twenty-One Years*, op. cit., p. 37.

'who had devoted ... recovered', 'so shattered ...', Lewis, pp. 224–225.

'sources of infection', letter from Eunice Frost, n.d., to AL (Bristol), EEF; DM1843.

'inclined to get ...', letter from W.E. Williams, 23 Mar. 1953, to AL; Bristol DM1819.

'a problem in ...', 1 May 1949, letter from AL to Eunice Frost (Bristol), EEF; DM1843.

'inclined to rattle ...', letter from W.E. Williams, 18 Dec. 1959, to AL; Bristol DM1819.

'weak', letter from AL, 31 Dec. 1957, to RL; Bristol DM1819/20/2.

'rather lost ...', letter from AL, Jul. 1947, to RL (private collection); Lewis, p. 247.

'terrible contempt', 'ruthless denigration', Tony Godwin, statement, n.d. (Bristol); Lewis, p. 387.

'developed a cold ... satisfiable', handwriting analysis, 18 Aug. 1956; Bristol DM1819/22/3/2/26.

'pay no attention ...', J.E. Morpurgo, *Master of None*, op. cit., p. 196 and p. 300.

'He makes a better ...', letter from David Herbert, 8 May 1985, to Eric Norris; Bristol DM1294/3/2/9/6.

'making a mess ...', letter from AL to Eunice Frost, 10 Aug. 1956 (Bristol), EEF; DM1843.

'let it be known ... having', Morpurgo, p. 255.

'unflattering and ...', Morpurgo, p. 303.

'The first question...', cited by Jean Mascord, Voluntary Aid Detachments, in 'Australians at War' (http://www.australiansatwar.gov.au). Betty Snow appears in a photograph in Melanie Oppenheimer's book, *All Work No Pay: Australian Civilian Volunteers in War*.

The letters from RL to Betty are from the Lane collection, Melbourne.

'in no mood ... unfortunately', letter from Bob Maynard, 30 Jun. 1948, to AL; LCM.

'I do think ... *Good God*', Bob Maynard; Hare, p. 31.

'Allen was a man ...', Max Mallowan, *Mallowan's Memoirs* (HarperCollins: 2010), p. 288.

'a sense of reserve ... thinking', Peter Calvocoressi, op. cit., p. 182.

'always felt there ...', Bernard Venables; Steve Hare (ed.), *Lost Causes* (Penguin Collectors' Society: 1998), p. 47.

'pocket Napoleon', Richard Chopping; Steve Hare (ed.), *Lost Causes*, op. cit., p.18.

'Allen Lane, a ... the process', Frances Partridge, *Everything to Lose: Diaries 1945–1960* (Victor Gollancz: 1985), p. 52.

'was well aware ... Harmondsworth', Lewis, p. 292.

Chapter 21: Small Fry

'crack up', letter from Eunice Frost, 27 Feb. 1950, to Harry Paroissien (Bristol); EEF, DM1843.

'all that I may ... married life', Samuel Allen Gardiner Williams Lane, last will and testament, [Jan. 1950], LCM.

'I have not made ... mourning attire', Allen Williams Lane, note, [1950], LCM.

'Nora has agreed ... guardianship', Allen Williams Lane, note, [1950], LCM.

'anti-climax', letter from Eunice Frost, 27 Feb. 1950, to Harry Paroissien (Bristol); EEF, DM1843.

'strained of face ...', letter from AL, 12 Mar. 1950 (private collection); Lewis, p. 283.

'My dear Mother ... loving son, Allen', letter from AL to his mother, 22 Mar. 1950; LCM.

'a tired old ...', Agatha Christie; Janet Morgan, *Agatha Christie: A Biography* (Collins: 1984), p. 400.

'bloated', Robert Lusty, eulogy delivered at AL's memorial service, *The Bookseller*, 22 Aug. 1970; Bristol DM1819/20/2.

'half-frozen ...', Lewis, p. 290.

'You may be ... have you', letter from Bob Maynard, 11 Jul. 1949, to Eunice Frost; Hare, p. 270.

'combine business ...', Lewis, p. 290.

'the track is ...', AL quoted in a newspaper, Morpurgo, p. 257.

'personality, his ... every sort', letter from H.B. Muir, 3 Nov. 1955, to RL; LCM.

'One firm wanted ...', Bob Maynard, reminiscences; Bristol DM1294/4/5/1/6.

'were more sensitive ... forgive', Morpurgo, p. 258.

'His drinking was ... disappearance', Morpurgo, p. 259.

'convinced himself ...', Morpurgo, p. 260.

'Good evening ... I'm here', RLM, pp. 174–175; LCM.

'I had lunch ... ten days', letter from RL, 25 Feb. 1953, to AL; Bristol DM1819/20/2.

'Better a team ... cross-legged', Morpurgo, p. 276.

'like a gargoyle', Morpurgo, p. 277.

'only a visit', letter from RL, 23 Mar. 1956, to I.C. Dickson; Bristol DM1819/25/2.

'a visible, audible ...', 'instinctively responsive ...', 'to have a Lane ...', Morpurgo, p. 250.

'Finally it achieved ...', W.E. Williams, *Allen Lane: A Personal Portrait*, op. cit., p. 72.

'had always been ...', Bob Maynard; Geoffrey Dutton, *A Rare Bird: Penguin Books in Australia 1946–96* (Penguin Books: 1996), p. 19.

'I think it ... his own', letter from AL, 4 Nov. 1955, to RL; Bristol DM1819/20/2.

'a series of ...', Hare, p. 271.

'By his own ...', 'It was two years ... others', Morpurgo, p. 260.

'I am tired ...', letter from Bob Maynard, 28 Feb. 1955, to Eunice Frost; Bristol DM1843/1.

'No, no, no ... do that', AL; Geoffrey Dutton, op. cit., p. 21.

'with heavy irony', Lewis, p. 291.

'his ruthless ...', Morpurgo, p. 299.

'very deep ...', letter from H.B. Muir, 3 Nov. 1955, to RL; LCM.

'would not be ...', Geoffrey Dutton, op. cit., p. 22.

Chapter 22: A Personal Letter

'greater efficiency', letter from AL, 3 Feb. 1956, to RL; Bristol DM1819/28/2.

'entirely responsible ...', letter from AL, 3 Feb. 1956, to RL; Bristol DM1819/28/2.

'would be a very ...', letter from RL, 19 Nov. 1957, to AL; Bristol DM1819/25/2.

'They think the ... the moment', letter from AL, [1955], to RL; Bristol DM1819/20/2.

'unbusinesslike', 'cardinal sin', Lewis, p. 395.

'accompanying it with ...', Morpurgo, p. 287.

'gaunt', 'ugly', Lewis, p. 260.

'didn't see that ... out well', letter from AL, [c.1955], to RL; Bristol DM1819/28/2.

'all seemed so ... love Lettice', letter from AL, 10 Aug. 1956, to Eunice Frost (Bristol), EEF; DM1843.

'I am convinced ... vastly separated', letter from AL, 1 Aug. 1958, to Eunice Frost (Bristol), EEF; DM1843.

'round the bend', letter from AL, n.d., to Joan Collihole (private collection); Lewis, p. 287.

'You may hardly ... moment', letter from RL, 5 May 1957, to AL; Bristol DM1819/22/3/2/13.

'We had already ... telephone', letter from AL, 14 May 1957, to RL; Bristol DM1819/22/3/2/14.

'friendly decisions ... of mind', letter from RL, 5 May 1957, to AL; Bristol DM1819/22/3/2/13.

'the only thing ... Clovelly', letter from RL, [Nov. 1956], to AL; LCM.

'three weeks ...', letter from RL, n.d., to AL; Bristol DM1819/20/2.

'possibly the worst ... imprint', letter from RL, 15 Aug. 1960, to AL; LCM.

'a masterly effort', letter from RL to AL; Geoffrey Dutton, op. cit., p. 28.

'"RL would continue ... salary', letter from RL, n.d., to AL; Bristol DM1819/20/2.

'too destructive ...', letter from RL to AL; Geoffrey Dutton, op. cit., p. 28.

'the milk in ...' letter from RL, 24 Aug. 1959, to AL; LCM.

'the unhappy atmosphere ...', letter from A.H. Reynolds, 12 Mar. 1960, to AL; Bristol DM1663/36.

'as a business letter ... per cent fit', letter from RL, n.d., to AL; Bristol DM1819/20/2.

'You will now ... years' time', letter from AL, 21 Aug. 1959, to RL; Bristol DM1819/22/3/2/22.

Chapter 23: Gamesmanship

'to the sick ... indeed', T.S. Eliot, *After Strange Gods: A Primer of Modern Heresy* (Faber: 1934), p. 61.

'rather absurd', letter from Graham Greene, 22 Aug. 1960, to W. E. Williams (Bristol); Lewis, p. 323.

'I put my feet ... prosecute', Mervyn Griffith-Jones; Richard Hoggart, *An Imagined Life: Life and Times, 1959–91* (Chatto & Windus: 1990), p. 53.

'My own view ... was it', letter from AL, 7 Mar. 1960, to RL (Bristol); Lewis, p. 316.

'all right, but ...', letter from Clare Lane, n.d., (Bristol); Lewis, p. 331.

'A Rev. Gordon Powell ... the title', letter from RL, 15 Dec. 1960, to AL; LCM. The book was *The Innkeeper of Bethlehem*.

'You say you ... against you', letter from RL, 3 Oct. 1960, to AL; LCM.

'the most celebrated ...', Lewis, p. 316.

'was manifestly ... lower down', W.E. Williams, *Allen Lane: A Personal Portrait*, op. cit., p. 24.

In the early '70s Penguin Australia had its own 'Chatterley trial' (in fact a series of trials) after John Michie and the Australian and British boards decided to publish Philip Roth's *Portnoy's Complaint* in Australia.

'Did you see ... Martins', letter from AL, 17 Jul. 1947, to RL; Bristol DM1819/22/3/2/5.

'If father wants ... Monday', letter from AL, 24 Jul. 1947, to RL; Bristol DM1819/22/3/2/8.

'permanent finance ... consideration', letter from W.R.T. Whatmore, 9 Nov. 1955, to AL; Bristol DM1819/11/3.

'Unfortunately rumours ... under discussion', letter from AL, 23 Apr. 1958, to RL; Bristol DM1819/20/2.

'seldom dealt ... counsellors', Morpurgo, p. 326.

'does not seem ...', letter from W.R.T. Whatmore, 10 Jun. 1958, to AL; Bristol DM1819/11/3.

'to bring serious ... the staple diet', *The Economist*, 3 Dec. 1938.

'In reply to your ... instalments', letter from RL, 23 Aug. 1960, to AL; Bristol DM1819/20/2.

'You may have ... ordinary way', letter from AL, 25 Oct. 1960, to RL; LCM.

'They were obviously ... business life', letter from AL, 27 Jan. 1961, to Harry Paroissien; Bristol DM1819/Box 16. The £1 million valuation corresponded to a price per share of approximately eight shillings and included capital raised by issuing some new shares for cash.

'We had a Board ... ten shillings', letter from AL, 21 Mar. 1961, to Harry Paroissien; Bristol DM1819/Box 16.

'used the planned ... with it', Lewis, p. 336.

'it would be better ... new form', W. Lionel Fraser, letter to AL, 27 Jan. 1961, Bristol DM1819/Box 16.

Chapter 24: Shock Troops

'The idea of ... on capital', letter from RL, 17 Sept. 1959, to AL; Bristol DM1819/20/2.

'In order to help ... further five', letter from AL, 22 Sept. 1959, to RL; LCM.

'HAVE DISCUSSED YOUR ... IMMEDIATELY', telegram from RL, [c.1960], to AL; LCM.

'I replied giving ... Paroissien', letter from RL, 9 Jun. 1960, to AL; Bristol DM1819/Box 16.

'Naturally it was ... expenses', letter from RL, 28 Jul. 1960, to AL; Bristol DM1819/Box 16.

'On the question of ... precaution!', letter from AL, 12 Oct. 1960, to RL; LCM.

'your letter to ... such state', letter from RL, 10 Jan. 1960, to AL; Bristol DM1819/22/3/2/23.

'it is hoped ... to Spain', letter from AL, 3 Feb. 1961, to RL; Bristol DM1819/11/3.

'I would like ... months later', letter from AL, 7 Feb. 1960, to RL; Bristol DM1819/22/3/2/28.

'total expenses to be ...', letter from Gordon H. Gunson, 28 Mar. 1961, to AL; Bristol DM1819/11/3.

'A large amount ... your comments', letter from AL, 7 Feb. 1961, to RL; Bristol DM1819/11/3.

'From a business ... 50/50 one', letter from RL, 14 Feb. 1961, to AL; Bristol DM1819/11/3.

'This is a very ... from it', letter from AL, 19 Feb. 1961, to RL; Bristol DM1819/11/3.

'I feel that it ... Board as well', letter from AL, 20 Feb. 1961, to RL; Bristol DM1819/11/3.

'In reply to your ... shares myself', letter from RL, 27 Feb. 1961, to AL; Bristol DM1819/11/3.

'(1) If RL resigns ... if necessary', minutes taken by AL from telephone conversation, 8 Mar. 1961, with RL; Bristol DM1819/11/3.

'REORGANISATION OF ENTIRE ... FORTHWITH', draft telegram from AL, 8 Mar. 1961, to RL; Bristol DM1819/Box 16.

'I am in daily ... troop operation', letter from AL, 9 Mar. 1961, to Harry Paroissien; Bristol DM1819/Box 16.

'misleading', Lewis, p. 337.

'OK LET'S THROW ... AND ADVISE', telegram from RL, 9 Mar. 1961, to AL; Bristol DM1819/Box 16.

'AM WILLING TO ... COMPANIES', telegram from AL, 9 Mar. 1961, to RL; Bristol DM1819/Box 16.

'AGREE OUR CONDITIONS ...' telegram from RL, 10 Mar. 1961, to AL; Bristol DM1819/Box 16.

Chapter 25: Chatterleys

'FURTHER MY CONVERSATION ...', telegram from C.T. Hyland, 10 Mar. 1961, to AL; Bristol DM1819/Box 16.

'now settled with ...', letter from AL, 9–10 Mar. 1961, to Harry Paroissien; Bristol DM1819/Box 16.

'Your brother ... May next', letter from Cecil Hyland, 10 Mar. 1961, to AL; Bristol DM1819/11/3.

'My brother, who ... Australian Boards', memo from AL, 14 Mar. 1961, to Penguin staff; Bristol DM1819/24/2.

'My present plan ... a cable', letter from AL, 17 Apr. 1961, to RL; Bristol DM1819/11/3.

'To begin with ... pro-rata basis', memo from AL, 19 Apr. 1961, to Penguin staff; Bristol DM1819/Box 16.

'in only five ... five per cent', Morpurgo, pp. 328–329.

'I am not sure ... and FORGET', letter from Nancy Mitford, 23 Apr. 1961, to AL; Bristol DM1819/Box 16.

'Here's to the Penguins ... the bag', letter from D. Crawley, 26 Apr. 1961 to
    Directors, Messrs. Helbert, Wagg & Co. Ltd and J. Henry Schroder & Co.
    Ltd; Bristol DM1819/Box 16.
'I am writing to ... Auld lang syne!', letter from J.L. Gledhill, 24 Apr. 1961, to
    AL; Bristol DM1819/Box 16.
'No, I am ... for shares', letter from AL, 26 Apr. 1961, to J.L. Gledhill; Bristol
    DM1819/Box 16.
'His position as ... daughters', Morpurgo, p. 329.
'Do you know ... every minute', letter from David Herbert, 8 May 1985, to
    Eric Norris; Bristol DM1274/3/2/9/6.
'The operation was ... popularity', letter from R.T. Whatmore, 1 May 1961,
    to AL; Bristol DM1819/Box 16.
'male members ...', Lewis, p. 338.
'I have thought ... rude health', letter from AL, 19 Jun. 1961, to RL; Bristol
    DM1663/29.
'I am very concerned ... envisages', letter from AL, 7 Aug. 1961, to Leslie
    Paisner; Bristol DM1663/29.
'with a handshake ...', W.E. Williams, *Allen Lane: A Personal Portrait*, op.
    cit., p. 89.
'I'm not a very ...', AL, cited in Lewis, p. 397.

Chapter 26: The Great Adventure

'invitation after invitation ...', Morpurgo, p. 299.
'there had been comments ... well-wishers', Morpurgo, pp. 262–263. See also
    Lewis and Dutton. There are numerous extant versions of this departure
    story. In most of them, John Michie was in, and John Stephens was out.
'Get rid of ...', Geoffrey Dutton, op. cit., p. 52.
'prodigious', Morpurgo, p. 393.
'bucked as ...', letter from AL, 5 Mar. 1946, to Victor Weybright; Bristol
    DM1819/28/3.
'The kindness ... writing them', letter from James Ronald, 6 May 1964, to AL;
    LCM.
'To work with ...', W.E. Williams, *Allen Lane: A Personal Portrait*, op. cit.,
    p. 31.
'Sir Allen suggested ... this on?', letter (on AL's behalf), 23 Mar. 1965, to
    Reynolds Stone; Bristol DM1819/20/2.
'As he was an ... notebook', Chris Dolley recollection, in Hare, p. 347.
'It may easily ... leader', graphology report for AL, Bristol, cited in Morpurgo,
    p. 287. There are numerous other fascinating graphological and
    astrological reports in the Bristol Penguin archive.

'subtle plot . . .', W.E. Williams, *Allen Lane: A Personal Portrait*, op. cit., p. 72.

'a gentleman . . .', Tony Godwin statement, n.d., (Bristol); Lewis, p. 364.

'Not Chris! . . .', Susanne Lepsius, quoted in Morpurgo, p. 359.

'Poor Bill', letter from AL, 14 Aug. [1956], to RL; LCM.

'Yes, I've got . . . closing-time!', letter from AL, 15 Jan. 1964, to RL; LCM.

'Yes, your guess . . . his loyalty', letter from AL, 24 Mar. 1960, to RL; LCM.

'ended up with . . .', letter from AL, Easter Monday 1966, to RL; LCM.

'more an inconvenience . . . look-see', letter from AL, 3 Dec. 1959, to RL; LCM.

'I have now . . .', letter from AL, 7 Oct. 1966, to RL; Bristol DM1819/20/2.

'My drink . . . weeks ago', letter from AL, 18 Jan. 1965, to RL; LCM.

'[this] mode of . . . centre', graphology report for AL, quoted in Morpurgo, p. 287.

'no close collaborator . . .': During this period, Allen did confide, to a degree, in the former delivery driver Ron Blass, who was widely referred to as Allen's 'henchman'.

'ignored or humiliated', Maggie Fergusson & Michael Morpurgo, *Michael Morpurgo: War Child to War Horse* (Fourth Estate: 2012), p. 120.

'just did not . . .', Clare Morpurgo; Maggie Fergusson & Michael Morpurgo, op. cit., p. 119.

'without consulting . . .', Morpurgo, p. 307.

'and then blow . . .', Maggie Fergusson & Michael Morpurgo, op. cit., p. 119.

Maggie Fergusson & Michael Morpurgo (op. cit.) provide more details about Clare's pregnancy and the pressure to abort.

'what all the . . .', Morpurgo, p. 301.

'occasionally embarrassed . . .', Morpurgo, p. 233.

'her bedroom . . .', letter from AL, 17 Mar. 1965, to RL; LCM.

'I was in Julie . . . dentist', letter from AL, 19 Dec. 1963, to RL; LCM.

'The greatest . . . years ago', letter from AL, 28 Sept. 1965, to RL; Bristol DM1819/22/3/2/29.

'The news in . . . any longer', letter from RL, 15 Oct. 1965, to AL; Bristol DM1819/20/2.

'expensive failure', Lewis, p. 395.

'I dwell often on . . . memories', letter from AL, 23 Nov. 1958, to RL; LCM.

'I wonder if you . . . the years', letter from AL, 30 Jul. 1965, to RL; LCM.

'shook Allen badly', W.E. Williams, *Allen Lane: A Personal Portrait*, op. cit., p. 89.

'a step which . . .', W.E. Williams, *Allen Lane: A Personal Portrait*, op. cit., p. 60.

'He used to . . . mere £70,000', W.E. Williams, *Allen Lane: A Personal Portrait*, op. cit., p. 25.

'I sometimes think . . .', letter from Lettice Lane, 6 Aug. 1968, to Eunice Frost (Bristol), EEF; DM1843.

'It goes without . . .', letter from AL, 18 Mar. 1970, to RL; LCM.
'I am a very untidy . . .', letter from AL, 4 Nov. 1958, to RL; LCM.
'unprecedented affluence', Morpurgo, p. 333.
'Who are all . . . fuckers', Lewis, p. 374.
'could all too . . .', Lewis, p. 400.
'greedy', letter from Bill Williams to Richard Lane, 3 May 1971, LCM.

Chapter 27: The Master Builder

'I never got . . .', RLM, p. 86; LCM.
'Small almonds . . . lanterns', RLD, 9 & 22 Sept. 1924; LCM

INDEX

Abdy, Richard Combe 83–88, 124
Adams, Evangeline 133
Albatross Verlag 120–23, 126–27,
    136, 147, 178, 197, 199
Aldridge, Alan 206
All Saints Choir School 78
Allen, Ashton 131, 291
Allen Lane Foundation 292–93
Allen Lane The Penguin Press
    290–91
Allen, Paul 121
Allen, W. E. D. 190
Anne, Princess Royal 289
Angus & Robertson 245
Apple 121
Arno, Peter 114, 296
Arnold, H. A. W. 120–21, 126
Askwith, Billie 26, 28–30
Asprey & Co. 224
Atkins, Robert 79–80, 82, 87–89, 112
Australian Red Cross 284
Avati, James 206
Avon Books 148, 206

Baillie, Albert 101
Baillieu, Everard 284

Ballantine, Ian 147, 201
Ballet Rambert 230
Bannister, Estrid 207, 238, 286
Bantam Books 201, 252
Barker, B. T. P. 22
Barton, J. E. 20, 22
Barton, Sydney 175
Barwell, Henry 22
Beach, Sylvia 114
Beales, Lance 137–38, 170, 176, 289
Beames, Mr ('Billy') 10, 296
Beardsley, Aubrey 15, 17, 75
Beatles, The 251, 285
Beaton, Peggy 100
Bechstein, Carl 19
Beer, Robert J. 38, 47–49, 60
Belcher, Julie 288, 290
Bingham, Mr 8, 24
Bird, Frank 149, 153, 228, 242
Bird, Nora 2–5, 8–10, 12, 16, 24,
    32, 39, 41, 71–72, 76–77, 86–87,
    97, 133, 145–46, 148–49, 153,
    157–58, 175, 178, 185–86, 215,
    224, 228, 242, 246, 259, 293
Blackwell, Basil 250
Blue Cross 8

Bluth, Karl 238
Boar's Head Press 290
Bodley Head, The xi, 15–17, 18, 23–24, 66–67, 69, 70, 73–76, 78, 88, 95, 98–100, 102–9, 111–18, 120–23, 128, 130–31, 135–37, 167, 169, 172, 174, 177, 210–13, 243, 249, 252, 263, 283, 290, 296–97
Bodley, Sir Thomas 17
Boston Conservatory of Music 19
Boswell, Ronald 69, 75, 137, 268–69
Bourne, 'Loony' 27, 30, 174
Boyle, Edward 291
Brahms, Johannes 19
Braun, Carl 204
Bristol Grammar School 9–11, 13, 20, 78
Bristol University xii, 13, 14
British Broadcasting Corporation 153, 272
Brown, Arnold 54–59, 61
Brunel, Isambard Kingdom 5
Bullcraig & Davis 109
Bumpus Bookshop 129, 186
Butt, Dame Clara 4
Buxton Forman, Harry 17

Caldwell, Erskine 202, 249
Calvocoressi, Peter 210, 220
Cambridge University 72, 176, 184
Camus, Albert 190–91
Cape, Jonathan 115, 118, 128, 298
Carpentier, Georges 11, 116
Carr-Gomme, Hubert 69, 75
Cazenove & Co. 253
Cerf, Bennett 115
Chalmers-Mitchell, Peter 137
Champion de Crespigny, Mrs Philip 73
Chandler Moulton, Louise 19

Charles, Prince of Wales 289
Chatto & Windus 124, 128, 210, 227
Cheltenham Boys' Grammar School 9
Cherry-Garrard, Apsley 136
Chivers, Stanley 71
Chopping, Richard 220
Christie, Agatha 69, 73, 74, 109, 118–19, 127, 187, 207, 220, 226, 296, 298
Churchill, Winston 225, 284
Clarendon, Douglas 95
Clark, Margaret 209–11
Clayton, Owen 218
Clifton, Bob 52, 60, 62
Clifton Brothers College 9
Coles, Joan 102, 124, 135
Collihole, Evelyn 10, 242
Collihole, Frances 10, 12
Collihole, Joan 10, 239
Collihole, William 12
Conan Doyle, Arthur 73, 101
Conan Doyle, Kingsley 73
Crawford, Mr 8
Crawley, D. 273
Crowther, Geoffrey 277
Cudmore, Collier Robert 30, 34–35, 47, 88
Curtis, Neil 79–80
Curwen Press 104, 197, 200

Darantière, Maurice 115
Davies, Bob 133
Davies, Peter 117, 250
Davis, Fred 214
Davis, Reverend (of Moorook) 35
da Vinci, Leonardo 121–22, 181
De Courcy Ireland, Stanley 34, 72
de Graff, Robert 148
Dell Books 148, 206
Dempsey, William Harrison 'Jack'

11, 116
Dene, Arundel 23
Department of Migration and
    Settlement 22, 37, 269
Disney, Walt 113
Dolley, Chris 285–86
Donnelly, Gaylord 92
Downside School 9
Drinkwater, John 68
Drummond, Lindsay 69, 75, 269
Dunlop Tyres 131
Dutton, Geoffrey 246, 280–81

Economist Newspaper Ltd, The
    252–54, 277
Egoist Press 115
Eichberg, Annie Philippine *see*
    Lane, Annie Philippine
Eichberg, Julius 19
Eliot, T. S. 115, 248
Elizabeth II 180, 289–90
Enoch, Kurt 120, 178, 201–2,
    204–5, 213, 249, 261, 263, 269
Ernst, Morris 115
Evans, Ifor 207
Everett, R. W. H. 159

Faber & Faber 115, 117
Facebook x, 301
Farouk, King of Egypt 83, 88
Fawcett Books 203
First Edition Club 72, 103–5, 115,
    117, 182, 197
Flower, Desmond 103
Forces Book Club x, 182–83, 188
Fortey, Mr ('Fifty') 10–11, 296
France, Anatole 19, 68, 78, 124, 220
Fraser, Lionel 253, 255, 277
Freud, Sigmund 137
Friends' School, Saffron Walden
    9–10, 71–72, 76

Frost, Eunice 138, 147, 170, 177,
    181, 187, 190, 193–94, 196, 198,
    201–2, 205, 207, 211–13, 215,
    221, 223–24, 227–28, 230, 234,
    237, 239, 259, 261, 292
Fry's Chocolates 7

Gael, Doug 10, 15, 24, 150
Gael, Roma 15–16, 100
Gael, Rosemary 15–16, 100
Garrick Club 221
Garvie, Keith 28, 29, 72, 107
Gates, Bill 121
Gill, Eric 115, 127
Gledhill, J. L. 274
Glover, A. S. B. 232–33
Godwin, Tony 211, 279, 285–86
Golden Cockerel Press 103, 290
Goldsack, Sydney 130
Gollancz, Victor 147, 199
Gray, Thomas 5, 7, 9
Greene, Graham 189–91, 206, 248,
    298
Grenville, Richard 142, 284
Grieg, Edvard 19
Griffith-Jones, Mervyn 249, 272
Gunson, Gordon H. 255, 263

Hall, W. F. 203–4
Harben, Joan 80
Harben, Philip 80
Hardy, Thomas 68, 74, 220
Hare, Steve ix, 191, 234
Harrap, George 117
Harrap, Walter 117, 182
Harris, Bob 2
Haynes, Annie 73
Hazell, Raymond 110, 122, 128, 130
Hazlett, Wyndham 92
Heinemann Books 250
Helbert, Wagg & Co. 253, 255, 263,

270–71
Herbert, David 213, 275
Higham, David 190
Higson, Sylvanie 227
Hill, Jack 52
Hine, Hubert 79, 81, 83, 92, 107, 131
Hine, Muriel 73, 79
Hogarth Press 115
Hoggart, Richard 202
Holroyd-Reece, John 120–21, 123,
    197
Holt, Harold 280
Houghton Mifflin 252
Hornibrook, F. A. 172
Horwitz, Israel 244–45
Hutchings, Mr ('Eggy') 10–11, 296
Hutchinson & Co. 136
Hutchinson, A. S. M. 106
Hyland, Cecil 259, 265–67, 270

Insel Verlag 147

Jas Smith 282
J. Henry Schroder & Co. 253, 267,
    271
Jobs, Steve 121
John Lane Bequest 284
Johnson, Samuel 88
Johnston, Edward 127
Jonas, Robert 206
Joyce, James 114–15

Keats, John 17
Kent, C. S. 181
Kent, Tatyana ('T. K.') *see* Schmoller,
    Tatyana
Kilgour, French and Stanbury 232
King, Annie Philippine *see* Lane,
    King, Annie
King, Lenden Athelburt 22, 30–33,
    35–37, 56

King, Tyler Batcheller 19
Kite, Peter 131
Knottenbelt, Eva 154, 282

Ladyman, Phyllis 189
Lambert, J. W. 74, 112
Lanchester, Elsa 101
Lane, Allen Lane Williams ix–xi,
    1–12, 13, 15–16, 20, 23–24, 29,
    32, 39, 41, 49, 66–76, 78–79,
    86–87, 90–96, 100–3, 105–31,
    133–40, 142–51, 167–78, 180–
    88, 190–215, 217–96, 299–301
Lane, Anna 204, 207–8, 238, 291,
    293, 295
Lane, Annie Philippine (née
    Eichberg) 19–21, 34, 39, 48,
    51, 66–67, 69–72, 76, 78, 87, 90,
    102, 128, 135, 169, 300
Lane, Betty 214–20, 227, 233, 242,
    262, 281–82, 292–93, 295–96,
    299–300
Lane, Camilla Matilda Williams
    2–4, 6, 11, 15–16, 21, 23, 30, 32,
    39, 63, 71, 73, 76, 86, 103, 142,
    153, 179, 185, 215, 223–25, 239,
    243, 247, 264, 300
Lane, Christine *see* Teale, Christine
Lane, Clare *see* Morpurgo, Clare
Lane, Elizabeth xii, 227, 233, 242–
    43, 250, 262, 279, 281–82, 284,
    289, 292–93, 295–96, 300–1
Lane, John (junior) ix–xi, 2–4, 8,
    11, 13, 24, 32, 39, 68–72, 76, 78,
    86–88, 91–99, 108–19, 122–25,
    127–29, 131–32, 134–39, 143–55,
    157–69, 171–88, 192–93, 204,
    207–9, 227–28, 243, 251, 258,
    261, 274, 289, 294, 296, 299, 301
Lane, John (senior) 15–18, 19, 20,
    23–24, 34, 39, 49–52, 67–70, 72,

74–76, 78, 88, 90, 98, 100, 102–
3, 105–8, 112–14, 118, 121–22,
169–70, 172, 177, 189, 226, 232,
240, 251, 29, 296, 300
Lane, Lettice 175–78, 184, 204,
207–8, 238–39, 288, 291–93, 295
Lane, Nora *see* Bird, Nora
Lane, Richard Grenville Williams
ix–xi, 1–12, 13–16, 19, 20,
22–65, 70–73, 75–76, 78–96,
98, 101–203, 205–24, 226–28,
230–71, 274, 276–84, 286–301
Lane, Samuel Allen Gardner
Williams 2–8, 12, 16, 21, 23,
27–30, 32, 37, 39, 40–41, 63,
70–71, 73, 76, 86–88, 139, 142,
179, 185, 212, 223–26, 251, 282
Larkin, Philip 251
Laughton, Charles 101
Lawrence, D. H. 192, 248, 275, 285,
298
Leavis, F. R. 248
Ledig-Rowohlt, Heinrich Maria 238
Le Galliene, Richard 17–18
Lehmann, John 232
Lepsius, Susanne 238, 239, 286, 288
Lewis, Brian 229, 282
Lewis, Jeremy ix, 74, 182, 209, 222,
242, 256, 267, 293
Linklaters & Paines 246, 253, 266,
268
Lloyd, George 83
Locke, W. J. 68
London and Lancashire Insurance
Company 90, 92, 94
London School of Economics 137,
176
Longmans & Co. 252, 260, 295
Lothian Press 150, 227
Lothian, Lord (Philip Henry Kerr)
150–51, 178

Low, David 150, 174
Lusty, Robert 122, 171

~

Machell, R. A. 253, 277
Machiavelli, Niccolò 271
McInnes, Robert 206
McLean, Rauri 220
McMinn, 'Mac' 21, 24–25, 28–30,
50–51, 80
McPhee, Hilary 272–73, 280–81
Mailey, Arthur 282
Mallowan, Max 118, 220, 276
Mannin, Ethel 101, 122, 169
Mansfield, Katherine 213
Mardersteig, Hans 120–22, 181
Marsh, Ngaio 216
Martin, Peggy 157
Martin, Peter 158
Martin, Ralph 'Tubby' 154–57,
161–62, 165, 227
Martins Bank 128, 140, 253, 264,
271, 299
Maschler, Tom 285–86
Mascord, Jean 214
Mathews, Elkin 17, 18, 24
Matthews, Mr and Mrs (of 'Meyrah')
34–36, 55, 103
Maurois, André 68, 127
May, James Lewis 52, 78
Maynard, Bob 131, 151, 167, 182,
200–1, 214–19, 227–30, 233–36,
245, 261, 269, 272, 293, 298
Maynard, Edith 227, 229, 230
Maynard, Leander 293
Menon, V. K. Krishna 137, 269, 288,
301
Methuen Books 278
Microsoft 121
Milbank, Mark 288–89
Milton, Ernest 80, 82
Milton, John 78

Minney, Rubeigh 195
Mitford, Nancy 273
Monckton, Ivor 92
Morison, Stanley 192
Morpurgo, Clare 184, 187, 191, 214, 235, 250, 252, 280, 287–88, 293, 295
Morpurgo, Jack ix, 101, 148, 172, 176, 182–83, 213, 232, 234, 280, 282, 287, 293
Morpurgo, Michael 287–88
Mott, Tony 293
Mount, Don 45–46, 48, 50, 189
Moynihan, Rodrigo 226, 231–32
Murray, Kate 133, 168, 256
Muir, Harry 229, 235
Muspratt Eric, 131

National Bank of Egypt 87–88
National Gallery of Victoria 288
Nichols, Beverley 72, 127
Nichols, Paul 72, 95
Nonesuch Press 103
Nunn, Tom 38, 49, 64

O'Grady, Dr 90–91
Olney, Stan 121, 126, 131, 182, 211
Orioli, Giuseppe 248
Orr, Lettice *see* Lane, Lettice
Osborne, Jean 138
Oxford University 171

P&O Steam Navigation Company 25, 54, 96, 145
Paisner, Leslie 253, 255, 257, 266–68, 270, 277–79, 293
Palgrave, Francis 5
Palmer, Stuart 124
Pan Books 206
Paroissien, Harry 196, 205, 211, 236–37, 255, 258–60, 267, 285

Partridge, Frances 221
Paton, Alexandra 300
Paton, Hugh 295
Paton, Louise 300
Paton, Richard 300
Peall, Cyril 92
Pearson, Hesketh 74–75
Pearson Longman Ltd 295
Peat, Marwick, Mitchell & Co. 251, 253
Penguin Australia 150, 175, 200–1, 214, 227–30, 233–36, 243–47, 256, 265–67, 270, 280–81
Penguin Books Ltd
    Brand, logo and design 123–25, 127–28, 136, 172, 176, 196–99, 205–6, 298–99
    Corporate culture 131, 141, 170, 173, 176, 177, 194, 195, 209–13, 220–22, 231–34, 236–38, 284, 285–87, 297
    Editorship 128, 136–38, 147, 173, 189, 193–96, 237, 297–98
    Flotation and takeovers xi, 251–79
    Founding of 1, 116–27, 135, 291, 297–99
    Premises 130–32, 139, 145–46, 149–50, 188, 262, 272, 285, 290
    Production standards 182, 189, 191–96, 297–99
    Profitability and sales performance x, 126–30, 134, 136–38, 140, 150, 167, 174, 181–82, 189, 192, 194, 201, 233–34, 237–38, 251, 271–72, 292
    Series 136, 140–41, 181–84, 189, 193, 199, 206, 232, 272, 297

Social impact 137, 182–84, 272–73, 297–98
Penguin Canada 200–1, 236
Penguin Inc. (United States) 147–48, 150, 173, 178, 181, 200–6
Pevsner, Nikolaus 84, 207
Pleydell & Smith 73
Pocket Books 148, 206
Porteous, Alexander 101
Potter, Stephen 250
Powell, Reverend Gordon 250
Prescott, E. Clifford 130
Priestman, Miss (Florence) 9–10
Prince Philip, Duke of Edinburgh 180, 289–90
Pritchard, Dr Owen 90–91
Purbrick, Eric 98
Puxley, Dorothy Oceana ('Ducka') 66, 239–40, 293
Puxley, Florence 66
Puxley, George (senior) 66
Puxley, George (junior) ('Pat') 66–68
Puxley, Richard 66

Rainsford, W. H. 105
Random House xi, 115, 252
Rapley, Bill 131–32, 185–86, 211
Raymond, Harold 122
Reynolds, A. H. 245–46, 259
Rhodes, Cecil 21, 28, 74
Rieu, E. V. 282
Rieu, Nellie 282
Rodd, Rennell 74
Rolfe, Frederick 105
Ronald, James 283
Rota, Bertram 290
Rothenstein, William 19
Rowlands, Doug 52, 54, 61
Rowlands, Esme 52–53, 64
Rowlands, Fred 52–53

Rowlands, Netta 51, 69, 103
Rowlands, Thomas Henry 51–52, 54–55, 61, 63, 69, 88, 98, 103
Royal College of Art 232
Royal Navy Volunteer Reserve 143, 150, 167, 176, 274
Ryan, Victor 30–31, 35–37, 47, 60, 269

Sackville-West, Vita 190
Samuel, Howard 278
Scarisbrick, Tony 214
Schmoller, Hans 200, 206, 249, 284
Schmoller, Tatyana 196, 200, 207, 215
Secker and Warburg 136
Selfridges 107, 129, 214
Senior, Elizabeth 147
Shakespeare & Co. 114
Shakespeare, William 78–79, 88–89, 95, 129, 190
Shankland, Mr 140
Shaw, George Bernard 68–69, 74, 98–99, 116, 121–122, 136–37, 191–92, 199, 220, 223, 238, 248, 251, 262, 274, 297–98
Simon, André 103
Simon, Oliver 197–98, 200, 207
Simon, Ruth 197, 207
Sime, Dawn 288
Siné (Maurice Sinet) 286
Slade School of Fine Art 226
Smedley, Rule & Co. 108
Smith, Geoffrey 221
Smith, Lily 66
Smith, Ted 66
Snow, Betty *see* Lane, Betty
Snow, Ruby 214
Snow, Sydney 214–15, 282, 296
Snow's Department Stores 214
Spenser, Edmund 5, 14

Steinberg, S. H. 127

Stone, Reynolds 284–85

Stonier, Brian 245

Summers, Jack 131, 291

Symons, Alphonse James Albert 72, 103–5, 120, 138

∽

Tabouis, Geneviève 140–41

Tauchnitz 121

Tawney, R. H. 272

Teale, Christine (née Lane) 207, 214, 280, 288, 293, 295

Teale, David 288

Tellisford House 8–9

Tink, Margaret 227

Thomas Tilling Ltd 252–53, 259

Travers, Ben 23, 29, 67, 72, 103, 122, 221, 282

Tschichold, Jan 197–200, 206, 227, 281

Twain, Mark 5, 74, 220

Tytler, Reverend Donald 250

∽

University of Melbourne 229

Unwin, Stanley 116–17, 125, 136, 226, 250, 298

∽

Venables, Bernard 220

Von Kamptz, Fritz 7

∽

W. D. & H. O. Wills 4, 45

Wallace, Edgar 117

Walter, Wilfred 80, 82

Ward, Lewis 244, 261

Watson, William 18, 69

Watts, Erb 15, 21

Waugh, Evelyn 248

Wayne, Ronald 121

Weaver, Harriet 115

Wegner, Max 120

Wells, H. G. 74, 192

Wendell Holmes, Oliver 5, 220

Westbrook, Eric 288

Weybright, Victor 201–5, 213, 249, 261, 263, 269

Whatmore, Walter ('Whatty') 251–53, 255, 259, 267, 270, 275, 277

White, Patrick 281

Whitten, Wilfred 5

Wilde, Oscar 15, 17–18, 52, 69, 103–4, 135, 220, 232

Williams, Gladys 224

Williams, Camilla *see* Lane, Camilla

Williams, Samuel *see* Lane, Samuel

Williams, William Emrys ('Bill') 118–19, 137–38, 147, 170, 182–83, 195–96, 205, 207, 210–12, 221, 233, 237–38, 249, 259, 279, 284–87, 291–93

Willett, Basil 108

Willings Denton Library 73

Wilmott, Ernest 9

Wilson, John Gideon 129

Wise, Thomas 17

Withers, A. B. 36–38, 40–43, 47, 49, 55, 60, 81, 88, 98, 219, 284, 296

W. M. Drummond & Co. 219

Wood, Peggy 100

Woolf, Leonard 115, 190

Woolf, Virginia 115, 190–91, 298

Woolworths 113, 116, 121, 130, 136, 299

Wozniak, Steve 121

Wyndham Lewis, D. B. 227

∽

Young, Edward 120, 123, 125–27, 138, 188

∽

Zuckerberg, Mark x–xi

MR. W. HEATH ROBINSON'S IDEA OF 'A BUSY